British Architects,
1840-1976

ART AND ARCHITECTURE INFORMATION GUIDE SERIES

Series Editor: Sydney Starr Keaveney, Associate Professor, Pratt Institute Library, Brooklyn, New York

Also in this series:

AMERICAN ARCHITECTS TO THE FIRST WORLD WAR—*Edited by Lawrence Wodehouse*

AMERICAN ARCHITECTS FROM THE FIRST WORLD WAR TO PRESENT—*Edited by Lawrence Wodehouse*

AMERICAN DECORATIVE ARTS AND OLD WORLD INFLUENCES—*Edited by David M. Sokol**

AMERICAN DRAWING—*Edited by Lamia Doumato**

AMERICAN PAINTING—*Edited by Sydney Starr Keaveney*

AMERICAN SCULPTURE—*Edited by Janis Ekdahl*

ANCIENT EGYPTIAN ART AND ARCHITECTURE—*Edited by Eleanore Wedge**

ART EDUCATION—*Edited by Clarence Bunch*

COLOR THEORY—*Edited by Mary Buckley*

EUROPEAN PAINTING, 1870-1910—*Edited by Timothy Daum**

HISTORIC PRESERVATION—*Edited by Arnold L. Markowitz**

INDIGENOUS ARCHITECTURE WORLDWIDE—*Edited by Lawrence Wodehouse*

POTTERY AND CERAMICS—*Edited by James E. Campbell*

STAINED GLASS I—*Edited by Darlene A. Brady and William Serban**

STAINED GLASS II—*Edited by Darlene A. Brady and William Serban**

TWENTIETH-CENTURY EUROPEAN PAINTING—*Edited by Ann-Marie Cutul**

VICTORIAN ART: ARCHITECTURE, SCULPTURE, DECORATIVE ARTS—*Edited by Marlene A. Palmer**

VICTORIAN ART: PAINTING, DRAWING, GRAPHIC ART—*Edited by Marlene A. Palmer**

*in preparation

The above series is part of the
GALE INFORMATION GUIDE LIBRARY

The Library consists of a number of separate series of guides covering major areas in the social sciences, humanities, and current affairs.

General Editor: Paul Wasserman, Professor and former Dean, School of Library and Information Services, University of Maryland

Managing Editor: Denise Allard Adzigian, Gale Research Company

British Architects, 1840-1976

A GUIDE TO INFORMATION SOURCES

Volume 8 in the Art and Architecture Information Guide Series

Lawrence Wodehouse

Lecturer, Department of Architecture
Jordanstone College
University of Dundee, Scotland

Gale Research Company
Book Tower, Detroit, Michigan 48226

Library of Congress Cataloging in Publication Data

Wodehouse, Lawrence.
   British architects, 1840-1976.

   (Art and architecture guide series ; v.8)
   Bibliography ; p. 375
   Includes indexes.
   1. Architecture--Great Britain--Bibliography.
2. Architects--Great Britain--Bibliography. I. Title.
Z5944.G7W66   [NA961]   016.72'0941   78-54116
ISBN 0-8103-1393-6

VITA

Lawrence Wodehouse is by training an architect, city planner, and architectural historian with degrees from the universities of Durham (England), London, and Cornell respectively. His major field of interest is nineteenth-century American architecture, notably architects who designed public buildings. He taught for a number of years in the United States succeeding Sibyl Moholy-Nagy as professor of architectural history at Pratt Institute, New York, 1969-74. Since returning to Britain, his birthplace, his interests have centered around Anglo-American architectural relationships. He is a member of the Royal Institute of British Architects.

Wodehouse is the author of AMERICAN ARCHITECTS FROM THE CIVIL WAR TO THE FIRST WORLD WAR (Gale, 1976) and AMERICAN ARCHITECTS FROM THE FIRST WORLD WAR TO THE PRESENT (Gale, 1977). He has also published more than a score of articles in journals of learned societies including: ANTIQUES, ARCHITECTURAL HISTORY, ART JOURNAL, HISTORIC PRESERVATION, JOURNAL OF THE SOCIETY OF ARCHITECTURAL HISTORIANS, and OLD TIME NEW ENGLAND. He has contributed sixteen entries to the McGRAW-HILL DICTIONARY OF WORLD BIOGRAPHY, 1973.

CONTENTS

ABBREVIATIONS OF ORGANIZATIONS CITED

AAL	Architectural Association, London
AIA	American Institute of Architects
BM	British Museum
EAA	Edinburgh Architectural Association
GLC	Greater London Council
HMC	Historic Manuscripts Commission
IAS	Incorporation of Architects of Scotland (later RIAS)
LCC	London County Council (later GLC)
NMRS	National Monuments Record of Scotland
NRA	National Register of Archives
RAL	Royal Academy, London
RIAI	Royal Institute of the Architects of Ireland
RIAS	Royal Incorporation of Architects of Scotland
RIBA	Royal Institute of British Architects
V&A	Victoria and Albert Museum

MAGAZINES, NEWSPAPERS, AND PERIODICALS CITED, WITH ABBREVIATIONS WHERE APPLICABLE

Architect	A
American Architect	AA
American Architect and Architecture	
American Architect and Building News	AA&BN
Ancient Monument Society Transactions	
Annual Register	
Apollo	
Archaeologia Aeliana	
Archaeological Journal	
Archigram	
Architect and Builder	
Architect and Builder (South Africa)	
Architect and Building News	A&BN
Architect and Contract Reporter	
Architect and Engineer	
Architects' and Builders' Journal	
Architectural Association Journal	AAJ
Architectural Association Notes	AAN
Architectural Association Quarterly	AAQ
American Art Review	AAR
Architectural Design	AD
Architectural Forum	AF
Architectural History	AH
American Institute of Architects' Journal	AIAJ

Magazines, Newspapers, Periodicals Cited

Architects' Journal	AJ
Architectural Review	AR
Architectural Review (Boston)	
Architectural Record	A Rec
Architecture North West	
Arena	
Art Journal	
Artwork	
Birmingham Archaeological Society	
Blackmansbury	
Brickbuilder	
British Archaeological Association Journal	
British Architect	
Builder	B
Building Design	BD
Building News	BN
Built Environment	
The Cambridge Review	
Canadian Architect	
Concrete	
Connoisseur	
Construction News	
Cornhill Magazine	
Country Life	CL
Design	
Design (Bombay)	
Design Quarterly	
Domus	
Ecclesiologist	
Edinburgh Architecturel Association Yearbook	EAAY
Ekistics	
Elseviers Maandschift	
Engineer	
Essays of the London Architectural Association	
Furniture History	

Gentleman's Magazine

Glasgow Evening News

Glasgow Institute of Architects' Yearbook

Glasgow Philosophical Society

Glasgow Review

Hobby Horse

Housing Review

!deal Home

Indian Institute of Architects' Journal

Industrial Archaeology

Interiors

International Studio

Irish Builder

Iron

Journal of Hellenic Studies

Journal of the Royal Architectural Institute of Canada   JRAIC

Journal of the Society of Architectural Historians   JSAH

Journal of Transport History

Lancashire and Cheshire Antiquarian Society Transactions

Landscape and Garden

Listener

· Liturgical Arts

London Studio

Magazine of Art

Marg

Metu

Newcomen Society Transactions

New International Yearbook   NIY

New York Times

Observer

Official Architect and Planner   OA&P

Pax: The Monthly Review of the Benedictines of
    Prinknash, Glos.

Paxton's Magazine of Botony and Register of Flowering Plants

Pencil Points

Perspecta

The Planner

Proceedings of the Royal Philosophical Society of Glasgow

Program

Progressive Architecture   PA

Prospect

Quarterly Bulletin of the Irish Georgian Society

Quarterly of the Royal Incorporated Architects of Scotland   QRIAS

Royal Institute of British Architects' Journal (including the   RIBAJ
Transactions and Proceedings)

Scotsman

Scottish Art Review

Scottish Education Journal

Scottish Field

Scottish Georgian Society Bulletin

South African Architectural Record

Studies: An Irish Quarterly Review of Letters, Philosophy
and Science

Studio, or Studio International

Studio Yearbook of Decorative Art

Times

Town and Country Planning   T&CP

Town Planning Institute Journal   TPIJ

Town Planning Review   TPR

Transactions of the Jewish Historical Society of England

Transactions of the Scottish Ecclesiological Society

Urban Structure

Western Architect

Yearbook of the Royal Institute of the Architects of Ireland

Zodiac

INTRODUCTION

The United Kingdom of Great Britain includes England, Scotland, Wales, and Northern Ireland, although prior to 1914 the whole of Ireland was governed by the British monarchy. Scotland, Wales, and Ireland have small populations compared to that of England, where the major concentration of people is in the southeast, surrounding London. Most major buildings and innovative movements have therefore tended to center in the same area and most architects emanate from London and the London schools. It is thus not surprising that there is a proliferation of books on English architecture and, until comparatively recently, all too few publications on nineteenth- and twentieth-century developments in other areas of Great Britain. Of the architects listed in this information guide, thirty-two who have biographies are English, ten listed wrote their own autobiographies--the first was George Gilbert Scott--and six others have monographs on their works. Only one Irishman has a biography--VICTORIAN ARCHITECT: THE LIFE AND WORK OF WILLIAM TINSLEY by John D. Forbes in 1953. This book was published by the Indiana University Press, a midwestern American publisher because Tinsley worked in Ohio after 1851, the year he immigrated to the United States. The Scots fare better with biographies of seven architects, but these include three who are best known for their work in England--John Burnet, Basil Spence, and James Stirling. Stirling was trained at Liverpool University and practices in London, although he was born in Glasgow. Of the remainder, Charles Rennie Mackintosh is not merely the best known but has thirteen publications on his life and work if one includes catalogs of major exhibitions. Furthermore, he has had more signed articles written about his work than any other British architect from 1840 to the present although Lutyens comes a close second.

When, however, one begins to browse into the history of British architecture, the books are few and give scant mention of buildings north of Hadrian's Wall, or west of Edward I's castles on the border dividing England and Wales; all too little mention is made of buildings across the Irish Sea. Banister Fletcher's all inclusive HISTORY OF ARCHITECTURE (18th ed. New York: Charles Scribner's Sons, 1975) provides an extensive survey of "English Mediaeval Architecture," followed by "Scottish and Irish Architecture," but the "English Renaissance" is not followed by the Scottish and Irish renaissances. Robert Adam (1728-92), Scotland's most famed eighteenth-century architect is listed under "English Renaissance," where we find that "among collegiate buildings of this period may be mentioned . . . Edinburgh University (1789-91) substantially by Robert Adam, completed (1815-34) by W.H. Playfair." Ireland fares worse, with a listing of the Casino at Marino by the English architect William Chambers; James Gandon (1742-1823), Chambers's pupil is also listed, since both were "famous for their Dublin buildings." Of more recent vintage, Mackintosh gains greater coverage in Banister Fletcher's survey with a listing and description of six of his buildings and comments upon his influence in Europe.

In the realm of architectural dictionaries, emphasis is again placed on English rather than British architecture. John Harvey published his ENGLISH MEDI-EVAL ARCHITECTS: A BIOGRAPHICAL DICTIONARY DOWN TO 1550 (London: B.T. Batsford) in 1954, and Howard M. Colvin, his A BIOGRAPHICAL DICTIONARY OF ENGLISH ARCHITECTS, 1660-1840 (London: John Murray) in 1963; J. Mordaunt Crook is to continue where Colvin concluded his dictionary. Even Nikolaus Pevsner, that Germanic fiend for detail, has stopped short at the borders in his forty-six-volume series, The Buildings of England. "It is Sir Nikolaus's intention that Wales, Scotland and Ireland shall have their 'Buildings', but he himself will not be hoofing around the Celtic fringes. . . . The young scholars are there. There's one who thinks he can do the whole of Ireland, and there are two for Scotland and three for Wales," wrote Ena Kendall in the British Sunday OBSERVER MAGAZINE ("Every Building Worth Knowing," 14 April 1974, pp. 13-19). Kendall indicates her skepticism with such phrases as "there's one who thinks . . .," which imply that whoever "he" may be, he will not have the perseverance of a Pevsner, nor perhaps the authoritative pull with Penguin Books, which, like most publishers, is now playing safe, although its early ventures were experimental.

Although a considerable number of books have been published on Scottish architecture, most tend to emphasize its medieval, Renaissance, and Georgian phases. During the years 1921-33, for example, the Scottish National Art Survey published EXAMPLES OF SCOTTISH ARCHITECTURE FROM THE NATIONAL ART SURVEY DRAWINGS, PUBLISHED BY A JOINT COMMITTEE OF THE NATIONAL GALLERY OF SCOTLAND AND THE R.I.A.S. (Glasgow, 4 vols.), which includes examples from only the twelfth to the seventeenth centuries, as though no Scottish art after the seventeenth century was worthy of consideration. Likewise, the Royal Commission on the Ancient Monuments of Scotland tended, until quite recently, to stop short of the nineteenth century. Its publication THE CITY OF EDINBURGH (Edinburgh: Her Majesty's Stationery Office, 1951) excludes the nineteenth century but mentions (p. 33) Robert Lorimer's Thistle Chapel and vestries at St. Giles Cathedral, 1910, as "modern additions." T.W. West's A HISTORY OF ARCHITECTURE IN SCOTLAND (London: University of London Press, 1967) is superficial and inaccurate. Even Henry-Russell Hitchcock had preconceptions of what he would find when he visited Glasgow. In his ARCHITECTURE, NINETEENTH AND TWENTIETH CENTURIES (Baltimore, Md. and Harmondsworth, Mdx.: Penguin Books, 1969), he discusses the architecture of Glasgow after having "come from Edinburgh looking for more examples of what is done so supremely well there. And of course it is not to be found." (Andor Gomme and David M. Walker. ARCHITECTURE OF GLASGOW. London: Lund Humphries,

1968, p. 12). Adding to the fact that so little is written on recent Scottish architecture is the confusion over the true identities of the designers of Scottish buildings since so many minor architects had similar and almost identical names. Nikolaus Pevsner wrote the foreword to Gomme and Walker's ARCHITECTURE OF GLASGOW, pointing out that there were seven architects by the name of Thomson and only two of them related. The famous Alexander "Greek" Thomson was one of them. He partnered at different periods with two different architects, both with the name of John Baird, neither of whom were related. Pevsner's list is quite extensive.

Outside of Scotland the name of William Burn is not well known even though he designed approximately seven hundred buildings, many in England. J. Mordaunt Crook's THE GREEK REVIVAL (London: John Murray, 1972) evaluates the work of Burn, who transposed to Scotland what he learned from his teacher Robert Smirke in London and who, with William Henry Playfair and Alexander Hamilton, forwarded the classical tradition until it was supplanted by the High Victorian Gothic style. Crook states: "Neither Wales nor Ireland produced a native Greek Revival and tradition. Things were different in Scotland. Here the dissemination of the style was less rapid than in England but much more complete" (p. 104).

David M. Walker has also been researching the Subject of Burn, Bryce and the Scottish Country House, and an essay with this title was planned at least as early as 1969 when it was advertised by the publishers Thames and Hudson, London, for a projected book on eight Victorian architects. Mark Girouard refers to the same essay in his THE VICTORIAN COUNTRY HOUSE (Oxford: Clarendon Press, 1971) but by 1974 the book was scheduled as SEVEN VICTORIAN ARCHITECTS, to be published in 1976-77 with an introduction by Nikolaus Pevsner (see A37).

David Bryce began his training with Burn in the mid-1820s and partnered with him during 1841-44, until the latter transferred his practice to London.

Various local authorities have attempted to prepare lists of buildings of special architectural or historical interest as required under the Town and Country Planning (Scotland) Act of 1947. Invariably the towns, cities, and counties describe the buildings and list ownership, lessees, and occupiers but little more. Dates of construction and the name of the architect are almost always omitted. Should an application be submitted to demolish a listed building, the local authority is bound to inform the Scottish Georgian Society to ascertain its views and opinions.

One major source of information on Scottish architecture is the National Monuments Record of Scotland, 54 Melville Street, Edinburgh. This organization begun in 1941 as the Scottish National Buildings Record and, originally privately funded, became part of the Ministry of Works in 1966. It now has one hundred forty thousand photographs, fifty thousand drawings, and a library of five thousand volumes. The drawings include those from the National Art Survey, those collected by Robert Rowand Anderson and Robert Lorimer, and, those transferred from the Royal Institute of British Architects, by William Burn.

Introduction

For a listing of other research sources on Scottish architecture, one can do no better than browse through the bibliography section (p. 315) of Gomme and Walker's ARCHITECTURE OF GLASGOW, in which are listed "Official Records and Collections of Unpublished Material," "Newspapers, Periodicals and Journals," in addition to annuals and books.

Even less can be said for the architecture of Wales than of Scotland for Wales has always retained closer ties with England and has always been dominated by English architects; moreover, England is often cited as the location of Welsh buildings. G.E. Kidder Smith, for example, discussed the Brynmawr Rubber Company plant in Brednockshire in his THE NEW ARCHITECTURE OF EUROPE (London: Prentice-Hall International, 1962, p. 61-62). Designed by the Architects Copartnership in 1951, it was described as "the first postwar building in England [sic] to command world attention."

Ireland includes not only Eire (the Irish Free State), but also the six counties of the Republic of Northern Ireland, which seceded from the Free State in 1921. Irish architecture was a unified whole long before the Act of Union of 1801 and to a certain extent spans beyond Home Rule in 1914. When the Institute of the Architects of Ireland was founded in 1839, it included architects of the whole of Ireland, and when in 1863 it became (and still is) the Royal Institute of the Architects of Ireland, its charter was granted by Queen Victoria. By 1871 there were thirty-eight fellows and twenty-three members of the institute, a comparatively small body of professionals for such a sizeable country.

Little interest has been taken in the architecture of Ireland from the Victorian period to the present although eighteenth-century Ireland is reasonably well documented: the Irish Georgian Society, founded in 1958 publishes a quarterly bulletin and there are numerous publications on various aspects of Georgian architecture in Ireland. Little, however, exists on the nineteenth or the twentieth centuries. Maurice Craig's IRELAND OBSERVED: A HANDBOOK TO THE BUILDINGS AND ANTIQUITIES (Cork: Mercier Press, 1972) is brief but provides the most thorough architectural survey of the whole of Ireland to date. There are, of course, archaeological surveys, including those on industrial archaeology. Craig has also written specifically on Dublin in DUBLIN, 1660-1860 (London: Cresset Press, 1952), but this book covers only a few years of Victoria's reign. There are two articles on Cork and similar contributions on Waterford and Limerick (of the early nineteenth century and thus omitted from section C), but the only other book on an Irish city is that on Belfast--Charles Brett's BUILDINGS OF BELFAST, 1700-1914 (London: Weidenfeld and Nicholson, 1967), which is very much a catalog but invaluable for source material. Brett has also contributed HISTORIC BUILDINGS, GROUPS OF BUILDINGS, AREAS OF ARCHITECTURAL IMPORTANCE IN THE GLENS OF ANTRIM (Belfast: Ulster Architectural Heritage Society, 1972) as one of eighteen surveys published or to be published by the society of the nine counties of the province of Ulster. Two titles in this proposed series that have already been published are Brett's SURVEY AND RECOMMENDATIONS FOR JOY STREET AND HAMILTON STREET DISTRICT

OF BELFAST (Belfast: 1971) and D. Girvan, R. Oram, and A. Rowan's LIST OF HISTORIC BUILDINGS, GROUPS OF BUILDINGS, AREAS OF ARCHITEC-TURAL IMPORTANCE IN ANTRIM AND BALLYMENA (Belfast: 1969). The remaining fifteen surveys will constitute QUEEN'S UNIVERSITY AREA OF BELFAST, LURGAN AND PORTADOWN, MOIRA RURAL DISTRICT COUNCIL, LISBURN, BANBRIDGE, PORTAFERRY AND STRANGFORD, CRAIGAVON URBAN DISTRICT, DOWNPATRICK, CITY OF DERRY, TOWN OF MONA-GHAN, WEST ANTRIM, NORTH ANTRIM, and DERRY-RURAL AREAS. These surveys are, in many respects, short catalogs but comparable to Nikolaus Pevsner's series, The Buildings of England.

The Ulster Architectural Heritage Society inventories will be invaluable to the author(s) of the projected Buildings of Ireland. So, too, will be the Architectural Record Society of the National Library of Ireland, founded in 1928 to record buildings in danger of extinction. In his book on Belfast, Brett states that "the only Belfast architect to appear in the DICTIONARY OF NATIONAL BIOGRAPHY is Sir Charles Lanyon" (p.31). Other than that, the only other three to gain mention in the dictionary seem to be James Pain of Cork, Charles Lanyon of Dublin, and Thomas Drew of Dublin. Background information on Irish architects is thus sparse, for detailed information has never been researched. Benjamin Woodward, the designer of the Trinity Col-lege Museum, Dublin, and the partner of the famous Thomas Deane is often referred to as the "little known" architect from Cork who was "apparently" born in 1815. Nothing is known of Woodward's parentage or education. In listing the works of William Smith, Brett states: "There were in 1829 two architects called W. Smith working in Belfast" (. . . BELFAST, p. 18), but no one seems to have sorted them out. Discussing "Three Centuries of Commerce: City of Waterford, Ireland--III," Mark Girouard states with reference to the Waterford Courthouse:

> According to Edmund Downey, the Waterford historian, the builder was a Waterford man Terrance O'Reilly. Was he also its architect? He is described as 'architect' in a Waterford directory of 1839 (COUNTRY LIFE, 22 December 1966, pp. 1695-98).

Thus, much more local research needs to be done, not only into the history of buildings, but also into the factual information concerning their architects. Rarely does one find the dates of architects given in published books, arti-cles, or even obituaries. In the yearbooks of the Royal Institute of the Ar-chitects of Ireland (sometimes published biannually), the date of death is sometimes omitted and the date of birth, rarely mentioned, for the simple reason that they are usually not known.

THE DIRECTORY OF THE AMERICAN INSTITUTE OF ARCHITECTS provides complete factual information (when it is provided by the member) of the lives and works of its members. However, the yearbooks of the Royal Institute of the Architects of Ireland and the KALENDAR of the Royal Institute of British Architects list only name, address, registration number, and date of member-ship.

Introduction

Historical architectural research invariably has to begin at the local level. Historical societies and local historians will have to begin the mammoth task of sifting through local courthouse and building department records, through insurance inventories, parish registers, and the like. Only then will an accurate regional and, ultimately, a national picture begin to emerge. T.J. McNamara described the "Burning of Blackrock Church Destroyed Gem of Famous Monk-Architect" in the CORK EVENING ECHO, 11 May 1962, p. 5. The fact that Blackrock Church burned led McNamara to research the building and thereby he discovered that it was not built by G.R. Pain, to whom it was usually attributed, but by Brother Michael Augustus Riordan, about whom little is known. This is the type of local research which needs to be done on an extensive scale. Both architects practiced in County Cork where any kind of historical research has been made difficult by the burning of the City and County Courthouse in 1890 and the City Hall in 1920.

The Irish Georgian Society is sponsoring the BIOGRAPHICAL DICTIONARY OF IRISH ARCHITECTS, SIXTEENTH CENTURY TO 1914, initiated by Rolf Loeber and modeled on Howard Colvin's BIOGRAPHICAL DICTIONARY OF ENGLISH ARCHITECTS, 1540-1840. Less than six hundred of the four thousand suggested entries will be included and considerable financial assistance will be needed even when the material is ready for publication. Six sample biographical sketches for the dictionary were published in the IRISH GEORGIAN SOCIETY QUARTERLY BULLETIN, January-June 1974.

Three doctoral dissertations have been written on Irish architecture and all three end in the mid-nineteenth century: E.J. McParland's Cambridge University dissertation, "Public Architecture in Ireland, 1750-1850," completed in 1975, concentrates on neoclassical architecture; Joseph Masheck's Columbia University dissertation of 1973, "Irish Church Building between the Treaty of Limerick and the Great Famine," covers the years 1691 to 1845. In his study Masheck states that "British and American scholars are beginning to take Irish Gothic Revival architecture seriously although little has as yet appeared in print on the subject" (p. 187). Douglas Scott Richardson's Yale dissertation, "Gothic Revival Architecture in Ireland," 1970, considers late eighteenth and early nineteenth century manifestations of the style. Hopefully, other aspects of more recent Irish architecture will stimulate historians to research and to publish on its significant aspects. Irish architecture came of age when Michael Scott was awarded the gold medal of the Royal Institute of British Architects in 1975, an award of international consequence.

This volume normally includes only those architects whose works have been evaluated by architectural critics. For example, Leonard Manasseh has been excluded although he is quite a well-known architect who has produced a reasonable corpus of work, for though his designs have been illustrated and described in print, neither his work as a whole nor his individual buildings have been the subject of a signed article. Architects with a city-planning bias, such as Patrick Abercrombie, Barry Parker, or Raymond Unwin, have also been excluded and so, too, have theorists such as William Morris, John

Ruskin, and Patrick Geddes. On the other hand, foreign architects working in Britain, notably those escaping from Nazi Germany in the 1930s--Walter Gropius, Marcel Breuer, and Eric Mendelsohn--have been included. Others in this last group are the Russian-born, British-educated Serge Chermayeff, Berthold Lubetkin, and the Swiss-born William Lescaze, who practiced in the United States and was commissioned to design at Dartington Hall, Devonshire. The American government employed John Johansen in Dublin and Eero Saarinen in London and American business engaged Skidmore, Owings and Merrill at Hayes Park, Middlesex; the Danish Arne Jacobson was commissioned to design St. Catherine's College, Oxford, and the German Peter Behrens was employed to design a house at Northampton.

A limited number of civil engineers have also been included. One is Francois Hennebique, whose system of concrete construction was patented in Britain and utilized in Dundee as early as 1904 and in Glasgow two years later.

Where information is available, brief biographical sketches are included for each architect providing date of birth and death, education, training, employment, partnerships, writings, depositories of drawings and research material, obituary notices, and notations of undergraduate and graduate theses and dissertations. Undergraduate theses are occasionally of a sufficiently high standard to justify inclusion. J.H. Gould's MODERN HOUSES IN BRITAIN, 1919-39, to be published in 1977, began as an undergraduate B.A. thesis at the University of Newcastle. This, and most other theses, has been abstracted from the RESEARCH REGISTER (no. 4, 1975), which is published by the Society of Architectural Historians of Great Britain and provides author and title of thesis but sometimes omits the date of submission. Obituary notices have been taken directly from the card catalog of the Avery Library at Columbia University; Adolf K. Placzek's AVERY OBITUARY INDEX OF ARCHITECTS AND ARTISTS of 1963 now needs to be completely updated and a new edition to be published, which is likely in the not too distant future. The AVERY INDEX TO ARCHITECTURAL PERIODICALS, 1973, and the CATALOG OF THE AVERY ARCHITECTURAL LIBRARY OF COLUMBIA UNIVERSITY, 1968, have been useful in providing books and articles to annotate.

For ease of reference, a numbering system for each architect has been used in this information guide with a subnumber for each annotation listed. In the general section, each notation has a key letter and number in order to make index references easier to locate.

Part 1

BRITISH ARCHITECTURE

Section A

GENERAL REFERENCE WORKS ON BRITISH ARCHITECTURE

The terms "British" and "English" are invariably used synonymously. Thus, as in the Dewey Decimal Library System, all books on English architecture are listed under British architecture. Books on Irish and Scottish architecture are listed in sections C and D.

A1   Addleshaw, G.W.O. "Architects, Sculptors, Designers and Craftsmen, 1770-1970, Whose Work Can Be Seen in Chester Cathedral." AH 14 (1971): 74-112.

Addleshaw, dean of Chester Cathedral lists 106 men and their work at the cathedral. He begins with 1770 because what was left prior to that date cannot be attributed to any one person; most of the pre-1770 work was anonymous.

A2   Aslin, Elizabeth. THE AESTHETIC MOVEMENT. London: Elek, 1969. 192 p.

Subtitled "Prelude to Art Nouveau," Chapter Two: "Red Brick and Sunflowers" briefly incorporates the arts-and-crafts innovations of the 1870s and '80s.

A3   Association of Special Libraries and Information Bureaus. INDEX TO THESES, edited by Geoffrey M. Paterson and Joan E. Hardy. London: Vol. 1-- , 1949/50-- .

Lists all theses "accepted for higher degrees by the universities of Great Britain and Ireland and the Council for National Academic Awards." They are listed alphabetically under subject by author but no exact date or pagination is provided.

A4   Atkinson, Thomas Dinham. A GLOSSARY OF TERMS USED IN ENGLISH ARCHITECTURE. London: Metheun and Co., 1928. 335 p., 270 figs.

Historical terms used notably in the construction of residential and religious architecture form the major portion of the glossary.

A5   Avery Architectural Library of Columbia University. AVERY INDEX
       TO ARCHITECTURAL PERIODICALS. 15 vols. Boston: G.K. Hall,
       1973. One-volume supplement, 1975.

       Lists all articles in periodicals on architecture, worldwide,
       and in journals on allied subjects. Indexing is under sub-
       ject, author, designer, and geographic location headings.

A6   _____. CATALOG. Boston: G.K. Hall, 1968. Supplements in
       1973 and 1975.

       Avery Library has collected publications by architects as
       well as about them and their buildings. It is thus more
       catholic than the RIBA Library.

A7   Banham, Reyner. GUIDE TO MODERN ARCHITECTURE. London:
       Architectural Press, 1962. 160 p. Reprinted as AGE OF THE MAS-
       TERS: A PERSONAL VIEW OF MODERN ARCHITECTURE, 1975.
       170 p.

       The elements of modern architecture, worldwide, are pre-
       sented with considerations of function, form, construction,
       and space.

A8   _____. THE NEW BRUTALISM. London: Architectural Press, 1966.
       196 p.

       A phase of British architecture beginning about December
       1953. A small, but influential group of architects practiced
       in a "brutal" manner. Their antecedents are carefully ex-
       amined and their work explained.

A9   Benton, Tim, and Millikin, Sandra. ART NOUVEAU, 1890-1902.
       Milton Keynes, Mdx.: Open University Press, 1975. 64 p., 132 figs.
       Units 3-4 of the Open University's course A305: "History of Archi-
       tecture and Design 1890-1939."

       Although the book covers the European art nouveau move-
       ment, almost half of it is devoted to "The British Arts and
       Crafts Architects": C.F.A. Voysey, M.H. Baillie Scott,
       and Charles Rennie Mackintosh.

A10   Betjeman, John. FIRST AND LAST LOVES. London: John Murray,
       1952. 244 p.

       A selection of articles which have been published elsewhere
       are gathered together and republished within one cover.
       The subject matter is mainly, but not wholly, Victorian ar-
       chitecture, places, building types, and personal opinions
       about them.

A11   . GHASTLY GOOD TASTE: OR, A DEPRESSING STORY OF THE RISE AND FALL OF ENGLISH ARCHITECTURE. London: Chapman and Hall, 1933. Reprint. London: Anthony Blond, 1970. 112 p.

> A condemnation of "refeenment" and speculation in "colossal hideosities," at the expense of tradition and environment. The architectural purse has passed from the aristocrats to the middle class and beyond.

A12   . A PICTORIAL HISTORY OF ENGLISH ARCHITECTURE. London: John Murray, 1970. 112 p.

> The excellent photographs, many in color, enhance Betjeman's view of architecture: "I have always had so much pleasure from looking at buildings that I have wanted to convey my pleasure to others."

A13 Bird, Eric L., ed. ONE HUNDRED YEARS OF BRITISH ARCHITECTURE, 1851–1951. London: RIBA, 1951. 48 p.

> The RIBA held an exhibition in 1951 in connection with the Festival of Britain that year. Six well-illustrated essays are included.

A14 Boase, Thomas Sherrer Ross. ENGLISH ART: 1800–1870. London: Oxford University Press, 1959. 352 p., 96 pls.

> Covering painting, sculpture, and architecture, this volume surveys the major movements, protagonists, and styles and their place in English history. It includes most of the recent developments in architectural history and interpretation of the period.

A15 Braun, Hugh Stanley. ELEMENTS OF ENGLISH ARCHITECTURE. Newton Abbot, Devon.: David and Charles, 1973. 194 p.

> Developments in construction, materials, design, interiors, planning, and restoration are covered in a historical survey of English architecture.

A16 Briggs, Martin S. BUILDING TO-DAY. London: Oxford University Press, 1944. 112 p.

> Building as practiced in all its types in 1939 "and as we hope it will be resumed as soon as circumstances permit after peace is attained."

A17 Brockman, H.A.N. THE BRITISH ARCHITECT IN INDUSTRY, 1841–1940. London: George Allen and Unwin, 1974. 186 p.

> During the period considered, engineers and architects became

more closely associated in their work. Industrialization itself is not considered; rather the architectural and social aspects lead on to totally integrated building design.

A18   Buchanan, R.A. INDUSTRIAL ARCHAEOLOGY IN BRITAIN. Harmondsworth, Mdx.: Penguin Books, 1974. 446 p.

"One omission needs a word of explanation. Eire can be legitimately excluded from a survey of British industrial archaeology, but strictly speaking there should be some treatment of Ulster, which is both British and part of the United Kingdom."

A19   Casson, Hugh M[axwell]. AN INTRODUCTION TO VICTORIAN ARCHITECTURE. London: Art and Technics,

"It is hoped that this modest survey will act as an introduction to those more complete studies which are to come, and that meanwhile it will help to stimulate the respect, interest, even the affection, which the fabulous architecture of this truly fabulous age so emphatically deserves."

A20   Cement and Concrete Association. STRUCTURAL CONCRETE BUILDINGS. 2d ed. London: 1962. 56 p.

The whys and wherefores of using reinforced concrete illustrated by post-Second World War buildings in Britain.

A21   Chatterton, Frederick, ed. WHO'S WHO IN ARCHITECTURE, 1923. London: Architectural Press, 1923. 408 p. (Other editions by Technical Journals, London, 1914 and 1926.)

The amount of information on the various architects listed is sometimes meager with no explanation as to why.

A22   Clark, Kenneth. THE GOTHIC REVIVAL. 2d ed. Baltimore, Md. and Harmondsworth, Mdx.: Penguin Books, 1950. 308 p.

The developments of the Gothic revival movement and the major architects after 1840, including Barry and Pugin on the Houses of Parliament and George Gilbert Scott and those associated with the Ecclesiological Society, are discussed. The period from as far back as the mid-eighteenth century to 1840 is also covered.

A23   Clarke, Basil F.L. CHURCH BUILDERS OF THE NINETEENTH CENTURY: A STUDY OF THE GOTHIC REVIVAL IN ENGLAND. London: Society for Promoting Christian Knowledge, 1938. 296 p.

This book covers all the major architects, their buildings, and the variations of the Gothic. Appendix 1: "Some

Nineteenth-Century Architects and Their Churches" and appendix 2: "Some Towns and Their Churches," are useful reference sources.

A24   Clifton-Taylor, Alec, et al. SPIRIT OF THE AGE. London: British Broadcasting Corporation, 1975. 240 p.

Only the last three of the eight contributions to this volume are relevant to the nineteenth and twentieth centuries. Mark Girouard's "All that Money Could Buy," Patrick Nuttgens's "A Full Life and an Honest Place," and Hugh Casson's "Dreams and Awakenings" are well-illustrated, but brief, surveys since they are the transcripts of hour-long television programs.

A25   Collins, Peter. CHANGING IDEALS IN MODERN ARCHITECTURE, 1750-1950. London: Faber and Faber, 1965. 309 p.

The modern movement in all its flavors and the styles of the nineteenth century in Europe and America are considered with strong injections and interweavings of the influence of British architects.

A26   Colvin, H.M. A BIOGRAPHICAL DICTIONARY OF ENGLISH ARCHITECTS 1660-1840. London: John Murray, 1954. 821 p.

This biographical dictionary of more than one thousand architects and master-builders from the seventeenth century into the nineteenth does include architects who lived after 1840. Although all lived and worked in England, several designed structures in Scotland, Wales, and Ireland. "The dates 1660-1840 were chosen because they cover the whole history of English classical architecture in its mature phase."

A27   Crook, J. Mordaunt. THE GREEK REVIVAL. London: John Murray, 1972. 204 p.

"A general survey of that neglected phase of British history," neoclassicism from 1760 to 1870, covering all the major protagonists.

A28   _____. VICTORIAN ARCHITECTURE: A VISUAL ANTHOLOGY. London and New York: Johnson Reprint Corporation, 1971. Unpaged, 300 pls.

"This volume is merely a selection of buildings actually erected in Britain during the years of Queen Victoria's reign and illustrated in contemporary architectural journals."

A29   Curl, James Stevens. VICTORIAN ARCHITECTURE: ITS PRACTICAL

ASPECTS. Newton Abbot, Devon.: David and Charles, 1973. 128 p.

Victorian architecture reflective of its period has much to teach those who lament the passing of nineteenth-century structures. All building types and their architects are considered.

A30   Curtis, William. LE CORBUSIER. ENGLISH ARCHITECTURE 1930's. Milton Keynes, Mdx.: Open University Press, 1975. 74 p., 104 figs. Units 17-18 of the Open University's course A305: History of Architecture and Design 1890-1939.

The book is divided into two sections, the first on Le Corbusier and the second on his impact on England during the late 1920s and '30s. His was not the only influence, but the International Style, of which he was part, was a dominant movement.

A31   Dalzell, W.R. ARCHITECTURE: THE INDISPENSABLE ART. London: Michael Joseph, 1962. 263 p.

The last three chapters are devoted to a reasonably in-depth study of "Regency and Victorian Architecture," "The Twentieth Century," and "Architecture since the Second World War."

A32   Dannatt, Trevor. MODERN ARCHITECTURE IN BRITAIN. London: Batsford, 1959. 216 p.

This book is the outgrowth of an exhibition held at the Arts Council of Great Britain in London, 1956, surveying British architecture, 1945-55. Buildings of 1956-59 are also considered in photographs and accompanying text.

A33   Dickinson, P.L. AN OUTLINE HISTORY OF ARCHITECTURE OF THE BRITISH ISLES. London: Jonathan Cape, n.d. 320 p.

Chapter 11 covers the major styles of the nineteenth century, industrialization, and slums and the remedies. Chapter 12 deals with the present-day position in both architecture and town planning.

A34   Eastlake, Charles Locke. A HISTORY OF THE GOTHIC REVIVAL. London: Longmans, Green, and Co., 1872. 209 p. Reprint. Edited by J. Mordaunt Crook. Leicester: Leicester University Press; New York: Humanities Press, 1970.

The Crook edition provides an introduction, a minibiography of Eastlake, and an analysis of the origins of the Gothic revival in its earliest phases. This is followed by Eastlake's

"Selected Examples of Gothic Buildings Erected between 1820 and 1870," with all the influences, movements, and allied attitudes.

A35   Eaton, Leonard K. AMERICAN ARCHITECTURE COMES OF AGE: EUROPEAN REACTION TO H.H. RICHARDSON AND LOUIS SULLI-VAN. Cambridge, Mass.: MIT Press, 1972. 256 p.

This book examines Richardson's and Sullivan's presence and influence. After an introduction on "American Architecture and the Problem of Cultural Maturity," Eaton considers the subject "The American Strain in British Architecture."

A36   Esher, Viscount. RECENT ENGLISH ARCHITECTURE, 1920-1940: SELECTED BY THE ARCHITECTURE CLUB. London: Country Life, 1947. 65 pls.

The Architecture Club was founded in 1921 "to encourage intelligent criticism and review of modern buildings and to enlarge public appreciation of good architecture and the allied arts." Viscount Esher was chairman of the club in 1946 and this selection by building type is essentially of architects' architecture. It is thus an invaluable commentary of the period.

A37   Fawcett, Mary. SEVEN VICTORIAN ARCHITECTS. Introduction by Nikolaus Pevsner. London: Thames and Hudson, 1976. 160 p., 121 illus.

To include essays on Bodley by D.C.W. Verey; William Burn and David Bryce, when they partnered together, by D.M. Walker; Philip Hardwick by H. Hobhouse; Lutyens by R. Gradidge; J.L. Pearson by D.W. Lloyd; Sydney Smirke by J. Mordaunt Crook; and Alfred Waterhouse by Stuart Smith.

A38   Fergusson, James. HISTORY OF MODERN STYLES OF ARCHITEC-TURE. 3d rev. ed. Vol. 2. London: John Murray, 1891. 453 p.

Chapter 4: "Classical Revival"; chapter 5: "Gothic Revival"; and chapter 6: "Recent Architecture" of book 4, volume 2 are devoted to English architecture. Chapter 6 covers 1851-80. Examples of Scottish and Irish architecture are included.

A39   Ferriday, Peter, ed. VICTORIAN ARCHITECTURE. London: Jonathan Cape, 1963. 306 p.

A compendium of major articles, some published elsewhere and in journals, of C.R. Cockerell, Charles Barry, A.W.N.

Pugin, Joseph Paxton, William Butterfield, George Gilbert Scott, William Burges, G.E. Street, R.N. Shaw, Philip Webb, C.F.A. Voysey, and J.F. Bentley, in addition to essays on nineteenth-century houses and the architectural profession as a whole.

A40   Gardiner, Stephen. "Architects: Profession in Need of Rebuilding?" OBSERVER MAGAZINE, 7 November 1976, pp. 20-35.

The OBSERVER surveyed the professions in a series of articles over a number of weeks. After a brief statement by Gardiner, twenty-five "architects speak out for their profession." Biographical information on the twenty-five provided.

A41   Gardner, A.H. OUTLINE OF ENGLISH ARCHITECTURE. London: B.T. Batsford, 1945. 122 p.

A score of pages for the general reader are devoted to the nineteenth and twentieth centuries.

A42   Gibberd, Frederick. THE ARCHITECTURE OF ENGLAND FROM NORMAN TIMES TO THE PRESENT DAY. London: Architectural Press, 1938. 48 p.

A brief, but well-illustrated, pictorial survey. It is meant for a general audience and is especially suited to a young person with an interest in architecture.

A43   Gloag, John. BRITISH ARCHITECTURE OF TODAY. London: RIBA, n.d. 21 p.

A photographic exhibition of 150 examples of "contemporary" architecture.

A44   _____. THE ENGLISH TRADITION IN ARCHITECTURE. London: Adam and Charles Black, 1963. 258 p.

Twenty-four pages of chapter 8 are devoted to "Revivals and the Hidden Style."

A45   _____. VICTORIAN TASTE: SOME SOCIAL ASPECTS OF ARCHITECTURE AND INDUSTRIAL DESIGN, 1820-1900. 2d ed. Newton Abbot, Devon.: David and Charles, 1972. 175 p.

Victorian style, taste, theory, and the "virile generative powers" that produced architecture and industrial design in Britain from 1820 to 1900. Social implications, patronage, and the final outcome are assessed.

A46   Gomme, A.H., and Gomme, Mrs. UNPUBLISHED RESEARCH IN AR-
        CHITECTURAL HISTORY. Keele, Staff.: Society of Architectural
        Historians, Research Register no. 4 (Autumn 1975). 22 p.

        A listing of research, theses, and dissertations in progress
        throughout Britain and of those that have been completed
        but not published. Research Registers 1-3 have been in-
        corporated into number 4. Dates of completed projects not
        always given.

A47   Goodey, Brian. URBAN WALKS AND TOWN TRAILS: ORIGINS,
        PRINCIPLES AND SOURCES. Birmingham: Centre for Urban and Re-
        gional Studies, University of Birmingham, 1974. [118 p.]

        The subject "Origins" of walks takes up seventeen pages;
        of "Principles," twenty-three pages; and the remaining
        seventy-eight pages is titled "An Annotated List of Avail-
        able Trails and Walks" throughout towns and areas of Brit-
        ain.

A48   Goodhart-Rendel, H.S. ENGLISH ARCHITECTURE SINCE THE RE-
        GENCY: AN INTERPRETATION. London: Constable, 1953. 296 p.

        An amplification of a lecture series given at Oxford Uni-
        versity in 1934. The book reassesses the architecture of
        the Victorian period and its most elaborate structures.
        Major architects, their designs, and the contribution of
        engineering are all considered. The book stops with the
        early 1930s.

A49   Gotch, J.A., ed. THE GROWTH AND WORK OF THE ROYAL IN-
        STITUTE OF BRITISH ARCHITECTS 1834-1934. London: RIBA, 1934.
        187 p., photographs and biographical notes of all presidents of the
        RIBA.

        At the RIBA's centenary, this survey, including H.S.
        Goodhart-Rendell's essay "Architecture of the Past Hun-
        dred Years," of all RIBA activities was published.

A50   Gowan, James. "AA 125: A Decade of AA Architecture." AAQ 5
        (January/March 1973): 4-39.

        "James Gowan makes a personal selection of architects and
        their buildings from the formative period of the Architec-
        tural Association, 1958-68. The survey includes the work
        of established British architects who had an influence on
        the architecture of the period as well as the later work of
        those trained at the AA during the period." A certain
        amount of biographical material has been abstracted from
        this article.

A51   Gradidge, Roderick. "Checklist of Architects, 1820-1939: Compiled
       for the Society for the Protection of Ancient Buildings." Mimeographed.
       London: Victorian Society, n.d. 21 p.

       "Architects Whose Work Should Be Looked at Carefully
       Before Alterations or Destruction." An extensive listing.

A52   Gray, A.S. EDWARDIAN ARCHITECTURE (provisional title). London:
       Duckworth, forthcoming. A biographical dictionary.

A53   Harbron, D. AMPHION, OR THE NINETEENTH CENTURY. London:
       J.M. Dent and Sons, 1930. 179 p.

       When this book was published, little research had been
       undertaken concerning Victorian architecture. "When a
       dynasty has been dethroned, its gods--discarded--become
       the devils of the next administration." Some of the high-
       lights "to express the century" are presented.

A54   Harris, John. CATALOGUE OF BRITISH DRAWINGS FOR ARCHITEC-
       TURE, DECORATION, SCULPTURE AND LANDSCAPE GARDENING,
       1500-1900, IN AMERICAN COLLECTIONS. Upper Saddle River,
       N.J.: Gregg Press, 1971. 355 p.

       Henry-Russell Hitchcock wrote the introduction of this illus-
       trated catalog.

A55   Hatje, Gerd. ENCYCLOPAEDIA OF MODERN ARCHITECTURE. Lon-
       don: Thames and Hudson, 1963. 336 p., 446 illus.

       Worldwide manifestations, materials, movements, individual
       architects, and schools are presented but with a strong em-
       phasis on British architecture.

A56   Hersey, George L. HIGH VICTORIAN GOTHIC: A STUDY IN AS-
       SOCIATIONISM. Baltimore: Johns Hopkins University Press, 1972.
       234 p.

       "Through a detailed examination of the contemporary litera-
       ture, he [Hersey] shows that associationism led Victorians
       to see buildings emotionally and dramatically . . . as
       sources of moral correction and punishment." All aspects
       of nineteenth-century Gothic are examined in relation to
       Hersey's associational interpretations.

A57   Hitchcock, Henry-Russell. ARCHITECTURE: NINETEENTH AND
       TWENTIETH CENTURIES. Baltimore: Penguin Books, 1969. 682 p.

       Although concerned with architecture worldwide, all British
       movements of the period are covered.

A58 _____ . EARLY VICTORIAN ARCHITECTURE IN BRITAIN. 2 vols. London: Architectural Press; New Haven: Yale University Press, 1954. Vol. 1: 635 p.; vol. 2: 17 sections of illustrations.

This detailed and thorough study covers only the beginning of Victoria's reign of the second quarter of the nineteenth century. All movements and styles are considered, with the account of the major protagonists and their architecture complemented by a description of the lesser-known architects and their works.

A59 Hitchcock, Henry-Russell, Jr., and Bauer, Catherine. MODERN AR-CHITECTURE IN ENGLAND. New York: Museum of Modern Art, 1937. Reprint. New York: Arno Press, 1969. 102 p.

In this exhibition catalog, Hitchcock ties the nineteenth to the twentieth century and Bauer specifically discusses hous-ing. The exhibition consisted of seventy-seven photographic segments, many of which are illustrated in the catalog's seventy-two plates.

A60 Holford, William, and White, Gabriel. ARCHITECTURE TODAY. London: Arts Council and RIBA, 1961. 52 pls.

Essentially shows the best of all types of British architecture from about 1955 to 1961. This was a catalog of an exhibition held in London at the time of the meeting of the Congres Internationaux d' Architecture Moderne.

A61 Jackson, Anthony. THE POLITICS OF ARCHITECTURE: A HISTORY OF MODERN ARCHITECTURE IN BRITAIN. London: Architectural Press, 1970. 219 p.

Aesthetic and sociological aspects of British architecture are considered, from the advent of modern architecture in 1930 to the major designs of local-authority architects of the im-mediate past.

A62 Jamilly, Edward. "Anglo-Jewish Architects, and Architecture in the 18th and 19th Centuries." TRANSACTIONS OF THE JEWISH HISTOR-ICAL SOCIETY OF ENGLAND 18 (1954): 127-41, 6 pls.

This article emphasizes, but, especially with regard to the more nationally famous Jewish architects, is not exclusively on synagogues and Jewish buildings. Ten architects and their patrons are noted.

A63 Jencks, Charles. MODERN MOVEMENTS IN ARCHITECTURE. Har-mondsworth, Mdx.: Penguin Books, 1973. 432 p.

Chapter 7: "Recent British Architecture: Pop-Non Pop" (pages 239-98), considers public, symbolic, and other types of architecture over the past thirty years.

A64   Jenkins, Frank. ARCHITECT AND PATRON: A SURVEY OF PROFES-
SIONAL RELATIONS AND PRACTICE IN ENGLAND FROM THE SIX-
TEENTH CENTURY TO THE PRESENT DAY. London: Oxford University
Press, 1961. 254 p.

This book assesses the creative designer's human relationships. Chapter 10 covers the nineteenth century and 11,
"The Modern Scene," when the patron changed, to some
extent, from the private client to the local authority.

A65   Joedicke, Jurgen. ARCHITECTURE SINCE 1945: SOURCES AND DI-
RECTIONS. London: Pall Mall Press, 1969. 179 p.

Although covering modern architecture worldwide, English
architects predominate in the first part of the section "The
Second Phase, 1958-66." The book has a thorough bibliography.

A66   _____. A HISTORY OF MODERN ARCHITECTURE. London: Architectural Press, 1959. 243 p.

In the section "The Contribution of the Nations," the immediately pre- and post-World War II architecture of Britain
is presented on pages 154-60.

A67   Kaye, Barrington. THE DEVELOPMENT OF THE ARCHITECTURAL
PROFESSION IN BRITAIN: A SOCIOLOGICAL STUDY. London:
George Allen and Unwin, 1960. 223 p.

An attempt "to show what the functions of the architectural
profession have been, and how it has set about fulfilling
them," this book analyzes professionalism, from its rise
during the controversial battle of the styles to the legal
implications of the twentieth century.

A68   Kidson, Peter, and Murray, Peter. A HISTORY OF ENGLISH ARCHI-
TECTURE. London: George G. Harrap and Co., 1962. 256 p.

The last eighteen pages briefly survey "Victorian and Modern Architecture."

A69   Lambert, Sam. "Historic Pioneers: Architects and Clients." AJ 151
(11 March 1970): 594-97.

Lambert selects a number of London buildings from the period 1914 to 1939 and their architects. Included are Berthold
Lubetkin, Maxwell Fry, William Crabtree, and Erno Goldfinger.

A70 Landau, Royston. NEW DIRECTIONS IN BRITISH ARCHITECTURE.
London: Studio Vista; New York: George Braziller, 1968. 126 p.

Landau examines the philosophies and explaines the new
building trends.

A71 Little, Bryan. ENGLISH HISTORIC ARCHITECTURE. London: B.T.
Batsford, 1964. 256 p.

Stylistic and constructional innovations in English architecture up to about 1920 are analyzed. Thereafter architecture has been based less upon historical precedents.

A72 Lubetkin, Berthold. "Modern Architecture in England." AMERICAN
ARCHITECT AND ARCHITECTURE 150 (February 1937): 29-42.

"England has become almost the only country in which modern architecture can flourish in comparative freedom. This
circumstance has naturally attracted many foreign architects,
fleeing from political restrictions or economic stagnation in
other countries."

A73 Macleod, R. STYLE AND SOCIETY: ARCHITECTURAL IDEOLOGY
IN BRITAIN, 1835-1914. London: RIBA, 1971. 144 p.

A study of the ideals and intentions of the major designers
of the stylistic revivals of the Victorian and Edwardian eras.

A74 Marriott, Charles. MODERN ENGLISH ARCHITECTURE. London:
Chapman and Hall, 1924. 268 p.

An appreciation and explanation of Edwardian architecture
as seen through the eyes of a man who admired the architecture of his day. The most elaborate public building and
the simplest domestic buildings are considered. The last
twenty-five pages contain biographical material on architects of the period.

A75 MARS (Modern Architecture Research Society) Group. NEW ARCHI-
TECTURE. London: 1938. 25 p.

A catalog of an exhibition of modern architecture, British
and European, held at the New Burlington Galleries, London. The MARS Group also published the reports, "What
Is Modern Architecture," no. 2, 1944, and no. 3, 1945
(proceedings of a meeting of the group held in December
1944).

A76 Maxwell, Robert. NEW BRITISH ARCHITECTURE. London: Thames
and Hudson, 1972. 200 p.

Fifty examples of British architecture since 1950 are examined by building type. All raise new issues, on the function of buildings. Well illustrated with plans, sections, axonometrics, and photographic coverage.

A77 Mills, Edward David. 1946-1953: THE NEW ARCHITECTURE IN GREAT BRITAIN. London: Standard Catalogue Co., 1953. 209 p.

Reprint of a series of special articles commissioned by the magazine AD. They comprise the "best contemporary architecture" in the fields of religious, civic, educational, and domestic buildings. Brief biographical notes are given on the respective designers. The book begins with a discussion and listing of significant buildings in Great Britain, 1925-45.

A78 Morris, Francis O. A SERIES OF PICTURESQUE VIEWS OF SEATS OF THE NOBLEMEN AND GENTLEMEN OF ENGLAND AND IRELAND. 6 vols. London: William Mackenzie, 1866-80.

Worth looking at since it lists and illustrates early nineteenth-century additions and rebuildings.

A79 Muthesius, Stefan. HIGH VICTORIAN MOVEMENT IN ARCHITECTURE, 1850-1870. London and Boston: Routledge and Kegan Paul, 1972. 246 p.

This movement evolved from the Gothic revival into a period characterized by "massiveness combined with a varied outline and by vigorous handling of decorative forms with polychromatic contrasts of material." All these qualities are either medieval in derivation or are part of nineteenth-century architectural theory. All the "big guns" are considered.

A80 NRA. ARCHITECTURAL HISTORY AND THE FINE AND APPLIED ARTS: SOURCES IN THE NATIONAL REGISTER OF ARCHIVES. London: HMC, 1969-- .

Vol. 1, edited by T.W.M. Jaine, 1969. 82 p.

Vol. 2, edited by T.W.M. Jaine, 1970. 98 p.

Vol. 3, edited by T.W.M. Jaine and R.A. Storey, 1971. 89 p.

Vol. 4, edited by Brenda Weeden, 1972. 80 p.

Vol. 5, 1974. 71 p.

"The intention of this SOURCE LIST is to note and describe all references to art and architectural history in the lists of manuscript accumulations which comprise the National Register

of Archives." Collections of designs from the "lists" have
generally been incorporated into this Gale information guide,
under biographical date of architects, but minor information,
such as a letter from a client to an architect thanking him
for a drawing, has generally been excluded. Client ownership of material has also generally been omitted.

A81   Nellist, John B. BRITISH ARCHITECTURE AND ITS BACKGROUND.
London: Macmillan and Co., 1967. 361 p.

Chapter 11 surveys the nineteenth century and 12 "The
Modern Movement," but more space is devoted to "background" developments in Europe and America than to British
architecture.

A82   Papworth, Wyatt, ed. THE DICTIONARY OF ARCHITECTURE. 9
vols. London: Architectural Publication Society, 1852-92. Reprint.
New York: DaCapo Press, 1969.

An invaluable source of general architectural information
with much biographical material.

A83   Parris, Henry. "British Transport Historical Records and Their Value
to the Architectural Historian." AH 2 (1959): 50-62.

These records, with the exception of those of the Public
Record Office, constitute the "largest single collection relating to architecture in this country in the nineteenth century." The collection established by the British Transport
Commission, founded in 1951, is kept in London, York,
and Edinburgh (see also JOURNAL OF TRANSPORT HIS-
TORY 2 [1956-57]: 129).

A84   Pevsner, Nikolaus. "Nine Swallows--No Summer." AR 91 (May
1942): 109-12.

"A selection of British examples is shown and discussed to
clarify Britain's role in this first stage of twentieth century
architecture." Examples range from 1900 to 1912, a period
usually associated with the Edwardian baroque, Tudor tradi-
tionalism, and the Georgian revival. Most of the innovations were in the fields of commercial and industrial architecture and engineering, and the introduction of reinforced
concrete.

A85   _____. PIONEERS OF MODERN DESIGN FROM WILLIAM MORRIS
TO WALTER GROPIUS. London: Faber and Faber, 1936. 254 p.
Later paperback edition, partly rewritten, for Penguin Books, Harmonds-
worth, Mdx., 1960.

Covering the modern movement in Europe and America, this
book emphasizes the British arts-and-crafts and art nouveau
movements.

A86   . SOME ARCHITECTURAL WRITERS OF THE NINETEENTH
CENTURY. Oxford: Clarendon Press, 1972. 338 p.

All the major British architectural theorist-writers are considered but so too are non-British writers.

A87   . THE SOURCES OF MODERN ARCHITECTURAL DESIGN.
London: Thames and Hudson, 1968. 216 p.

British developments are concentrated in chapter 3, "New
Impetus From England" (pages 115-45), emphasizing the
contribution of Britain to European trends.

A88   Placzek, Adolf K. AVERY OBITUARY INDEX OF ARCHITECTS AND
ARTISTS. Boston: G.K. Hall and Co., 1963. 338 p.

Approximately 13,500 entries taken from major American
and English journals on architecture, 1865 to 1963. The
card index of Avery Architectural Library, Columbia University, is continuously updated and all post-1963 obituaries
have been abstracted from that index.

A89   Reilly, Charles H. REPRESENTATIVE BRITISH ARCHITECTS OF THE
PRESENT DAY. London: B.T. Batsford, 1931. 172 p.

Reilly has selected a dozen architects, because of their
personalities, and representative examples of their work.
Reilly seems to be against the "anonymity of the modern
architect," which he considers "rather pretentious."

A90   RIBA. ANNUAL REVIEW OF PERIODICAL ARTICLES. 7 vols. London: Superceded by ARCHITECTURAL PERIODICAL INDEX, vol. 1,
1973-- .

Lists all articles in architectural magazines by subject but
additionally in the ARCHITECTURAL PERIODICAL INDEX,
with an author and architect index for cross referencing.

A91   . CATALOGUE OF THE DRAWINGS COLLECTION OF THE
ROYAL INSTITUTE OF BRITISH ARCHITECTS. Vol. 1-- . London:
Gregg International Publishers, 1968-76. (Editors vary.)

A lavishly illustrated catalog with detailed explanation of
each drawing and the architect concerned. Eight volumes
are devoted to the works of nine architects or architect-
families, including Lutyens, Voysey, and the Wyatt family.

Other volumes are to be published on the Scott family, the Papworth family, the Pugin family and Andrea Palladio.

A92 _____. CATALOGUE OF THE ROYAL INSTITUTE OF BRITISH AR-CHITECTS LIBRARY. 2 vols. London: 1937. Reprint. Folkestone and London: 1972. Vol. 1, AUTHOR CATALOGUE OF BOOKS AND MANUSCRIPTS, 1138 p. Vol. 2, CLASSIFIED INDEX AND ALPHABETICAL SUBJECT INDEX OF BOOKS AND MANUSCRIPTS, 514 p.

Very much out of date but does provide information on the early collection. It is hoped that an updated RIBA library catalog will be published in the near future similar to that of Avery Architectural Library.

A93 _____. DIRECTORY OF MEMBERS. London: 1973-- . Annual. Various sections separately numbered.

Lists all members, with their degrees, awards, and home or office address, but provides none of the additional material common to its counterpart in the United States. There is also a DIRECTORY OF PRACTICES and together they re-place what was known as the KALENDAR published from 1886-1965 in seventy-four editions. It was replaced by the DIRECTORY from 1966-72.

A94 _____. "Index of Architects of Several Countries and Many Periods." Mimeographed. London: 1956. 66 p.

A listing "containing nearly 4,000 names and 10,000 ref-erences."

A95 Richards, J.M. ARCHITECTURE TODAY. London: Arts Council, 1961. [58 p.], 26 pls.

Fifty-six buildings by a representative sampling of British architects are listed and described; twenty-six of these buildings are illustrated.

A96 _____. THE FUNCTIONAL TRADITION IN EARLY INDUSTRIAL BUILDINGS. London: Architectural Press, 1958. 200 p.

Mainly a photographic survey organized by building type.

A97 Richardson, Albert E. MONUMENTAL CLASSIC ARCHITECTURE IN GREAT BRITAIN AND IRELAND DURING THE EIGHTEENTH AND NINETEENTH CENTURIES. London: B.T. Batsford, 1914. 124 p.

Surveys classical architecture in Britain from early seven-teenth century to mid-nineteenth. Richardson thoroughly

illustrates and describes all the major examples in each
phase of development.

A98   Service, Alastair, ed. EDWARDIAN ARCHITECTURE AND ITS ORI-
        GINS. London: Architectural Press, 1975. 504 p.

        Covering the period 1870 to 1914, this book considers the
        pioneers, their stylistic traditions, and the types of struc-
        tures which they built. The book similarly treats the archi-
        tects of the early twentieth century who were influenced
        by the pioneers but who also established their own creative
        atmosphere.

A99   Sharp, Dennis. SOURCES OF MODERN ARCHITECTURE. Architec-
        tural Association Papers, no. 2. London: 1967. 56 p.

        A selected bibliography on modern architects worldwide.
        Additionally, there is a section devoted to books on na-
        tional trends.

A100   _____. A VISUAL HISTORY OF TWENTIETH CENTURY ARCHITEC-
        TURE. London: Heinemann, 1972. 304 p.

        Architecture worldwide, with British examples and a chron-
        ological table.

A101   Spain, Geoffrey, and Dromgoole, Nicholas. "Theatre Architects of
        the British Isles." AH 13 (1970): 77-89.

        Theaters are listed numerically per year from 1840 to 1920,
        by location, and under the names of sixteen architects.
        There is an additional listing of "other architects" in and
        outside of London.

A102   Statham, Heathcote. MODERN ARCHITECTURE: A BOOK FOR AR-
        CHITECTS AND THE PUBLIC. London: Chapman and Hall, 1897.
        281 p.

        Essentially a survey of late Victorian architecture of Britain,
        with added European and American examples.

A103   Stephen, Douglas; Frampton, Kenneth; and Carapetian, Michael.
        BRITISH BUILDINGS, 1960-1964. London: Adam and Charles Black,
        1965. 103 p.

        Thirteen modern buildings by twelve British architects are
        carefully analyzed with plans, sections, interior and exte-
        rior photographs, and descriptions.

A104   Summerson, John. '45-'55: TEN YEARS OF BRITISH ARCHITECTURE. London: Arts Council of Great Britain, 1955. 60 p.

This exhibition catalog surveys all building types in this ten-year period, with a brief introduction to each of nine sections.

A105   _____. VICTORIAN ARCHITECTURE: FOUR STUDIES IN EVALUA-TION. New York: Columbia University Press, 1970. 131 p.

This book consists of the 1968 Bampton Lectures, a series of four, given at Columbia University, New York. The first lecture evaluates Victorian architecture; the second, "Two Victorian Stations" (King's Cross by Lewis Cubitt and St. Pancras by G.G. Scott); the third, "Two Victorian Churches" (St. James the Less by G.E. Street and St. Martin's by Edward Buckton Lamb, both in London); and, finally, the Law Courts Competition, won by G.E. Street.

A106   Trent, Christopher. ENGLAND IN BRICK AND STONE. London: Anthony Blond, 1958. 272 p.

Chapter 10, "The Victorian Age and After," and chapter 11, "Today and Tomorrow," briefly cover these periods in thirty pages.

A107   The Trussed Concrete Steel Co., Ltd. REINFORCED CONCRETE--A PICTORIAL RECORD. London: [1946?]. 47 p.

Interesting because it illustrates architecture in Britain of the period between the two world wars.

A108   Turnor, Reginald. NINETEENTH CENTURY ARCHITECTURE IN BRITAIN. London: B.T. Batsford, 1950. 118 p.

All the major movements, famous architects, and important buildings of the period are well covered. The nineteenth century looked backward for precedents and forward toward the future but the "Romantic Movement, paradoxically ended by killing the romance of architecture among other arts."

A109   Ware, Dora. A SHORT DICTIONARY OF BRITISH ARCHITECTS. London: George Allen and Unwin, 1967. 312 p.

A brief dictionary of British architects from the twelfth century to the present, emphasizing major architects and their principal, extant, and, mostly, London works.

A110   Webb, Michael. ARCHITECTURE IN BRITAIN TODAY. London: Country Life Books, 1969. 256 p.

"The aims of the book are to illuminate, to guide and to provoke." It covers a ten-year period prior to 1969 and analyzes 140 buildings of all types with regard to functional and visual qualities. Numerous plans, sections, and photographs.

A111   West, Thomas Wilson. A HISTORY OF ARCHITECTURE IN ENGLAND. London: University of London Press, 1963. 176 p.

Forty pages, a few photographs, and some crude drawings cover the nineteenth and twentieth centuries.

A112   Wood, K.M. "Precast Concrete in the U.K." CANADIAN ARCHITECT 11 (July 1966): 51-62.

Seventeen examples of the use of precast concrete are illustrated. The aim of using this material has been to produce greater architectural effect with less weight.

A113   Yarwood, Doreen. THE ARCHITECTURE OF ENGLAND FROM PREHISTORIC TIMES TO THE PRESENT DAY. London: B.T. Batsford, 1963. 672 p.

A major and detailed survey with numerous line drawings and some photographs. Each chapter considers a period of history in detail giving a general statement about the period; discussing its major movements, leading theorists and practitioners, minor masters, and building types.

A114   Yorke, F.R.S., and Penn, Colin. A KEY TO MODERN ARCHITECTURE. London and Glasgow: Blackie & Son, 1939. 180 p.

All architecture was at one time "modern." In this book the new structural techniques, materials, and production techniques available to architects; the "New Aesthetic"; and the theories attached to the English interpretation of the International Style are presented. One of its authors—Colin Penn—worked for William Lescaze in the United States and at Dartington Hall, England.

A115   ZODIAC. "Selection of Architectural Works by British Architects." 18 (1968): 64-118.

The most recent work of twenty-six major firms of architects is illustrated and described.

Section B

TOWNS, CITIES, AND COUNTIES OF ENGLAND

Book references only since the number of articles is too extensive. For minor publications, see Goodey A47.

B1   AAL. GUIDE TO MODERN ARCHITECTURE IN LONDON, 1927-1957. London: 1957. 12 p., index, foldout map.

    The index is keyed to the foldout map to indicate the location of modern buildings in London that are worth seeing.

B2   Allsopp, Bruce. HISTORICA ARCHITECTURE OF NEWCASTLE-UPON-TYNE. Newcastle upon Tyne: Oriel Press, 1967. 96 p.

    From earliest times to the early twentieth century.

B3   Allsopp, Bruce, and Clark, Ursula. HISTORIC ARCHITECTURE OF NORTHUMBERLAND. Newcastle upon Tyne: Oriel Press, 1969. 96 p.

    Roman to Victorian architecture, plus vernacular examples, are presented in approximately three hundred annotated photographs.

B4   Ayers, John. ARCHITECTURE IN BRADFORD. Bradford: Bradford Civic Society, n.d. 108 p.

    A selection of significant buildings is described and illustrated by photographs, sketches, and original drawings. The city is considered as six geographic areas, mainly developed in the nineteenth century but earlier and later periods of growth are also recognized.

B5   Balfour, Alan. PORTSMOUTH. London: Studio Vista, 1970. 95 p.

    A book covering the region and docks, including their naval and defense structures, in addition to the town's other architecture.

B6   Betjeman, John, and Piper, John. MURRAY'S BUCKINGHAMSHIRE
ARCHITECTURAL GUIDE. London: John Murray, 1948. 132 p.

A presentation of good, representative examples of all periods of architecture in 112 pages of photographs; includes
a "Gazetteer To All Parishes," pp. 113-28.

B7   Bolton and District Civic Trust. THE BUILDINGS OF BOLTON.
N.p., n.d. 34 p.

Examples essentially of nineteenth century architecture in
various areas of the city are illustrated and described.

B8   Booth, Philip, and Taylor, Nicholas. CAMBRIDGE NEW ARCHITEC-
TURE. London: Leonard Hill, 1970. 209 p.

A survey of all major buildings built in Cambridge, 1945-
68. For each building the date of construction, names of
architect and contractor, cost, requirements, and description are provided.

B9   _____. A GUIDE TO CAMBRIDGE NEW ARCHITECTURE: THREE
WALKS FROM THE MARKET PLACE. London: Leonard Hill, 1972.
75 p.

Not intended to be a comprehensive survey, this book attempts "to show a typical cross-section of what has been
built in the last twenty years, by the city, by the university
and by individuals, and to place this in the context of the
town as a whole."

B10   Burrough, T.H.B. BRISTOL. London: Studio Vista, 1970. 96 p.

This maritime port was heavily damaged during the Second
World War and has been raped during the succeeding years.
Nevertheless, it still has representative examples of buildings of all historic periods in Britain. One hundred seventy-
two examples selected from the medieval period to the present are described and illustrated.

B11   Cantacuzino, Sherban, et al. CANTERBURY. London: Studio Vista,
1970. 90 p.

Canterbury is thought of as a medieval city, but subsequent
developments, including comprehensive changes after the
Second World War, have produced a city of wider interest.
One hundred and thirty buildings are illustrated and noted.

B12   Casson, Hugh [Maxwell]. NEW SIGHTS OF LONDON: THE HANDY
GUIDE TO CONTEMPORARY ARCHITECTURE. London: London Transport, 1930. 54 p.

B13   Clunn, Harold P. THE FACE OF LONDON. Rev. ed. London:
       Phoenix House, 1951. 630 p., 200 illus.

       An extensive history of the architectural development of
       London "from the dawn of the nineteenth century down to
       the year 1951." Earlier aspects are also considered.

B14   _____. LONDON REBUILT, 1897-1927. London: John Murray,
       1927. 316 p.

       "An attempt to depict the principal changes which have
       taken place with some suggestions for the further improve-
       ments of the metropolis." Each district of the city is con-
       sidered and the book is well illustrated.

B15   Coard, Peter, and Coard, Ruth E. VANISHING BATH: BUILDINGS
       THREATENED AND DESTROYED. 2d ed. Bath: Kingsmead Press,
       1973. xx, 313 p., pls.

       "This book is a record of some of the Bath buildings destroyed
       or threatened with demolition during the last ten years."
       The book consists of 311 plates of sketches by Peter Coard
       of Georgian and Victorian buildings and their details.

B16   Crawford, David. THE CITY OF LONDON: ITS ARCHITECTURAL
       HERITAGE. London: Woodhead-Faulkner in association with Commer-
       cial Union, forthcoming.

       Two walks of an hour or so, each covering a total of sixty
       buildings of all periods.

B17   Crick, Clare. VICTORIAN BUILDINGS IN BRISTOL. Bristol: Bristol
       and West Building Society, 1975. 72 p.

       The various phases and styles of Victorian architecture in
       Bristol are considered, with a special emphasis on commer-
       cial and residential buildings. Engravings and architects'
       original drawings are used as illustrations of buildings ex-
       tant and demolished.

B18   Crossland, James Brian. LOOKING AT WHITEHAVEN. Whitehaven:
       Whitehaven Borough Council, 1971. 74 p.

       Concerns the borough of Whitehaven and the county of
       Cumberland, placing greater attention on nineteenth- and
       twentieth-century and vernacular architecture. Ninety-
       nine examples are specified.

B19   Dale, Antony. FASHIONABLE BRIGHTON, 1820-1860. Newcastle
       upon Tyne: Oriel Press, 1947. 192 p.

25

This book concentrates on post-Regency Brighton, the period
which has justly made the town famous. The work of
Charles Augustus Busby (1788-1834) and of Amon Henry
Wilds (-1850) is carefully considered. A good bibliography lists publications by Busby.

B20   Dougan, David. NEWCASTLE--PAST AND PRESENT. Newcastle upon
      Tyne: Frank Graham, 1971. 64 p.

      "This book tells Newcastle's story through the ages as shown
      in her historic architecture. It also describes some of the
      best of the new modern buildings."

B21   Hanson, Michael. FAMOUS ARCHITECTS OF THE CITY OF LON-
      DON. London: City Press Publication, 1971. 70 p.

      Thirty-two buildings from the Renaissance to the present are
      considered, each with a full-page illustration and a full-
      page discussion. The book comprises a series of articles
      first published in the CITY PRESS.

B22   _____. 2000 YEARS OF LONDON. London: Country Life, 1967.
      232 p.

      Photographs, engravings, maps, and explanatory text present
      a wide range of architectural history, with strong emphasis
      on the last two hundred years.

B23   Hickman, Douglas. BIRMINGHAM. London: Studio Vista, 1970.
      96 p.

      "Birmingham has much to offer and rewards careful study."
      Well-known and lesser-known buildings are presented chron-
      ologically with an emphasis on those of the last two hun-
      dred years.

B24   Hilling, John Bryan. CARDIFF AND THE VALLEYS. London: Lund
      Humphreys, 1973. 184 p.

      A well-illustrated survey of nineteenth-century architecture
      with a few preindustrial and twentieth-century examples.
      A list of 230 buildings in the region with architectural
      significance are listed on pages 166-70.

B25   Hinton, David Alban. OXFORD BUILDINGS FROM MEDIEVAL TO
      MODERN: EXTERIORS. Oxford: Oxford Archaeological Excavation
      Committee, 1972. 64 p.

      Fifty-six buildings, of which eleven are post-1839, are
      considered.

B26   Hughes, J. Quentin. LIVERPOOL. London: Studio Vista, 1969. 143 p.

         A photographic and textual description of significant buildings in Liverpool dating from nineteenth century to 1969.

B27   _____. SEAPORT: ARCHITECTURE AND TOWNSCAPE IN LIVERPOOL. London: Lund Humphries, 1964. 179 p.

         A photographic and textual survey of Liverpool with a strong emphasis on its nineteenth-century industrial and commercial architecture.

B28   Jenkins, Simon. A CITY AT RISK. London: Hutchinson, 1970. 190 p.

         "This book is about the streets of London. It is intended partly as a guide, partly as an essay, and partly as a call to arms." The streets of London are considered as total entities of design even though they have taken centuries to develop. The "call to arms" is for a concerted attack on those who would destroy the unity of such spaces.

B29   Kent, Arnold. NORWICH IN PICTURES. Norwich: Jarrold, 1971. 73 pls.

         Seventy-three plates of buildings from the medieval period to the present.

B30   Lambert, Sam. NEW ARCHITECTURE OF LONDON: A SELECTION OF BUILDINGS SINCE 1930. London: British Travel and Holidays Association in collaboration with the Architectural Association, 1965. 100 p.

         One hundred eighty good examples of modern architecture have been selected, illustrated, and described, with a location map provided for each region covered within an eight-mile radius from the center of London.

B31   Lewis, Whitfield. BATTLE OF STYLES. London: RIBA. London Region, 1975. 96 p.

         A committee of the London Region of the RIBA has recommended the listing of buildings, 1914-39, which "represent all facets of the inter-war architectural scene." All the buildings are illustrated. Whitfield Lewis wrote "Preamble."

B32   Linstrum, Derek. HISTORIC ARCHITECTURE OF LEEDS. Newcastle upon Tyne: Oriel Press, 1969. 96 p.

         "Leeds is a city of many fine buildings, most of them dating

from the vigorous and exciting nineteenth century." There
are 215 illustrations and accompanying commentary.

B33 Little, Bryan. BATH PORTRAIT: THE STORY OF BATH, ITS LIFE
AND ITS BUILDINGS. 2d ed. Bristol: Burleigh Press, 1968. 130 p.

To a discussion of the earlier modern period, "Victorian
Variations," and the earlier phases of the city's growth,
the second edition adds a chapter on developments in the
1960s.

B34 _____. BIRMINGHAM BUILDINGS: THE ARCHITECTURAL STORY
OF MIDLAND CITY. Newton Abbot, Devon.: David and Charles,
1971. 128 p.

This survey of Birmingham's heritage includes most of the
one hundred examples belonging to the nineteenth and
twentieth centuries. A lengthy essay, with a brief mention
of earlier periods, complements the photographs. Pages
123-25 provide biographies of "Victorian and Later" architects of the area.

B35 _____. THE BUILDINGS OF BATH, 47-1947: AN ARCHITECTURAL
AND SOCIAL STUDY. London: Collins, 1947. 176 p.

"Grecian and Gothic (1800-1850)," "Modern Bath (1850-
1944)," and "The New Plan" are briefly considered in the
last three chapters.

B36 _____. CHELTENHAM IN PICTURES. Newton Abbot, Devon.:
David and Charles, 1967. 112 p.

The photographs illustrate not only the Regency terraces of
this historic city but also the problems of the present day.

B37 Liverpool, City and County Borough of. LIVERPOOL BUILDS, 1945-
65. Liverpool: 1967. 157 p., index.

All aspects of public architecture are described and illustrated.

B38 McCallum, Ian Robert More. A POCKET GUIDE TO MODERN BUILD-
INGS IN LONDON. London: Architectural Press, 1951. 128 p.

"The Establishment of a New Architecture" and "The Reformation of Environment" are the themes of this book, which
presents the best architecture by the most talented designers
from the 1930s to 1950.

B39   McKean, Charles, and Jesticoe, Tom. GUIDE TO MODERN BUILD-
       INGS IN LONDON, 1965-75. London: Warehouse Publishing (Stu-
       dio International) 1976. 109 p., 3 maps.

       Nine trails of 101 London buildings built within the last
       decade, with an appendix of a further one hundred build-
       ings.

B40   Markham, Felix. OXFORD. London: Weidenfeld and Nicolson,
       1967. 191 p.

       A rather general book but discusses specific examples of
       modern architecture in the last chapter; "Oxford In the
       Twentieth Century."

B41   Metcalf, Priscilla. VICTORIAN LONDON. New York and Wash-
       ington, D.C.: Praeger Publishers, 1972. 190 p.

       Man's exploitation of the environment and man's physical
       surroundings are examined. Beginning with "The Fabric of
       London in 1837," the book devotes one chapter to each
       decade, ending with the 1890s.

B42   Morris, Jan. BATH: AN ARCHITECTURAL GUIDE. London: Faber
       and Faber, 1975. 150 p.

       A few Victorian buildings in this essentially eighteenth-
       century city are illustrated and described.

B43   Nairn, Ian. MODERN BUILDINGS IN LONDON. London: London
       Transport, 1964. 127 p.

       This book describes 250 buildings and contains thirty-six
       pages of illustrations.

B44   _____. NAIRN'S LONDON. Harmondsworth, Mdx.: Penguin
       Books, 1966. 167 p.

       A personal selection of about 150 examples of "the best
       things in London. . . . Everything in the book is acces-
       sible."

B45   Nuttgens, Patrick. YORK. London: Studio Vista, 1970. 94 p.

       The rich nineteen hundred years of development in York have
       resulted in a book of great variety. It covers many of the
       most recent developments too.

B46   _____. YORK: THE CONTINUING CITY. London: Faber and
       Faber, 1976. 130 p.

Townscape from the first century to the twentieth is the basis of this book, which also considers the social, political, and economic aspects of the city.

B47   Pevsner, Nikolaus. BEDFORDSHIRE AND THE COUNTY OF HUNT-INGDON AND PETERBOROUGH. The Buildings of England. Harmondsworth, Mdx.: Penguin Books, 1968. 414 p.

B48   BERKSHIRE. 1966. 355 p.

B49   BUCKINGHAMSHIRE. 1960. 340 p.

B50   CAMBRIDGESHIRE. 2d ed. 1970. 209 p.

B51   CHESHIRE (with Edward Hubbard). 1971. 442 p.

B52   CORNWALL. 2d ed. Revised by E. Radcliffe. 1970. 282 p.

B53   COUNTY DURHAM. 1953. 279 p.

B54   CUMBERLAND AND WESTMORELAND. 1967. 339 p.

B55   DERBYSHIRE. 1953. 282 p.

B56   DEVON NORTH. 1952. 200 p.

B57   DEVON SOUTH. 1952. 351 p.

B58   DORSET (with J. Newman). 1972. 354 p.

B59   ESSEX. 2d ed. Revised by Enid Radcliffe. 1965. 482 p.

B60   GLOUCESTERSHIRE: THE COTSWOLDS (with D. Verey). 1970. 545 p.

B61   GLOUCESTERSHIRE: THE VALE AND THE FOREST OF DEAN (with D. Verey). 1970. 456 p.

B62   HAMPSHIRE (with D. Lloyd). 1967. 832 p.

B63   HEREFORDSHIRE. 1963. 366 p.

B64   HERTFORDSHIRE. 1953. 313 p.

B65   KENT, NORTH EAST AND EAST (with John Newman). 1969. 529 p.

B66   KENT, WEST AND THE WEALD (with John Newman). 1969. 645 p.

B67   LANCASHIRE, NORTH. 1969. 306 p.

B68   LANCASHIRE, SOUTH. 1969. 480 p.

B69   LEICESTERSHIRE AND RUTLAND. 1960. 371 p.

B70   LINCOLNSHIRE (with John Harris). 1964. 770 p.

B71   LONDON 1: THE CITIES OF LONDON AND WESTMINSTER. 3d ed. Revised by Bridget Cherry. 1973. 753 p.

B72   LONDON 2: EXCEPT THE CITIES OF LONDON AND WESTMINSTER. 1952. 496 p.

B73   MIDDLESEX. 1951. 204 p.

B74   NORTH-EAST NORFOLK AND NORWICH. 1962. 392 p.

B75   NORTH-WEST AND SOUTH NORFOLK. 1962. 438 p.

B76   NORTHAMPTONSHIRE. 2d ed. Revised by Bridget Cherry. 1973. 543 p.

B77   NORTHUMBERLAND (with Ian A. Richmond). 1957. 362 p.

B78   NOTTINGHAMSHIRE. 1951. 248 p.

B79   OXFORDSHIRE (with Jennifer Sherwood). 1974. 936 p.

B80   SHROPSHIRE. 1958. 368 p.

B81   SOMERSET, NORTH AND BRISTOL. 1958. 510 p.

B82   SOMERSET, SOUTH AND WEST. 1958. 394 p.

B83   STAFFORDSHIRE. 1974. 376 p.

B84   SUFFOLK. 2d ed. Revised by E. Radcliffe. 1974. 555 p.

B85   SURREY (with Ian Nairn). 2d ed. Revised by Bridget Cherry. 1971. 600 p.

B86   SUSSEX (with Ian Nairn). 1965. 692 p.

B87   WARWICKSHIRE (with A. Wedgwood). 1966. 529 p.

B88   WILTSHIRE. 1963. 578 p. (1976 ed. revised by Bridget Cherry).

B89   WORCESTERSHIRE. 1968. 376 p.

B90   YORKSHIRE: THE EAST RIDING. 1972. 416 p.

B91   YORKSHIRE: THE NORTH RIDING. 1966. 454 p.

B92   YORKSHIRE: THE WEST RIDING. 1967 (2d ed. Revised by E. Radcliffe). 654 p.

> This forty-six-volumed series provides inventories of architectural features from prehistory to the present day, adjudging aesthetic qualities and the placing of buildings within the historical context surveyed in the introduction to each volume.

B93   Plummer, Desmond. DO YOU CARE ABOUT HISTORIC BUILDINGS. London: Greater London Council, n.d. 58 p.

> A case for the partial preservation of the environment of London as it existed prior to modern developments. "More drastic changes have taken place in this century than in the last thousand years."

B94   Salvadori, Renzo. 101 BUILDINGS TO SEE IN LONDON. Translated by Brenda Balich. Venice: Canal Books, 1969. 91 p.

> "This book is intended as an instrument to guide the visitor interested in architecture" with photographs, notes, and

some plans of London's buildings, ranging from the most famous examples of Roman remains to samples of twentieth-century architecture.

B95   Sharp, Dennis. MANCHESTER BUILDINGS. London and Manchester: Architecture North West, The Official Journal of the Liverpool Architectural Society, the Manchester Society of Architects, and the North Lancashire Architectural Society, no. 19, October-November 1966. 60 p.

A publication commemorating the centenary of the Manchester Society of Architects. Two hundred buildings are mentioned and 150 are illustrated. Maps and a gazetteer are provided.

B96   _____, et al. MANCHESTER. London: Studio Vista, 1969. 143 p.

Two hundred representative nineteenth-century buildings--familiar and unfamiliar--in Manchester are described and illustrated.

B97   Stewart, Cecil. THE STONES OF MANCHESTER. London: Edward Arnold, 1956. 144 p.

A thorough and detailed history of nineteenth-century architecture in Manchester.

B98   Summerson, John. THE ARCHITECTURE OF VICTORIAN LONDON. Charlottesville: University Press of Virginia, 1976.

A lucid interpretation of the period for layman and scholar alike, based upon the 1972 Page-Barbour Lectures at the University of Virginia.

B99   _____. THE LONDON BUILDING WORLD OF THE EIGHTEEN-SIXTIES. London: Thames and Hudson, 1973. 60 p.

This fifth Walter Neurath Memorial Lecture given at the University of London studies the men who actually built the major architectural examples of the 1860s.

B100   Taylor, Nicholas. CAMBRIDGE NEW ARCHITECTURE. Edited by Nicholas Hughes, Grant Lewison, and Tom Wesley. Cambridge: 1964. 140 p.

All major postwar college and other buildings and a few prewar projects are illustrated and described by area. There is a map, list of architects and buildings, and photographic coverage.

B101   Whittaker, Neville, and Clark, Ursula. HISTORIC ARCHITECTURE
        OF COUNTY DURHAM. Newcastle upon Tyne: Oriel Press, 1971.
        96 p.

> A history of the architectural heritage of county Durham
> from earliest religious examples to the nineteenth century,
> with an additional section on vernacular architecture. An-
> notations accompany the 270 photographs.

B102   Wilkes, Lyall, and Dodds, Gordon. TYNESIDE CLASSICAL: THE
        NEWCASTLE OF GRAINGER, DOBSON AND CLAYTON. London:
        John Murray, 1964. 159 p.

> Thomas Grainger was the speculative builder, John Clayton,
> the town clerk of Newcastle, and Dobson, the architect.
> Together they transformed an essentially medieval town into
> one of grand nineteenth-century concepts; which is now
> being threatened by the twentieth century.

B103   Wilson, Aubrey. LONDON'S INDUSTRIAL HERITAGE. Newton
        Abbot, Devon.: David and Charles, 1967. 160 p.

> A cross section of a wide variety of buildings and sites
> covering all aspects of trade, industry, and commercial
> activity in London.

B104   Wright, Lance. "An Account of the Bristol Society of Architects,
        1850–1950." RIBAJ 57 (April 1950): 225–9.

> "This study represents the first scholarly study of Victorian
> architecture in Bristol."

Section C

IRISH ARCHITECTURE, INCLUDING TOWNS, CITIES, AND GEOGRAPHIC AREAS

C1   AJ. "Ireland's Modern Buildings." Vol. 144 (7 September 1966): 611-28.

> The president of the RIAI drew up a list of architects who were each asked by the AJ to send one photograph of his own work and nominate one building by another architect. This process of selection produced a representative sampling of modern buildings.

C2   Bell, Thomas. THE ORIGIN AND PROGRESS OF GOTHIC ARCHITECTURE IN IRELAND. Dublin: W.F. Wakeman, 1828. 270 p.

> Section 20, pp. 246-60, is titled "On the Revival of Gothic Architecture in Modern Times."

C3   Brett, Charles Edward Bainbridge. BUILDINGS OF BELFAST, 1700-1914. London: Weidenfeld and Nicolson, 1967. 72 p.

> A catalog of information.

C4   _____. COURT HOUSE AND MARKET HOUSES OF THE PROVINCE OF ULSTER. Belfast: Ulster Architectural Heritage Society, 1973. 108 p.

> All periods up to the present are covered and organized by county.

C5   _____. HISTORIC BUILDINGS, GROUPS OF BUILDINGS, AREAS OF ARCHITECTURAL IMPORTANCE IN THE GLENS OF ANTRIM. Belfast: Ulster Architectural Heritage Society, 1972. 56 p.

> A building-by-building survey of the towns in the area. The architects of many structures seem to be unknown.

C6   Brett, Charles Edward Bainbridge, and McKinstry, R. SURVEY AND

RECOMMENDATIONS FOR JOY STREET AND HAMILTON STREET DISTRICT OF BELFAST. Belfast: Ulster Architectural Heritage Society, 1971. 16 p.

> A brief survey, mainly of anonymous, domestic architecture.

C7   Craig, Maurice. DUBLIN, 1660-1860. London: Cresset Press, 1952. 362 p.

> The most useful parts of this book, particularly with regard to nineteenth-century architecture, are chapter 24, "The End of a Tradition," pp. 291-306; appendix 1, "List of Streets and Buildings," pp. 319-332; and an excellent bibliography.

C8   _____. IRELAND OBSERVED: A HANDBOOK TO THE BUILDINGS AND ANTIQUITIES. Cork: Mercier Press, 1970. 120 p.

> Brief mention of numerous structures from all periods of Irish history. Good bibliography and glossary.

C9   Craig, Maurice, et al. IRISH ARCHITECTURAL DRAWINGS: AN EXHIBITION TO COMMEMORATE THE 25TH ANNIVERSARY OF THE IRISH ARCHITECTURAL RECORDS ASSOCIATION. Dublin: Irish Architectural Records Association, 1965. 44 p.

> A collection of mainly eighteenth- and early nineteenth-century drawings in various collections, listed by the Irish Architectural Records Association, founded in 1939. "Brief Lives" refers to fifteen architects, whose drawings are noted and illustrated in the catalog.

C10   Cuffe, Luan P. ARCHITECTURAL SURVEY. Dublin: Parkside Press, 1953. 64 p.

> Surveys Irish architecture of the early 1950s, which was influenced by the "technical press of other countries."

C11   De Breffny, Brian, and ffolliott, Rosemary. THE HOUSES OF IRELAND. London: Thames and Hudson, 1975. 240 p.

> Chapter 8 surveys material on "Victorian and Edwardian Buildings in Ireland, 1846-1914." It is concerned more with who lived in the mansions than with who designed them.

C12   Delany, Patrick M. ARCHITECTURAL SURVEY 1966. London: Parkside Press, 1966.

> A survey of Dublin's buildings for 1966 with a directory of architects of the Republic of Ireland.

C13   Dixon, Hugh. ULSTER ARCHITECTURE 1800-1900. Belfast: Ulster
        Architectural Heritage Society, 1973. 32 p., 23 unpaged illus.

> This is a catalog of 159 architectural drawings and nine
> portraits, exhibited in the new extension to the Ulster Mu-
> seum, 27 October 1972-2 January 1973. The introduction
> is brief.

C14   Girvan, D.; Oram, R.; and Rowan A. LIST OF HISTORIC BUILD-
        INGS, GROUPS OF BUILDINGS, AREAS OF ARCHITECTURAL IMPOR-
        TANCE IN ANTRIM AND BALLYMENA. Belfast: Ulster Architectural
        Heritage Society, 1969. 34 p.

> A detailed survey but with a marked omission of architects'
> names, even for twentieth-century buildings.

C15   Harvey, John. DUBLIN: A STUDY IN ENVIRONMENT. London:
        B.T. Batsford, 1949. Reprint. East Ardsley Wakefield, Yorkshire:
        S.R. Publishers, 1972. 126 p.

> A brief history, giving numerous facts, most of which can
> more readily be located elsewhere, on the historical archi-
> tecture.

C16   Killanin, Lord, and Duignan, M. THE SHELL GUIDE TO IRELAND.
        2d rev. ed. London: Ebury Press, 1967. 478 p.

> Not intended as an architectural survey, this publication
> provides only minimal information although it does mention
> architects and their works. This edition has a more com-
> prehensive index than the 1962 edition.

C17   McNamara, T.F. "The Architecture of Cork, 1700-1900." YEAR-
        BOOK OF THE ROYAL INSTITUTE OF THE ARCHITECTS OF IRELAND
        (1960): 15-39.

> "Valuable civic papers were burned in the fire of the old
> City and County Courthouse in 1890. Even more recent
> records were destroyed in the burning of the former City
> Hall in 1920." A great city of Greek and Gothic revival
> buildings, many of which are described in detail.

C18   McParland, E.J. "Public Architecture in Ireland, 1750-1850." Doc-
        toral dissertation, Cambridge University, 1975. 507 p.

> A survey of neoclassical architecture.

C19   Masheck, Joseph. "Irish Church-Building between the Treaty of Lim-
        erick and the Great Famine." Doctoral dissertation, Columbia Univer-
        sity, 1973. 423 p.

Covering the years 1691 to 1845, this dissertation is especially valuable for chapters 9, "Greek Churches in Dublin and the Provinces"; 13, "Roman Catholic Gothic"; and 14, "The Early Mediaeval Revival."

C20   Northern Ireland, Government of.   AN ARCHAEOLOGICAL SURVEY OF COUNTY DOWN.   Belfast: Her Majesty's Stationery Office, 1966.   478 p., 213 pls.

Numerous nineteenth-century houses and churches.

C21   O'Connell, Dermot.   "The Irish Architectural Scene."   B 211 (9 September 1968): 113-17.   See also "Architecture in Ireland," pp. 118-26 of the same issue.

"The city grows old gracelessly" is the estimate by O'Connell on Dublin: it is losing its eighteenth-century charm without establishing a twentieth-century character.   "Urban planning in the Republic has been a story of non-planning."

C22   O'Gorman, John.   "Architecture."   In IRISH ART HANDBOOK, pp. 63-66.   Dublin: Cahill and Company, 1943.

Discusses the emergence of modern architecture in Ireland as well as "bogus modernism"--the art deco stylistic trends by speculative builders and others.   O'Gorman's discussion of the ideas of Walter Gropius is followed by a listing of a few notable architects and their works.

C23   QUARTERLY BULLETIN OF THE IRISH GEORGIAN SOCIETY.   "Biographical Dictionary of Irish Architects."   (January-June 1974): 1-2.

An announcement that in 1973 Rolf Loeber had initiated the compilation of a dictionary of Irish architects to cover the period of the sixteenth century to 1914.   Four thousand entries were planned and included craftsmen, but the ultimate numer will probably be nearer six hundred.

C24   RIAI.   SESSIONAL PAPERS, 1863-4 TO 1869-70.   Dublin: 1871. 59 p.

This publication contains papers read to the institute from 1863 to 1870.   It lists and names the seventy-nine members of the institute in 1871:   thirty-eight fellows, twenty-three associates, and eighteen other classes.   Avery Architectural Library, Columbia University holds this volume and the yearbooks for 1943-4, 1946, 1955, 1956-57, 1958, 1959, 1960-61, 1962, 1963, 1964, 1965-66, 1967, 1968, and 1969-71.   The RIBA has only the yearbooks of 1962, 1963, 1968, and 1969-71.   The secretary and librarian of the

RIAI refuses to answer correspondence concerning any holdings which the RIAI may have.

C25   Richardson, Douglas Scott. "Gothic Revival Architecture in Ireland." Doctoral dissertation, Yale University. 1970. 838 p.

Political, social, and cultural history provides the backdrop for the late eighteenth and early nineteenth century Gothic revival of a distinctive Irish flavor for both Protestant and Catholic religious architecture.

C26   Wright, Lance, and Browne, Kenneth. "A Future for Dublin." A R 156 (November 1974): 269-330.

"This is not a 'Guide to Dublin' nor is it about conservation in the currently accepted meaning of the word. It is about Urbanisim." The article is about a changing Dublin and is illustrated with plans, aerial views, drawings, and numerous photographs.

Section D
SCOTTISH ARCHITECTURE, INCLUDING TOWNS, CITIES, AND GEOGRAPHIC AREAS

D1   Aitken, George S. "History and Reminiscences of the Edinburgh Architectural Association." Typewritten. Edinburgh: 13 February 1913. 306 p.

Compiled from the association's books of minutes--recollections of senior members of the EAA--this manuscript is a major source of material on Edinburgh architecture and the association, founded in 1858.

D2   Beazley, Elisabeth, and Lambert, Sam. "The Astonishing City." AJ 139 (1964): 1006-36.

A survey of Glasgow's most historical structures, with an essay on "Greek Thomson," pp. 1014-16, and references to VILLA AND COTTAGE ARCHITECTURE, an 1868 publication of Blackie, the Glasgow publisher (see E74). There are also the essays "James Salmon Junior," pp. 1017-18; "Charles Rennie Mackintosh," pp. 1019-22; and "Some Ware-Houses," pp. 1023-27; a detailed map, p. 1028; and the section titled "Others Worth Visiting," pp. 1029-36.

D3   Butt, John. THE INDUSTRIAL ARCHAEOLOGY OF SCOTLAND. Newton Abbot, Devon.: David and Charles, 1967. 344 p.

One in a series of books on industrial archaeology published by David and Charles. This particular volume on Scotland intends to stimulate local historians to a deeper study of regional histories. Industries described include agriculture, textiles, mining, metal working, chemicals, and transport. Regrettably, in numerous cases designers' names have been omitted although it might have been easy to locate them. The text is followed by a gazetteer (pp. 193-320) of fifteen hundred sites, for which some entries are brief: "The following is an all-too-brief selection from an embarrassingly splendid list of sites" (p. 260). When Butt says "built by" he sometimes means "constructed by," "designed by," "founded by," or "built for."

D4   Cant, Ronald G. HISTORIC BUILDINGS OF ANGUS. Forfar, Angus: Angus Historic Buildings Society, 1974. 40 p., map.

Although brief and with only about ten pages devoted to architecture after about 1800, this publication does list numerous buildings not mentioned elsewhere; however, it does not always list architects. Other small local guides such as this are needed.

D5   Crossland, James Brian. VICTORIAN EDINBURGH. Letchworth: Wayfair Publishers, 1966. 93 p.

Aspects and sketches of the nineteenth-century architecture of Edinburgh as originally published in the SCOTSMAN.

D6   EAA. EDINBURGH: AN ARCHITECTURAL GUIDE. Edinburgh: 1969. Unpaged.

Beginning with the medieval period and ending with modern structures, this guide contains 254 entries that provide facts and data about Edinburgh's architectural heritage.

D7   _____. EXHIBITION CATALOGUE. Edinburgh: 1907. xxii, 67 p.

The EAA was founded in 1858 for professional architects who were not members of the Architectural Institute of Scotland. This exhibition, held from 19 June 1907 through August of that year, surveyed fifty years of work by Scottish architects. The catalog lists the exhibitors and 474 drawings. At the end of the catalog (pp. i-xxii), "Memoirs of Deceased Scottish Architects Whose Portraits Are Exhibited," provides brief biographical data.

D8   Finlay, Ian. THE STORY OF SCOTS ARCHITECTURE. Edinburgh: Douglas and Foulis, 1951. 64 p.

Four broadcasts on Scottish architecture of which the last is concerned briefly (pp. 50-64) with the eclecticisms of the nineteenth century, Mackintosh at the turn of the century, and the architecture of the 1930s.

D9   Gardner, Alexander. "Some Notable Scottish Architects." PROCEEDINGS OF THE ROYAL PHILOSOPHICAL SOCIETY OF GLASGOW 39 (1907-8): 73-91.

As part of the jubilee celebrations of the Glasgow Architectural Society, Gardner presents notes on four eighteenth-century architects and eleven who were alive or practicing after 1840: Peter Nicholson, David Hamilton, J. Gillespie-Graham, Thomas Hamilton, William Burn, William Henry

Playfair, George Meikle Kemp, David Bryce, Charles
Wilson, J.T. Rochead, and Alexander Thomson.

D10   Gomme, Andor, and Walker, David [M.] ARCHITECTURE OF GLAS-
GOW. London: Lund Humphries, 1968. 320 p.

> A detailed study of architecture from the medieval period
> to the early twentieth century, but with an emphasis on
> the Victorian period since Glasgow is a Victorian city with
> an independent tradition. Well illustrated.

D11   Hay, George. THE ARCHITECTURE OF SCOTTISH POST-REFORMA-
TION CHURCHES, 1560–1843. Oxford: Clarendon Press, 1957.
299 p., 47 pls.

> Chapter 5, "Late Georgian and Early Victorian, 1800–43,"
> provides historical background, and appendix A, an "In-
> ventory and Index of Churches, 1560–1843," also records
> dates of the churches and architects concerned. Two-fifths
> of the ministers of the Established Church left to found the
> Free Church in 1843, the terminal date of this work. Dur-
> ing the next eighty years, few parish churches were built.

D12   Hume, John R. INDUSTRIAL ARCHITECTURE OF GLASGOW. Glasgow and London: Blackie and Son, 1974. 327 p., 96 pls.

> Considerable research into Glasgow's industrial past had
> been undertaken long before the demolitions and redevelop-
> ments of the 1960s. The emphasis of the book is on indus-
> trial processes but a major portion is also devoted to a de-
> tailed gazetteer of the city's areas. Most of the plates
> reproduce buildings.

D13   Keppie, John. THE STORY OF THE GLASGOW INSTITUTE OF AR-
CHITECTS FOR THE FIRST FIFTY YEARS. Glasgow: Glasgow Institute of Architects, 1921. 56 p.

> "Being Two Lectures Delivered by Ex President John Keppie,
> FRIBA, ARSA, at the Opening of the Session 1919 and
> 1920." After a brief introduction Keppie lists members,
> deaths, and affairs of the institute year by year, 1869–
> 1919.

D14   Lindsay, Ian Gordon. THE CATHEDRALS OF SCOTLAND. London:
W. and R. Chambers, 1926. 256 p.

> All cathedrals of Scotland, including those of the Roman
> Catholic church are listed. Nineteenth-century restora-
> tions, new works, and the architects employed are men-
> tioned.

D15   Macaulay, James. THE GOTHIC REVIVAL, 1745-1845. Glasgow and London: Blackie, 1975. 451 p.

Concentrating more upon "Gothick," than Gothic revival buildings in northern England and Scotland, Macaulay first describes the background of the area and the revival movement there and then its numerous architectural examples.

D16   Nicoll, James, ed. DOMESTIC ARCHITECTURE OF SCOTLAND. Aberdeen: Daily Journal Offices, 1908. xix p., 66 pls.

The plates consist of plans, elevations, and photographs.

D17   Petzsch, Helmut. ARCHITECTURE IN SCOTLAND. London: Longman, 1971. 146 p.

Chapters 11 and 12, on the nineteenth and twentieth centuries, are brief but well illustrated. Each chapter has a lengthy, representative list "Buildings to See" and a "Further Reading" bibliography.

D18   Reid, J.M. GLASGOW. London: B.T. Batsford, 1956. 176 p.

Brief mention is made of architects throughout the book but notably in chapter 6--"The Age of Grey Ashlar"--in which "Greek" Thomson figures prominently.

D19   Royal Scottish Academy of Painting, Sculpture and Architecture. CENTENARY EXHIBITION OF THE ROYAL SCOTTISH ACADEMY OF PAINTING, SCULPTURE AND ARCHITECTURE 1826-1926. Edinburgh: 1927. 114 p., 116 pls.

Exhibits 512-59 list the "Architectural Works in Members' Gallery."

D20   Steer, Kenneth. RECORDING SCOTLAND'S HERITAGE. Edinburgh: Her Majesty's Stationery Office, 1975. 16 p.

This is not a catalog but a lengthy statement on the origins, working methods, and progress of the work of the Royal Commission on the Ancient and Historical Monuments of Scotland. The archive known as the National Monuments Record of Scotland has about one hundred forty thousand photographs and fifty thousand drawings.

D21   Walker, David M. ARCHITECTS AND ARCHITECTURE IN DUNDEE 1770-1914. Abertay Historical Society Publication no. 3. Dundee: 1955. 32 p.

A thorough survey of Dundee architecture with meaty footnotes and detailed information in the "Index of Architects and Engineers," pp. 31-32.

D22 _____. "The Architecture of Dundee." In DUNDEE AND DISTRICT, edited by S.J. Jones, pp. 284-300. Dundee: Dundee Local Executive Committee of the British Association, 1968.

> The first four pages are devoted to prenineteenth-century architecture. The remainder surveys various building types and parallel developments in Dundee to 1968.

D23 _____. NINETEENTH CENTURY MANSIONS IN THE DUNDEE AREA. Dundee: College of Art, 1958. 8 p., 24 pls., frontispiece.

> Sketches by Walker accompanied by explanatory text.

D24 West, T.W. A HISTORY OF ARCHITECTURE IN SCOTLAND. London: University of London Press, 1967. 208 p.

> Chapters 9 and 10--"Engineering and Revivalism, c.1800-c.1900" and "The Twentieth Century"--briefly survey the period.

D25 Young, Andrew McLaren, and Doak, A.M. GLASGOW AT A GLANCE. Rev. ed. Glasgow: Collins, 1971. Unpaged.

> A series of 231 structures, each photographed, annotated, and listed chronologically from the medieval period to 1970.

Section E

BUILDING TYPES

E1   Abercrombie, Patrick, ed. THE BOOK OF THE MODERN HOUSE:
A PANORAMIC SURVEY OF CONTEMPORARY DOMESTIC DESIGN.
London: Hodder and Stoughton, 1939. 378 p., 244 pls.

    Fourteen authors have contributed articles, which comple-
ment the book's illustrations on all aspects of housing, including furniture and interiors, at home and abroad, in
town and in country.

E2   Allen, Gordon. THE CHEAP COTTAGE AND SMALL HOUSE: A
MANUAL OF ECONOMICAL BUILDINGS. London: B.T. Batsford,
1919. 143 p.

    This book surveys all aspects of the small house, notably
those by Gordon Allen.

E3   Architectural Press. THE SMALLER HOUSE: BEING SELECTED EX-
AMPLES OF THE LATEST PRACTICE IN MODERN ENGLISH DOMES-
TIC ARCHITECTURE. London: 1924. 191 p.

    This book offers photographs, plans or drawings, and a de-
scription of numerous examples of smaller houses. One of
many publications on this subject.

E4   Barman, Christian. AN INTRODUCTION TO RAILWAY ARCHITEC-
TURE. London: Art and Technics, 1950. 104 p.

    Railway architecture is "a complete epitome of the archi-
tectural movements of nineteenth century England . . . an
architecture of revolution. Moreover, architects educated
in the humanist tradition were employed in . . . a fascinating mixture of engineering design and vernacular architecture strengthened here and there with an infusion of
high architectural skill." Examples are provided from periods throughout the nineteenth century to the Second World
War.

E5   Barr, A.W. Cleeve. PUBLIC AUTHORITY HOUSING. London: B.T. Batsford, 1958. 287 p.

> This book is concerned with the design, construction, standards, services, and density of housing schemes and, in pages 153-280, examines fifty-six examples of housing throughout Britain.

E6   Barton, Stuart. MONUMENTAL FOLLIES: AN EXPOSITION ON THE ECCENTRIC EDIFICES OF BRITAIN. Worthing, Sussex: Lyle Publications, 1972. 271 p.

> An attempt to "define the undefinable" in the range of sham, elaborate, and enormous architectural edifices. The follies are considered in geographical order by country in England, Scotland, and Wales, with maps, photographs, and brief descriptions.

E7   Berriman, S.G., and Harrison, K.C. BRITISH PUBLIC LIBRARY BUILDINGS. London: Andre Deutsch, 1966. 260 p.

> From roughly 1960-65 private and public architects built a large number of well-designed public libraries in Britain. A commentary is supplemented by fifty plans, more than two hundred photographs, and a listing of libraries built on pp. 247-58.

E8   Betjeman, John. COLLINS GUIDE TO ENGLISH PARISH CHURCHES. London: Collins, 1958. 480 p.

> A well-illustrated, annotated, county-by-county, selective survey of English parish churches, most of which were built in the nineteenth century.

E9   _____. LONDON'S HISTORIC RAILWAY STATIONS. London: John Murray, 1972. 126 p.

> The space, materials, taste, architectural features (and follies), function, and structure of twelve London stations are analyzed and illustrated.

E10   Biddle, Gordon. VICTORIAN STATIONS. Newton Abbot, Devon.: David and Charles, 1973. 256 p.

> Covering the years 1830 to 1923 and emphasizing the golden age of railway building--the 1840s and '50s--this text discusses many of the outstanding examples out of a possible ninety thousand Victorian stations in Great Britain. Also discussed is the work of seven major railway architects. Well illustrated with line drawings and photographs.

E11   Birchett, Denis. "Review of Some Parking Buildings." AJ 144 (6 July 1966): 45–60.

"Most available information on design of parking buildings is based on American or European experience." Thirteen British examples completed prior to the Building Regulations of 1965 are examined.

E12   Birks, Tony. BUILDING THE NEW UNIVERSITIES. Newton Abbot, Devon.: David and Charles, 1972. 128 p.

All aspects of university buildings designed since 1959 "in the biggest wave of university expansion in the nation's history" are considered. Seven major new campuses are critically evaluated.

E13   Boyne, Colin. "Churchill College, A Science College: But Is Its Design Based on Scientific Principles?" AJ 130 (3 September 1959): 118–42.

The competition for the design of Churchill College, Cambridge, was won by Richard Sheppard, Robson and Partners. This lengthy article presents sixteen of the unsuccessful designs giving each's general and specific planning details.

E14   Brawne, Michael. "The New Universities." AR 147 (April 1970): 237–313.

Eleven British universities are examined, compared, and appraised, with considerations of their landscapes, their architectural contributions to education, activities, space, and location.

E15   Bruckmann, Hansmartin, and Lewis, David L. NEW HOUSING IN GREAT BRITAIN. London: Alec Tiranti, 1960. 131 p.

The text, in English and German, forwards the idea that England has much to offer in the field of housing mainly due to her experience of rapid industrial expansion and, then, well-planned redevelopment and new town programs. Sociological, technical, economic, and artistic solutions are presented. Multistoried and individual houses are well illustrated.

E16   Cantacuzino, Sherban. "New Uses for Old Buildings." AR 151 (May 1972): 261–327.

Churches and educational and commercial buildings seem to be the building types most likely to be adapted to new uses. European examples begin this survey, which comprises this whole issue of AR.

49

E17 _____. "Offices." AR 148 (October 1970): 219-50.

"The fact that most people spend a large proportion of their lives at work would be enough to justify the REVIEW devoting half an issue to offices," and to the individuals, as opposed to organizations, who use them. Numerous examples throughout Britain are cited and illustrated.

E18 Clarke, Basil F.L. CHURCH BUILDERS OF THE NINETEENTH CENTURY: A STUDY OF THE GOTHIC REVIVAL IN ENGLAND. 2d ed. Newton Abbot, Devon.: David and Charles, 1969. 296 p.

At the time of its original publication in 1938, this book "was a pioneer application of the buildings of the High Victorian period." Two appendixes list architects and their churches and the churches' locations.

E19 _____. PARISH CHURCHES OF LONDON. London: B.T. Batsford, 1966. 312 p.

A reference guide to every parish church in London (excluding cathedrals, mission churches, and some chapels), including the "thin, cheap, brick churches of the 1830's and early '40's" and the bomb-damaged churches that were repaired in the 1950s.

E20 Clay, Felix. MODERN SCHOOL BUILDINGS. 3d ed. London: B.T. Batsford, 1929. 208 p.

Providing numerous examples, especially of plans, this book is essentially "A Handbook on the Planning Arrangement, and Fitting of Day and Boarding Schools."

E21 Crawford, Alan, and Thorne, Robert. BIRMINGHAM PUBS, 1890-1939. Birmingham: University of Birmingham Centre for Urban and Regional Studies, in association with the Victorian Society, 1976. 32 p.

During the two major periods of pub building in Birmingham--1897-1907 and 1920-35--all pubs were constructed by cabinetmakers and the elitest of building contractors.

E22 Crawford, David, ed. A DECADE OF BRITISH HOUSING. London: Architectural Press, 1975. 252 p.

After a general introduction to the "fast-changing" housing layouts of the decade 1963-73, twenty-one examples are studied in detail. Bibliography, pp. 249-50.

E23 Crook, J. Mordaunt. THE BRITISH MUSEUM. London: Allen Lane--

Penguin Press, 1972. 251 p.

> The title of the book should really be THE MUSEUM IN BRITAIN since the book is not solely concerned with the British Museum--it also covers architectural politics, taste, and the economic pressures of public, secular, and national museums.

E24 Davison, Thomas Raffles. MODERN HOMES. London: George Bell and Sons, 1909. 248 p.

> Sixty examples of domestic architecture by a wide range of architectural talents are illustrated and commented upon, in the hope that the layman will be influenced "toward the attainment of a higher ideal" in domestic architecture.

E25 Donat, John. "Living in Universities." AD 36 (December 1966): 589-635.

> This special issue of AD asks: who decides what the living environment of students should be and how do they differ in countries other than Britain? Most of the major projects for university dormitories in Britain over a ten-year period are examined; so too are a few foreign examples.

E26 Dutton, Ralph. THE VICTORIAN HOME. London: B.T. Batsford, 1954. 206 p.

> The book's whole emphasis is on the effect of the family's activities and attitudes on the inside and outside of the residence, 1837-1901.

E27 Friedman, Bernard, ed. FLATS: MUNICIPAL AND PRIVATE ENTERPRISE. London: Ascot Gas Water Heaters, 1938. 287 p.

> A series of essays on the design of flats that considers in detail nineteen housing developments, giving their plans, photographs, costs, construction, special features, equipment, and other characteristics.

E28 Gauldie, Enid. CRUEL HABITATIONS: A HISTORY OF WORKING-CLASS HOUSING, 1780-1918. London: George Allen and Unwin, 1973. 363 p.

> A history of working-class housing in Britain related to "the decay of towns and the unsuccessful attempts to better their condition by public health reforms."

E29 _____. "Lists of Houses Built in Dundee, 1867-1913." Photocopy. N.p., n.d. Copy held at the Jordanstone College Library, Dundee.

This listing of houses, including tenements, was abstracted from records of the Dundee Buildings Department. Each entry has the following information: date, place, built by, built for, number of houses per block, number of rooms per house, sanitation arrangements, and other remarks. Street addresses are sometimes given but street numbers are not. The compilation is approximately six hundred pages long with three entries per page and may have been undertaken in preparation for the author's previous listing, CRUEL HABITATIONS: A HISTORY OF WORKING-CLASS HOUSING, 1780-1918 (see E28).

E30   Girouard, Mark. THE VICTORIAN COUNTRY HOUSE. Oxford: Clarendon Press, 1971. 218 p.

Although this book is primarily concerned with England and Wales, it makes numerous references to Scottish and Irish country houses.

E31   _____. VICTORIAN PUBS. London: Studio Vista, 1975. 223 p.

"In the 1890's London pubs were rich in architectural beauty and in the colourful, often bizarre characters who served and drank in them." There is a chapter titled "The Architects," and, toward the end of the book, pubs outside of London are also considered. The book is well illustrated, occasionally with color reproductions.

E32   Glasstone, Victor. VICTORIAN AND EDWARDIAN THEATRES: AN ARCHITECTURAL AND SOCIAL SURVEY. London: Thames and Hudson, 1975. 136 p., 210 illus.

The elaborate splendor of British theaters, ignored for so long, is now being widely admired and research and preservation societies are being formed. Evolution in design, numerous elaborate examples, and the decline of the theater are the topics considered.

E33   Goodhard-Rendel, H.S. "The Churches of Brighton and Hove." AR 44 (August 1918): 23-29; (September 1918): 59-63; (October 1918): 75-79.

"The churches of a modern seaside town may seem unlikely to prove fruitful for architectural study especially to a generation (1918) not yet awakened to a perception of what was great in the 'Gothic Revival.'" The well-illustrated first part of the article discusses the contributions by R.C. Carpenter, Charles Barry, and Somers Clarke; the second discusses Bodley, Butterfield, and lesser architects; and the third returns to Carpenter and Clarke and comments on John L. Pearson and William Emerson.

E34   Gould, J.H. MODERN HOUSES IN BRITAIN, 1919-39. London: Society of Architectural Historians, forthcoming. 72 p., 40 pls., 24 plans.

> The publisher's announcement states that the book "includes an analytical essay," gazetteering three hundred houses of the period into three distinct movements. This book was an outgrowth of a 1973 B.A. thesis at the University of Newcastle.

E35   Harris, John. A COUNTRY HOUSE INDEX: AN INDEX TO OVER 2,000 COUNTRY HOUSES IN 107 BOOKS OF COUNTRY VIEWS PUBLISHED BETWEEN 1715 AND 1872, TOGETHER WITH A LIST OF BRITISH COUNTRY HOUSE GUIDES AND COUNTRY HOUSE ART COLLECTION CATALOGUES FOR THE PERIOD 1726-1870. Shalfleet Manor, Isle of Wight: Pinhorns, 1971. 43 p.

E36   House and Cottage Exhibition. THE BOOK OF THE EXHIBITION OF HOUSES AND COTTAGES. London: [House and Cottage] Exhibition Committees, 1911. 150 p.

> This exhibition by one hundred architects was held at Romford Garden Suburb, Gidea Park, with houses costing £500 and cottages costing £375.

E37   Howard, Diana. LONDON THEATRES AND MUSIC HALLS, 1850-1950. London: Library Association, 1970. 290 p.

> Each major theater in London is listed, with its date of opening; its former names; the names of its architect and builder; its dates of renovations; the name of its management; its literature; and contemporary historical, and other, accounts of it. A valuable information source.

E38   Jensen, Rolf. HIGH DENSITY LIVING. London: Leonard Hill, 1966. 245 p.

> All aspects are covered in this worldwide survey, which, however, emphasizes twenty-seven British examples.

E39   Jones, Barbara. FOLLIES AND GROTTOES. London: Constable, 1953. 459 p.

> The eccentricity of folly building was a craze of the eighteenth century throughout Britain. "New fashions emerged in the nineteenth century. Sham castles were built to hide a factory or a farm rather than to complete a view, but the true eccentricity always survived." The book is in two parts, the first tracing the history of the folly and the second, "Follies by County," in which 830 are listed, with brief descriptions and photographs or drawings.

E40   Jordan, Robert Furneaux, et al. SCHOOL CONSTRUCTION, 1955-56. London: Councils and Education Press, 1956. 154 p.

School buildings from the mid-1930s for all levels of education are analyzed in a period of changing constructional techniques by both private and public architect.

E41   Leacroft, Richard. THE DEVELOPMENT OF THE ENGLISH PLAYHOUSE. London: Eyre Methuen, 1973. 354 p.

About half of this book is devoted to the post-1840 theater. Cut-away drawings, plans, photographs, and a discussion of the economic, social, and technical aspects of its development provide a comprehensive picture of the theater.

E42   Little, Bryan. CATHOLIC CHURCHES SINCE 1623. London: Robert Hale, 1966. 256 p.

Numerous Catholic churches were built as a result of the Catholic Emancipation Act of 1829, but liturgical changes, which have produced many different architectural expressions and solutions since 1945, have perhaps had an even more significant impact on church design. A thorough survey, well-illustrated.

E43   Lloyd, David, and Insall, Donald. RAILWAY STATION ARCHITECTURE. N.p., n.d. 60 p.

Originally prepared for the Victorian Society, this is a selective survey of individual companies and their lines, which includes sixty examples of railway stations (listed in a schedule on pp. 41-44).

E44   Lloyd, Nathaniel. A HISTORY OF THE ENGLISH HOUSE: FROM PRIMITIVE TIMES TO THE VICTORIAN PERIOD. London: Architectural Press, 1931. Reprint. New York: Architectural Book Publishing Co., 1975. 487 p.

This book is packed with information and is thoroughly illustrated.

E45   Macartney, Mervyn E., ed. RECENT ENGLISH DOMESTIC ARCHITECTURE. London: Architectural Review, 1908. 200 p.

This book was intended to satisfy the great contemporary interest shown at home and abroad in English domestic architecture. A selection of fifty examples is described, with photographs, plans, and other information.

E46   McGrath, Raymond. TWENTIETH CENTURY HOUSES. London: Faber and Faber, 1934. 232 p.

Of these 128 examples worldwide, the first thirty-two are British. A series of chapters covering all aspects of house design complements the examples.

E47   Martin, Bruce. SCHOOL BUILDINGS, 1945-1951. London: Crosby Lockwood and Son, 1952. 128 p.

Plans, photographs, and descriptions of schools. Mainly English, but also a few European and American, examples are provided.

E48   Meeks, Carroll L.V. THE RAILWAY STATION: AN ARCHITECTURAL HISTORY. New Haven: Yale University Press, 1956; London: Architectural Press, Conn. 1957. 203 p.

A study of railway architecture in the Western world, 1800-1956. The emphasis is on style, structure, and construction. A considerable number of British stations are surveyed.

E49   Mills, Edward D. THE MODERN CHURCH. London: Architectural Press, 1956. 189 p.

Emphasizing the design and construction of churches, this book fits into this section only because it illustrates numerous British examples.

E50   Mullins, William, and Allen, Phyllis. STUDENT HOUSING: ARCHITECTURAL AND SOCIAL ASPECTS. London: Crosby Lockwood and Son, 1971. 248 p.

An international survey of students' requirements and needs, with fifty-nine schemes, a large number of which are British, analyzed in depth.

E51   Newton, Ernest, and Newton, W.G. ENGLISH DOMESTIC ARCHITECTURE. London: Technical Journals, [1923]. 176 p.

H.S. Goodhard-Rendel added an essay to the book entitled "Modern British House Planning: A Note on Recent Tendencies" and states "I doubt that any house-plan among the works of our contemporaries is better of its sort than the best of Shaw's and of Nesfield's were of theirs. . . . It is possible for the picturesque to be almost as uncomfortable as sublime." To Goodhard-Rendel the work by Lutyens had a "system of balance between arrangement and appearance." This book consists almost wholly of plans, descriptions, and photographs of 107 houses for town and country.

E52   Park, June. HOUSES AND BUNGALOWS. London: B.T. Batsford, 1958. 191 p.

"This book is intended to help you discover what those possibilities [of having a residence designed] are and where you need professional advice in order to make the best of them." Thirty-seven examples, all but five, British, are analyzed, with site, plan, construction, and services explained.

E53   Pevsner, Nikolaus. A HISTORY OF BUILDING TYPES. London: Thames and Hudson, 1976. 352 p.

An expansion of the Mellon Lectures given at the National Gallery, Washington, in 1970, investigating public buildings worldwide.

E54   Phillips, R. Randal. THE MODERN ENGLISH HOUSE. London: Country Life, n.d. xxii p., 192 pls.

By "modern" the author means recent since these houses cover all aspects of architecture between the two world wars. Some should be considered modern, but many are derivative of historic styles and vernacular traditions.

E55   Physick, John, and Darby, Michael. MARBLE HALLS. London: Victoria and Albert Museum, 1973. 220 p.

This catalog from the exhibition, "Drawings and Models for Victorian Secular Buildings," is wide ranging, covering 152 examples of all building types except ecclesiastical. All are illustrated, a few in color.

E56   Pidgeon, Monica, and Crosby, Theo. AN ANTHOLOGY OF HOUSES. London: B.T. Batsford, 1960. 174 p.

"Our intention is to show houses that really attempt to solve the problem of the mid-twentieth century dwelling." A dozen British examples are included in this worldwide survey. Good photographic coverage with plans and commentary.

E57   Pite, [Arthur] Beresford. "A Review of the Tendencies of the Modern School of Architecture." RIBAJ 8 (1900-1901): 82-84.

A survey of the development from the medieval revival styles to the arts-and-crafts movement. The evolution considers Burges, Godwin, Sedding, Butterfield, Webb, Shaw, and Bodley.

E58   Port, M.H. SIX HUNDRED NEW CHURCHES: A STUDY OF THE CHURCH BUILDING COMMISSION, 1818-1856, AND ITS CHURCH

BUILDING ACTIVITIES. London: Society for the Propagation of Christian Knowledge, 1961. 208 p.

> This book is valuable for appendix 1, "Grants Made by the Church Building Commission, 1818–56, List of Churches."

E59   Price, Barbara. TECHNICAL COLLEGES AND COLLEGES OF FURTHER EDUCATION. London: B.T. Batsford, 1959. 160 p.

> Twelve English examples of technical colleges are thoroughly considered, with background information on their design, planning, and accommodation provided.

E60   Richards, Timothy M., and Curl, James Stevens. CITY OF LONDON PUBS: A PRACTICAL AND HISTORICAL GUIDE. Newton Abbot, Devon.: David and Charles, 1973. 216 p.

> A guide to the densest area of public houses in Britain is divided into ten convenient walking sections, each full of descriptions.

E61   Robson, Edward Robert. SCHOOL ARCHITECTURE. London: John Murray, 1874. 440 p. Reprint. Introduction by Malcolm Seaborne. Leicester: Leicester University Press; New York: Humanities Press, 1972. [37 p.]., [8 figs.], 440 p.

> Robson integrated the educational and architectural aspects of school design, which he investigated while traveling in Europe and America. It was from that travelling that he "formulated a distinctive rationale for the design of his new London Schools," 1871–89.

E62   Seaborne, Malcolm. ENGLISH SCHOOL: ITS ARCHITECTURE AND ORGANIZATION, 1370–1870. London: Routledge and Kegan Paul, 1971. 317 p., 235 pls.

> "This book is . . . not only a major contribution to architectural history but also a study in the development of educational ideas and practices."

E63   Sharp, Dennis. THE PICTURE PALACE--AND OTHER BUILDINGS FOR THE MOVIES. London: Hugh Evelyn, 1969. 224 p.

> This book examines the evolution of the movie theater, a twentieth-century building type, concentrating on examples by architects in Britain and the United States although a few continental European samples are thrown in for good measure.

E64   Smithells, Roger, ed. MODERN SMALL COUNTRY HOUSES. London: Country Life, 1936. 192 p.

Forty-eight examples, each with at least one photograph, plan, and description, are studied.

E65   Sparrow, Walter Shaw, ed. THE BRITISH HOME OF TODAY. London: Art and Life Library, 1904. Unpaged.

Referring to "specimens of good workmanship . . . at once useful to the general householder and attractive to the professional student," this book is selective and does not intend to be representative. It includes seven essays and a wide variety of illustrations, some in color, of a large number of architects' works.

E66   _____. THE MODERN HOME. London: Studio, 1906. 176 p.

"The aim of the present book is to continue the scheme of work begun in THE BRITISH HOME OF TODAY, appealing to a wider public and presenting "various types of the best contemporary design." There are five essays and numerous illustrations, many in color.

E67   Spiller, Brian. VICTORIAN PUBLIC HOUSES. Newton Abbot, Devon.: David and Charles, 1972. 112 p.

Public houses are of Victorian origin and this book surveys them in all their decorative magnificence in Britain and Ireland.

E68   Sugden, Derek. "The Anatomy of the Factory." AD 38 (November 1968): 513-52.

This whole issue of AD is devoted to "single storey factories in which the structural framework is used to support the roof and services to machinery." The article covers historical and present-day examples, mainly British, but occasionally foreign.

E69   Tarn, John Nelson. FIVE PER CENT PHILANTHROPY: AN ACCOUNT OF HOUSING IN URBAN AREAS BETWEEN 1840 AND 1914. Cambridge: At the University Press, 1973. 211 p.

"Housing of the working man and his family was one of the last considerations in the Victorian town." Opinion and reform changed this priority, but the results of reform were sufficiently unsatisfactory so as to make additional measures ultimately necessary.

E70   _____. WORKING-CLASS HOUSING--NINETEENTH CENTURY BRITAIN. London: Architectural Association, 1971. 105 p.

Tarn considers all, but notably the social and economic, aspects of working-class housing. Much of this housing was anonymous but the architectural profession was active in the field, as chapter 4, "Housing and the Professional Architect," indicates.

E71   Taylor, Derek, and Bush, David. THE GOLDEN AGE OF BRITISH HOTELS. London: A Northwood Publication, 1974. 166 p., index.

What was the reason for the hotel boom in Britain during 1837-1900, who built these hotels, and why have many disappeared? Why are the years 1914-74 considered less than glorious?

E72   Thompson, Anthony. LIBRARY BUILDINGS OF BRITAIN AND EUROPE. London: Butterworths, 1963. 326 p.

Thompson realizes that the topic of library design is richly documented but nevertheless, that few good books exist on British libraries. In part 1, he treats synthetically the subject of library design; in part 2, he analyzes existing library buildings of all categories.

E73   Turnor, Reginald. THE SMALLER ENGLISH HOUSE, 1500-1939. London: B.T. Batsford, 1952. 216 p., 190 figs.

Chapters 5 through 7 concentrate upon the Victorian domestic revival and the "modern" aspects of the 1930s International Style.

E74   VILLA AND COTTAGE ARCHITECTURE: SELECT EXAMPLES OF COUNTRY AND SUBURBAN RESIDENCES RECENTLY ERECTED, WITH A FULL DESCRIPTIVE NOTICE OF EACH BUILDING. London and Glasgow: Blackie and Sons, 1868. 112 p., 80 pls.

This book discusses some of the lesser-known residential works of notable architects of the mid-nineteenth century.

E75   Ward, Colin, ed. BRITISH SCHOOL BUILDINGS--DESIGNS AND APPRAISALS, 1964-74. London: Architectural Press, 1976. 249 p.

Nineteen appraisals are abstracted from the AJ. Minimum standards, open planning, and a reversal to the good old days are discussed.

E76   Whiting, Penelope. NEW HOUSES. London: Architectural Press, 1964. 168 p.

Numerous examples of residential architecture throughout the British Isles are illustrated and described, using photographs of interior and exterior views and occasionally of details, site plans, and building plans.

E77   _____. NEW SINGLE-STOREY HOUSES. London: Architectural Press, 1966. 176 p.

Thirty-one examples of houses are described and illustrated.

E78   Wright, H. Myles. SMALL HOUSES, £500-£2,500. 2d ed. London: Architectural Press, 1946. 112 p.

Architect-designed houses could be built for less than £2,000 prior to 1937 and one of this book's eighty examples cost as little as £285.

E79   Yorke, F.R.S. "The Modern English House." AR 80 (December 1936): 237-314.

Fifteen houses of brick, four of frame construction, and eleven of concrete are illustrated with plans and notes. Yorke considered them to be as typical of the work of the mid-1930s as the houses illustrated in the December 1928 issue of AR were typical of their period of British domestic architecture.

E80   _____. THE MODERN HOUSE IN ENGLAND. 3d ed. London: Architectural Press, 1948. 140 p.

A sequel to the earlier edition, THE MODERN HOUSE, which dealt with houses worldwide, this volume considers only British examples. Each edition added more examples and in the 1948 edition there are twenty-three of brick and stone, thirteen of frame construction, and sixteen of concrete, all from the period 1934-48.

E81   Yorke, F.R.S., and Gibberd, Frederick. MODERN FLATS. . London: Architectural Press, 1958. 208 p.

The introduction begins: "This is really a picture book in which are recorded in photographs, plans and diagrams some of the more distinguished flat buildings which have been built in recent years throughout the world." Most of the examples are, however, from England. This book is very similar to its authors' THE MODERN FLAT, 3d ed., London: Architectural Press, 1950, 208 p., and its two previous editions, of 1937 and 1948.

E82   Yorke, F.R.S., and Whiting, Penelope. THE NEW SMALL HOUSE. London: Architectural Press, 1953. 144 p.

Sixty-four houses built between 1939 and 1953 illustrate the opinion that "the problem of the small house is a live and still a stimulating one" though few "have an appearance that expresses a new way of living, or the new use of materials."

Part 2
SELECTED ANNOTATED BIOGRAPHICAL
BIBLIOGRAPHY OF BRITISH ARCHITECTS, 1840-1976

SELECTED ANNOTATED BIOGRAPHICAL BIBLIOGRAPHY
OF BRITISH ARCHITECTS, 1840-1976

1:1   ABERDEEN, DAVID DU RIEU (1913-)

Studied at the University of London where he also taught, 1947-50.
Won the competition for the Trades Union Congress Memorial Building,
London, 1953.

1:2   Richards, J.M.   "Criticism: TUC Memorial Building." AJ 126 (19
December 1957): 912-14.

Although slightly jazz moderne and with a few shortcomings,
the building has a very high standard of finish throughout.
Pages 915-24 illustrate the building in more detail and provide factual information.

2:1   ADSHEAD, STANLEY DAVENPORT (1868-1946)

Trained under George Sherrin, Ernest George, and William Flockart.
Publications: MODERN METHODS OF BUILDING, 1937; A NEW
ENGLAND, 1941; and several books on town and regional planning
schemes. Obituaries: RIBAJ 53 (May 1946): 53; TPIJ 32 (May/
June 1946): 157; Lionel B. Budden, TPR 19 (Summer 1947): 121-22.

2:2   Parkes, Kineton.   "Draughtsmen of Today." AJ 66 (3 August 1927):
175-77.

An appreciation of sketches, watercolors, and pen and ink
drawings.

3:1   AHRENDS, BURTON AND KORALEK (Partnership 1961-)

Peter Ahrends (1933-   ), Richard Burton (1933-   ), and Paul G.
Koralek (1933-   ).   All three studied at the AAL, 1951-56. Burton

worked for Powell and Moya. Koralek worked in New York for Marcel Breuer. He submitted and won the competition for the library at Trinity College, Dublin, 1961, while living in New York.

3:2   Burton, Richard, and Koralek, Paul. "Small Group Design and the Idea of Quality." RIBAJ 78 (June 1971): 232-39.

Two members of the firm discuss their office environment. "Like many architects, we work in a general atmosphere of uncertainty about what we are doing. We can no longer function within the context of certainty and conviction of the modern movement, and are surrounded by doubts and questions." Their two buildings at Trinity College, Dublin, in addition to nine projects in England, one in Israel, and another in Australia, are illustrated.

3:3   Colquhoun, Alan. "Library, Trinity College, Dublin." AR 142 (October 1967): 264-77.

The library should be full of books in forty-five years. Then how will it expand? It is a symbolic building with an emphasis on ceremony rather than function. After discussing organizational weaknesses, Colquhoun states that "the handling of the masses in their plastic relationships shows great skill." Thoroughly illustrated.

3:4   Cornforth, John. "A Threat to Trinity College, Dublin." CL 150 (19 August 1971): 430-31.

A discussion of Koralek's design for the new Arts Building, to be sited on the southern part of the Fellows' Garden at Trinity College to accommodate forty-five hundred people. Cornforth is sympathetic but has reservations concerning its scale and loss of trees.

3:5   Delaney, Patrick. "Trinity College Library, Dublin." AD 37 (October 1967): 459-68.

Delaney, an architect and journalist for the IRISH TIMES, comments on higher education in Dublin, and focusing upon Trinity College and its new library.

3:6   Donat, John. "Magic Box: Trinity College Library in Dublin." AF 127 (October 1967): 459-68.

"Almost by definition Ahrends, Burton and Koralek are anti-box architects; so what could they do with a winning scheme that was clearly, unmistakably and irrevocably a box?" It became a box of tricks and by transformation was no longer a box. Plans, sections, and photographs illustrate how the building is "a virtuoso orchestration of light."

3:7   Haddock, Mary. "Architects and Their Offices." B 211 (11 No-
       vember 1966): 115-17.

           "The firm turns down most small work because they find it
           difficult to afford the disproportionate amount of time in-
           volved."

3:8   McGrath, Norman. "New Setting for Rare Books." AF 131 (De-
       cember 1969): 70-75.

           After having its new library built, Trinity College, Dublin,
           decided to hire Ahrends, Burton and Koralek to renovate
           the two hundred fifty-year-old library and to construct an
           east pavilion.

3:9   Silver, Nathan. "Translating the Root Form for Today's Campus."
       PA 47 (April 1966): 156-57, 168-77.

           Chichester Theological College, Sussex, is small with a
           "loving attention to materials, details and appropriate se-
           quence of space."

3:10   Wright, Lance. "Building Revisited." AJ 156 (26 July 1972):
       205-16.

           The library at Trinity College, Dublin, is reappraised as a
           reader's library and not a librarian's library. The building
           is inflexible but an interesting place in which students can
           use books as they were never allowed in the old facilities.

4:1   AITCHISON, GEORGE, JR. (1825-1910)

       Educated at the RAL and University of London, 1853-55. Articled to
       his father, of the same name, and practiced with him, 1859-61, after
       which the younger Aitchison branched out on his own. RIBA gold
       medalist, 1898. RIBA has drawings. Obituaries: AA&BN 97 (1
       June 1909): 3; RIBAJ 17 (1909-10): 583.

4:2   Girouard, Mark. "The Victorian Artist at Home." CL 152 (16 No-
       vember 1972): 1278-81.

           In 1865 Aitchison designed one of the first artist's houses
           for Frederick Leighton in London.

4:3   Stell, C.F. "Leighton House, Kensington." ARCHAEOLOGICAL
       JOURNAL 114 (1957): 122-25.

           Aitchison was a lifelong friend of Frederick, Lord Leighton,
           for whom he built this house. Plans only.

5:1　　AITKEN, GEORGE SHAW (1836-1921)

Wrote: "History and Reminiscences of the Edinburgh Architectural Association." Typewritten manuscript owned by the EAA (See D1). Publication: ABBEYS OF ARBROATH, BALMERINO AND LINDORES. 1884. Obituary: AR 50 (October 1921): xlvi.

5:2　　Dunbar-Nasmith, James. "George S. Aitken, President, 1858-59." EAAY 3 (1959): 73-75.

Born in Dundee, Aitken worked for J. Dick Peddie of Peddie and Kinear in Edinburgh. He was a founding member of the EAA because the IAS did not admit pupils to membership. Aitken returned to Dundee, where he partnered with McLaren and Sons until 1880.

6:1　　ANDERSON, ADAM (1783-1847)

6:2　　Nasmith, R.J., and A.S. "Propriety at Perth Waterworks." AR 121 (April 1957): 271-73.

Adam, rector of Perth Academy, was asked by the Perth Water Commission to submit a scheme for a new waterworks in 1832. Adam's reasoning and his design are described. The building was in operation until 1862. See also AR "SOS from Perth," 141 (March 1967): 233, written when the building was threatened with demolition--it has since been restored.

7:1　　ANDERSON, ROBERT ROWAND (1834-1921)

Trained in law but became a pupil of the School Board of Manufacturers (a forerunner of the schools of architecture). He worked in Holland under J.H. Cuypers and in London with George Gilbert Scott. Partnered with David Bryce prior to practicing independently ca. 1875; later practiced as Rowand Anderson, Kininmonth and Paul. Knighted, 1902. RIBA gold medalist, 1916. The RIBA has one drawing of St. John's church, Alloa. Publication: with Robert Lorimer, EXAMPLES OF SCOTTISH ARCHITECTURE FROM THE 12TH TO THE 17TH CENTURIES, 4 vols., 1921-33. Obituary: RIBAJ 28 (1920-21): 457-58, 471, 511.

7:2　　Murdoch, William Garden Blaikie. "A Scottish Revival of Mediaevalism." QRIAS 35 (1931): 69-78.

". . . Sir Rowand Anderson made a departure. For it would seem to have been he who led the way in contending that Scottish Baronial with certain modifications is suitable

for villa architecture. And an illustration lies in the residence he built for himself, Allermuir, Colinton, Edinburgh."

8:1 ARCHIGRAM (1961-)

A group of architects consisting of Warren Chalk (1927-), Peter
Cook (1936-), Dennis Crompton (1935-), David Greene
(1937-), Ron Herron (1930-) and Michael Webb (1937-).
Published ARCHIGRAM, nos. 1-7 (1961-December 1966), a magazine
whose format changed with each issue and which was filled mostly
with illustrations of the ideas of the six members of Archigram.

8:2 Banham, Reyner. "A Clip on Architecture." AD 35 (November
1965): 534-35.

Sources of Archigramers' thought processes are presented
with an especial emphasis on the contribution of Alison
Smithson and Peter Smithson.

8:3 _____. "A Clip-On Architecture." DESIGN QUARTERLY. 63
(1965): 1-32.

This whole issue is devoted to an expanation of the "end-
less" or "indeterminate" architecture of Archigram.
Thoroughly illustrated.

8:4 _____. "Monaco Underground." AJ 152 (2 September 1970):
506-9.

Archigram "has landed a really big fish at last." It won
a competition for a multifunctional space right on the sea-
shore at Monaco.

8:5 Chalk, Warren. "Architecture as Consumer Product." ARENA 81
(March 1966): 228-30.

Chalk has contributed "some notes on housing, which continue the argument [begun in 'Some Notes on Archigram.'
ARENA 81 (January 1966): 171-72] and should lead to a
greater understanding of Archigram's ideals."

8:6 Chapman, Priscilla. "The Plug-In City." EKISTICS 20 (November
1965): 279-80.

An explanation of what "Plug-In City" is all about and of
who is involved in Archigram.

8:7 Cook, Peter. "Control-and-Choice Living." In URBAN STRUCTURE,
edited by David Lewis, pp. 124-31. New York: John Wiley and
Sons, 1968.

"The overriding concern being a search for systems, organization and techniques that permit the emancipation and general good life of the individual." Drawings illustrate Cook's regard for family units.

8:8 _____. "Some Forays by the Archigram Group into the World of Exhibitions." AAQ 1 (July 1969): 84-89.

"Elation and irritation come out of exhibiting. Elation, when it is the first chance to expose ideas to people by every dimension possible. Irritation, when it is read as a formula or a bit of showbiz."

8:9 _____. "A Summer's Evening at the AA When We Tried to Show the Many-Sided Nature of Archigram." AAQ 2 (October 1970): 40-41.

A visual, aural happening.

8:10 Cook, Peter, ed. ARCHIGRAM. London: Studio Vista, 1972. 144 p.

ARCHIGRAM magazine, which brought six architects together, evolved into their means of presenting their ideas of experimental developments as opposed to "definitive" architecture, which they distrust. This book is a collection of those ideas.

8:11 Cook, Peter, and Greene, David. "Metamorphosis." EKISTICS 28 (August 1969): 104-6.

This is an extract by the editors of ARCHIGRAM of their magazine's eighth issue (1969). This selection explains, amongst other things, an ideas circus of five or six vehicles, which plug into the big top.

8:12 Sharp, Dennis. "Forecasting Tomorrow's World." RIBAJ 74 (December 1967): 537-41.

"In a very real sense the utopian concept means destroying existing systems and values." Archigram accepts "the notion of the supercity without spending the time and effort in considering its social, financial, psychological and physical implications."

9:1 ARCHITECTS' CO-PARTNERSHIP (1953-)

The successor to Architects' Cooperative Partnership, begun in 1939 by the following six architects: Kenneth Capon, Peter Cocke; Michael Cooke-Yarborough; Leo de Syllas (-1964); John Grice; and Michael Powers. All were born during the First World War and trained at the AAL. They were joined soon after 1953 by Anthony Cox. Their first major commission was the Brynmawr Rubber Company in Wales. Publication: ST. ALBANS AND MID-HERTFORDSHIRE HOSPITAL, 1944. De Syllas's obituary: AR 135 (May 1964): 315.

9:2   Cement and Concrete Association. FACTORY AT BRYNMAWR. London: 1952. 24 p.

Design considerations, layout, structure, and finishes are discussed and accompanied by numerous drawings and photographs to explain this rubber and plastics manufacturing business.

9:3   Donat, John. "Dunelm House, Durham." AR 139 (June 1966): 451-61.

A bold concrete clubhouse for students and staff (the accommodations of each are separate), which is tucked into the site of this historic city. Well illustrated.

9:4   RIBAJ. "Architects' Approach to Architecture." Vol. 74 (June 1967): 230-38; A&BN 231 (15 February 1967): 272-73.

The AAL took a new stand in the 1930s and members of the firm were part of it. Their work is explained by three unnamed partners. Le Corbusier was their great inspiration.

10:1 ARUP, OVE NYQUIST (1895-)

Practiced engineering since the early 1930s. Knighted, 1971. RIBA gold medalist, 1966. Publications: WORKING-CLASS RESIDENTIAL FLATS, 1937, and SAFE HOUSING IN WAR TIME, 1941. Arup Associates has practiced architecture since 1953, with Philip Dowson (1924-   ), as the driving force of this division of Ove Arup and Partners. Dowson trained at Cambridge University and the AAL.

10:2   Bendixson, T.M.P. "Oxford's New Physics Laboratories." AJ 133 (8 June 1961): 837-38.

Sketches, plans, and photographs of a model of this proposed building with a brief explanation.

10:3   Dowson, Philip. "Architects' Approach to Architecture." RIBAJ 73 (March 1966): 105-15.

After the Second World War, "the urgent question then was how to reconcile the demands of industrialized method with those of an environment worth living in." The answer was formulated in Dowson's approach to design.

10:4 _____. "Building for Science: University of Birmingham Mining and Metallurgy Building." AD 37 (April 1967): 160-70.

Growth and adaptability are related to flexible modular planning grids, which allow for expansion in two directions. Construction, structure, and services are integrated into the initial design process. Numerous diagrams and photographs illustrate the system.

10:5 _____. "A Room of One's Own." AD 38 (April 1968): 164-72.

At Somerville College, Oxford, the Wolfson Hall of residence allows "for self-expression, and the need to plan against loneliness," since student rooms are multifunctional.

10:6 Nuttgens, Patrick. "One for the Planners." RIBAJ 78 (March 1971): 107-9.

Arup Associates won the limited competition to coordinate the two precincts at the University of Sheffield, and create a unity from a variety of buildings located there.

10:7 O'Hare, Michael. "Office Profile: Arup Associates and the Group Practice Experiment." PA 52 (April 1971): 102-5.

"The usual description of Ove Arup is that he is an architect at heart who happens to be one of the best engineers in the world." His group practice is of about twenty-five architects and engineers who integrate well in the design process notably of mechanical systems related to structure.

10:8 Rawstorne, Peter. "Ove Arup." RIBAJ 72 (April 1965): 176-83.

Rawstorne interviews Arup, the design engineer of many notable structures in Britain since the 1930s, including Lubetkin and Tecton's Highpoint Flats, London, 1934, where Arup was employed by the contractor. Topics also discussed include the collaboration of architects and engineers, systems building, and the quality of design.

11:1 ASHBEE, CHARLES ROBERT (1863-1942)

Studied under G.F. Bodley. King's College, Cambridge owns his journals (see 11:2-3). The V & A owns his journal, 1886-87, and a typescript of his memoirs, 1938-40. The RIBA has drawings. Publications: AMERICAN SHEAVES AND ENGLISH SEED CORN, 1901; CARICATURES, 1928; CRAFT-MANSHIP IN COMPETITIVE INDUSTRY, 1908; AN ENDEAVOR TOWARD THE TEACHING OF JOHN RUSKIN AND WILLIAM MORRIS, 1901; FRANK LLOYD WRIGHT, 1911; HAMPTONSHIRE EXPERIMENT IN EDUCATION, 1914; MODERN ENGLISH SILVERWORK, 1909; A REPORT TO THE COUN-CIL OF THE NATIONAL TRUST FOR PLACES OF HISTORIC INTEREST AND NATURAL BEAUTY, 1901; A SURVEY OF LONDON, 1900; THE TRINITY HOSPITAL IN MILE END, 1896; WHERE THE GREAT CITY STANDS, 1917; and translated THE TREATISES OF BENVENUTO CEL-LINI ON GOLDSMITHING AND SCULPTURE, 1896. Obituaries: A&BN 170 (29 May 1942): 123, (5 June 1942): 137; B 152 (29 May 1942): 476; RIBAJ 49 (June 1942): 134. G.M. Thompson is preparing a B. Arch. thesis at the University of Belfast on C.R. Ash-bee and the Guild of Handicrafts. Alan Crawford and S. Bury are researching Ashbee's life.

11:2 Crawford, Alan. AN INDEX TO THE ASHBEE JOURNALS AT KING'S COLLEGE, CAMBRIDGE. Leicester: University of Leicester Victorian Studies Centre, 1965. 58 p.

11:3 _____. "Ten Letters from Frank Lloyd Wright to Charles Robert Ash-bee." AH 13 (1970): 64-76.

These letters, edited and with minor omissions, have been abstracted from the forty volumes of Ashbee's journals owned by King's College, Cambridge.

12:1 ASLIN, CHARLES HERBERT (1893-1959)

Studied at Sheffield University and was county architect for Hertford-shire, 1945-58. Obituaries: A&BN 215 (29 April 1959): 532; AIAJ 33 (June 1960): 138; AJ 129 (23 April 1959): 613; B 196 (24 April 1959): 769; RIBAJ 66 (June 1959): 296.

12:2 Davies, Richard Llewelyn, and Weeks, John R. "The Hertfordshire Achievement." AR 111 (June 1952): 367-72.

"Architecture does in fact result from that long-expected revolution, the impact of industrial production on building." Technologically and economically prefabricated unit con-struction was an answer to the postwar school building pro-gram.

12:3 Hertfordshire County Council. BUILDING FOR EDUCATION. N.p.: 1962. 42 p.

One hundred schools had been completed in Hertfordshire by 1948, and two hundred by 1961, "to keep pace with the continuous growth of the county's population . . . and

. . . to provide for the rapidly developing conception of educational needs." A listing of new schools and extensions is provided at the end of the book.

13:1 ATKINSON, ROBERT (1883-1952)

Worked for John Belcher prior to practice in London. The RIBA has four drawings. Publication: REPORT ON THE EDUCATION OF THE ARCHITECT IN THE UNITED STATES OF AMERICA, 1922. Obituaries: AAJ 68 (April 1953): 176; A&BN 203 (8 January 1953): 33; AJ 117 (1 January 1953): 6, (8 January 1953): 31; B 184 (2 January 1953): 21; RIBAJ 60 (January 1953): 117.

13:2 Chermayeff, Serge. "The New Building for the DAILY EXPRESS." AR 72 (July 1932): 3-12.

Ellis and Clarke designed the building but Atkinson was architect of the entrance hall.

13:3 Oswald, Arthur. "A Wren Church Reborn." CL 110 (2 November 1951): 1464-65.

Atkinson built a "modern" All Hallows Church at Twickenham, with the Wren tower of All Hallows, Lombard Street, London, reerected on the same site, linked by a cloister walk.

14:1 BAIRD, JOHN (1798-1859)

Apprenticed in Dalmuir, Scotland, to an architect whom he succeeded at the age of twenty.

14:2 Hitchcock, Henry-Russell. "Early Cast Iron Facades." AR 109 (February 1951): 113-16.

Although the article discusses cast iron architecture in Britain and America, Hitchcock admits that Glasgow has been "from the eighteenth century a major center of the iron trade." The Jamaica Street Warehouse is illustrated and mentioned. Hitchcock quotes a description, in B 21 (1863): 713, of a Glasgow iron framework on Argyle Street and says that it would fit the description of Paisleys, a known work by John Baird and James Thomson.

15:1 BAKER, BENJAMIN (1840-1907)

Apprenticed to H.H. Price and John Fowler with whom he later partnered.

15:2   "Sir Benjamin Baker." AA&BN (8 June 1907): 226-27.

The Firth of Forth Bridge was not innovative design and the
construction of the London Underground system, with John
Fowler, was engineered with extreme caution. Baker's major projects are evaluated.

16:1   BAKER, HERBERT (1862-1946)

Trained at the RAL and the AAL, Baker was articled to his uncle
Arthur Baker in 1879. He became an assistant to Ernest George in
1882 and began to work in South Africa in 1892. Knighted, 1926.
RIBA gold medalist, 1927. Partnered with A.T. Scott in 1931 and
became official architect to the government of South Africa. Collab-
orated with Lutyens at New Delhi, India. The RIBA has five drawings.
See also 16:7,11. Publications: ARCHITECTURE AND PERSONALI-
TIES, 1944, and INDIA HOUSE, LONDON, 1930. Obituaries:
A&BN 185 (15 February 1946): 95; B 170 (15 February 1946):
158; RIBAJ 53 (March 1946): 189-90.

16:2   Aylwin, G. Maxwell. "An Imperial Architect," B 167 (17 November 1944): 387.

A review of Baker's ARCHITECTURE AND PERSONALITIES,
"a wealth of interest to be found through the very breadth
of the author's experiences."

16:3   Bagenal, Hope. "The Acoustics of the Legislative Chamber at Delhi."
A&BN 121 (28 June 1929): 851-53.

A tall interior space is usually good for ventilation but
poor for acoustics. Bagenal, an expert acoustician, explains how Baker compromised.

16:4   Byron, Robert. "New Delhi." AR 69 (January 1931): 1-30.

See 161:5.

16:5   Chipkin C.M. "New Delhi." SOUTH AFRICAN ARCHITECTURAL
RECORD 43 (November 1958): 21-28.

The plan for New Delhi is illustrated and discussed. Patrick Geddes, who criticized the plan, gained a retort from
Lutyens: "A certain Professor Geddes who has come over
here to lecture on town planning, 'a crank' who 'talked
rot in an insulting way.'" See also 161:6.

16:6   Collingwood, Frances. "Sir Herbert Baker." B 202 (8 June 1962):
1181-82.

A tribute on the centennial of his birth (9 June). Baker met Lutyens in the office of Ernest George and was later to collaborate with him in India.

16:7   Earle, L. Marriott. "The Work of Herbert Baker." ARCHITECT AND BUILDER (South Africa) 17 (October 1967): 22-27.

Earle presented drawings by Baker to the University of Cape Town. Baker's importance, practice, and work are mentioned.

16:8   Greig, Doreen Edith. "The Work of Sir Herbert Baker from 1892 until 1912 and His Contribution in South Africa." SOUTH AFRICAN ARCHITECTURAL RECORD 48 (January 1963): 3-6; (February 1963): 3-6; (March 1963): 3-6; (April 1963): 9-12; (May 1963): 9-11; (June 1963): 5-9; (July 1963): 11-19; (August 1963): 11-20; (September 1963): 13-18; (October 1963): 17-21; (November 1963): 23-26; (December 1963): 13-16.

Baker's training, pupilage, travel, activities to 1892, practice, theory, arrival in South Africa, and buildings are described and his work in the Cape is assessed.

16:9   Hussey, Christopher. "London House: A Hall of Residence for Dominion Students in London." CL 97 (22 June 1945): 1080-83.

Begun in 1930 for the University of London, and left unfinished due to the war, London House is to be completed, this 1945 article reports.

16:10   Knapp-Fisher, A.B. "Sir Herbert Baker." AJ 65 (16 February 1927): 251-62.

More of Baker's work is illustrated in this article than most, including his work in South Africa and at New Delhi.

16:11   Wenland, W. "Architectural Drawings and Records of Sir Herbert Baker's Firm." SOUTH AFRICAN ARCHITECTURAL RECORD 52 (November 1967): 21-22.

L. Marriott Earle presented six thousand drawings and fifteen thousand other records, 1890-1930, by twenty leading architects, including Baker, to the University of Cape Town libraries.

17:1   BARLOW, WILLIAM HENRY (1812-1902)

17:2   Ferriday, Peter. "The Greatest Folly of Them All: The Architecture of St. Pancras Station and Hotel." CL 138 (18 November 1965): 1314-17.

> For the St. Pancras train shed, opened in 1868, Barlow designed the largest space in Britain of the period. To this space Scott added his hotel, 1865-76.

18:1 BARRY, CHARLES (1795-1860)

Articled to Middleton and Bailey, Lambeth surveyors, 1810-16. Set up practice in London, 1820, after three years of travel. Publications: ILLUSTRATIONS OF THE NEW PALACE OF WESTMINSTER, 1849; THE TRAVELLER'S CLUB HOUSE, 1839. The RIBA library has various sketches, drawings, notebooks, diaries, journals of various tours, letters, specifications, and reports of competition projects. The Treasury Department and Office of Works published reports on the Houses of Parliament, London, and Edward Welby Pugin published a pamphlet WHO WAS THE ART ARCHITECT OF THE HOUSES OF PARLIAMENT?, 1867. Avery Architectural Library, Columbia University, has some autograph letters and "A Perspective View of an Unexecuted Large Public Building of the Renaissance Style." Obituaries: B 18 (19, 26 May; 2, 9 June; 21 July 1860): 305-7, 315, 322-24, 342-44, 347, 367, 459. Utilizing source materials from the clubs, I.L. Campbell wrote a B. Arch. thesis, "Charles Barry and the Italianate Style of the London Clubs, 1829-65," at the Aberdeen School of Architecture in 1975. P. Hodson is researching Barry's architecture.

18:2 Barry, Alfred. MEMOIR OF THE LIFE AND WORKS OF SIR CHARLES BARRY, R.A., F.R.S. London: J. Murray, 1867. 407 p.

> Relying upon personal recollections and those of his father's friends to supply the deficiencies of the journals and letters, the Reverend Alfred Barry presents his father's early life, education, travel, professional career, Italianate and Gothic phases, and unexecuted projects but centers the major portion of his text upon the Houses of Parliament, the "Palace of Westminster." His father's works are listed, pp. 355-37.

18:3 Binney, Marcus. "The Travels of Sir Charles Barry." CL 146 (28 August; 2, 11 September 1969): 494-98, 550-52, 622-24.

> Barry, a Greek revivalist, traveled widely in Italy in early life but was unmoved by Italian architecture until later life when he established a whole new mode of design--the Italianate.

18:4 Chancellor, E. Beresford. "A New Westminster: The Vision of Sir

Charles Barry." AR 61 (June 1927): 207-9.

> City planning "has always been a favorite occupation of both professional and amateur architects." In this respect, the plans and sections of the Houses of Parliament are illustrated and explained.

18:5 _____. "Pioneers of London Development." AR 49 (May 1921): 123-26.

> This last of four articles devoted to London's growth is concerned with Barry's clubs.

18:6 Collingwood, Frances. "Sir Charles Barry: Architect and Gothic Revivalist." B 198 (13 May 1960): 904-5.

> In March 1960, members of parliament were discussing the need for additional space. Barry had planned 237 additional members' rooms in 1855 at a cost of five million pounds. A resume of Barry's life is provided.

18:7 Copeland, G.W. "Designed by Barry." CL 114 (22 October 1953): 1308.

> This is a letter to the editor of CL concerning the tower of Trenham Hall, Staffordshire, added by Barry to a sixteenth-century house and demolished, 1911-12. Its topmost stage was reerected at Sandon Park, Staffordshire.

18:8 Cornforth, John. "Bowood, Wiltshire, Revisited." CL 151 (8, 15, 22 June 1972): 1448-51, 1546-50, 1610-13.

> Numerous architects, including Barry, built at Bowood (see especially the third segment of this article), but a large portion of this expansive residence was demolished in 1955. Barry's entrance lodge is illustrated, p. 1612.

18:9 _____. "Stafford House, Revisited." CL 144: (14 November 1968): 1188-91, 1257-61.

> Barry succeeded Benjamin Dean Wyatt as architect for Stafford (now Lancaster) House after arguments between the architect and client. See also AH 1 (1958): 17-30.

18:10 Ferriday, Peter. "Sir Charles Barry: 1795-1860." AR 128 (December 1960): 393.

> An appreciation of Barry's Palace of Westminster and concern for his buildings likely to be demolished.

18:11   Girouard, Mark.   "Charles Barry: A Centenary Assessment."   CL
        128:   796-97.

        A review of an exhibition, held at the RIBA in 1960, of
        portraits, original drawings, notebooks, photographs, and a
        model. See also RIBAJ 68 (November 1960):   12-13.

18:12   Port, M.H., ed. THE HOUSES OF PARLIAMENT. London: Yale
        University Press, 1976.   352 p., 212 illus., 11 pls.

        The publisher's announcement states: "This authoratative
        study of design, construction and decoration of the building
        takes into consideration political, social, technological and
        economic factors, as well as artistic ones." In addition to
        one by Port, there are articles by eight other contributors.

18:13   Statham, H. Heathcote.   "The Architectural Genius of Sir Charles
        Barry."   B 80 (5 January 1901): 3-8.

        "The life of Sir Charles Barry is a highly instructive one
        in the example it affords of untiring pains in studying and
        perfecting his designs in every detail." A selection of his
        works are presented.

18:14   _____. "Sir Charles Barry." AAN 17 (July 1902): 97-99.

        Character, design ability, and other qualities are surveyed
        and his major buildings are discussed.

18:15   Whiffen, Marcus. THE ARCHITECTURE OF SIR CHARLES BARRY IN
        MANCHESTER AND NEIGHBORHOOD. Manchester: Royal Man-
        chester Institution, 1950.   19 p.

        A detailed survey based upon local correspondence and re-
        search material. Illustrated.

18:16   Wyatt, Matthew Digby. ON THE ARCHITECTURAL CAREER OF THE
        LATE SIR CHARLES BARRY. N.p., n.d.. 20 p.

        "Read at the Royal Institute of British Architects, May 21st,
        1860." A tribute to a major architect who designed a ma-
        jor building--the Houses of Parliament. "No public build-
        ing in Europe possesses a more ingenious and effective plan,
        a more perfect homogeneity of parts and style, a more
        graceful outline under every point of view, and greater
        technical excellence and beauty."

19:1 BARRY, CHARLES, JR. (1823-1900)

        Trained under his father. Charles Barry, began practice ca. 1847, and partnered with Robert R. Banks (-1872). The RIBA has draw-ings.

19:2   A.   "Charles Barry."   63 (1900):   362.

"With him we lose a link which unites the present with a former and most memorable period of architecture." The styles of his major works and his awards are listed.

19:3   Stratton, Arthur.   "The Royal Exchange, London."   AR 42 (September 1917):   45-50.

Barry won the competition to cover the courtyard of the Royal Exchange with a glass roof, built 1883-84 and illus-trated in this article.

20:1   BARRY, EDWARD MIDDLETON (1830-80)

Third son of Charles Barry; trained at the RAL, 1848; worked for Thomas Henry Wyatt (1807-80) and for Barry's father, completing the Houses of Parliament after his father's death in 1860.   The RIBA has drawings.   Obituaries: AA&BA 7/8 (1880): 41,66,83-84; AAR 1 (1880): 201-4; B 38 (31 January; 7, 14 February 1880): 123, 147-50,169,203-4; RIBAJ (1879-80): 275.

20:2   Cornforth, John.   "The Fitzwilliam Museum, Cambridge."   CL 132 (22, 29 November 1962):   1278-81, 1340-43.

George Basevi's competition-winning scheme of 1835, in-cluding drawings of the interiors, is illustrated.   However, these interiors were not carried out until the 1870s by Barry.   Basevi's schemes were not as rich or as elaborate in decoration, materials, and color as those by Barry. Reference is made to Carl Winter's publication on the building.

20:3   Hussey, Christopher.   "Covent Garden Opera House."   CL 103 (25 June 1948):   1278-81.

The third theater on this site was by E.M. Barry and opened in 1858.   "The auditorium deserves to be recognised as one of the most successful creations of mid-Victorian architec-ture."   Numerous interior photographs.

21:1   BARTHOLOMEW, ALFRED (1801-45)

Articled to J.H. Good.   The RIBA has a volume of drawings.   Publications: CYCLOPEDIA OF THE NEW METROPOLITAN BUILDING ACT, 1844; HINTS RELATIVE TO THE CONSTRUCTION OF FIREPROOF BUILDINGS, 1839; SACRED LYRICS, 1831; SPECIFICATIONS FOR PRACTICAL ARCHITECTURE, 1840.

21:2   Pace, George G. "Alfred Bartholomew: A Pioneer of Functional Gothic." AR 92 (October 1942): 99-102.

        He was a Gothicist who sought a structural logic in past historic styles. "Pure taste in architecture has in past ages been purely structural."

21:3   Pevsner, Nilolaus. "Bartholomew and Garbett." AR 152 (October 1972): 239-41.

        Pevsner discusses Bartholomew's theories of architecture as contained in SPECIFICATIONS FOR PRACTICAL ARCHITECTURE.

22:1   BASEVI, GEORGE (1794-1845)

        Articled to John Soane, 1810, and entered the RAL, 1813. Began practice in 1819. The RIBA has drawings.

22:2   Bolton, Arthur Thomas. ARCHITECTURAL EDUCATION A CENTURY AGO: BEING AN ACCOUNT OF THE OFFICE OF SIR JOHN SOANE, RA., . . . WITH SPECIAL REFERENCE TO THE CAREER OF GEORGE BASEVI. Sir John Soane Museum Publication no. 12. London: [1924]. 19 p.

        Basevi began his pupilage with the fifty-eight-year-old Soane and remained for five years. During that period he made numerous drawings, now owned by the Sir John Soane Museum. Three of Basevi's drawings--one is dated 1818; the second, 1819, and the third--later are illustrated. Two of the drawings relate to Basevi's travels after leaving Soane.

22:3   Cornforth, John. "The Fitzwilliam Museum, Cambridge." CL 132 (22, 29 November 1962): 1278-81, 1340-43.

        Basevi won this building's competition against twenty-six other competitors, who had submitted thirty-five designs (some are illustrated) in 1835. When Basevi died, the work was incomplete. C.R. Cockerell continued the job until 1847, but E.M. Barry was responsible for the interiors when work resumed in 1870.

22:4   Hobhouse, Hermione. "The Building of Belgravia." CL 145 (8, 22 May 1969): 1154-57, 1312-14.

Basevi produced new designs, which differed from the earlier designs, which had already been agreed upon, for that area of London known as Belgravia. They are described and illustrated.

22:5   Hussey, Christopher. "Beechwood, Highgate, Middlesex: The Home of Mr. and Mrs. Oswald Lewis." CL 111 (7 March 1952): 652-55.

The trees predate the 1780 house, which was demolished in 1828. Basevi's residence, built in 1834 on the same site, thus has a magnificent setting.

22:6   Ramsey, Stanley C. "London Clubs." AR 35 (March 1914): 56-59.

The eighth in a series of articles on London clubs, this article refers to Basevi's Conservative Club. This club was completed in 1845, the year of his accidental death at Ely Cathedral.

23:1   **BEAZLEY, SAMUEL (1786-1851)**

Trained under his uncle Charles Beazley (ca.1756-1829) in London. The RIBA has drawings. Publications: THE ROUE, 1828; THE OXONIAN, 1840; and "On the Rise and Progress of Gothic Architecture," in ESSAYS OF THE LONDON ARCHITECTURAL SOCIETY, 1808. Obituary: B 9 (1851): 694-95.

23:2   Harbron, Dudley. "Minor Masters of the XIXth Century: Samuel Beazley, A Victorian Vanbrugh." AR 79 (March 1936): 131-34.

Lesser-known architects were apparently not written about in their own day because "popular taste was for saintliness and success" and for moral appeal. An architect, traveler, and playwright, Beazley worked in Wales and London. His theatrical writings are discussed.

24:1   **BECKETT, EDMUND (1816-1905)**

A lawyer and architect, he added Denison to his name and was also known as Lord Grimthorpe when he succeeded to his father's baronetcy in 1874. Publications: A BOOK OF BUILDING, CIVIL AND ECCLESIASTICAL: WITH THE THEORY OF DOMES AND OF THE GREAT PYRAMID, 1876; LECTURES ON CHURCH BUILDING, 1856; LECTURES ON GOTHIC ARCHITECTURE CHIEFLY IN RELATION TO ST. GEORGE'S CHURCH, DONCASTER, 1855.

24:2   Beckett, O.R. "Father of Big Ben: An Account of Some Incidents in the Life and Work of Edmund Beckett Denison, First Lord Grimthorpe." CL 105 (13 May 1949): 1108-10.

> Big Ben has a crack in it because Beckett fitted a seven instead of a four hundred-weight hammer for striking the bell. He "eventually triumphed over all obstacles save that of his own truculence."

24:3   Ferriday, Peter. LORD GRIMTHORPE, 1816-1905. London: John Murray, 1957. 230 p.

> "The mere recital of Lord Grimthorpe's interests makes it evident that a complete biography could not be written. . . . Everything that Lord Grimthorpe did caused controversy; he had an unequalled knack of bringing out the worst in his fellow men. His letters to the press were brutish, bullying and libellous." He was involved mainly in restoration and public works--the clock of Big Ben at Westminster Palace, London, is one example.

24:4   _____. "Lord Grimthorpe versus Architects and Others, or All That Money Can Buy." AR 117 (April 1955): 260-66.

> St. Albans Cathedral "was a patchwork of old repairs when Grimthorpe first interested himself in it, and he left it, in defiance of everyone, the tidy, pinnacled and gabled structure it now is."

25:1 BEDFORD, FRANCIS W. (1866-1904)

Obituary: RIBAJ 12 (1904-5): 116.

25:2   Thorp, William H. "F.W. Bedford." AAN 20 (January 1905): 12-14.

> Thorp was Bedford's employer and Bedford was articled to Thorp for three years. He (Bedford) designed Brahan in Perth, in the arts-and-crafts mode. From 1897-1903, he partnered with Sydney D. Kitson in the Leeds area.

26:1 BEHRENS, PETER (1868-1940)

Famous German architect who designed one house in Britain. The RIBA has numerous drawings of that house, called New Ways, at 508 Wellingborough Road, Northampton. Susan Wheeler wrote a thesis at the AAL in 1966 on the house.

26:2   Silhouette. "New Ways." AR 60 (November 1926): 175-79.

> The plan, exterior, and series of art deco interiors of this Northampton house, "the latest continental model--though not strictly of concrete" are illustrated.

27:1 BELCHER, JOHN (1841-1913)

Trained under, assisted, and became a partner of his father in 1865. Practiced with Arthur Beresford Pite (see 196:1) in 1885 and with John James Joass (1868-1952), 1905-13. RIBA gold medalist, 1907. President, RIBA, 1904-6. The RIBA has drawings. Publications: THE INSTITUTE OF CHARTERED ACCOUNTANTS IN ENGLAND AND WALES, 1893; LATE RENAISSANCE ARCHITECTURE IN ENGLAND, 1897-99; and with Mervyn Macartney, ESSENTIALS OF ARCHITECTURE, 1893. Obituaries: RIBAJ 21 (1913-14): 50, 55, 75; AIAJ 2 (1914): 251. Joass, also the son of an architect, worked for J.J. Burnet and later for Belcher prior to their partnership. Joass's obituaries: B 182 (16 May 1952): 748; RIBAJ 59 (August 1952): 385-86.

27:2   Harper, Charles G. "The Work of John Belcher, Architect." AR 4 (1898): 130-33, 201-6, 237-47, and supplement foldout drawings.

> Belcher's background, stylistic development, and major works are described and fifteen of these works illustrated.

27:3   James, J.W. "The Late John Belcher: A Biographical Notice." RIBAJ 21 (1913-14): 75-77.

> Gives Belcher's background, education, partnerships, literary and musical interests, and contributions and list his major works.

27:4   Jelly, F.R. "Six More of the Best." B 212 (10 March 1967): 110.

> Considerations of Belcher's ESSENTIALS IN ARCHITECTURE, 1907 (reprint ?) as unobtrusive, concise, factual, and almost personal.

27:5   Joass, J[ohn] J[ames]. "The Work of the Late John Belcher, RA." RIBAJ 22 (1914-15): 97-106.

> Belcher rejected the Gothic revival as being "unsuitable to the requirements of his time" and instead, designed in the early English Renaissance revival style. He did, in fact, design in a wide variety of styles; numerous buildings are listed.

27:6   Macartney, Mervyn. "A Personal Note on the Late John Belcher."
        AR 34 (December 1913): 127-28.

> Belcher's stylistic developments, authorship of books, and
> service to the profession are the main points covered.

27:7   Service, Alastair. "Belcher and Joass." AR 148 (November 1970):
        282-90. Reprinted in EDWARDIAN ARCHITECTURE AND ITS ORIGINS,
        edited by Alastair Service, pp. 310-27. London: Architectural Press,
        1975.

> Theirs was the grand manner in the turn of the century
> baroque revival. Belcher began the revival with the aid
> of Arthur Beresford Pite, who also introduced him to the
> arts-and-crafts tradition, and then continued with Joass.

28:1   BENNETT, HUBERT (1901-)

> Trained at the University of Manchester in the 1930s. Served as
> county architect of Yorkshire, 1945-56, and then as architect to the
> London County Council (subsequently known as the Greater London
> Authority), 1956-71. Knighted, 1970.

28:2   Blake, Peter Thomas. "Housing Design: Quality Returns to the City."
        AF 123 (July/August 1965): 40-47.

> Canada Estate, London, is one example of housing "which
> seems to reflect the kind of quality of urban architecture
> and urban design that can produce such 'cities of equal
> chance.'"

28:3   Campbell, Kenneth. "Erith." In THE PEDESTRIAN IN THE CITY,
        edited by David Lewis, vol. 11, pp. 197-202. Princeton: D. Van
        Nostrand Co., 1965.

> The proposed layout of this area, situated within the City
> of London, is presented through sketches and written inten-
> tions.

28:4   Carter, John. "Building Revisited: Hayward Art Gallery on the South
        Bank, London SE1." AJ 153 (3 February 1971): 243-54.

> Its fortress-like character, inflexibility, inaccessibility, con-
> flict between fire regulations and security precautions, im-
> pressive internal space, and related aspects are covered in
> this critical analysis.

28:5   Chalk, Warren. "South Bank Arts Centre, London." AD 37 (March
        1967): 120-23.

Proposals date back to 1955 and plans were announced in 1960. The separation of vehicular and pedestrian circulation was of the utmost importance. Its construction and acoustics are treated very briefly.

28:6 Greater London Council. GLC ARCHITECTURE, 1965/70. London: 1970. 119 p.

Bennett was architect to the council during this period and thur takes credit for all the housing, educational architecture, buildings for special and other services, civic design, and historic preservation by his department. GLC ARCHITECTS REVIEW 2, covering later work was published 1976 by Academy Editions.

28:7 Haddock, Mary. "Sir Hubert Bennett: A 'Retirement' into Property Development." B 220 (15 January 1971): 83.

Upon retirement at sixty-five, Bennett became a property developer. In so doing he had to resign from the RIBA and the Architects Registration Council of the United Kingdom, thereby forfeiting the right to call himself an architect.

28:8 Huxtable, Ada Louise. "Two in Trouble." NEW YORK TIMES, 22 June 1969, sec. 2, p. 30.

Hayward Gallery, London, has "bad lighting, inept installation" and its entrance is not easily discovered because of its organized confusion. The extension to the Tate Gallery by Richard Llewelyn Davies and others is, by comparison, readily accessible.

28:9 Killick, John [Alexander Wentzel]. "Paddington Maintenance Depot." OA&P 32 (February 1969): 151-57.

"The solution of a complicated problem . . . has resulted from a brilliant collaboration between architect and engineer." Location, planning, and services are explained.

28:10 London County Council. THE PLANNING OF A NEW TOWN [Hook]. London: 1961. 182 p.

Hook, Hampshire, was the site of a proposed new town, sixty miles west of London, with good communication links. All aspects concerning the planning of the town were considered in great detail. [For political reasons the town did not materialize--Wodehouse.]

28:11 Moro, Peter. "Queen Elizabeth Hall: An Appraisal." RIBAJ 75 (June 1968): 251-57.

Moro publicly discusses a building by another architect for two reasons: he was originally asked to collaborate in the design in 1947, and some national newspapers are dispensing with architectural critics. Moro comments on the faceted building which complements rather than conflicts with the Royal Festival Hall, the traffic, materials, circulation, and features of the accommodation provided. The article ends with a series of statements by those who use the hall.

28:12 Pike, Alexander. "Thamesmead Report." AD 39 (November 1969): 602-13.

The project for a new town on the river Thames for twenty-five thousand people began in 1962. It "has a scale comparable with the natural landscape. The decision to design Thamesmead to match this scale is the basic philosophy behind the scheme." General plans, as well as detailed considerations, of the housing are illustrated.

28:13 Scott, N. Keith. "Queen Elizabeth Hall: Appraised." A&BN 231 (29 March 1967): 538-39.

"Someone has been thinking hard all the time, but has lacked the ultimate gift of making it all add up." The complex is described as "a jumble of irrelevancies" with a "tonal flatness." Pages 540-42 analyze the building in detail and contain plans and numerous illustrations.

28:14 Webb, Michael. "The Arts Council's New Gallery." CL 144 (11 July 1968): 70-71.

The Hayward Gallery has "harsh textures and ponderous forms" but is a logical design with "a versatile series of spaces."

29:1 BENTLEY, JOHN FRANCIS (1839-1902)

Became a pupil of Henry Clutton in 1858 and began practice in the 1860s, designing mostly Roman Catholic church buildings. The RIBA has drawings. Obituary: RIBAJ 8 (1901-2): 219, 437-41.

29:2 Bell, E. Ingress. "John Francis Bentley: A Sketch from Memory." AAN 18 (January 1903): 1-3.

Bell was a member of a small group interested in church art and wrote this recollection of Bentley, who was also a member of Bell's group and his near neighbor.

29:3   Butler, Arthur Stanley George. JOHN FRANCIS BENTLEY: THE ARCHITECT OF WESTMINSTER CATHEDRAL. London: Burns and Oates, 1961. 31 p.

> Bentley's background, training, and early works are discussed, followed by a description of Westminster Cathedral, to which Bentley was appointed architect in 1894. There is a ground plan and a section of the cathedral.

29:4   Girouard, Mark. "Carlton Towers, Yorkshire." CL 141 (26 January; 2, 9 February 1967): 176–80, 230–33, 280–83.

> The third part of this article concentrates on Bentley's sumptuous interiors of 1875–79, designed within E.W. Pugin's extensions of 1873–75.

29:5   Hadfield, Charles. "The Late John Francis Bentley: A Retrospect." AR 11 (1902): 115–17.

> Hadfield knew Bentley for thrity years and during that period, they had corresponded. Their correspondence forms the basis of this article.

29:6   _____. "Westminster Cathedral." RIBAJ 10 (1902-3): 249–76.

> A detailed assessment, with photographs and fold-out plans. The structure was unfinished when this paper was presented.

29:7   Harbron, Dudley. "Centenary: John Francis Bentley." AJ 89 (26 January 1939): 159–60.

> Bentley's background, contemporaries, and works are discussed. He died 2 March 1902, the day before the RIBA gold medal could have been awarded to him.

29:8   Lethaby, W[illiam] R[ichard]. "Westminster Cathedral." AR 11 (January 1902): 3–19.

> A general appreciation, with description and numerous photographs.

29:9   L' Hospital, Winefride de. WESTMINSTER CATHEDRAL AND ITS ARCHITECTS. 2 vols. New York: Dodd, Mead and Co., 1919. 694 p.

> All aspects of the design and construction of the cathedral are covered and are illustrated by numerous plates and figures. Written by Bentley's daughter, this monograph has an introduction by W.R. Lethaby, who states: "It is a building notably planned, carefully balanced and soundly constructed."

29:10 Mansford, F. Herbert. "The New Cathedral at Westminster." AR 12 (August 1902): 317-37.

> "Mr. Bentley has come as near the development of a new style as it is probably one man ever can, without the invention of some new method of construction." The building is compared to others and is described and illustrated in detail.

29:11 Ricardo, Halsey. "John Francis Bentley." AR 11 (May 1902): 155-64; 12 (July 1902): 18-31. Reprinted in VICTORIAN ARCHITECTURE, edited by Peter Ferriday, pp. 289-300. London: Jonathan Cape, 1963.

> The first part of this article considers Bentley's churches during a great period of religious architecture and the second, his collegiate and residential contributions. Good photographic coverage.

29:12 Richards, J.M. "Inside Westminster Cathedral." AR 115 (March 1854): 202-5.

> The unadorned interior brickwork of Westminster was to Bentley the bare bones of the building. Now it "accords so well with our own aesthetic preferences," a fact which Lethaby had recognized more than a half a century earlier. Several errors of judgment have, however, crept into the development of the interior since the demise of Bentley.

29:13 Scott-Moncrieff, W.W. JOHN FRANCIS BENTLEY. London: Benn; New York: Charles Scribner's Sons, 1924. 28 p., 34 pls.

> Bentley's life and times and their historical background. Scott-Moncrieff leaves the descriptions and criticisms of Bentley's architecture to others. Most illustrations are of Westminister Cathedral and a few are of other religious and residential architecture.

29:14 Willson, T.J. "John Francis Bentley: A Memoir." RIBAJ 9 (1901-2): 437-41.

> Bentley's father attempted to channel his son's talents into the direction of engineering, but at his father's death Bentley began the study of architecture. His work is surveyed.

30:1 BLASHILL, THOMAS (1831-1905)

Publication: SUTTON-IN-HOLDERNESS: THE MANOR, THE BEREWIC, AND THE VILLAGE COMMUNITY, 1896. Obituary: RIBAJ 12 (28 January, 11 March 1905): 211-12, 309-11.

30:2   Matthews, J. Douglas. "Thomas Blashill." RIBAJ 12 (28 January, 11 March 1905): 211-12, 309-11.

> His early life and the appointments which he held until becoming architect to the London County Council are listed. He built working-class housing to replace slums and fought to improve working conditions within buildings.

31:1 BLOMFIELD, ARTHUR WILLIAM (1829-99)

Articled to Philip Charles Hardwick, 1852-55; traveled with Frederick Pepys Cockerell prior to beginning practice in London in 1856. Knighted, 1889. RIBA gold medalist, 1891. The RIBA owns one drawing. Obituaries: A 62 (1899): 276-77; AA&BN 66 (1899): 74; RIBAJ 7 (1899-1900): 19-20, 36-37.

31:2   Street, Arthur Edmund. "Sir Arthur Blomfield." RIBAJ 7 (1899-1900): 36-37.

> His father was a bishop and his major commissions were from the church.

32:1 BLOMFIELD, REGINALD THEODORE (1856-1942)

Nephew of Arthur William Blomfield, under whom he trained. Began practice in 1884. President, RIBA, 1912-14. RIBA gold medalist, 1913. Knighted, 1919. The RIBA has drawings. Publications: ARCHITECTURAL DRAWING AND DRAUGHTSMEN, 1912; BYWAYS: LEAVES FROM AN ARCHITECT'S NOTE BOOK, 1929; THE FORMAL GARDEN IN ENGLAND, 1892; A HISTORY OF FRENCH ARCHITECTURE FROM THE REIGN OF CHARLES VIII TILL THE DEATH OF MAZARIN, 1494-1661, 1911; A HISTORY OF FRENCH ARCHITECTURE FROM THE DEATH OF MAZARIN TILL THE DEATH OF LOUIS XV, 1661-1774, 1921; A HISTORY OF RENAISSANCE ARCHITECTURE IN ENGLAND, 1500-1800, 1897; MEMOIRS OF AN ARCHITECT, 1932; THE MISTRESS ART, 1908; MODERNISMUS, 1934; RICHARD NORMAN SHAW, 1940 (see 234:4); SEBASTIEN LE PRESTRE DE VAUBAN, 1633-1707, 1938; SIX ARCHITECTS, 1935; A SHORT HISTORY OF RENAISSANCE ARCHITECTURE IN ENGLAND, 1900; STUDIES IN ARCHITECTURE, 1905; THREE HUNDRED YEARS OF FRENCH ARCHITECTURE, 1494-1794, 1936; THE TOUCHSTONE OF ARCHITECTURE, 1925; and with Percy Gardner, GREEK ART AND ARCHITECTURE: THEIR LEGACY TO US, 1922. Obituaries: AJ 97 (7 January 1943): 3-4; A&BN 173 (8 January 1943): 26; RIBAJ 50 (January 1943): 65-67.

32:2   Blomfield, Reginald Theodore. MEMOIRS OF AN ARCHITECT. London: Macmillan and Co., 1932. 314 p.

"In the following pages, I have described more or less typical incidents of my life. These have only a personal interest." After chapters on training and travel, the whole book is devoted to an explanation of Blomfield's works.

32:3 Briggs, Martin S. "Voysey and Blomfield: A Study in Contrast." B 176 (14 January 1949): 39-42.

Having studied the two men, Briggs shows similarities in their backgrounds but differences in their temperaments, ideals, ambitions, and outlooks, even though they died within a year or two of each other. Their works are compared.

32:4 Collingwood, Frances. "Sir Reginald Blomfield." B 191 (21 December 1956): 1057-58.

His life and works are assessed and his autobiography is quoted: "If I am to be remembered, I hope it may be by the Menin Gate [Ypres, France], my design for the completion of the Quadrant [Regent Street, London], and Lambeth Bridge."

32:5 Hussey, Christopher. "Godinton Park, Kent." CL 132 (6, 20 December 1962): 1396-1400, 1600-1603.

The gardens of this seventeenth-century house were laid out by Blomfield in the Jacobean style in 1902. Most of the written and photographic material of the article is concerned with Godinton Park of an earlier period.

32:6 Jelley, F.R. "Six More of the Best." B 213 (28 July 1967): 74.

In a series on architectural writers, Jelley considers Blomfield's A SHORT HISTORY OF RENAISSANCE ARCHITECTURE, a vehicle used to attack rival historians and others with whom Blomfield did not agree.

33:1 **BLORE, EDWARD (1787-1879)**

Topographer and antiquarian as well as architect. Illustrated: HISTORY OF RUTLAND, 1811, written by his father, Thomas Blore, a local historian. Publication: THE MONUMENTAL REMAINS OF NOBLE AND EMINENT PERSONS: COMPRISING THE SEPULCHRAL ANTIQUITIES OF GREAT BRITAIN, 1826. The V&A has drawings of ca. two thousand designs and Cambridge University Library has his account books, 1818-50, see 33:4. For holdings at the BM and the RIBA, see 33:3. In 1948 P. Horsburgh wrote an undergraduate thesis

"The Life and Works of Edward Blore, 1789-1879," at the AAL. H. Meller wrote an MA thesis in 1975 at the Courtauld Institute, London, titled "The Country Houses of Edward Blore."

33:2 Cornforth, John. "Hill Court, Herefordshire." CL 139 (27 January; 3, 10 February 1966): 180-83, 228-31, 286-89.

Hill Court, built ca.1700, was engulfed by eighteenth-century developments. Blore added Goodrich Court from 1828 to 1833 and it was demolished in 1946. The third portion of this article mentions and illustrates the interiors.

33:3 Crook, J. Mordaunt. "Xanadu by the Black Sea: The Woronzow Palace at Aloupka." CL 151 (2 March 1972): 513-17.

Woronzow Palace in Aloupka, Turkey, was built in the Moorish and Gothic revival styles, 1837-40, for the vicere-gent to the tzar, Michael Woronzow. RIBA and BM have preliminary drawings for the palace.

33:4 Girouard, Mark. "Merevale Hall, Warwickshire." CL 145 (13, 20 March 1969): 598-601, 662-65.

One of the most inspired Elizabethan revival buildings in Britain, 1838-44. Sketches and drawings for it are in the V&A, and account books in the Cambridge University Library.

33:5 Hussey, Christopher. "From Stable-Yard to Principal's House: The Clock House, Keele, Staffordshire." CL 127 (14 January 1960): 72-73.

It was originally intended that Blore would rebuild Keele Hall but he built only the stables; drawings, ca.1832 illustrated. The structures have now been converted to the Principal's House, Keele University.

33:6 Smith, H. Clifford. "Vicissitudes of the Marble Arch." CL 112 (4 July 1952): 38-39.

Blore was appointed successor to John Nash for the erection of the Marble Arch, London, to commemorate victories at the battles of Trafalgar and Waterloo. Plaster models of the arch were discovered in a storeroom at the V&A. They illustrate the differences between the projected and the completed arches.

34:1 BLOW, DETMAR JELLINGS (1867-1939)

Partnered with F. Billerey in London. Obituaries: A&BN 157 (10

February 1939): 183; B 156 (10 February 1939): 305; RIBAJ 46 (3 April 1939): 571.

34:2 Hussey, Christopher. "Hilles, Stroud, Gloucestershire: The Home of Detmar Blow." CL 88 (7, 14 September 1940): 212-16, 234-37.

> Designed for Blow's own use in 1914, Hilles was never completed. "The treatment of the interior reflects many of the intentions of William Morris."

34:3 _____. "Holcombe House, Gloucestershire: The House of the Dowager Countess Plymouth." CL 88 (21 December 1940): 542-46.

> Blow added to and restored this Jacobean mansion in 1925. He mainly added gables "dear to the Cotswold builder."

34:4 Nares, Gordon. "Wootton Manor, Sussex." CL 117 (7 April 1955): 920-23.

> Blow added a new wing and built a staircase of eighteenth-century design linking the new and the original portions of this Jacobean mansion.

35:1 BODLEY, GEORGE FREDERICK (1827-1907)

A pupil of George Gilbert Scott, 1845-50, Bodley practiced alone beginning in 1860 and with Thomas Garner (1839-1906), 1869-97. RIBA gold medalist, 1899. Garner has also been articled to Scott. Cecil Greenwood Hare (1875-1932) took over the practice on Bodley's death. The HMC's Wolseley Collection has fifty letters of Bodley, 1885-1902. The RIBA has a few sketches. Obituaries: AA&BN 92 (1907): 137; RIBAJ 15 (1907-8): 13-14, 79, 145-52. David C.W. Verey is researching Bodley's work.

35:2 Cole, David. HANDLIST OF THE WORKS OF BRITISH ARCHITECTS. Vol. 1, G.F. BODLEY, T. GARNER, & C.G. HARE. London: Union Publications, 1972. 18 p.

> "The purpose of this publication is to provide a compact handlist of the architectural works of" Bodley, Garner, and Hare. The chronological listing of their works is alphabetical by town and geographical by county. The alphabetical list names the architect as "B, G, H, or in combination."

35:3 Hussey, Christopher. "Country Homes: Powis Castle." CL 79 (30 May, 6, 13, 20 June 1936): 564-72, 598-604, 624-30, 652-58.

Of the four parts of this article, only the last illustrates the oak drawing room that received its present form from Bodley, who was responsible for the paneling and the plaster ceiling (p. 655, fig. 7).

35:4   Verey, David [C.W.] "Two Early Churches of Bodley." CL 149 (20 May 1971): 1246-49.

Bodley's first commission for a complete religious building was the Baptist church at France Lynch, Gloucestershire, 1854, and was followed by All Saints, Selsley, Gloucestershire, 1861-62. These were the early works of "the most influential ecclesiastical architect in England" at the end of the century.

35:5   Washington Cathedral Executive Committee. WASHINGTON DC.: CATHEDRAL OF ST. PETER AND ST. PAUL. Washington, D.C.: 1930. 75 p.

An almost totally pictorial essay illustrating "parts of the fabric and some of its related buildings completed, under construction, and to be built."

36:1 BRODERICK, CUTHBERT (1822-1905)

After studying with Henry Lockwood, 1837-44, Broderick set up practice in Hull, at some time with George Corson (1829-1910). The RIBA has drawings. Obituary: B 88 (1905): 272.

36:2   Harbron, Dudley. "Minor Masters of the XIXth Century." AR 79 (January 1936): 33-35.

Broderick's background, education, travel, and major commissions are mentioned and a few of his sketches and designs are illustrated.

36:3   Linstrum, Derek. "Architecture of Cuthbert Broderick." CL 141 (1 June 1967): 1379-81.

"One of the architects who benefitted from the competition system of building a large pracrice on the foundations of his first success was Cuthbert Broderick." He began in Bradford, designed most of his buildings in Leeds, and built the Grand Hotel in Scarborough, Yorkshire.

36:4   Wilson, T. Butler. TWO LEEDS ARCHITECTS: CUTHBERT BRODERICK AND GEORGE CORSON. Leeds: West Yorkshire Society of Architects, 1937. 80 p.

The life and work of the two men are described and are
also organized into "Chronological Charts."

37:1 BROOKS, JAMES (1825-1901)

Worked for Lewis Stride, 1847-49, after which he entered the RAL.
Brooks began his practice in 1852. Obituaries: AA&BN 74 (1901):
33-34; B 81 (1901): 321; RIBAJ 8 (1900-1901): 504. R.E. Dixon
is preparing a doctoral dissertation at London University, on Brooks.

37:2 Adkins, J. Standen. "James Brooks: A Memoir." RIBAJ 17 (1909-
10): 493-516.

> A lengthy well-illustrated article on this Gothicist. Appendix
> A contains a "List of the Principal Works Carried out by
> Mr. James Brooks," 1851-96, and appendix B enumerates
> "Exhibits" at various galleries and lists his "Published Draw-
> ings."

37:3 Baggallay, Frank T. "The Late James Brooks." AR 10 (1901): 218-
24.

> This church architect has "more power and originality than
> the present generation is quite aware of."

37:4 Hyland, Anthony. "James Brooks, Architect (1825-1901)." B 196
(2 January 1959): 6-7.

> An appreciation of Brooks's twenty-five new churches and
> of his restorations and alterations, many in London's East
> End.

38:1 BRYCE, DAVID (1803-76)

After an education at Edinburgh High School, Bryce worked for his
father, a builder, and then beginning ca.1824, for William Burn (see
44:1), with whom Bryce partnered from 1841 until 1844, when Burn
moved to London. Obituary: B 34: 499, 507-8. David M. Walker
is researching Bryce's residential architecture; N. Jackson is also researching his work.

38:2 Fiddles, Valerie, et al. MR. DAVID BRYCE. Edinburgh: University
of Edinburgh, 1976. 131 p.

> An exhibition catalog, listing more than two hundred works
> by Bryce and including five essays on various aspects of his
> designs.

38:3   Rowan, Alistair. "Capenoch, Dumfriesshire." CL 148 (13 August 1970): 394–97.

> Plan, sketches, and photographs of the Bryce additions, 1847–54, complement the description.

38:4   _____. "Penicuick House, Midlothian." CL 144 (15, 22, 29 August 1968): 383–87, 448–51, 492–94.

> To this original design of 1761–69, Bryce made additions "with remarkable restraint." He was adding to several similar houses at the time.

39:1   BRYDON, JOHN McKEAN (1840-1901)

Trained under John Bryce in Edinburgh and Campbell Douglas in Glasgow, Brydon assisted Shaw, and Nesfield in London. Obituaries: AA&BN 72 (1901): 82; RIBAJ 8 (1900–1901): 381.

39:2   Gibson, James Sivewright. "The Late John McKean Brydon." RIBAJ 8 (1900–1901): 400–405.

> In praise, his work is listed and illustrated. His private hospital buildings contrast strikingly with those built by public bodies.

39:3   Loftie, Rev. W.J. "Brydon At Bath." AR 18 (July 1905): 3–9, 50–59, and 146–54.

> Seventeenth-century architecture inspired Brydon in most of his work at Bath. He was not well known in London but was given the commission for new government offices in Parliament Street (completed 1912) just prior to his death in May 1901. "The Office of Works have [sic] been actuated by a single-minded desire to fulfill the deceased architect's wishes and adhere to his ideas."

39:4   _____. "The Late John McKean Brydon." AR 10 (1901): 30–31.

> Although Scots-trained, most of his works are in England, where he practiced. Eulogized as an architect whose career seems "never to have been fully set forth."

40:1   BUCKLER, JOHN (1770-1851)

Obituary: B 10 (3 January): 7. The RIBA has drawings. C. Arno is preparing a Ph.M. thesis, at the Courtauld Institute, University of London, on Buckler's drawings.

40:2   Oswald, Arthur. "Blithfield, Staffordshire." CL 116 (28 October, 4, 11 November 1954): 1488-92, 1576-79, 1664-67.

Medieval Blithfield was Gothicized in the 1820s. Exterior battlements and turrets and quite magnificent, elaborately vaulted interior spaces are thoroughly illustrated.

41:1   BUNNING, JAMES BURNSTONE (1802-63)

Trained under George Smith and began practice in 1822. Obituary: B 21 (1863): 782-83.

41:2   RIBAJ. "The London Coal Exchange." Vol. 68 (July 1961): 344.

The alarm was raised that the Coal Exchange, London, would be demolished, and it was. Its interior is illustrated.

42:1   BURGES, WILLIAM (1827-81)

Studied under Edward Blore, 1844, and was an assistant of Matthew Digby Wyatt. In 1856 Burges and Henry Clutton (1819-93) won the international competition for Lille Cathedral, France. Clutton completed the Cathedral at Cork, Ireland, after Burges's death. Publications: ARCHITECTURAL DRAWINGS, 1870; ART APPLIED TO INDUSTRY, 1865; VENISE: ICONOGRAPHIE DES CHAPITEAUX DU PALAIS DUCAL, Paris, 1857. Burges's notebooks are owned by the RIBA, and his contract book, 1875-80, is on loan to the V&A, which has other material. Obituaries: AA&BN 9-10 (1881): 236-37; B 40 (1881): 531-32, 534, 581, 648, 811; BN (1881): 473, 480; RIBAJ (1881-82): 17-30. J. Mordaunt Crook and Charles Handley-Read (see 42:9) are preparing monographs on Burges. Clutton was also a pupil of Blore. Clutton's publications: EXAMPLES OF ECCLESIASTICAL PERPENDICULAR ROOFS, 1845; ILLUSTRATIONS ON THE DOMESTIC ARCHITECTURE OF FRANCE FROM THE ACCESSION OF CHARLES VI TO THE DEMISE OF LOUIS XII, 1853. Obituaries: AAR 2 (1881): 95; RIBAJ 9 (20 July 1893): 460. G. McHardy wrote an M.A. thesis, "Henry Clutton and His Early Eccesiastical Work," in 1969 at the Courtauld Institute, London; P. Hunting is preparing a Ph.M. thesis, at the University of London, on Clutton's domestic architecture.

42:2   Briggs, R.A. "The Art of William Burges, ARA: An Appreciation." RIBAJ 23 (9 February 1916): 131-39.

The RIBA was given by Burges's niece a series of drawings of Burges's own house. His work "was founded on the thirteenth century style" and if he had not designed his house in that style, it would have been in the Pompeiian style. Eight of the drawings, which were exhibited, are illustrated and described.

42:3   Crook, J. Mordaunt. "Patron Extraordinary: John Marquess of Bute." In VICTORIAN SOUTH WALES--ARCHITECTURE, INDUSTRY AND SOCIETY, pp. 3-22. Victorian Society Conference Report no. 7. London: 1969.

"The quality of Burges's work in consistently superb . . . [in interiors where] enthusiasm and romance run riot." Crook concentrates on the work of Burges around Cardiff.

42:4   Floud, Peter. CASTELL COCH. London: Her Majesty's Stationery Office, 1954. 28 p., fold-out plan.

"Though the foundations of the castle date back 700 years, almost everything to be seen today was built in the 1870's as a result of the collaboration of two remarkable men: John Patrick Crichton-Stuart, third Marquess of Bute (1848-1900), as patron and William Burges (1827-81), as architect."

42:5   Girouard, Mark. "Cardiff Castle, Glamorganshire." CL 129 (6, 13, 20 April 1961): 760-63, 822-25, 886-89.

Burges renovated and added to this Roman structure with its twelfth-century keep during 1867-72 and added stables in 1876. Description of and attitudes toward Burges's work complement a whole series of interior photographs. A plan on p. 823 keys the phases of building and some of Burges's notebook sketches are illustrated.

42:6   _____. "Castell Coch, Glamorgan." CL 131 (10, 17 May 1962): 1092-95, 1174-77.

"The first view of Castell Coch leaves one in no doubt that it was the work of someone who knew what architecture was about." Burges added on to medieval foundations. His earlier work in Wales is listed and his aspirations for Castell Coch are discussed. Exterior considerations are given in the first article, interior ones in the second and both aspects are well illustrated.

42:7   Godwin, E[dward] W[illiam]. "The Home of an English Architect." ART JOURNAL (1886): 170-73, 301-5.

Number 9, Melbury Road, Kensington, 1875-80.

42:8   Handley-Read, Charles. "Aladdin's Palace in Kensington: William Burges's Tower House." CL 139 (17 March 1966): 600-604.

Burges's own house, where the interior design is outstanding for the period.

42:9 _____. "St. Fin Barre's Cathedral." AR 141 (June 1967): 422-30.

Handley-Read is writing a biography on Burges. This article concerns Burges's remarkable cathedral in Cork, built during 1862-83 in a High Victorian Gothic style. The article's coverage, both written and illustrative, is thorough and includes reference to two books on the building: Richard Caulfield, HAND-BOOK TO THE CATHEDRAL OF ST. BARRE, 1881; and Andrew C. Robinson, ST. FIN BARRE'S CATHEDRAL, 1887.

42:10 Howell, W.G. "Castell Coch." AR 109 (January 1951): 39-46.

Castell Coch of 1262-95, with later medieval keep and gateway, was restored, remodelled, and made habitable from 1875 onward by Burges. His High Victorian Gothic style was not without an Oriental flavor. Well illustrated.

42:11 Marks, Percy L. "William Burges." AAN 18 (March 1903): 31-33.

Obituary covering Burges's life, partnership with Clutton, competitions, and personal qualities.

42:12 Pullan, Richard Popplewell. ARCHITECTURAL DESIGNS OF WILLIAM BURGES. London: B.T. Batsford, 1883. 21 p., 75 pls.

The plates illustrate twenty projects, each descirbed by Burges. The descriptions are edited, however, by his brother-in-law, also an architect. All of the illustrations had previously been published in architectural magazines having been drawn under the supervision of Burges.

42:13 _____. THE DESIGNS OF WILLIAM BURGES, ARA. London: B.T. Batsford, 1886. 23 pls.

Photographs of ecclesiastical and domestic furniture and ornaments, executed in wood, stone, and metal.

42:14 _____. DETAILS OF STONEWORK BY W. BURGES, ARA. London: B.T. Batsford, 1887. 8 p., 39 pls.

Working drawings of six major projects by Burges have been reproduced photographically to illustrate his masterly detailing of stonework "exactly as a thirteenth century architect would have carried them out."

42:15 _____. THE HOUSE OF WILLIAM BURGES, ARA. London: B.T. Batsford, 1886. 40 pls.

> A portfolio of forty photographs, mounted on boards, of Burges's own house on Melbury Road.

42:16 _____. "Works of the Late William Burges." RIBAJ (1881-82): 183-95.

> "It may be safely asserted that it is but seldom that any great artist attains the full measure of his fame or receives his due tribute of praise during his life-time." After this disclaimer, the author assesses some of Burges's major projects and also some of his designs unsuccessfully submitted in various nineteenth-century competitions.

42:17 Rees, William. CARDIFF CASTLE. [Cardiff: Cardiff Corporation], n.d. 15 p.

> This illustrated handbook is for the aid of the tourist and provides a brief history of the castle, including its additions by Burges, executed mainly in 1870-75. The building was given by the Bute family to the Cardiff Corporation, 24 June 1948.

42:18 Rotch, Arthur. "William Burges." AA&BN 9 (1881): 236-37.

> "His personality was so original that he could not fail to be a marked man in the community where eccentricity is at a premium."

42:19 Taylor, Nicholas, and Symondson, Anthony. "Burges and Morris at Bingley." AR 144 (July 1968): 35-38.

> Burges's "Book of Drawings" for the interior of Oakwood, Yorkshire, adds another design to his list of works. Many drawings are illustrated.

43:1 BURN, WILLIAM (1789-1870)

Son of Robert Burn, the architect. Trained in London under Robert Smirke. Thereafter Burn practiced in Edinburgh, ca.1824-44, and partnered with David Bryce (see 38:1), 1841-44. Burn's works total ca.seven hundred buildings. Obituaries: B 28 (5, 12 March 1870): 189, 231; RIBAJ (1869-70): 121-29. Depositories of drawings: William Salt Library, Cornwall Records Office, Glouchester Records Office (see 43:5), NMRS, RIBA. David M. Walker is researching his domestic work.

43:2   Donaldson, T[homas] L[everton]. "Obituary." RIBAJ (1869-70): 121-29.

> A lengthy obituary, invaluable for the list of two hundred houses on which Burn worked, including forty new houses in Scotland, sixty in England, and four in Ireland.

43:3   Hussey, Christopher. "Harlaxton Manor, Lincolnshire." CL 121 (11, 18 April 1957): 704-7, 764-67.

> Salvin was replaced at Harlaxton "in 1848 by William Burn. He, it is presumed, was responsible for the Baroque and Rococo decoration of astounding quality and elaboration attributed to about 1855."

43:4   _____. "Prestwold Hall, Leicestershire." CL 125 (16, 23, 30 April 1959): 828-31, 890-93, 948-51.

> Burn remodeled this eighteenth-century house in 1843. The interiors are Italianate (see second installment of article). The third installment concerns the work of ca. 1875, not by Burn.

43:5   _____. "Stanway, Gloucestershire." CL 136 (3, 10, 17 December 1964): 1490-94, 1646-49, 1708-11.

> The house dates back to the sixteenth century and has had various additions (and demolitions--see plan, p. 1492), including the work of Burn, 1859, which is described in the third part of the article. Working drawings are now in the Gloucester Record Office.

43:6   Macaulay, James. "William Burn and the Country House." In THE GOTHIC REVIVAL, 1745-1845, pp. 318-37. Glasgow and London: Blackie, 1975.

> Macaulay's chapter 7 concerns Scottish country houses by Burn and his contemporaries, ca. 1815-39.

43:7   Rowan, Alistair. "Raby Castle, Co. Durham." CL 147 (1, 8, 22 January 1970): 18-21, 66-69, 186-89.

> A history of the house from 1626, through its reconstructions of 1768-88, to the completion of the interiors by Burn and others, 1844-48.

44:1 BURNET, JOHN JAMES (1859-1938)

Attended the Ecole des Beaux-Arts, Paris, 1874-77. In 1878 became his father's partner in Glasgow. From 1886 to 1897 the partnership was known as Burnet, Son and [J.C.] Campbell; it later changed to Burnet, Son and [Norman] Dick. In 1905 the younger Burnet moved to London, where his partners became Thomas S. Tait and Francis Lorne. Starting in the early 1920s the partnership was known as Sir John Burnet, Tait and Lorne, whose publications are: THE ARCHITECTS' JOURNAL LIBRARY OF PLANNED INFORMATION, 1936; THE INFORMATION BOOK OF SIR JOHN BURNET, TAIT AND LORNE. Burnet obituaries: A&BN 155 (8 July 1938): 29, 31; AJ 88 (8 July 1938): 6; B 155 (8 July 1938): 59; RIBAJ 45 (18 July, 15 August 1938): 893-96, 941-43. In 1976 at the University of Dundee Gordon Fraser wrote a B. Arch. thesis, "Early Influences on the Work of Sir John James Burnet," which refers to the influence of the Chicago School. Andor Gomme and David M. Walker are researching the work of Burnet.

Thomas S. Tait obituaries: AJ 120 (22 July 1954): 97; AR 116 (September 1954): 141; B (23 July 1954): 126; RIBAJ 61 (August 1954): 427. In 1972 J.H. Gould wrote a B.A. thesis, "T.S. Tait--Architect," at the University of Newcastle.

44:2   Edwards, A. Trystan. THE ARCHITECTURAL WORK OF SIR JOHN BURNET AND PARTNERS. Geneva: Masters of Architecture, 1930. xvi, 115 pls.

> The designer of the London-based firm from about 1920 to 1930 was Thomas S. Tait, although both in London and Glasgow buildings designed by the firm have "a blending of the Classic and modern spirit." Its work has a "combination of experience" and "a freshness of outlook."

44:3   Emberton, Joseph. "Adelaide House." A 113 (9 January 1925): 24-31.

> Adelaide House, London, an office block, "should have a tremendous influence on our younger generation of architects. It proves beyond all doubt that the design of a modern building is . . . a true and reasonable expression of the structure of the building." The building is described in detail.

44:4   Goodhart-Rendel, Harry Stuart. "The Work of Sir John Burnet." AJ 57 (27 June 1923): 1065-1110.

> Goodhart-Rendel thinks that Burnet is the "greatest British architect of the present time [1923]. His careful considerations with relation to design are propounded." Good photographic coverage and a detailed listing of his works by building type.

44:5   Rees, Verner O. "Glasgow University Zoological Building." AJ 66 (21 September 1927): 383-87.

>A handsome design to contain classrooms and a museum. Illustrations, plans, and description.

44:6   Robertson, Howard. "Two Great London Buildings of 1924." AJ 61 (7 January 1925): 4-12.

>Lutyens's Britannic House, and John Burnet and Partners' Adelaide House, both office blocks, "are probably the most important architectural events of the London year."

44:7   Smith, William James. "An Architectural Anthology: Glasgow-- 'Greek' Thomson, Burnet and Mackintosh." QRIAS 85 (1951): 11-13, 56-60.

>"Burnet's early work has a French-Italian flavour always distinguished by originality of composition and good proportion."

44:8   Wakefield, Lord. "Memorial Chapel, Glasgow University." AJ 70 (11 December 1929): 906-11.

>Described and illustrated with plan.

44:9   _____. "Royal Masonic Hospital." AR 74 (August 1933): 50-58.

>A well-illustrated article including some working drawings of this London hospital. Planning, structure, equipment, and the reasons for these design elements are explained.

44:10 Walker, David M. "Sir John James Burnet." In EDWARDIAN ARCHITECTURE AND ITS ORIGINS, edited by Alastair Service, pp. 192-215. London: Architectural Press, 1975.

>Burnet's Beaux-Arts training and influence from America are obvious in all of his work, which is here well illustrated and described.

45:1 BURTON, DECIMUS (1800-1881)

Trained under his father, James Burton, and under George Maddox (1760-1843), prior to entering the RAL, 1817. Began practice in 1821. Obituaries: AA&BN 11-12 (1882): 14; B 41 (24 December 1881): 779-81. The RIBA and V&A have drawings of some of his projects. P.A. Clarke wrote an RIBA thesis, "James and Decimus Burton, 1761-1837," in 1949. W.A. Eden wrote a B. Arch. thesis "James and Decimus Burton, 1761-1807," at Liverpool University in 1928.

45:2   Bohan, Peter John. "James and Decimus Burton: Architectural Trends in England Exemplified by Their Work, 1790-1860." Doctoral dissertation, Yale University, 1961. 368 p.

        Picturesque planning came from John Nash in the initial work of Decimus Burton but thereafter Burton designed in the Italianate and Gothic styles. From 1835 to 1860 he was concerned with alterations and speculative developments.

45:3   Ferriday, Peter. "Palm House at Kew." AR 121 (February 1957): 127-28.

        Richard Turner of Dublin erected the Palm House and was its designer even though Burton supervised its construction and had originally planned the building. But Burton's plan had a "superabundance of pillars--plenty of taste but no room for the palms." So Turner redesigned it, but posterity usually gives the credit to Burton.

45:4   Graig, Gordon. "Before His Time--Mr. Decimus Burton." APOLLO 4 (1926): 140-44.

        Burton designed the Colosseum, Regent's Park, London, 1823, with a panoramic view, as from the top of St. Paul's Cathedral, on the interior of the drum. It was forty-six thousand square feet in extent and was painted by E.T. Parris and his assistants. Two of Burton's 1823 illustrations-- THE GEOMETRICAL ASCENT TO THE GALLERIES IN THE COLOSSEUM, REGENT'S PARK and the BIRD'S-EYE VIEW . . .," from the top--accompany this article.

45:5   Honour, Hugh. "The Regent's Park Colosseum." CL 113 (2 January 1953): 22-24.

        Opened in 1829, the Colosseum had painted on its interior a 360-degree panorama of London, as from the top of St. Paul's Cathedral. In the center of the space was a vertical, cylindrical shaft containing staircases and a hand-operated elevator.

45:6   Hussey, Christopher. "Calverley Park, Tunbridge Wells." CL 145 (1, 8 May 1969): 1080-83, 1166-69.

        Calverley Park, 1827-50, was based upon Regent's Park, London, by John Nash. Burton designed the crescents, lodges, shopping promenades, and hotel all in the spirit of Nash, making them both classical and picturesque.

45:7   _____. "Country Homes, Gardens, Old and New: Grimston Park, Yorkshire." CL 87 (9, 16 March 1940): 252-56, 276-80.

Burton rebuilt and Italianized the house, 1840, and W.A. Nesfield was responsible for the gardens.

45:8   Jones, Ronald P. "The Life and Work of Decimus Burton." AR 17 (March and April 1905): 108-18, 154-64.

Original drawings and photographs of a bygone era are used in discussing Burton's work in Regent's Park, Hyde Park, the Athenaeum Club, all three in London, and some of his residential work.

45:9   McRae, J.F. "Burton's Tunbridge Wells." AJ 65 (9, 16 February 1927): 214-16, 249-50.

This "straightforward, high principled and cultured man" lacks a biographer, so a brief resume of his life and work precedes McRae's consideration of Burton's public and private commissions at Tunbridge Wells.

45:10   Nares, Gordon. "The Athenaeum." CL 109 (6 April 1951): 1018-22.

Burton designed the Athenaeum, its furniture, and its fittings, 1827-30. It was redecorated, 1891-92, and an attic story was added by T.E. Collcutt, 1899.

45:11   Ramsey, Stanley C. "London Clubs." AR 34 (September 1913): 54-58.

This article on Burton's Athenaeum is the fourth article in a series on London's clubs.

45:12   Taylor, G.C. "Country Homes, Gardens, Old and New: Holme House, Regent's Park." CL 86 (28 October 1939): 444-48.

"Imitating the Palladian villa . . . and its general style [is] half way between the moderate pretensions of the ornamental cottage and the stately magnificence of the mansion."

46:1 BUTTERFIELD, WILLIAM (1814-1900)

Apprenticed to a London builder and later articled to a Worcester architect, he established a practice in London, ca.1844. RIBA gold medalist, 1884. The RIBA has drawings and the V&A has various designs. Publications: ELEVATIONS, SECTIONS AND DETAILS OF SAINT JOHN BAPTIST CHURCH AT SHOTTESBROKE, BERKSHIRE, 1844 and numerous articles in ECCLESIOLOGIST. Obituaries: AA&BN 67 (1900): 65; ARCHITECT AND CONTRACT REPORTER 63 (2 March

1900): 138-39; RIBAJ 7 (1899-1900): 240-48. For his 1963 B.A. W. Brackenbury wrote a thesis, "William Butterfield," at Cambridge University.

46:2   Girouard, Mark. "Milton Ernest Hall, Bedfordshire." CL 146 (23 October 1969): 1042-46.

Butterfield's only country house was a commission obtained from the employer of his sister, a governess. He designed interiors, furniture, and a boathouse (now gone), all of which this article illustrates with plans, sections, and elevational drawings.

46:3   Harris, E. Swinfen. "The Life and Work of William Butterfield." ARCHITECT AND CONTRACT REPORTER 83 (1910): 129-30 and 145-47.

Swinfen lists Butterfield's buildings known from drawings, observations, and the periodical BUILDER and presents Butterfield "the man" and "friend."

46:4   Langham-Carter, R.R. "St. Saviour's Church, Claremont: Cape." ARCHITECT AND BUILDER (South Africa) 22 (September 1972): 8-11.

Begun in 1845 by Robert Gray, first Anglican bishop of Cape Town, who died in 1872, this church was completed in 1880 from designs by Butterfield. Herbert Baker added a larger chancel in 1904.

46:5   Pite, [Arthur] Beresford. "A Review of the Tendencies of the Modern School of Architecture: The Influence of William Butterfield and Mr. Philip Webb." RIBAJ 8 (1900-1901): 89-90.

Butterfield has been misjudged but his genius will be appreciated when it is realized that he "expressed his own thought in his materials for its modern purpose, with absolutely new art."

46:6   Redfern, Harry. "Some Recollections of William Butterfield and Henry Woodyer." A&BN 178 (14, 21, 28 April 1944): 21-22, 44-45, 58-60.

Redfern joined Butterfield's office in 1877 and worked under Henry Woodyer (1816-96). Redfern's recollections provide an insight into the workings of an architect's office of the period.

46:7   RIBAJ. "The Late William Butterfield." Vol. 7 (1899-1900): 241-48.

An odd article, claiming among other things that the Gothic revival never caught on in America! Butterfield's individuality and some of his works are mentioned.

46:8   Ricardo, Halsey. "Melbourne Cathedral: A Comment." AR 3 (1897-98): 187.

There is a difference between Butterfield's design and the manner in which it has been executed by others. "The difference is great and disastrous." The cathedral's interior is dark and details have been misinterpreted.

46:9   _____. "William Butterfield." AR 7 (January-June 1900): 258-63; 8 (July-December 1900): 15-23.

A general appreciation with emphasis on his output.

46:10 Summerson, John. "The Gothic Revival Number: Act 3: Christian Gothic; Scene 1: William Butterfield." AR 98 (December 1945): 166-75.

Summerson "finds it difficult to write down a clear and sensible explanation of the fascination" that Butterfield exercises. The phases of his development and his influence, work methods, and major buildings are described. This article interprets Butterfield's architecture as the glorification of the ugly.

46:11 _____. "Pugin and Butterfield." AR 152 (August 1972): 97-99.

Paul Thompson (see 46:14) questioned Summerson's evaluation that "the first glory of Butterfield is, to me his utter ruthlessness. How he hated 'taste.'" (46:10). Summerson defends his attitude of 1945 when he had just completed his book GEORGIAN LONDON with the resultant judgement.

46:12 Thompson, Paul. "All Saints' Church, Margaret Street, Reconsidered." AH 8 (1965): 73-94.

Thompson asks and answers many questions. Did Butterfield adapt the ideas in the design of All Saints', London, "through travelling, or reading, or did he invent them? Are the faults in the building, as well as its powerful inventiveness, due to naive ignorance or an inability to coordinate the work of fellow artists, or to a deliberate and sadistic hatred of beauty?"

46:13 _____. "Butterfield's Masterpiece Re-Assessed: All Saints', Margaret Street." CL 137 (14 January 1965): 60-62.

A key building of the third stage of the Gothic revival,
"of conscious originality grounded in scholarship." It was
assumed to be an ugly discordant building, but is it?

46:14 _____. WILLIAM BUTTERFIELD. London: Routledge and Kegan
Paul, 1971. 526 p.

A thorough biography of Butterfield, his personality, style,
works, and the patrons, fellow architects, and builders with
whom he came into contact. His designs are analyzed with
regard to the elements of construction and aesthetic criteria.
There is a Chronology and Select Gazetteer at the end of
the book.

46:15 _____. "William Butterfield's Australian Cathedrals." CL 150 (9,
16 September 1971): 622-24, 686-90.

"The most favoured architect of the Cambridge Ecclesiolo-
gists," Butterfield "was never given important work in an
English cathedral." Instead he designed Perth Cathedral,
Scotland, 1847; Frederickton Cathedral, Canada; and three
cathedrals in Australia: two in Adelaide, dated 1847 and
1868, and one in Melbourne, in 1878.

47:1 BYRNE, BARRY (1883-1967)

American architect who designed the Church of Christ the King, Cork,
Ireland. For his American work, see: Wodehouse, Lawrence. AMER-
ICAN ARCHITECTS FROM THE CIVIL WAR TO THE FIRST WORLD
WAR. Detroit: Gale Research Company, 1977.

47:2 B. "The Lighting of Ecclesiastical Building: Lighting a Concrete
Church." Vol. 142 (4 March 1932): 423-24, 641.

The Church of Christ the King, Cork, is described with
respect to artificial and natural lighting and its plan, elevation, and section are reproduced; photographs of the
building are included. For further coverage, see A Rec 65
(May 1929): 463-66.

48:1 BYRNE, PATRICK (1783-1864)

Son of the architect John Byrne, he studied under Henry Aaron Baker
and at the Dublin Society School. Began practice, ca.1815, and
built numerous suburban and country churches. Of his three architect
sons, Hugh became Dublin's city architect from ca.1840 until 67.
The National Library, Dublin, has Patrick Byrne's drawings in its

Joly Print Collection, including three watercolors from his student days.

48:2   Curran, Constantine P. "Patrick Byrne, Architect." STUDIES: AN IRISH QUARTERLY REVIEW OF LETTERS, PHILOSOPHY, AND SCIENCE, 33 (June 1944): 193-203.

        Byrne began as a classicist but converted to the Gothic revival and was a pioneer of that style in Dublin. Toward the end of his life he reverted back to the classical.

48:3   Raftery, Patrick. "The Last of the Traditionalists: Patrick Byrne, 1783-1864." QUARTERLY BULLETIN OF THE IRISH GEORGIAN SOCIETY 7 (April-December 1964): 48-66.

        Biographical material for 48:1 was abstracted from this article.

49:1 CARPENTER, RICHARD HERBERT (1841-1893)

Articled to and partnered with William Slater (1819-72). The RIBA has drawings. Obituary: B 64 (1893): 303, 310, 319; RIBAJ 9 (1892-93): 339.

49:2   Bernard, John Henry. THE CATHEDRAL CHURCH OF SAINT PATRICK [Dublin]: A HISTORY AND DESCRIPTION OF THE BUILDING. London: G. Bell and Sons, 1905. 88 p.

        Carpenter rebuilt the Chapter House as a chapel for the Knights of St. Patrick "reproducing the original design with very considerable success."

50:1 CASSON, HUGH MAXWELL (1913-)

Studied at the University of Cambridge and practiced from 1937 to 1946 with C. Nicholson and from 1946 on with Neville Condor. Knighted, 1952. The RIBA has drawings. Publications: HOUSES BY THE MILLION: AN ACCOUNT OF THE HOUSING ACHIEVEMENT IN THE USA, 1940-1945, 1946; AN INTRODUCTION TO VICTORIAN ARCHITECTURE, 1948 (see A19); NEW SIGHTS OF LONDON, 1930 (see B12). Edited: BRIDGES, 1963; FOLLIES, 1963.

50:2   Brock, Dave. "Conversation with Casson." JRAIC 37 (February 1960): 72-73.

        Jottings of a talk that Casson gave in Vancouver, Canada, concerning architecture, the automobile, and the city.

50:3   Richards, J.M.   "Criticism: Youth Hostel at Holland Park, London."
        AJ 131 (18 June 1959): 911–15.

        Richards is mainly concerned with scale and detailing in
        this lengthy criticism of a new hostel adjacent to a Jaco-
        bean house.

50:4   Wharton, Kate.   "Talking to Sir Hugh Casson." A&BN 2 (29 Janu-
        ary 1969): 27.

        As a nation we are not encouraged to look and there are
        not enough good architects about--so says Sir Hugh.

50:5   Woodward, Christopher.   "Public Buildings for Public Activities."
        RIBAJ 78 (February 1971): 50–57.

        Casson's firm won first prize in a limited competition for
        the redevelopment of the market place at Derby. Thirteen
        firms were invited to compete and several schemes are il-
        lustrated.

51:1   CHAMBERLIN, POWELL AND BON (Partnership 1952-)

        Peter Hugh Girard Chamberlin (1919-   ), trained at the Kingston
        School of Art; Geoffrey Powell (1920-   ), trained at the AAL;
        Christopher Bon (1921-   ), trained in Zurich and Milan. Publica-
        tions: REPORT TO THE COURT OF COMMON COUNCIL OF THE
        CORPORATION OF THE CITY OF LONDON, 1959; UNIVERSITY OF
        LEEDS DEVELOPMENT PLAN, 1960.

51:2   Chamberlin, Peter.   "Architects' Approach to Architecture." RIBAJ
        76 (June 1969): 228–35.

        "To search for the solution within the problem; the problem
        being to provide environment for a specific human activity
        with the resources available, both physical and financial."

51:3   Gillespie, Bernard.   "Barbican Project for the City of London."
        CANADIAN ARCHITECT 16 (January 1971): 38–42.

        Materials and forms have been restrained and thus the dif-
        fering scales of historic and infill buildings complement
        each other in a unifying whole. It is a town within the
        city.

51:4   Richards, J.M.   "Criticism: Housing at Golden Lane, City of Lon-
        don." AJ 125 (20 June 1957): 911–15.

        In praise of the inward-looking urban space, the high stan-
        dard of finishes, and a sculptural roof on the high block of

and the internal relationships within the residential accommodation for fourteen hundred people on seven acres.

51:5   Webb, Michael. "Eclectic Design for a Cambridge College." CL
        139 (28 April 1966): 1004-7.

        New College, to cater to three hundred women, was begun
        in 1962. It captures the "traditional splendour of Cambridge
        in modern times."

52:1   CHAMPNEYS, BASIL (1842-1935)

        Articled to John Prichard of Llandaff and began private practice in
        1867. RIBA gold medalist, 1912. Publications: HENRY MERRITT:
        ART CRITICISM AND ROMANCE, 1879; MEMOIRS AND CORRESPON-
        DENCE OF COVENTRY PATMORE, 1900; A QUIET CORNER OF EN-
        GLAND, 1875. Obituaries: NIY (1935): 493; RIBAJ 42 (27 April
        1935): 737-38.

52:2   Girouard, Mark. "Victorian Sweetness and Light: Newnham College,
        Cambridge." CL 150 (16 December 1971): 1704-6.

        Designed in the Queen Anne revival, 1892-93, its build-
        ings are illustrated and described.

52:3   John Rylands Library, Manchester. JOHN RYLANDS LIBRARY, MAN-
        CHESTER. 1900. 29 photographs.

52:4   Stokes, Leonard. "The Royal Gold Medal, 1912: Presentation to
        Mr. Basil Champneys." RIBAJ 19 (1911-12): 585-92.

        He practiced mainly in the Gothic revival mode and many
        of his buildings are listed. One of his most recent struc-
        tures was Oriel College, Oxford, in the Queen Anne re-
        vival.

53:1   CHATWIN, JULIUS ALFRED (1830-1907)

        Articled to Charles Barry, 1851, and practiced in Birmingham begin-
        ning in 1855. See T. Hutton, KING EDWARD VI SCHOOL BIR-
        MINGHAM 1552-1952 for his major work. Oxford: Blackwell, 1952.
        240 p. Obituary: RIBAJ 14 (1906-7): 556.

53:2   Chatwin, Philip B. LIFE STORY OF J.A. CHATWIN, 1830-1907.
        Oxford: University Press, 1952. 52 p.

"My father was so well known as a church architect and,
by some, as a successful designer of houses that his other
work is often forgotten." His life, education, and practice
are presented.

54:1 **CHERMAYEFF, SERGE (1900-)**

Born in Russia and educated in England, he began practice in 1930
and was associated with Eric Mendelsohn (see 172:1), 1933-36. Thereafter he practiced alone in England and the United States. The RIBA
has drawings. Publications: A CHILDREN'S CENTRE OR NURSERY
SCHOOL, 1944; and with C. Alexander, COMMUNITY AND PRI-
VACY: TOWARD A NEW ARCHITECTURE OF HUMANISM, 1963.
See also Wodehouse, Lawrence, AMERICAN ARCHITECTS FROM THE
FIRST WORLD WAR TO THE PRESENT. Detroit: Gale Research Co.,
1977.

54:2 Cordingley, R.A. "Building for Industry: The Role of the Architect."
AR 83 (March 1938): 117-26.

This article considers the fact that an architect is limited
in designing an industrial building because of the dictates
of the plant. Chermayeff's first unit of a long-term building project for laboratories at Blackley, Manchester, is examined in detail.

54:3 Hussey, Christopher. "Bentley, near Halland, Sussex." CL 88 (26
October, 2 November 1940): 368-71, 390-93.

Originally refused permission to build this design, Chermayeff
persevered in this timber residence for himself of 1935.

55:1 **CHRISTIAN, EWAN (1814-95)**

Worked for John Brown (flourished 1832-51) of Norwich and William
Railton. Began to practice in the late 1830s. RIBA gold medalist,
1887. Publications: ARCHITECTURAL ILLUSTRATIONS OF SKELTON
CHURCH, YORKSHIRE, 1846. Illustrated: Matthew Habershon's THE
FINEST EXISTING SPECIMENS OF ANCIENT HALF-TIMBERED HOUSES
IN ENGLAND, 1836. Obituary: B 68 (1895): 170; RIBAJ 2
(1894-95): 313, 331-34, 377.

55:2 Adkins, J. Standen. "Ewan Christian: A Memoir." RIBAJ 18 (1910-
11): 711-30.

The family tree, training, and major works of this eclectic
architect are discussed and, in the latter cases, illustrated
and a "List of Principal Works," 1841-94, is included.

55:3   Fleetwood-Hesketh, Peter. "Future of the National Portrait Gallery." CL 148 (20 August 1970): 446-48.

> The National Portrait Gallery adjoins William Wilkins's National Gallery at the northeast corner. Christian and J.K. Colling "adapted a style very different from Wilkins's work, but not discordant with it." The portrait gallery was opened in 1896. Fears were growing in 1970 concerning the ultimate fate of the building at a time when the National Gallery was physically expanding.

56:1   **CLARK, H. FULLER (fl. early twentieth century)**

56:2   Taylor, Nicholas. "The Black Friar." AR 136 (November 1964): 373-76. Reprinted in THE ANTI-RATIONALISTS, edited by Nikolaus Pevsner and J.M. Richards, pp. 181-86. London: Architectural Press, 1973.

> The Black Friar is a pub at 174 Queen Victoria Street, London. Its detailing is thoroughly art nouveau.

57:1   **CLARKE, JOSEPH (1819-88)**

Publication: SCHOOLS AND SCHOOL HOUSES, 1852. Obituary: B 54 (1888): 197-98.

57:2   Cornforth, John. "The House of St. Barnabas in Soho." CL 130 (6 July 1961): 18-21.

> The house dates from 1754, but a French Gothic-style chapel was added in 1862-64. Clarke had also intended to add cloisters and a dormitory, as his drawing (fig. 8) illustrates.

CLARKE-HALL, DENNIS. See HALL, DENNIS CLARKE

58:1   **COATES, WELLS WINTEMUTE (1895-1958)**

Born in Japan and educated in Canada, Coates studied for his doctorate in engineering at the University of London. Practiced architecture in London, 1929-39, but returned to Vancouver, Canada, to practice in 1956, and died there two years later. E.F. Elgohary wrote a doctoral dissertation, "Wells Coates and His Position in the Beginning of the Modern Movement in Britain," at the University of London in 1965. S.S. Adams wrote an undergraduate thesis, "Wells Coates," at the University of Newcastle in 1968.

58:2   Lambert, Sam. "Historic Pioneers: Architects and Clients." AJ   151
        (11 March 1970): 595.

        A very brief note quoting Jack Prichard, who was the client
        for Lawn Road Flats, London, 1934.

58:3   Richards, J.M. "Wells Coates, 1893 [sic]-1958." AR   124 (Decem-
        ber 1958): 357-60.

        Wells "was especially directed at exploring the common
        ground between architecture and engineering" because he
        was trained as an engineer.

59:1 COCKERELL, CHARLES ROBERT (1788-1863)

At sixteen he began architectural training under his father, Samuel
Pepys Cockerell (ca.1754-1827), and in 1809 he became an assistant
of Robert Smirke prior to travel to archaeological sites in the Mediter-
ranean area.   Cockerell practiced in London from 1819 on and was
professor of architecture at the RAL.   First recipient of the RIBA gold
medal, 1848.   Publications: ICONOGRAPHY OF THE WEST FRONT
OF WELLS CATHEDRAL, 1851; THE TEMPLE OF JUPITER PANHEL-
LENIUS AT AEGINA, AND OF APOLLO EPICURIUS AT BASSAE
NEAR PHIGALEIA IN ARCADIA, 1860; TRAVELS IN SOUTHERN EU-
ROPE AND THE LEVANT, 1810-1817, 1817.   He illustrated the 1825-
30 edition of James Stuart and Nicholas Revett, THE ANTIQUITIES
OF ATHENS.   Obituaries: B 21 (1863): 683-85; RIBAJ (1863-64):
1-3 and 17-26.   The V&A, RIBA and BM own drawings, lecture
notes, sketchbooks, and correspondence.   The RIBA also owns a manuscript by J.E. Goodchild, 1878.   E. Dodd is researching Cockerell
up to ca.1835.

59:2   Brydon, John McKean. "The Work of Professor Cockerell, RA."
        RIBAJ 7 (26 May 1900): 349-68.

        A general discussion of classical architecture and the per-
        sonalities of the period, the rival Gothic style, and his
        major works that includes biographical notes.

59:3   Cockerell, Robert Pepys. "The Life and Works of Charles Robert
        Cockerell." AR 12 (August and October 1902): 129-46.

        This account of Cockerell's background and travel includes
        the fact that he carried despatches for the foreign secre-
        tary.   The reasons for the emphasis on travel in the first
        segment of the article are that Cockerell's fame "rests not
        merely on his purely architectural work, but partly, if not
        equally, on his archaeological and artistic researches [sic]"
        and also because firsthand knowledge of Greek architecture
        was his inspiration.   The second segment of the article con-
        cerns his principal buildings.

59:4 Cornforth, John. "The Fitzwilliam Museum, Cambridge." CL 132 (22, 29 November 1962): 1278-81, 1340-43.

> George Basevi won the competition for the museum in 1835. At Basevi's death in 1845, Cockerell took charge and revised the scheme for the central staircase, which he had considered a weakness. In two years he had spent the twelve thousand pounds that had been raised, and work did not begin again until the 1870s under E.M. Barry.

59:5 Crook, J. Mordaunt. "Broomhall, Fife." CL 147 (29 January 1970): 242-46.

> Between 1766 and 1841 no fewer than eighteen architects were involved in schemes for the transformation of the house. Cockerell was but one of them and complained that Lord "Elgin wished to collect plans as amusement." One of Cockerell's elevations is illustrated.

59:6 Harris, John. "C.R. Cockerell's ICHNOGRAPHICA DOMESTICA." AH 14 (1971): 5-29.

> "As a survey of British architectural planning, the ICHNO-GRAPHICA DOMESTICA can only be compared to the more extensive collection of plans published in the various editions of VITRUVIUS BRITANICUS" by Colen Campbell, but the former is more catholic. Cockerell's diaries, 1821-32, are equally extensive since he wrote an average of 250 words per day, and some days wrote several thousand words.

59:7 Hussey, Christopher. "Oakly Park, Shropshire." CL 119 (1, 8 March 1956): 380-83, 426-29.

> The keeper's lodge, altered ca.1775, was remodeled by Cockerell, 1819-40. Cockerell's drawings are illustrated.

59:8 Hutton, C.A. "A Collection of Sketches by C.R. Cockerell, RA." JOURNAL OF HELLENIC STUDIES 29 (1909): 53-59, pl. 7.

> An account of a series of sketches, which Samuel Pepys Cockerell gave to the BM, that was made by Cockerell mainly in Greece and Italy, 1810-17.

59:9 NRA. COCKERELL MSS. London: Historical Manuscripts Commission, n.d.. 19 p.

> An annotated listing of lecture notes and professional correspondence held by the RIBA.

59:10 Prestwich, Ernest. "The Life and Work of Professor Cockerell." RIBAJ 18 (1910-11): 669-85.

Evolved from an undergraduate thesis presented at the University of Liverpool School of Architecture, it covers his life, education, travel, and major works.

59:11 Richardson, Albert E. "Design for Ionic Capital By Professor Cockerell." RIBAJ 25 (1917-18): 229-30.

Cockerell had explored the Temple of Apollo Epicurius at Bassae, Greece, by Ictinus. Eighteen years later in 1829, Cockerell prepared a drawing of a capital ("for the Bank of England?") and this was one of several designs given to the RIBA by Phene R. Spiers.

59:12 _____. "Some Early Drawings of Professor C.R. Cockerell, RA." RIBAJ 37 (1929-30): 722 and 725-27.

Drawings from as early as 1806 were given to the RIBA by Mrs. Frederick Pepys Cockerell, a daughter-in-law.

59:13 Smirke, Sydney. "Some Account of the Professional Life and Character of C.R. Cockerell." RIBAJ (1863-64): 17-28.

Smirke outlines Cockerell's life and work and lists his major projects and drawings. There are three handsome fold-out plates of drawings by Cockerell--of his restoration of the Roman Forum, drawn in 1817; his view of Athens dated 1816; and his 1843 sketch of a pediment for a public building.

59:14 Spiers, R. Phene. "Cockerell's Restoration of Ancient Rome." AR 29 (March 1911): 122-28.

Some drawings, "which had apparently been prepared as lecture diagrams," were discovered in 1906 at the RAL. They were probably made and used by Cockerell who was professor of architecture, 1839-60. Four are illustrated.

59:15 Watkin, David. THE LIFE AND WORK OF C.R. COCKERELL. London: A. Zwemmer, 1974. 272 p.

This biography is based partially upon newly discovered diaries. These, together with lecture notes and correspondence, provide an insight into the mind of a sensitive designer. His major works are thoroughly analyzed and are listed, pp. 249-53.

59:16 Worthington, Hubert. "Drawings by Charles Robert Cockerell, RA." RIBAJ 39 (1931-32): 268-71.

A review of his drawings exhibited at the RIBA and an assessment of the quality of draughtsmanship.

60:1   COGSWELL, A.E. (1858-1934)

60:2   Nash, Andy. A.E. COGSWELL: ARCHITECT WITHIN A VICTORIAN
       CITY. Portsmouth: Portsmouth Polytechnic School of Architecture,
       1975. 115 p.

       By far the most prolific architect of his era in and around
       Portsmouth, Cogswell designed in a great variety of styles
       and building types.

61:1   COIA, GIOVANI [JACK] ANTONIO (1891-)

       Born at Wolverhampton when his father, a Neapolitan musician, and
       his mother, a Florentine circus artist, were on their way to Glasgow.
       He trained at the Glasgow College of Art School of Architecture and
       worked for Herbert C. Welsh in London. A partner in the firm of
       Gillespie, Kidd and Coia since 1927. His first commission was for
       Leon, Gordon Street, Glasgow, 1928, which he designed in a latent
       art nouveau style. RIBA gold medalist, 1969.

61:2   Campbell, A.B. "Profile: Jack Coia, A.R.S.A., F.R.I.B.A." PROS-
       PECT 1 (Spring 1956): 25.

       Most of the above biographic material was abstracted from
       this article.

61:3   Sharp, Dennis. "A Craftsman's Architecture." CL 145 (19 June
       1969): 1590-92.

       Coia's work, including the ballroom of the Ca' Doro restau-
       rant, Glasgow; is presented and assessed.

61:4   Webb, Michael. "Scottish Homage to Le Corbusier." CL 142 (27
       July 1967): 212-14.

       The work of the firm Gillespie, Kidd, and Coia is briefly
       surveyed but special attention is given to St. Peter's Semi-
       nary at Cardross, commissioned 1958, inaugurated 1966.
       The seminary is described in relation to Le Corbusier's ar-
       chitectural expression.

62:1   COLLING, JAMES KENNAWAY (1816-1905)

       Worked for William Brooks, 1828-29; trained as an engineer; worked
       for Matthew Habershon, 1832-36, for John Brown of Norwich, 1836-
       40, and for Scott and Moffatt. Publications: ART FOLIAGE FOR
       SCULPTURE AND DECORATION, 1865; DETAILS OF GOTHIC ARCHI-
       TECTURE FROM EXISTING EXAMPLES, 1852-56; GOTHIC ORNAMENT,

1846-50; EXAMPLES OF MEDIEVAL FOLIAGE AND COLOURED DECORATION, 1874; SUGGESTIONS IN DESIGN, 1881. Obituaries: AA&BN 88 (1905): 106; AAJ 20 (October 1905): 224; B 89 (1905): 281; and RIBAJ 12 (30 September 1905): 19.

62:2 Fleetwood-Hesketh, Peter. "Future of the National Portrait Gallery." CL 148 (20 August 1970): 446-48.

See 55:3.

63:1 COMPER, JOHN NINIAN (1864-1960)

Born in Aberdeen; educated at the Ruskin School of Art, Oxford, and at the Royal College of Art, London, prior to being articled to Bodley and Garner; and then practiced in London. Knighted, 1950. The RIBA has a large, as yet uncatalogued, collection. Publication: OF THE CHRISTIAN ALTAR AND THE BUILDINGS WHICH CONTAIN IT, 1950. A. Symondson is working on a biography of Comper. Obituaries: A&BN 219 (4 January 1961): 5; AJ 133 (22 January 1961): 43; AR 129 (March 1961): 153-54; B 200 (6 January 1961): 22-23; RIBAJ 68 (February 1961): 145.

63:2 Anson, Peter F. "The Work of John Ninian Comper." PAX: THE MONTHLY REVIEW OF THE BENEDICTINES OF PRINKNASH, GLOS. 27 (November 1937): 177-84.

Described as a "pioneer in the modern Liturgical revival," because function plays an important part in his work. He presented a timeless quality, as did A.W.N. Pugin, except that Comper's architecture was "inclusive," incorporating almost all styles of architecture.

63:3 Betjeman, John. "A Note on J.N. Comper, Heir To Butterfield and Bodley." AR 85 (February 1939): 79-82.

A modest "out-and-out Medievalist" church architect, who relies upon color, presence, and proportion. "His father was a priest of the Scottish Episcopal Church and a leader of the Catholic Revival in that country. Catholicism was therefore the earliest as it is still the primary influence in his life." Both Bodley and Comper refused to join the RIBA.

64:1 CONNELL, WARD AND LUCAS (Partnership 1933-39)

Amyas D. Connell (1901-   ), Basil R. Ward (1902-76) and Colin A. Lucas (1906-   ). Connell and Ward were New Zealanders who came to Britain in 1924 and studied at the University of London and in Rome. Connell began practicing in 1928; Ward joined him in 1930, and Lucas in 1933. Lucas trained at Cambridge. Ward's obituary: BD, 6 August 1976, p. 1.

64:2 Hitchcock, Henry-Russell. "England and the Outside World." AAJ 72 (November 1956): 96-97.

This is the first detailed compilation of the firm's work. The article is thoroughly illustrated with photographs and a few plans.

64:3 Phillips, Randal. "A Modern House at Moor Park." CL 83 (2 April 1938): 358-59.

"A sincere and functional accomplishment." Illustrations of the inside and out, plus plan.

64:4 Smithson, Peter. "Connell, Ward and Lucas." AAJ 72 (December 1956): 138.

When Smithson was a student he discovered the work of the firm and still considers the partners the most important of the first generation of English modern architects.

64:5 Stevens, Thomas. "Connell, Ward and Lucas, 1927-1939." AAJ 72 (November 1956): 112-15.

Their twenty-one major commissions are tabulated, providing details of addresses of clients, the name of the partner responsible for the commission, and publications on each design.

64:6 Walford, Geoffrey. "A Client on His House." RIBAJ 46 (19 December 1938): 181-85.

The Walford house, 66 Frognal, Hampstead, London, is well illustrated and the client states what his requirements were. It seems that the house was designed prior to the choosing of the site.

65:1 COOPER, EDWIN (1873-1942)

Articled to and partnered with Hall and Davis, and later with S.B. Russell before practicing alone. Knighted, 1923. RIBA gold medalist, 1931. Obituaries: A&BN 171 (3 July 1942): 2; AF 77 (October 1942): 112; B 163 (3 July 1942): 3; CL 92 (3 July 1942): 18; RIBAJ 49 (July 1942): 49.

65:2   Newberry, John E. "The New Building for the Port of London Au-
        thority." AR 52 (December 1922): 160-68.

> Having taken eleven years to be built, this building, com-
> pleted in 1921, "successfully carries on and worthily upholds
> the traditions of English Renaissance." Photographs are
> mainly of its interiors and reproduce its plan.

65:3   _____. "Royal Mail House: The New Headquarters of the Royal
        Mail Steam Packet Company." AR 66 (September 1929): 121-32.

> This is one of the few enrichments of London "during the
> last few years." Plans and photographs.

65:4   Stratton, P.M. "Lloyds, 1688-1926: New Building Designed by Sir
        Edwin Cooper." AR 63 (June 1928): 223-39.

> Detailed considerations, mainly visual, of Lloyds of London.

66:1   **CRABTREE, WILLIAM (1905-)**

Designer of the Peter Jones department store in Sloane Square, London (one drawing in the RIBA collection).

66:2   Girouard, Mark. "Moving into the Kitchen Garden." CL 125 (8
        January 1959): 68-69.

> Crabtree designed this house, Scot's Acre, in Surrey, for
> his mother-in-law. It cost £10,600.

67:1   **CUBITT, JAMES (1914-)**

Born in Melbourne, Australia, and trained at the AAL. Practiced in
London since 1951.

67:2   Silverlight, John. "University in the Desert." OBSERVER, 13 June
        1976, Magazine Section, pp. 26-33.

> The discovery of oil in Libya in 1959 made the country
> wealthy. This new wealth attracted Cubitt, who in the
> 1960s had made a name for himself in school design. He
> designed the University of Benghazi in 1964 and by 1974
> it had seven thousand students. Since money is reasonably
> plentiful, he has been able to use durable materials, such
> as color-coded tiling.

68:1   **CUBITT, THOMAS (1788-1855)**

Started his own building firm about 1815 and built speculatively with

his brothers William and Lewis (1799–   ). The RIBA has drawings.
Obituaries: B 13 (29 December 1855): 629–30; 14 (9 February 1856):
72–73.

68:2   Dale, Antony. "The Centenary of Thomas Cubitt." CL 119 (1 March
1956): 388.

> Cubitt built thirty-seven houses at Kemp Town, Brighton,
> and lived at No. 13 Lewes Crescent, 1846–55. A plaque
> was placed on that house in 1953.

68:3   Fedden, Robin. "Polesden Lacey, Surrey." CL 103 (5, 12 March
1948): 478–81, 526–29.

> Replacing a seventeenth-century house, Polesden Lacey was
> built in 1824 (remodeled in 1906 in Edwardian sumptuous-
> ness).

68:4   Hobhouse, Hermione. "The Building of Belgravia." CL 145 (8, 22
May 1969): 1154–57, 1312–14.

> The original layout of Belgravia, London, was designed
> probably by James Wyatt in 1813, and as we know it today
> by Thomas Cundy, Sr. (1765–1825)--see also 69:1–2. Cu-
> bitt was one of its most important builders, developing nine-
> teen acres all told.

68:5   _____. "A Regency Survival in Clapham." CL 138 (16 December
1965): 1686–87.

> Crescent Grove, Clapham, London, is a Regency enclave
> attempting "to provide something attractive for every type
> of purchaser."

68:6   _____. THOMAS CUBITT: MASTER BUILDER. London: Macmillan,
1971. 568 p.

> Cubitt's fortune was made by speculative building in the
> best sense of the term, combining enterprise, high reputa-
> tion, and sound construction with an interest in the welfare
> of his workers. Complete archival material has provided
> Hobhouse with the wherewithall to present a thorough biog-
> raphy, well illustrated and footnoted.

68:7   Murray, Hubert. "Going to the Dogs: Guide Bleu to London's Isle
of Dogs." AAQ 4 (April-June 1972): 11–22.

> Christ Church of 1852 was the nucleus from which Cubitt
> Town, where the architect himself lived, developed. This
> article is rather general and not specifically about Cubitt.

68:8   Nares, Gordon. "Queen Victoria at Home: The Private Apartments at Osborne House." CL 116 (19 August 1954): 562–64.

> Begun in 1845, and its private apartments occupied the following year, Osborne House was not completed until 1890. It is Italianate.

69:1   CUNDY, THOMAS (1790-1867)

Eldest son of Thomas Cundy, Sr. (1765–1825), for whom he worked. Obituaries: B 25 (17 August 1867): 25; RIBAJ 3 (1895–96): 20.

69:2   Hobhouse, Hermione. "The Building of Belgravia." CL 145 (8, 22 May 1969): 1154–57, 1313–14.

> In 1821 the senior Thomas Cundy planned Belgravia, more or less as it is known today (see also 68:4). The younger Cundy designed several churches and other developments in the area.

70:1   DANNATT, TREVOR (1920-   )

Practiced in the office of Fry and Drew, 1943–48, and at the LCC, 1948–51; began private practice in 1952. Publications: BUILDINGS AND INTERIORS, 1951–72, 1972; MODERN ARCHITECTURE IN BRITAIN, 1959 (see A 32).

70:2   Dannatt, Trevor. "Architects' Approach to Architecture." RIBAJ 76 (March 1969): 98–105.

> Neither a socially nor a politically motivated architect, Dannatt states that he designs "from the love of buildings." He discusses his work.

70:3   Webb, Michael. "A Versatile Holiday House in Fife." CL 143 (30 May 1968): 1461–62.

> Built on the site of an earlier residence, Pitcorthie House, Fife, "combines originality of form with refinement of detail."

71:1   DARBOURNE AND DARKE (Partnership 1961-   )

John William Charles Darbourne (1935-   ) trained at the University of London and at Harvard University; Geoffrey James Darke (1929-   ) trained at the University of Birmingham. Darbourne won the Lillington Street, London, housing competition while studying at Harvard.

71:2   Chisholm, Judith. "People v. Architects." A 2 (February 1972): 48-49.

> Lillington Street, Westminster, is a three-stage project to provide two thousand residences, shops, a pub, a library, and old people's housing. Most of the conversations with "people" had no relevance to the architecture, except that standard cupboards were too narrow for dinner plates and not tall enough for bottles.

71:3   Lambert, Sam. "Lillington 3." AJ 155 (12 January 1972): 56-58.

> "The most illustrated, most visited, most eulogized housing scheme in London," with a density of 185 persons per acre and a garden with each house.

72:1 DARBYSHIRE, ALFRED (1839-1908)

Articled to P.B. Alley and practiced in Manchester beginning in 1862. Publications: AN ARCHITECT'S EXPERIENCES: PROFESSIONAL, ARTISTIC AND THEATRICAL, 1897; THE BOOKE OF OLDE MANCHESTER AND SALFORD, 1887; THE IRVING-DARBYSHIRE SAFETY PLAN, 1884. Obituary: RIBAJ 15 (1907-8): 540.

72:2   Darbyshire, Alfred. AN ARCHITECT'S EXPERIENCES: PROFESSIONAL, ARTISTIC AND THEATRICAL. Manchester: J.E. Cornish, 1897. 351 p.

> "I have written this book for my friends," who apparently requested it. Chapter 10 is titled "Architectural Practice-- Utilitarian and Artistic Clients." Darbyshire was involved in the theater and created stage designs.

72:3   Harbron, Dudley. "Minor Masters of the XIXth Century." AR 82 (July 1937): 31-33.

> Darbyshire sketched Gothic buildings and was convinced thereby that in "the revival of the Gothic lay the hope of English architecture." Even so, he played safe in architectural competitions by submitting other styles.

73:1 DAVIES, RICHARD LLEWELYN (1912-)

Trained at Cambridge University, the AAL and the Ecole des Beaux-Arts, Paris. Headed the division of architectural studies at the Nuffield Foundation, 1953-60; was professor of architecture, University of London, 1960-69, and professor of urban planning, 1969-75, University of London. Publications: STUDIES IN THE FUNCTIONS AND DE-SIGNS OF HOSPITALS, 1955; and with D.J. Petty, BUILDING ELE-MENTS, 1956.

73:2   Baird, George. "Paradox in Regent's Park: A Question of Interpre-tation." ARENA 81 (April 1966): 272-76.

> The Zoological Society, London, is one of two buildings used in this article to discuss the question of "meaning" in architecture.

73:3   Banham, Reyner. "Human Sciences." AR 127 (March 1960): 188-90.

> Experimental environments are being set up to program the needs and requirements of individuals. Social science is being introduced to study group behavior patterns.

73:4   Huxtable, Ada Louise. "Two in Trouble." NEW YORK TIMES 22 June 1969, sect. 2; 30.

> See 28:9.

73:5   Turner, Alan, and Buckhurst, Paul. "Racine: A Case Study of Revi-talization." BUILT ENVIRONMENT 1 (May 1972): 130-33.

> Eight thousand people housed in 104 city blocks which were rehabilitated by joint public and private collaboration. British planners based in New York made the analysis and supplied the know-how.

73:6   Weeks, John. "Multi-Strategy Buildings." AD 39 (October 1969): 536-40.

> The emphasis in hospital design is upon adaptability to changing programs based upon maintaining a balance among patient care, education, and research. A series of dia-grams show the progress from "linear to lattice communica-tion networks."

74:1 DAVIS, ARTHUR JOSEPH (1878-1951)

Trained at the Ecole des Beaux-Arts, Paris, and practiced with Charles Mewes, 1900-1914, and later with G.C. Gage. Obituary: RIBAJ 59 (November 1951): 35-36.

74:2   Corry, James. "The Architect of the RAC." CL 150 (4 November 1971): 1211.

Corry know Davis, the decorator, and corrects the confusion in the Fleetwood-Hesketh article (74:3) concerning the design of the Westminster Bank, Threadneedle Street, London.

74:3 Fleetwood-Hesketh, Peter. "The Royal Automobile Club." CL 150 (14 October 1971): 966-99.

"The Royal Automobile Club is the last and grandest of the great classic club houses" in Pall Mall, London, where at the end of the street, the earliest clubs were built. Its monumental and sumptuous interiors are illustrated.

74:4 Service, Alastair. "Arthur Davis of Mewes and Davis." In EDWARDIAN ARCHITECTURE AND ITS ORIGINS, pp. 432-42. London: Architectural Press, 1975.

Davis was a baroque-revival architect, notably of late seventeenth-century English architecture. Baroque revival of seventeenth-century England led to a French version of baroque through the Paris exhibition of 1900. Davis was the first British architect to practice in the new French mode and Charles Mewes, a Parisian architect, partnered with Davis in the task. Their major commissions, mostly in the London area, are described and illustrated.

75:1 DAWBER, E. GUY (1861-1938)

Educated at the RAL and articled to Thomas Deane in Dublin. He also worked for Ernest George and George Peto, prior to setting up practice in 1891. RIBA gold medalist, 1928. Publications: OLD COTTAGES AND FARMHOUSES, AND OTHER STONE BUILDINGS IN THE COTSWOLD DISTRICT, 1905; OLD COTTAGES AND FARMHOUSES IN KENT AND SUSSEX, 1900; HOUSING IN THE PEAK DISTRICT, 1934. Obituaries: AAJ 53 (May 1938): 522; A&BN 154 (29 April 1938): 112, 114; 155 (15 July 1938): 61; AJ 87 (28 April 1938): 685, 691; B 154 (29 April 1938): 824, 827; 156 (26 May 1938): 982; RIBAJ 45 (9 May 1938): 631, 633, 666-67; (23 May 1938): 720.

75:2 Collingwood, Frances. "Sir Guy Dawber, RA." B 201 (4 August 1961): 202-3.

Written at the centenary of his birth, this article comments upon his urban design and residential architecture, another speciality.

76:1 DAWKES, SAMUEL WHITFIELD (1811-80)

Practiced in Gloucester and Cheltenham.

76:2   Hussey, Christopher. "Witley Court, Worcestershire." CL 97 (8, 15 June 1945): 992–95, 1036–39.

> This Jacobean house, remodeled and Italianized in ca.1860 by Dawkes, had gardens by W.A. Nesfield. The house burned in 1937.

77:1   DEANE, THOMAS (1792-1871)

> Practiced with Benjamin Woodward (see 281:1), 1846–61. Together they won the competition for the museum of Trinity College, Dublin, 1853. Deane practiced at times with his two brothers Kearns Deane (-1847) and Alexander Sharpe Deane. His sons Thomas Newenham Deane (1828–99) and Thomas Manly Deane (-1932) were architects in practice, 1876–99. Thomas Deane's obituary: B 29 (14 October 1871): 804. Kearns Deane's obituary: B 5 (13 February 1847): 79. Thomas Newenham Deane was knighted, 1890. Thomas Newenham Deane's obituaries: AA&BN 66 (1899): 74; RIBAJ 7 (1899–1900): 39, 48. Thomas Manly Deane was educated at Trinity College, Dublin, and at the RAL. He trained under William Burges and practiced after his father's death, beginning in 1899, with Aston Webb (see 267:1). Thomas Manly Deane's obituary: RIBAJ 40 (1932-33): 557.

77:2   Bence-Jones, Mark. "Two Pairs of Architect Brothers." CL 142 (10 August 1967): 306–9.

> After the completion of the University of Cork, 1845–49, by Thomas Deane, with his son Thomas Newenham Deane and with Benjamin Woodward, the firm moved to Dublin. Famine and the depression reduced the amount of work available and at this point John Ruskin obtained for the firm the commission for the Oxford Museum.

77:3   Ferriday, Peter. "The Oxford Museum." AR 132 (December 1962): 408–16.

> This important historic national monument was threatened with demolition. Ferriday justifies its historical and architectural significance in describing the design and erection of the building.

77:4   Maxwell, Constantia. A HISTORY OF TRINITY COLLEGE, DUBLIN, 1591-1892. Dublin: University Press, 1946. 299 p.

> The museum is Venetian-Byzantine in style and uses a variety of Irish marbles. Although "little is known of Woodward, he was Mayor of Cork in 1830. In a recent article in the CORNHILL MAGAZINE (May 1944), Mr. Osbert Lancaster wrote of the Trinity Museum Building as 'one of

the greatest masterpieces of the Gothic Revival, the finest secular building the movement ever produced.'"

77:5   Roberts, H.V. Molesworth. "Notes on Some English Architects: The Puzzling Deane (and Woodward) Family." BLACKMANSBURY 7 (February and April 1970): 16-17.

Three generations of Deanes are discussed and some of their works are mentioned.

DENISON, EDMUND BECKETT. See BECKETT, EDMUND

78:1   DE SOISSONS, LOUIS JEAN GUY DE SAVOIE-CARIGNAN (1890-1962)

Born in Montreal, Canada; articled to J.H. Eastwood; and studied at the RAL and the Ecole des Beaux-Arts, Paris. Worked at various times with G. Grey Wornum (see 282:1); Peacock and Hodges, Robertson and Fraser; and A.W. Kenyon. Obituary: RIBAJ 69 (November 1962): 431.

78:2   Baker, C.V. "A Village for Old People: The Story of Miles Mitchell Village, Plymouth." HOUSING 21 (June 1959): 19-22.

Segregated housing for old people seems to be acceptable because "most are enthusiastic about having a little home of their own with modern fitments and pleasant surroundings."

78:3   Chambers, Theodore. "The Larkhall Estate." AR 66 (July 1929): 7-16.

In a period of population expansion, de Soissons and G.G. Wornum produced a density in courtyard housing development, three times as high as that which had existed on the same site in Clapham, London. Plans and photographs, general and detailed.

78:4   Lutyens, Robert. "Carlton House Terrace: The Facts." CL 109 (9 February 1951): 396-97.

The conversion of additions to Carlton House Terrace, London, into a proposed new foreign office is considered to be "inoffensive in relation to Nash's Terrace, but highly competent and intelligent in themselves."

78:5   Orfeur, Ronald. "New Wine: The Theatre at Welwyn." AR 63 (April 1928): 138-44.

De Soissons collaborated with A.W. Kenyon on this theater for eleven hundred persons in a town of six thousand (1928). It is Georgian in style although the interior (well illustrated) is art deco.

78:6   Oswald, Arthur. "Restoring Halls of the City Companies: Some Recent Work at Fishmongers' Hall and Leathersellers' Hall." CL 112 (14 November 1952): 1564–67.

Badly damaged during the Second World War, Leathersellers' was restored by de Soissons and his new reception room is illustrated.

79:1   DEVEY, GEORGE (1820-86)

Practice began about 1840. Obituary: B 51 (1886): 728. The RIBA has sketchbooks and an uncataloged collection of drawings. N. Taylor is researching his life and work.

79:2   Binney, Marcus. "Penshurst Place, Kent." CL 151 (4 May 1972): 1090–93.

This is the fourth article on "the finest and most complete surviving 14th-century manor house in England," and it mentions the additions by J.B. Rebecca and George Devey in the 1850s and '60s.

79:3   Girouard, Mark. "George Devey in Kent." CL 149 (1, 8 April 1971): 744–47, 812–15.

Devey designed several country houses in Kent at the peak of his career in the 1870s. His clients were Liberal in their politics. They disliked the town and sought the architectural vernacular revival of rural Kent as practiced by Devey.

79:4   Godfrey, Walter Hindes. "George Devey: A Biographical Essay." RIBAJ 13 (29 September 1906): 501–25.

Most of Devey's designs--cottages or mansions--were variants of the Elizabethan style with Dutch features and gables, which he seems to have introduced into nineteenth-century revival architecture.

79:5   _____. "The Work of George Devey." AR 21 (January, February, June 1907): 22–30, 83–88, 293–306.

Devey was a major exponent of the Queen Anne revival and this article discusses his works.

80:1   DICKSON, RICHARD (1792-1857)

Dunimarle Castle, Fife, owns ten elevations, 1837-45, by Richard and
Robert Dickson.

80:2   Rowan, Alistair. "Millearne, Perthshire." CL 151 (24 February, 2
March 1972): 452-56. 498-501.

Richard and Robert Dickson were the architects of this building even though no drawings or correspondence exists. The
"Gothick" house dates from 1821-29 although additions were
made in 1834 and 1838. Much of its architecture was based
upon copybooks of the period. Other more symmetrical designs by the Dicksons are listed.

81:1   DOBSON, JOHN (1787-1865)

A pupil of David Stephenson (1757-   ) of Newcastle upon Tyne,
1802-10, after which he left for London. There he studied under
John Varley, the painter, and became friendly with Robert Smirke.
Sydney Smirke married Dobson's eldest daughter. Dobson returned to
Newcastle to practice ca.1813. The RIBA has three drawings. Obit-
uary: B 23 (1865): 27. J.M. Ryder wrote an undergraduate thesis,
"Dobson's Railway Architecture," in 1964 at the University of New-
castle; D. Varty wrote an undergraduate thesis, "The Dobson and
Grainger Scheme for the Development of Newcastle," in 1955 at the
University of Newcastle.

81:2   Dobson, Margaret Jane. MEMOIR OF JOHN DOBSON. London:
Hamilton, Adams, 1885. 131 p.

After a brief memoir, Dobson's architecture is considered
under the headings "Domestic Architecture," "Ecclesiastical
Architecture," "Engineering Architecture," and "Town Improvements." The remaining fifty-eight pages list his works,
also by building type.

81:3   Girouard, Mark. "Dobson's Northumbrian Houses." CL 139 (17,
24 February 1966): 352-56, 406-9.

Less known than his urban townscape, some of his important
commissions in the countryside are presented.

81:4   Turley, Richard. "Early Victorian City Planning." AR 99 (May
1946): 141-46.

A detailed explanation of the growth of nineteenth-century
Newcastle by Dobson. Numerous plans and small illustrations.

81:5   Wilkes, Lyall, and Dodds, Gordon. TYNESIDE CLASSICAL: THE NEWCASTLE OF GRAINGER, DOBSON AND CLAYTON. London: J. Murray, 1964. 159 p.

          See B 102.

82:1   DONALDSON, THOMAS LEVERTON (1795-1885)

Trained at the RAL and practiced and taught in London. RIBA gold medalist, 1851. President of the RIBA, 1863-65. The RIBA has drawings. Publications: NUMISMATICA ARCHITECTURA: HAND-BOOK OF SPECIFICATIONS, 1857; MAXIMS AND THEOREMS, 1847.

82:2   Blutman, Sandra. "The Father of the Profession." RIBAJ 74 (December 1967): 542-44.

        Career and achievements, including major designs and publications, are recalled.

82:3   Gruning, Edward Augustus. "Memoir of the Late Professor Donaldson." RIBAJ 2 (1885): 123-24.

        Gruning was a pupil of Donaldson. A brief notice listing Donaldson's travel, publications, educational and professional commitment, and private life.

82:4   Papworth, Wyatt. "Professor Donaldson." RIBAJ 2 (1885): 121-23.

        Mainly concerned with the establishment of the Architectural Society (later to be named the RIBA) and with his publications.

83:1   DONTHORNE, WILLIAM JOHN (fl. 1817-53)

Pupil of Jeffrey Wyatt, 1817-20. The RIBA has drawings.

83:2   Arnold, Ralph. "Architect of Highcliffe." CL 123 (1 May 1958): 953.

        Highcliffe Castle, Hampshire, 1834, was by Donthorne, as quoted by J.C. Hare in THE STORY OF TWO NOBLE LINES, volume 2, no page reference provided.

83:3   Cooper, N. "Highcliffe Castle." ARCHAEOLOGICAL JOURNAL 123 (1966): 208.

        Donthorne was Lord Stuart's architect and gave form to his patron's ideas until he was dismissed in 1835. At that point A.W.N. Pugin was approached but thought Stuart's "arbitrary ignorance unsupportable."

83:4   Powell, J.H. "Highcliffe Castle, near Christchurch, Hampshire." ANCIENT MONUMENTS SOCIETY TRANSACTIONS 15 (1967-68): 83-94.

Built on the grounds of an older mansion in the style of a French sixteenth-century chateau, the building is examined and its owners listed.

84:1   DREW, THOMAS (1838-1910)

Trained under Charles Lanyon, worked for William George Murray, and began practice in Dublin in 1875. Knighted, 1900.

84:2   Bernard, John Henry. THE CATHEDRAL CHURCH OF SAINT PATRICK: A HISTORY AND DESCRIPTION OF THE BUILDING. London: G. Bell and Sons, 1905. 88 p.

On p. 35 Bernard notes that in the north transept "the beautiful staircase--designed in 1901 by Sir Thomas Drew, after the model of a similar structure of Mayence Cathedral [France]--leads to the new organ chamber."

84:3   Murray, Albert E. "Sir Thomas Drew, P.R.H.A., L.L.D.: A Memoir." RIBAJ 17 (27 August 1910): 737-40.

Married the sister of W.G. Murray and worked for the latter. His antiquarian and other interests are briefly noted.

84:4   Stalley, Roger. CHRIST CHURCH, DUBLIN. Ballycotton: Gifford and Craven, n.d. 45 p.

This book was recently advertised but since its publishers no longer exist at their address Meadow House, County Cork, the book seems to be totally unobtainable.

85:1   DUNN, JAMES BOW (1861-1930)

Obituaries: RIBAJ 37 (1929-30): 711-12; QRIAS 34 (1930): 53.

85:2   Royal Scottish Academy. ONE HUNDRED AND THIRD ANNUAL REPORT OF THE COUNCIL OF THE ROYAL SCOTTISH ACADEMY OF PAINTING, SCULPTURE AND ARCHITECTURE, pp. 19-21. Edinburgh: 1930.

Dunn's major works and competition entries are listed.

85:3   Browne, George Washington. "Obituary." RIBAJ 37 (1929-30): 711-12.

This obituary gives a summary of Dunn's background, life, works, and mentions that Dunn won second place in the Edinburgh Public Library competition (which Browne won). Dunn's works are to be found mainly in the southern counties of Scotland and northern counties of England.

85:4   Keppie, John. "Obituary. The Late Mr. J.B. Dunn." QRIAS 34 (1930): 53.

In partnership with J. Leslie Findlay, Dunn designed the SCOTSMAN's offices and George Watson College, both in Edinburgh.

86:1   **EASTLAKE, CHARLES LOCKE (1836-1906)**

Articled to P.C. Hardwick. He is best known for his influence on furniture style. The RIBA has a sketchbook, 1877-84. Publications: HINTS ON HOUSEHOLD TASTE, 1868; A HISTORY OF THE GOTHIC REVIVAL, 1872 (see A 34). The RIBA has correspondence in the Cockerell Collection and the HMC has correspondence in various collections. Obituary: RIBAJ 14 (1906-7): 59.

87:1   **EASTON AND ROBERTSON (Partnership 1919-75)**

John Murray Easton (1889-1975) and Howard Morley Robertson (see 215:1). Easton obituaries: AJ 162 (3 September 1975): 451; B 229 (29 August 1975): 19; RIBAJ 82 (September 1975): 6.

87:2   Geerlings, Gerald K. "The Royal Horticultural Hall, London, England." AF 54 (May 1931): 567-78.

"The Royal Horticultural Hall, the result of an unusual competition, illustrates new methods in design and construction to meet modern requirements."

87:3   McGrath, Raymond. "Light Opera." AR 67 (January 1930): 21-29.

"The Savoy [Theater, London] marks what one hopes will prove to be the turning point in the career of London theatres." Detailed photographic coverage.

87:4   Robertson, Howard.   "The British Pavilion, N.Y. World's Fair."   B
        156 (2 June 1939):   1030-32.

        How would one describe this building built for prestige and
        for the display of British goods? Is it contemporary, dated
        or modernistic?

88:1   ## ELLIS, BERTRAM CLOUGH WILLIAMS (1883-   )

        Knighted, 1971. Publications: THE ADVENTURE OF BUILDING, 1946;
        ARCHITECT ERRANT, 1971; COTTAGE BUILDING IN COB, PISE,
        CHALK AND CLAY, 1919. Republished with John Eastwick-Field as
        BUILDING IN COB, PISE, CHALK AND STABILIZED EARTH, 1947;
        ENGLAND AND THE OCTOPUS, 1928; ON TRUST FOR THE NATION,
        1947; PLAN FOR LIVING, 1941; PORTMEIRION, THE PLACE AND ITS
        MEANING, 1963; ROYAL FESTIVAL HALL, 1951; with Amabel William
        Ellis THE PLEASURES OF ARCHITECTURE, 1924; with John Summerson
        ARCHITECTURE HERE AND NOW, 1934. Edited with Amabel William
        Ellis the multiauthored series Vision of England begun 1947.

88:2   AR. "Bolesworth Castle and Its Renaissance." Vol. 57 (April 1925):
        149-53.

        In 1920 Ellis began the renovations that provided amenity,
        additional sunlight, modern conveniences and new functions,
        such as a nursery.

88:3   CL. "Houses after the War, II: For a Site on the Welsh Coast."
        Vol. 89 (4 January 1941): 16-17.

        Neither the site nor the client is mentioned, but plans and
        sketches of a crude, rambling house are illustrated.

88:4   Ellis, [Bertram] Clough Williams. ARCHITECT ERRANT. London:
        Constable, 1971. 291 p.

        Three months of training, plus the winning of an architec-
        tural competition for a "cheap cottage" of the best design,
        led Ellis into the practice of architecture. He covers all
        aspects of his life.

88:5   _____ . PORTMEIRION: THE PLACE AND ITS MEANING. Port-
        meirion, Wales: Portmeirion, 1963. Reprint. 1973. 95 p.

        Description and explanation of Portmeirion, an architect's
        dream village begun in 1926. Ellis is owner, developer,
        and architect of a design concept that nostalgically evolved
        against the current of modern architecture. Much of its
        success is due to the fact that Ellis is a creative landscape
        architect and town planner, as Christopher Hussey empha-
        sizes in the Prologue and Lewis Mumford in the Epilogue.

88:6   Gardiner, Stephen. "Nature: The Great Secret of Architecture." OBSERVER, 21 December 1975, magazine section, pp. 28-32.

> Although this is not an article specifically about Ellis, it does mention him twice: the article begins with one of his dictums: "My advice is always stay very young, and then live to be absurdly old.' He was not referring to the building of Portmeirion, the Italianate village of North Wales, commonly regarded as his life's work." The second reference states: "The architect who has made landscape in our century is, we find, a rare bird indeed: Clough Williams Ellis is one."

88:7   Wharton, Kate. "Passport to Pleasure." A&BN 6 (18 June 1970): 24-29.

> A "wonderful architectural poem" is the way in which the mixture of architectural styles at Portmeirion is described. Ellis "has been a tireless propagandist for the cause of physical beauty." Description and illustrations.

89:1   ELMES, HARVEY LONSDALE (1814-47)

Studied under his father, James Elmes; his uncle H.J. Elmes; and John Elger. Entered the RAL, 1831, and later practiced with his father. Avery Architectural Library, Columbia University, has two watercolor plans of the Assise Courts and St. George's Hall, Liverpool. The RIBA has drawings. S. Bayley wrote an M.A. thesis, "Harvey Lonsdale Elmes," in 1974 at the University of Liverpool.

89:2   Budden, Lionel B. "The St. George's Hall Controversy." AR 28 (November 1910): 216-18.

> An access by additional steps to the south portico of St. George's Hall, Liverpool, was rejected by St. George's Hall Committee ca. 1850 as unsatisfactory. There was a suggestion in 1910 to revert back to that unsatisfactory state of affairs, but those suggestions also had to be withdrawn.

89:3   Jones, Ronald P. "The Life and Work of Harry Lonsdale Elmes." AR 15 (June 1904): 230-45.

> "One of the few men in recent centuries whose ideas and conceptions were on the grand scale of Imperial Rome." Yet his Greek revival was freed "from antiquarian trammels," as seen in St. George's Hall, Liverpool, his major commission, which is thoroughly illustrated.

89:4   Tanner, J.A. "A Contemporary Account of St. George's Hall." AR 41 (June 1917): 122-25.

Tanner was a grandson of the resident superintendent of St. George's Hall. He based his article upon an account compiled by his grandfather.

89:5   Wainwright, David. "Elmes." AR 125 (May 1959): 349-50.

Shaw Street School, Liverpool, was won in competition by Elmes in 1840, but could he design it for fifteen thousand pounds? He first requested the return of his drawings for estimating purposes and then demanded his professional fee. The whole affair centered around professional etiquette and problems with a committee that had a businesslike attitude.

90:1   ELMES, JAMES (1782-1862)

Pupil of George Gibson until he entered the RAL, 1804. Publications: ANNALS OF THE FINE ARTS, 1816-20; THE ARTS AND ARTIST, 1825; A GENERAL AND BIBLIOGRAPHICAL DICTIONARY OF THE FINE ARTS, 1824; LECTURES ON ARCHITECTURE, 1823 (2d. ed.); MEMOIRS OF THE LIFE AND WORKS OF SIR CHRISTOPHER WREN, 1823; METROPOLITAN IMPROVEMENTS, 1827-29; A PRACTICAL TREATISE ON ARCHITECTURAL JURISPRUDENCE, 1827; A PRACTICAL TREATISE ON ECCLESIASTICAL AND CIVIL DILAPIDATIONS, 1829; A SCIENTIFIC, HISTORICAL AND COMMERCIAL SURVEY OF THE HARBOUR AND PORT OF LONDON, 1838; SIR CHRISTOPHER WREN AND HIS TIMES, 1852; LONDON AND ITS ENVIRONS IN THE NINETEENTH CENTURY, 1829. Avery Architectural Library, Columbia University, has a perspective sketch of St. Paul's Cathedral, London, James Elmes, del. 1811. The RIBA has drawings. Obituaries: B 20 (19 April 1862): 275; RIBAJ (1861-63): 11.

90:2   Chancellor, E. Beresford. "James Elmes: Architect and Author." B 149 (27 December 1935): 1139.

Brief synopsis of his life and work.

90:3   Musgrave, Clifford. "Sennicotts: A Regency Villa near Chichester." CONNOISSEUR 165 (June 1967): 69-73.

This building of 1809, attributed to Elmes, is described and illustrated; four interiors are reproduced in color.

91:1   EMBERTON, JOSEPH (1889-1956)

Worked for John Burnet and Partners and later partnered with P.J. Westwood, 1922-26, after which he practiced alone. He was the only British architect to have been represented in H.-R. Hitchcock and Philip Johnson's THE INTERNATIONAL STYLE, pp. 136-37, New York: W.W. Norton and Co., 1932. The RIBA has drawings. Obituaries: AJ 124 (29 November 1956): 57-58; B 191 (30 November 1956): 927; RIBAJ 64 (January 1957): 123.

91:2   Casson, Hugh [Maxwell]. "Blackpool." AR 86 (July 1939): 25-36.

"Not just another isolated modern building set down in somewhat incongruous solitude . . . but part of a well considered policy of developing an amusement area on rational and efficient lines." The New Casino is considered in all aspects and in considerable depth.

91:3   Ind, Rosemary. "Joseph Emberton, 1889-1956." 2 vols. Undergraduate thesis, AAL, 1974. 226 p., 212 illus.

A general account of Emberton's work and an attempt to place him historically.

92:1   ERSKIN, RALPH (1914-)

Trained at the Regent Street Polytechnic, London. Practices in Sweden and, more recently, also in Britain. Built Byker housing in Newcastle.

92:2   Andrews, Malcolm. "The Work of Ralph Erskin." AAJ 73 (May 1955): 226-47.

"Frustrated by the philistine architectural and social set-up immediately prior to the war, he landed up in Sweden." His designs there are illustrated.

93:1   FAIRLIE, REGINALD (1883-1952)

Obituary: B 183 (31 October 1883-1952)

93:2   Nuttgens, Patrick. REGINALD FAIRLIE, 1883-1952: A SCOTTISH ARCHITECT. Edinburgh: Oliver and Boyd, 1959. 58 p., 60 pls.

Nuttgens follows his discussion of Fairlie's life and work with a "List of Architectural Works," of all types.

94:1   FARMER AND DARK (Partnership 1934-)

Franklin Dark (1903-) trained at the RAL; Frank Quentery Farmer

(1879-1955) retired from the firm in 1952, but the firm still continues.
Obituaries of Farmer: B 188 (25 February 1955): 338; RIBAJ 62
(September 1955): 466-67.

95:1   FERGUSSON, JAMES (1808-86)

Publications: AN ESSAY ON THE ANCIENT TOPOGRAPHY OF JE-
RUSALEM, 1847; AN ESSAY ON THE MODE IN WHICH LIGHT WAS
INTRODUCED INTO THE TEMPLES OF THE GREEKS AND ROMANS,
1883; CAVE TEMPLES OF INDIA, 1880; AN HISTORICAL ENQUIRY
INTO THE TRUE PRINCIPLES OF BEAUTY IN ART, 1849; A HISTORY
OF ARCHITECTURE IN ALL COUNTRIES FROM THE EARLIEST TIMES
TO THE PRESENT DAY, 1865-67; THE HISTORY OF INDIAN AND
EASTERN ARCHITECTURE, 1876; A HISTORY OF THE MODERN STYLES
OF ARCHITECTURE, 1862 (A 37); THE HOLY SEPULCHRE AND THE
TEMPLE AT JERUSALEM, 1865; THE ILLUSTRATED HANDBOOK OF
ARCHITECTURE, 1855; ILLUSTRATIONS OF ROCK-CUT TEMPLES OF
INDIA, 1845; THE MAUSOLEUM OF HALICARNASSUS RESTORED,
1862; OBSERVATIONS ON THE BRITISH MUSEUM, 1849; ON A NA-
TIONAL COLLECTION OF ARCHITECTURAL ART, 1857; THE PALACES
OF NINEVEH AND PERSEPOLIS RESTORED, 1851; THE PARTHENON,
1883; PICTURESQUE ILLUSTRATIONS OF THE ANCIENT ARCHITEC-
TURE OF HINDOSTAN, 1848; REPORT ON THE BUDDHIST CAVE
TEMPLES AND THEIR INSCRIPTIONS, 1876-79; RUDE STONE MONU-
MENTS IN ALL COUNTRIES, 1872; THE TEMPLE OF DIANA AT
EPHESUS, 1883; TEMPLES OF THE JEWS, 1878; TREE AND SERPENT
WORSHIP, 1873 (2d. ed.); with T.C. Hope, ARCHITECTURE AT AHMEDA-
BAD, 1866. The RIBA has drawings. Obituaries: AA&BN 19 (16
January 1886): 25; B 4 (23 January 1886): 47.

95:2   Jelley, F.R. "Six More Of The Best: 3--James Fergusson." B 212
(7 April 1967): 94.

One of a series of articles in which Jelley assesses the
role of the architectural writers and in particular Fergusson's
A HISTORY OF ARCHITECTURE, 1865-67.

95:3   Winter, Robert W. "Fergusson and Garbett and American Architectural Theory." JSAH 17 (Winter 1958): 25-29.

Fergusson's progressivism took him beyond romantic common-
place. He was interested in economic buildings and forwarded organic architectural principles. The writings of
Fergusson and Edward Lacy Garbett are analyzed with this
thesis in view.

96:1   FERREY, BENJAMIN (1810-80)

A pupil of A.C. Pugin, Ferrey also studied under William Wilkins and set up practice in London, 1834. RIBA gold medalist, 1870. Publications: ANTIQUITIES OF THE PRIORY CHURCH OF CHRISTCHURCH, HANTS., 1834; RECOLLECTIONS OF A.N. PUGIN AND HIS FATHER AUGUSTUS PUGIN, 1861; A SERIES OF ORNAMENTAL TIMBER GABLES FROM EXISTING EXAMPLES IN ENGLAND AND FRANCE OF THE SIXTEENTH CENTURY, 1839. The RIBA has three drawings. Obituaries: AAR 1 (1880): 555; B 39 (28 August, 4 September 1880): 276, 281-83 (provides extensive list of works); RIBAJ (1879-80): 219-21 (repeated in AA 8 [25 September 1880]: 153).

96:2   Harris, John. "Bulstrode." AR 124 (November 1958): 319-20.

Begun in 1676, Bulstrode, Buckinghamshire, is to be seen today in the manner in which Ferrey left it in 1860. This article is concerned with its many alterations by numerous hands and Ferrey is only very briefly mentioned.

96:3   Howell, Peter, and Pritchard, T.W. "Wynnstay, Denbighshire." CL 151 (23, 30 March; 6 April 1972): 686-89, 782-86, 850-53.

This Jacobean house, largely rebuilt during 1736-39 by major eighteenth-century architects, burned down in 1858 and was rebuilt by Ferrey from 1858 to 1865. He was actually working at Wynnstay when the fire occured, having met his client while traveling first class by train--"he used afterwards to tell his pupils that it showed what a good idea it was always to travel first-class." The style chosen for Wynnstay was French seventeenth century. The second of the three parts of this article provides the most information.

97:1   **FIDLER, A.G. SHEPPARD (1909-)**

Trained at the University of Liverpool and was at one time city architect of Birmingham.

97:2   Richards, J.M. "Criticism: Teacher's Training College, Birmingham." AJ 126 (28 November 1957): 805-10.

Richards has very few negative criticisms about this building. Would the library be noisy? Is the residential accommodation tight, and should the sick quarters have been placed in the basement beneath staff living quarters?

98:1   **FITZGERALD, DESMOND**

Designed the Dublin Airport Terminal, 1939-41. For appreciation see:

CL 101 (7 March 1941): 420-21; RIBAJ 55 (September 1948): 500-501. Member of the RIBA since 1936.

99:1 FLETCHER, BANISTER FLIGHT (1866-1953)

Articled to his father, Banister Fletcher (1833-99), and educated at the AAL and the Ecole des Beaux-Arts, Paris. Worked for an array of architects. Publications: ANDREA PALLADIO, 1902; ARCHITECTURAL HYGIENE, 8th ed., 1944; THE ENGLISH HOUSE, 1910; A HISTORY OF ARCHITECTURE ON THE COMPARATIVE METHOD, 18th ed., 1975. The RIBA has notes and sketchbooks, 1895-1913. Obituaries: AAJ 69 (September/October 1953): 88; A&BN 204 (27 August 1953): 238; AJ 118 (27 August 1953): 251; AR 114 (October 1953): 211; B 185 (28 August 1953): 310-11; RIBAJ 60 (October 1953): 211.

99:2 Hanneford-Smith, W. THE ARCHITECTURAL WORK OF SIR BANISTER FLETCHER. London: B.T. Batsford, 1934. 291 p.

Fletcher's background, education, professional and literary works, numerous sketches made at home and abroad, student drawings, executed works, and submissions for competitions are presented.

100:1 FOSTER, NORMAN (1935-)

Studied at the University of Manchester and at Yale University. Has practiced since 1964.

100:2 Foster, Norman. "Architects' Approach to Architecture." RIBAJ 77 (June 1970): 246-53.

Teamwork and a fresh approach are the basis of all the firm's work.

100:3 Rabeneck, Andrew. "IBM Head Office." AD 41 (August 1971): 474-78.

Flexibility of services and allowance for future expansion in the International Business Machines head office building at Cosham, Hampshire, were prime considerations in its design. Diagrams, plans, and photographs.

101:1 FOWKE, FRANCIS (1823-65)

Born in Belfast and educated at the Royal Military Academy, Woolwich,

London. He was commissioned to serve in the Royal Engineers, 1842, and rose to the rank of captain. Publication: A DESCRIPTION OF THE BUILDING AT SOUTH KENSINGTON: ERECTED TO RECEIVE THE SHEEPSHANKS COLLECTION OF PICTURES, 1866. The RIBA has one perspective. Obituaries: B 23 (16 December 1865): 881-82; RIBAJ (1865-66): 29.

101:2 Binney, Marcus. "The Origins of the Albert Hall." CL 149 (25 March 1971): 680-83.

The frieze of the hall states: "This Hall was erected for the advancement of the arts and sciences and works of industry of all nations in fulfillment of the intentions of Albert Prince Consort," but associated with this ideal was the need for a chorus hall. This article offers a history of the motivations, the men concerned, the variety of projects forwarded, the abandoned schemes, and the completed building (a joint project of Fowke and Henry Cole), begun in 1867, two years after Fowke's death.

101:3 Bradford, Betty. "The Brick Palace of 1862." AR 132 (July 1962): 8, 15-21.

Fowke designed the building for the South Kensington International Exhibition of 1862. Twenty-four acres of exhibition space were erected in one year and machinery in motion was displayed. On the exhibition's centenary, the Victoria and Albert Museum staged an exhibition of photographs and drawings.

101:4 Clark, Ronald W. "The Royal Albert Hall of Arts and Sciences." In ROYAL ALBERT HALL, pp. 53-115. London: Council of the Royal Albert Hall, 1976.

This essay, providing a history of the hall, is one of many in a variety of similar publications on the building from the period of its inception.

102:1 FOWLER, CHARLES (1791-1867)

Publications: DESCRIPTION OF THE PLAN FOR THE REVIVAL OF HUNGERFORD MARKET WITH SOME PARTICULARS OF THE BUILDING PROPOSED TO BE ERECTED, 1829; ON THE PROPOSED SITE OF THE NEW HOUSES OF PARLIAMENT, 1836. Obituaries: B 25 (19 October 1867): 761; RIBAJ (1867-68): 1-15, 29.

102:2 Blake, Peter. "Shopping Streets under Roofs of Glass." AF 124

(January–February 1966): 68–75.

A survey of European and American arcades, including Fowler's Covent Garden, London.

102:3 Girouard, Mark. "Powderham Castle, Devon." CL 134 (4, 11, 18 July 1963): 18–21, 80–83, 140–43.

Descendants of the original owner still live in this early fifteenth–century castle. A plan on p. 19 shows its periods of growth. Fowler added castellated embellishments, including a new approach, 1848, which is described in the last section of this article.

102:4 Stratton, Arthur. "Covent Garden." AR 41 (April and May 1917): 67–72, 99–104.

Fowler designed the wholesale market in the center of Covent Garden, London, 1828–30. Externally built of granite, the internal structure is of iron with a glazed roof.

102:5 Taylor, Jeremy. "Charles Fowler (1792–1867): A Centenary Memoir." AH 11 (1968): 57–74.

Background of the period, Fowler's training in London, competitions which he entered, and his major commissions are discussed. An appendix lists "A Chronological Index of Fowler's Work."

102:6 _____. "Charles Fowler: Master of Markets." AR 135 (March 1964): 174–82.

Threatened with possible demolition in 1964, the market buildings at Covent Garden, London, and many of Fowler's other works, extant and demolished are discussed. His career and achievements are enumerated.

103:1 **FRY, EDWIN MAXWELL (1899–)**

Trained at the University of Liverpool and worked in London for Adams and Thompson. Partnered with Walter Gropius (see 120:1), 1934–36, and with his wife, Jane Beverly Drew (1911–   ), 1945–50. In 1951 the firm was known as Fry, Drew, Drake and Lasdun but in 1958 reverted back to Fry, Drew and Partners. Fry collaborated with Le Corbusier at Chandigarh, India, 1951–54. RIBA gold medalist, 1964. Jane Beverly Drew studied at the AAL and partnered with J.T. Allison, 1934–39 and worked independently, 1939–45. She married Fry in 1942 and partnered with him from 1945 to 1950. Publications: ARCHITECTURE FOR CHILDREN, 1944; ART IN THE MACHINE AGE, 1969; AUTOBIOGRAPHICAL SKETCHES, 1975; FINE

BUILDING, 1944; with J.B. Drew, ARCHITECTURE AND THE EN-VIRONMENT, 1976; with J.B. [Drew] Fry: TROPICAL ARCHITECTURE IN DRY AND HUMID ZONES, 1947; with J. [B] Drew and H. L. Ford: VILLAGE HOUSING IN THE TROPICS, 1947; with a variety of others, RECENT ADVANCES IN TOWN PLANNING, 1932. The RIBA owns drawings by Fry. See RIBAJ 75 (March 1968): 112.

103:2   Baines, Harry. "Sun House." DESIGN (Bombay) 10 (December 1966): 23-25.

Sun House, Hampstead, London, 1935, "is a perfect expres-sion of the spirit of the time." It was (in 1966) the resi-dence of the Indian deputy high commissioner to London.

103:3   Blutman, Sandra. "Drawings of the '30's." RIBAJ 75 (March 1968): 112.

The RIBA has acquired Fry's proposed additions to All Souls' College, Oxford, 1936. An axonometric drawing is illus-trated. Fry was a neo-Georgian designer in the 1920s.

103:4   Chipkin, C.M. "Chandigarh." SOUTH AFRICAN ARCHITECTURAL RECORD 43 (December 1958): 18-27.

This city was designed at the time of India's independence. It is described with relation to its climate, social back-ground, and sector planning.

103:5   Drew, Jane [B]. "On the Chandigarh Scheme." MARG 6, no. 4 (1953): 19-25.

Fry and Drew assisted Le Corbusier, advisor and chief plan-ner at Chandigarh. The biological, horizontal plan of the city is described and illustrated.

103:6   Fry, [Edwin] Maxwell. AUTOBIOGRAPHICAL SKETCHES. London: Elek Books, 1975. 167 p.

Fry prepared autobiographical sketches over a twenty-year period and they have been brought together within one cover. His education, move from Liverpool to London, practice, contemporaries, and the movements in which he was involved are all covered.

103:7   Fry, E. Maxwell. "A College in the Tropics." ZODIAC 2 (1958): 127-36.

Based upon the Oxbridge system of individual residential colleges, West African University at Ibadan, Nigeria, was proposed in 1944; construction began in 1950. Its scheme is described and illustrated in color, with black and white photographs, axonometric drawings, and a section.

103:8 Knight, Frank S. "Designing for Computers." B 215 (11 October 1968): 87-92.

> In buildings such as the Rolls-Royce Computer Centre, Derby, or the Gulf Oil Computer Centre, London, "conditions of temperature and humidity must be retained within narrow limits and the computer areas kept free from dust since this can adversely effect the equipment."

103:9 Korn, Arthur. "The M.A.R.S. Plan for London." PERSPECTA 13-14 (1971): 163-73.

> The Modern Architecture Research Group was the English wing of the Congres Internationaux d' Architecture Moderne, and its ideals were utopian and socialistic. The MARS plan for London was based upon "a 'grille' devised by Le Corbusier on which the divisions of Social activity evolved by the biologist-urbanist Patrick Geddes--work-relaxation-shelter-communication--" tied the dwelling to the city and the city to the region. It was to be a linear plan with open space in close vicinity to any urban strip.

103:10 Pevsner, Nikolaus. MAXWELL FRY. Manchester: Monks Hall Museum, 1964. (Unpaged 16 sides, including information on the cover), 14 illus.

> An exhibition catalog of Fry's work, listing forty illustrations held at Monks Hall Museum, Eccles, Manchester. The exhibition was held in June 1964.

103:11 Platts, Beryl. "The Architect as Collector: The Modern Collection of Maxwell Fry and Jane Drew." CL 140 (29 September 1966): 782-86.

> Mr. and Mrs. Fry live above the partnership's office at 63 Gloucester Place, London W.1. They own a few modern pieces.

103:12 Tyrwhitt, Jaqueline. "Chandigarh." JRAIC 32 (January 1955): 11-20.

> Background of the scheme, those involved, descriptions, planning attitudes, and architectural expression.

104:1 GANDY [DEERING], JOHN PETER (1787-1850)

Youngest brother of Joseph Michael Gandy (1771-1843)--see 105:1--and

Michael Gandy (1778-1862). He was a pupil of James Wyatt and entered the RAL in 1805. He assumed the name of Deering in 1828 and thereafter practiced to a limited extent. The RIBA has drawings. Publication: with William Gell, POMPEIANA, 3d ed. 1852. Obituary: B (16 March 1850): 130.

104:2 Hussey, Christopher. "Burghley House, Northamptonshire." CL 114 (3, 10, 17, 24, 31 December 1953): 1828-32, 1962-65, 2038-41, 2104-7, 2164-67.

Built in 1553-87 by Lord Burghley. The part of this article deals with the "notable unobtrusive modernization of the great building" of the 1830s.

105:1 GANDY, JOSEPH MICHAEL (1771-1843)

Began in the office of James Wyatt, ca. 1786, and entered the RAL, 1789. Worked for John Soane and practiced independently starting in 1801. Publications: DESIGNS FOR COTTAGES, 1805; THE RURAL ARCHITECT, 1805; with Benjamin Baud, ARCHITECTURAL ILLUSTRATIONS OF WINDSOR CASTLE, 1842. The RIBA has drawings. C. Nachman is preparing a doctoral dissertation at New York University, on Gandy.

105:2 Summerson, John. "Gandy and the Tomb of Merlin." AR 89 (May 1941): 89-90.

"Gandy's great architectural fantasy based on passages in the first canto of Ariosto's ORLANDO FURIOSO. The architecture--Norman, with a twist to Byzantium--is supposed to represent a primitive Christian type, but Gandy's taste does him more credit than archaeology." Other fantasies by Gandy are noted.

105:3 _____. "The Strange Case of J.M. Gandy." A&BN 145 (10 January 1936): 38-44.

Fifteen Gandy drawings accompany this brief article.

105:4 _____. "The Vision of J.M. Gandy." In HEAVENLY MANSIONS, pp. 111-34. London: Cresset Press, 1949.

"Gandy's life was, to a great extent, a struggle to emerge from the cave of poverty and dependence." He was an "architectural fantasist . . . a creator of designs and compositions reflecting in his own medium something of Wordsworth."

105:5   Tselos, Dimitris. "Joseph Gandy: Prophet of Modern Architecture."
MAGAZINE OF ART 34 (May 1941): 251-53, 281.

> Gandy "sought a structural purism and greater utility by
> eliminating many elements which had been retained as es-
> thetic embelishments long after their functional reasons for
> existence had disappeared." Simplicity of expression, her-
> alding the modern movement, is to be found in many of his
> designs.

106:1 GARNER, THOMAS (1839-1906)

Articled to George Gilbert Scott, 1856, and joined G. F. Bodley,
1869-97. Publication: with Arthur Stratton, THE DOMESTIC ARCHI-
TECTURE OF ENGLAND DURING THE TUDOR PERIOD, 1911. Obituary: AR 19 (June 1906): 275-76.

106:2   Warren, Edward. "Thomas Garner, Architect: Born 1838, Died 1906."
AR 19 (June 1906): 275-76.

> "Mr. Garner never received the full recognition to which
> his conspicuous abilities, scholarly knowledge and remark-
> able industry entitled him." His life and works are surveyed.

107:1 GEORGE, ERNEST (1839-1922)

Articled to Samuel Hewitt and partnered with Thomas Vaughan later
with Harold Peto, and also with Alfred Yeates. RIBA gold medalist,
1896. Knighted, 1907. Publications: COUNTRY HOMES IN ESSEX,
YORKSHIRE, WORCESTERSHIRE, SURREY, KENT, MIDDLESEX, 1895;
ETCHINGS OF OLD LONDON, 1884; LA FIERTE DE SAINT ROMAIN,
1893. Obituaries: AJ 56 (1922): 855, 857-60; B 133 (1922):
900-903; RIBAJ 30 (1922-23): 106. H.J. Grainger is preparing a
monograph on George. The RIBA has drawings.

107:2   Bradell, Darcy. "Architectural Reminiscences . . . 'Fugaces Anni.'"
B 168 (12 January 1945): 27-29.

> Bradell was a pupil of George and describes his office ex-
> periences, his fellow workers, and George's ability as a
> designer.

108:1 GIBBERD, FREDERICK (1908-)

Trained at the University of Birmingham and practiced since 1930.
Publications: THE ARCHITECTURE OF ENGLAND FROM NORMAN

TIMES TO THE PRESENT DAY, 1938 (A 41); TOWN DESIGN, 1953; THE MODERN FLAT, 1937 (E 81); with F.R.S. Yorke, MASTERWORKS OF INTERNATIONAL APARTMENT BUILDING DESIGN, 1959. The RIBA has drawings.

108:2 Mills, John Fitsmaurice. "The New Liverpool Metropolitan Cathedral." CONNOISSEUR 166 (December 1967): 225-31.

"The new Metropolitan is a statement of its time, a symbol to an expanding thought." The cathedral and its numerous art works are described and illustrated, a limited number in color.

108:3 Moon, R.C. "Nuneaton: A Plan for the Town Centre." AJ 108 (2 September 1948): 221-24.

A war-damaged town center was planned by Moon, the borough engineer, with Gibberd as consultant. Draft of the master plan, details of the center, and models illustrate the article.

108:4 Robson-Smith, N., and Tomlinson, A.H. "Environmental Qualities of Urban Open Space Challenged: An Appraisal of Queen's Gardens, Kingston upon Hull." B 219 (2 October 1970): 65-74.

Adding to an existing urban space, Gibberd has attained maximum pedestrianization, landscape, and access for his technical college.

108:5 Taylor, Nicholas. "Harlow Town Centre." AR 136 (September 1964): 220-22.

The first phase of Britain's first new town to be "substantially finished as its original plan intended" was completed in 1964.

108:6 _____. "Metropolitan Cathedral, Liverpool." AR 141 (June 1967): 436-48.

"It is indeed a mighty Pop landmark, . . . which in a sense [was] paid for . . . through diocesan football pools." The building, on Lutyens's foundations; the attitude of the church in Liverpool; and the uses of the building are all mentioned.

108:7 White, William. "The Altar and the Liturgy." RIBAJ 74 (July 1967): 281-85.

This article explains the planning and internal arrangement of the Liverpool Cathedral of Christ the King.

109:1 **GIBSON, DONALD EVELYN EDWARD (1908-   )**

Studied at the University of Manchester and was city architect of Coventry, 1939-55; county architect of Nottinghamshire, 1955-58; and director general of research and development in the Ministry of Public Buildings and Works since 1962. Publication: PLAN FOR NEW COVENTRY, 1942.

109:2 Wulff, Victor L. "The Replanning of Coventry." AIAJ 31 (January 1959): 30-33.

Gibson's plan for Coventry, 1947, was accepted over that of the city engineer because he departed from the "City that was" and because he advocated pedestrian precincts. Gibson was thus made planning officer in addition to being city architect.

110:1 **GILLESPIE-GRAHAM, JAMES (1777-1855)**

Born at Dunblane, Scotland, as James Gillespie, but added Graham, the family name of his wealthy wife to his own name. Practiced in Edinburgh. Publications: THE CHAPEL OF ST. ANTHONY, THE EREMITE, AT MURTHLY, PERTHSHIRE, 1850. Obituary: B 13 (7 April 1855): 166. James Macaulay is preparing a monograph on Gillespie.

110:2 Macaulay, James. "James Gillespie Graham." In THE GOTHIC REVIVAL, 1745-1845, pp. 229-52. Glasgow and London: Blackie, 1975.

Chapter 13 considers his Scottish castles and churches. He is indexed under "Gillespie."

110:3 _____. "James Gillespie Graham in Skye." THE SCOTTISH GEORGIAN SOCIETY BULLETIN 3 (1974-75): 1-14.

The Macdonald papers in the Register House, Edinburgh, reveal his involvement with buildings on the Isle of Skye.

110:4 Rowan, Alistair. "Dunninald, Angus." CL 146 (14, 21 August 1969): 384-87, 444-47.

Gillespie's projects began in 1819 and were symmetrical compositions. His ideas were pruned at Dunninald and an asymmetrical pile was completed in 1824.

110:5 _____. "Taymouth Castle, Perthshire." CL 136 (8, 15 October 1964): 912-16, 978-81.

Taymouth Castle or Taymouth tower house, dates from about 1550. William Adam designed the west wing; Archibald and James Elliot the main block, 1806-10; William Atkinson the east wing, 1818-21; and James Gillespie remodeled the west wing, 1838-39. The work, especially the rich interiors by Gillespie, at all stages is described and illustrated.

110:6 Stanton, Phoebe. In PUGIN, pp. 196, 198-200. London: Thames and Hudson, 1971.

A.W.N. Pugin produced fifty-eight drawings in September-October 1836 for Graham's entry in the Houses of Parliament competition. Pugin produced other drawings for unspecified purposes and places in 1837 and 1839-40 and was paid two hundred pounds in 1840-41. Was this for Pugin's interior work for Graham's St. Mary's Cathedral, Edinburgh?

111:1 GIMSON, ERNEST (1864-1919)

Obituaries: AR 46 (October 1919): 100; B 117 (1919): 84. The RIBA has drawings. G. Beaton is preparing a doctoral dissertation at the University of Leicester, on Ernest Gimson, the Barnsleys, and the arts-and-crafts movement.

111:2 Burrough, B.G. "Three Disciples of William Morris: Ernest Gimson." CONNOISSEUR 171 (August 1969): 228-32.

Gimson's father was an engineer in Leicester and when Morris visited the town to lecture in 1884, he was impressed by young Gimson's drawings. Morris introduced Gimson to J.D. Sedding, who employed Gimson. Gimson's furniture designs are illustrated.

111:3 Lambourne, Lionel. "The Art and Craft of Ernest Gimson." CL 146 (7 August 1969): 338-39.

Plaster and metalwork decorations by "one of the most highly original members of the Arts and Crafts Movement" are illustrated.

111:4 Lethaby, W.R.; Powell, Alfred H.; and Griggs, F.L. ERNEST GIMSON: HIS LIFE AND WORK. Stratford-upon-Avon: Shakespeare Head Press, 1924. 47 p.

This limited edition of five hundred copies contains three essays by the above-named authors--"Ernest Gimson's London Days," Ernest Gimson's Gloucestershire Days," "Ernest Gimson and His Work."

111:5 Russell, Gordon. ERNEST GIMSON. Leicester: Leicester Museum
and Art Gallery, 1969. 46 p.

An exhibition catalog, illustrated mainly with furniture.

112:1 GODWIN, EDWARD WILLIAM (1833-86)

Born in Bristol, Godwin was trained as an engineer prior to working
as an architect, first in Bristol and then in London after the death of
his first wife. He partnered with Henry Crisp, 1871-86. Publications:
ARTISTIC CONSERVATORIES AND OTHER HORTICULTURAL BUILD-
INGS, 1880; A HANDBOOK OF FLORAL DECORATIONS FOR
CHURCHES, 1865; TEMPLE BAR ILLUSTRATED, 1877. The V&A has
designs, drawings, and sketch-and notebooks and the RIBA has drawings
transferred from the V&A, 1962, and correspondence. Obituaries:
AA&BN 20 (1886): 202; B 5 (July-December 1886): 257. J. O'Cal-
laghan is preparing a doctoral dissertation at Yale University on Godwin.

112:2 Bence-Jones, Mark. "An Aesthete's Irish Castle." CL 136 (12
November 1964): 1274-77.

Built in 1866-67, Dromore Castle, County Limerick, Ireland, was demolished ca. 1954. Godwin studied and meas-
ured several Irish castles, including old Dromore, before designing a medieval revival pile. William Burges accompanied
Godwin on some of his Irish travels. Once built, the castle had many problems, including that of dampness. Godwin's advice to young architects was: "When offered a
commission in Ireland, refuse it." Godwin's notebook
sketches of Ireland are in the V&A.

112:3 Girouard, Mark. "The Victorian Artist at Home." CL 152 (23 November 1972): 1370-74.

"This article tells for the first time the full story of the
Chelsea, London, studio house designed by E.W. Godwin
for Whistler and his friends." Illustrated with original
drawings.

112:4 Greeves, T. Affleck. "London's First Garden Suburb: Bedford Park,
Chiswick." CL 142 (7, 14 December 1967): 1524-29, 1600-1602.

Godwin designed the first house in this speculative development, 1876.

112:5 Harbron, Dudley. THE CONSCIOUS STONE: THE LIFE OF EDWARD
WILLIAM GODWIN. London: Latimer House, 1949. 190 p.

Covers all aspects of his career, including the rather limited number of his architectural commissions mostly of a domestic nature.

112:6 _____. "Edward Godwin." AR 98 (August 1945): 48-52. Reprint. In EDWARDIAN ARCHITECTURE AND ITS ORIGINS, edited by Alastair Service, pp. 56-67. London: Architectural Press, 1975.

After condemning the Godwin entry in the DICTIONARY OF NATIONAL BIOGRAPHY as inadequate, Harbron considers Godwin's work in London, competition entries, and stylistic trends.

112:7 Hyde, H. Montgomery. "Oscar Wilde and His Architect, Edward Godwin." AR 109 (March 1951): 175-76. Reprint. In EDWARDIAN ARCHITECTURE AND ITS ORIGINS, edited by Alastair Service, pp. 68-76. London Architectural Press, 1975.

Godwin was employed by Wilde to design interiors and furniture for No. 16 (now No. 33) Tite Street, London, of 1884-85--Godwin's last commission. The correspondence between the two men was discovered in Godwin's papers in 1950.

112:8 Kaufmann, Edgar. "Edward Godwin and Christopher Dresser: The 'Esthetic' Designers, Pioneers of the 1870's." INTERIORS 118 (October 1958): 162-65.

"Talented, practical, and active beyond measure, Godwin and Dresser were in fact the first to break the ice for modern design in mass markets." Designs are illustrated.

112:9 NRS. GODWIN MSS. London: HMC, n.d. 14 p.

Miscellaneous papers, mainly of costume and antiquarian interest, are grouped and arranged alphabetically.

113:1 **GODWIN, GEORGE (1813-88)**

RIBA gold medalist, 1881. Obituary: B 64 (1888): 75-77, 101. Publications: ANOTHER BLOW FOR LIFE, 1864; THE CHURCHES OF LONDON, 1838; LONDON SHADDOWS: A GLANCE AT THE HOMES OF THOUSANDS, 1854; TOWN SWAMPS AND SOCIAL BRIDGES, 1859.

113:2 Ferriday, Peter. "George Godwin, the BUILDER and London: An Historic Appreciation." B 187 (31 December 1954): 1050, 1052.

The BUILDER began publishing in 1843 [sic, 1842] and Godwin was its third editor, 1844-83. He "rapidly built it up
into a paper of substance and authority."

113:3 King, Anthony. "Architectural Journalism and the Profession: The
Early Years of George Godwin." AH 19 (1976): 32-52.

His year of birth is established as 1813 and not as 1815,
as was previously thought. His editorial influence is evaluated.

113:4 _____. "George Godwin and the Reform of Working-Class Housing."
AR 136 (December 1964): 448-52.

Godwin and his reform-minded contemporaries had a great
impact on twentieth-century housing, health and safety
through their nineteenth-century publications. The hun-
dredth anniversary of ANOTHER BLOW FOR LIFE was 1964.

114:1 GOLDFINGER, ERNO (1902-62)

Born in Budapest, Hungary, and trained under Auguste Perret while
studying at the Ecole des Beaux-Arts, Paris; he practiced in England
beginning in 1934. Publications: BRITISH FURNITURE TODAY, 1951;
with E.J. Carter, THE COUNTY OF LONDON PLAN, 1943.

114:2 Lambert, Sam. "Historic Pioneers: Architects and Clients." AJ 151
(11 March 1970): 594-97.

Goldfinger is quoted concerning his houses at Willow Road,
Hampstead, London: "I really tried to build a late Georgian or Regency Terrace in a modern way."

114:3 Read, Herbert. "Erno Goldfinger." AD 33 (January 1963): 6-54.

Projects, 1924-62, are illustrated to provide and overall
picture of the total designer. A detailed chronology of
his life and works is provided.

114:4 Richards, J.M. "Criticism: Office Building in Albemarle Street,
London, W.1." AJ 126 (18 July 1957): 105-7.

Modest, distinguished, and carefully designed to provide
well-lighted rooms, this office building merges into the existing streetscape.

115:1 GOLLINS, MELVIN AND WARD (Partnership formed ca. 1945)

Frank Gollins (1910-   ) trained at the University of Birmingham;

James Melvin (1912–   ) trained at the AAL; Edmund Ward (1912–   ).

115:2   Aldous, Tony. ARCHITECTURE OF THE GOLLINS, MELVIN, WARD PARTNERSHIP. London: Lund Humphries, 1974. 147 p.

Thirty-two of the firm's major projects are presented through trilingual text (German, French, and English), photographs (many in color), plans, sections, and axonometric drawings.

115:3   Manser, Michael. "BOAC's Stake at Kennedy." A&BN 7 (1 October 1970): 33–35.

British Overseas Airways Corporation (now British Airway)'s is "probably one of the last permanently built airport buildings." Circulation and other aspects are described.

115:4   Martin, Bruce. "A Place in the City." BUILT ENVIRONMENT 1 (July 1972): 262–65.

Commercial Union Building, London, was built after the purchase of thirty properties. Two towers measure in height 387 and 191 feet. They are described and are evaluated as successful urban development.

115:5   Richards, J.M. "BOAC Bridgehead." AJ 152 (12 August 1970): 336–38.

An explanation of the limitations and requirements in designing this terminal at New York's Kennedy Airport.

116:1   GOODHART-RENDEL, HARRY STUART (1887-1959)

Studied music at the University of Cambridge under Donald Tovey. Articled to Charles Nicholson and began practice in London in 1910. President, RIBA, 1937–39. The RIBA has drawings. Publications: ENGLISH ARCHITECTURE SINCE THE REGENCY, 1953 (see A 48); FINE ART, 1934; HOW ARCHITECTURE IS MADE, 1947; NICHOLAS HAWKSMOOR, 1924; VITRUVIAN NIGHTS, 1932 (see also E 33). Obituaries: A&BN 216 (12 August 1959): 216; B 197 (14 August 1959): 17; RIBAJ 66 (September 1959): 405–7.

116:2   Ferriday, Peter. "A Great Critic: A Study of Mr. Goodhart Rendel." B 188 (7 January 1955): 4–5.

His expertise, reexamination, judgement, and critical abilities are assessed with relation to his lectures and writings.

116:3 Hobhouse, Christopher. "The Returning President: An Appreciation." A&BN 158 (30 June 1939): 346–47.

> Statesman and scholar, Goodhart-Rendel hated modernistic buildings but also felt that "there are probably quite enough Ionic and Corinthian columns in England to last us for a long time."

116:4 Hussey, Christopher. "Farleigh House, Hampshire." CL 90 (12, 19 September 1941): 476–79, 536–39.

> Additions to this 1731 house were made in 1935.

116:5 NRA. PAPERS OF H.S. GOODHART-RENDEL, C.B.E. London: HMC, 1973. 6 p. (an additional page dated July 1973 was added.)

> Personal correspondence on architecture, art, history of architecture, and office practice.

116:6 Pevsner, Nikolaus. "Goodhart-Rendel's Roll Call." AR 138 (October 1965): 259–64. Reprint. In EDWARDIAN ARCHITECTURE AND ITS ORIGINS, edited by Alastair Service, pp. 472–83. London: Architectural Press, 1975.

> Goodhart-Rendel wrote a series of articles on "rogue architects." Now Pevsner analyzes Goodhart-Rendel analyzing the "rogues." He was a rogue himself, listing no buildings in his WHO'S WHO entry.

116:7 Wiggin, Maurice. "The Squire of East Clandon: Harry Stuart Goodhart-Rendel." PAX: THE REVIEW OF THE BENEDICTINES OF PRINKNASH 64 (Autumn-Winter 1974): 55–59.

> This memoir of a Roman Catholic squire was extracted from Wiggin's book FACES AT THE WINDOW, London: Thomas Nelson and Sons, 1972.

117:1 GORDON, ALEX (1917-)

Worked for and partnered with T. Alwyn Lloyd (–1960) 1949-60; thereafter practiced independently.

117:2 Gordon, Alex. "Architects on Architecture." RIBAJ 75 (April 1968): 169–78.

> Gordon raises the question: "How does the modern architect maintain his creative function as the organizational demands on him increase?" Architecture is a service that balances commodity, firmness, delight, time, and cost. He explains

the workings of his office, its organization and structure. Many of his works are illustrated.

117:3 Haddock, Mary. "Architects and Their Offices: 8--Alex Gordon and Partners." B 212 (12 May 1967): 88-90.

Alex Gordon joined Alwyn Lloyd (-1960) ca. 1945, and their Cardiff firm now consists of six partners. They opened a London office in 1963. Their methods of running the office are explained.

117:4 Wharton, Kate. "Talking to Alex Gordon." A 1 (April 1971): 63.

Born in Scotland, Gordon was taken to Wales at the age of eight. As president of the RIBA he wanted to revitalize its annual conference and to forward greater coordination within the profession.

118:1 GOWANS, JAMES (1821-90)

Railway engineer and housing pioneer. Knighted, 1886. T.M. Davies is researching Gowans.

118:2 McAra, Duncan. SIR JAMES GOWANS: ROMANTIC RATIONALIST. Edinburgh: Paul Harris Publishing, 1975. 60 p.

McAra considers Gowans as a major Scottish architect of the last two hundred years, who "separately designed buildings unrivalled elsewhere in Great Britain." His "artistic verve, individual energy, professional confidence, and social concern for the welfare of the working class" made him both a romantic and a rationalist.

118:3 Taylor, Nicholas. "Modular Rockery." AR 141 (February 1967): 147-51.

Gowans's own house, Rockville, on Napier Road, Edinburgh, 1858, was demolished in 1966. Gowans had trained under the firm Moffat, Milne and Paterson, and also under David Bryce but joined his own father as a building contractor of railway engineering projects. He built four cottages at Colinton, Edinburgh, ca. 1855, a house for his daughter opposite his own, and many others. His own was described in B 18 (17 March 1860): 168.

GRAHAM, JAMES GILLESPIE. See GILLESPIE-GRAHAM, JAMES

119:1 **GREENE, GODFREY T.** (1807-86)

Director of engineering and architectural works for the Admiralty, 1850-64; held the rank of colonel.

119:2 Skempton, A.W. "The Boat Store, Sheerness (1858-60), and Its Place In Structural History." NEWCOMEN SOCIETY TRANSACTIONS 32 (1959-60): 57-78, pls. 4-15.

The men responsible for the design and construction of the building are documented. The building is thoroughly described and many drawings--including originals--are reproduced.

GRIMTHORPE, LORD. See BECKETT, EDMUND

120:1 **GROPIUS AND FRY** (Partnership 1934-36)

For Walter Adolph Gropius (1883-1969), see Wodehouse, Lawrence. AMERICAN ARCHITECTS FROM THE FIRST WORLD WAR TO THE PRESENT, Detroit: Gale Research Company, 1977. For Edwin Maxwell Fry, see 103:1. The RIBA has drawings of Isokon Company, St. Leonard's Hill, London.

120:2 Elliott, David. GROPIUS IN ENGLAND: A DOCUMENTATION OF THE YEARS 1934-7. London: Building Centre Trust, 1974. Unpaged ten-sided pamphlet.

Gropius first came to England from Germany in 1934 at the opening of an exhibition of his work at the RIBA. He settled in England on a more permanent basis later that year and all of his attempts to obtain commissions are noted. Most of the pamphlet is based upon material in the Bauhaus Archive in Berlin and in the Jack Prichard Papers at the University of Newcastle. Gropius's involvement at Dartington Hall, Devonshire, seems to have been judged solely by material in the Bauhaus Archive and is thus one-sided and partially inaccurate.

120:3 Gropius, Ise. ISE GROPIUS CAME TO THE BUILDING CENTRE ON THURSDAY 14 FEBRUARY 1974, AND TALKED ABOUT HER HUSBAND AND HIS WORK. London: Building Centre Trust, 1974. Unpaged four-sided pamphlet.

"Gropius' nature was not responsive to abstract, speculative thinking, divorced from practical experiment." Ise surveys her late husband's career and commitment.

121:1 HALL, DENNIS CLARKE (1910-)

Trained at the AAL, 1931-37, and practiced alone until the war.
Practiced as Hall, Scorer and Bright since 1954.

121:2 AAJ. "Dennis Clarke Hall." Vol. 74 (June 1958): 3-5.

His major completed works are listed and three are illustrated.

122:1 HAMILTON, THOMAS (1784-1858)

Born in Edinburgh, where he was apprenticed to his father, a carpen-
ter-builder. Obituary: B 16 (27 February 1858): 146.

122:2 McWilliam, Colin. "Thomas Hamilton, Architect, 1784-1855."
EAAY 5 (1961): 80-92. The RIBA has a plan of the High School,
Edinburgh.

An assessment of the architectural contribution by Hamilton
and his contemporaries to the city of Edinburgh after 1812.

123:1 HANSOM, JOSEPH ALOYSIUS (1803-82)

Born in Yorkshire, where he was apprenticed until he partnered with
Edward Welch in 1828. Patented the "safety cab" and founded the
periodical BUILDER in 1842. He then partnered with his brother
Charles, his sons Henry and Edward John (1842-1900), E.W. Pugin
(see 203:1), and Archibald Mathias Dunn (-1900). Denis Evinson
wrote an M.A. thesis, "Joseph Hansom," at the University of London
in 1966.

123:2 Williamson, R.P. Ross. "Minor Masters of the XIXth Century: 6--Jo-
seph Aloysius Hansom." AR 80 (September 1936): 117-19.

A successful architect who will be remembered mainly as a
coach builder.

124:1 HARDWICK, PHILIP (1792-1870)

Son of Thomas Hardwick (1752-1829), under whom he studied after
attending the RAL. Practiced starting ca. 1819. The RIBA has drawings. Obituaries: B 29 (14 January 1871): 24; RIBAJ (1871-72): 4.

124:2 Block, Geoffrey D.M. "London's Oldest Rail Terminus." CL 127 (17 March 1960): 554-56.

Aspects, especially the arch, of Hardwick's Euston Station, London, are considered. The Great Hall was completed by his son P.C. Hardwick (see 125:1).

124:3 Taylor, W.A. "Euston and the Hardwicks." CL 127 (25 February 1960): 390-91.

Taylor is the borough librarian of St. Pancras and announces that the Heal Collection of St. Pancras has "numerous cuttings and illustrations relating to the making of Euston Station."

125:1 HARDWICK, PHILIP CHARLES (1822-92)

Son of Philip Hardwick (see 124:1). Trained under Edward Blore before joining his father in 1852. He took over the practice in 1847 when his father's health declined. The RIBA has drawings. Obituaries: B 62 (1892): 108; RIBAJ 8 (1891-92): 174-75.

125:2 Carter, Paul. "St. Katharine Docks." LONDON ARCHAEOLOGIST 1 (Summer 1969): 51-55.

Built for safe anchorage and better repair facilities, the London docks indirectly increased trade and led to the building of St. Katharine Docks to accommodate 150 vessels and 210,000 tons of cargo.

125:3 Cornforth, John. "Adare Manor, Co. Limerick." CL 145 (29 May 1969): 1366-69.

This is the third article on Adare and concerns the building phase of 1850-62.

125:4 Gardner, Celia. "The Story of the London Dock." CL 150 (2 December 1971): 1591-92.

A history of the north bank of the river Thames and of the dock constructions of 1828. The renovation of those warehouses began in 1969.

125:5 London, Midland and Scottish Railway Co. OLD EUSTON: AN ACCOUNT OF THE BEGINNING OF THE LONDON AND BIRMINGHAM RAILWAY AND THE BUILDING OF EUSTON STATION. London: Country Life, 1938. 67 p.

A history of the railway company and of this particular line. Chapter 3, "The Doric Arch and Central Hall" describes the architecture of Euston Station, London and is followed by a watercolor illustration of the hall by P.C. Hardwick.

126:1 **HARRIS, EMANUEL VINCENT (1876-1971)**

Practiced at one time as Vincent Harris and Moodie. Obituaries: B 221 (6 August 1971): 66; OA&P 34 (August 1971): 607.

126:2 Summerson, John. "Recent Work of Mr. E. Vincent Harris." CL 75 (28 April 1934): 423-26.

"Contemporary classical" is the term used to describe a series of columned public buildings.

127:1 **HARRIS, THOMAS (1830-1900)**

Publications: EXAMPLES OF THE ARCHITECTURE OF THE VICTORIAN AGE, 1862; THREE PERIODS OF ENGLISH ARCHITECTURE, 1894; VICTORIAN ARCHITECTURE, 1860. Obituaries: B 79 (1900): 39; BN 79 (1900): 40; RIBAJ 7 (1899-1900): 450.

127:2 Donner, Peter F.R. "A Harris Florilegium." AR 93 (February 1943): 51-52.

The contents and attitudes of his books are discussed.

127:3 Goodhart-Rendel, H.S. "Rogue Architects of the Victorian Era." A&BN 195 (22, 29 April 1949): 359-62, 381-84; RIBAJ 56 (April 1949): 251-59.

"A fancy for queer shapes arbitrarily conceived. . . . But Harris's roguery lay in his empiricism, his impatience of rational restraint."

127:4 Harbron, Dudley. "Thomas Harris." AR 92 (September 1942): 63-66.

Harris as a young man was "intrigued by the methods" of Joseph Paxton. Thus, although he designed Gothic structures, he was careful to display their construction. His most interesting work was therefore in the industrial field. In his later residential work he tended to compromise his earlier attitudes.

128:1 **HAY, WILLIAM (1818-1888)**

Partner of George or William Henderson (1846-1905). Three obituaries follow:

128:2 BRITISH ARCHITECT. "Personal." Vol. 29 (8 June 1888): 409.

Hay assisted John Henderson and later worked for George Gilbert Scott before immigrating to Canada and the West Indies. Returning to Edinburgh in 1864, he partnered with William Henderson. Another reference--EAA (1907): vi-- confuses us by naming as Hay's partner yet a third Henderson--George Henderson, who had immigrated to Australia and then returned to Scotland.

128:3 B "The Late Mr. William Hay, Architect." Vol. 54 (9 June 1888): 414.

William Henderson is again listed as Hay's partner.

128:4 SCOTSMAN. "The Late Mr. William Hay." 1 June 1888, p. 4.

Hay went to Newfoundland on behalf of George Gilbert Scott and later practiced in Toronto.

129:1 HENNEBIQUE, FRANCOIS (1842-1921)

His system of construction is covered by Sigfried Giedion in SPACE, TIME AND ARCHITECTURE, pp. 325-26, Cambridge, Mass.: Harvard University Press, 1967; and by Jurgen Joedick in A HISTORY OF MODERN ARCHITECTURE, pp. 54-55, London: Architectural Press, 1959.

129:2 Kingsford, Peter Wilfred. "Francois Hennebique (1842-1921)." In BUILDERS AND BUILDING WORKERS, pp. 148-53. London: Edward Arnold, 1973.

Hennebique's life and background in France and works in Belgium, France, and Britain are enumerated.

130:1 HOLDEN, CHARLES HENRY (1875-1960)

Assisted C.R. Ashbee, studied at the RAL, and practiced in London with Harry Percy Adams (1865-   ), ca. 1907. Lionel G. Pearson (1879-   ) joined Holden and Adams in 1912 and the firm became known as Adams, Holden and Pearson. Holden was RIBA gold medalist, 1936. Publications: numerous city planning reports, including CITY OF LONDON, 1947, with William Holford. The RIBA has a couple of drawings. Obituaries: AAJ 76 (July-August 1960): 67; A&BN 217 (11 May 1960): 592; AR 127 (June 1960): 371; AR

128 (December 1960): 446-48 by Nikolaus Pevsner; RIBAJ 67 (August 1960): 383-84; TPIJ 46 (June 1960): 184.

130:2 Harris, Muriel. "Architectural Hopes and Difficulties in British Re-Planning." ARCHITECT AND ENGINEER 166 (21 July 1946): 16-19.

Appointed with W.G. Holford as consultants for the recon-struction of the city of London after the Second World War. Holden's architecture is human, direct, and simple and in a human, direct, and simple manner, he intended to proceed in city planning.

130:3 Pevsner, Nikolaus. "Charles Holden's Early Works." In EDWARDIAN ARCHITECTURE AND ITS ORIGINS, edited by Alastair Service, pp. 386-92. London: Architectural Press, 1975.

H. Percy Adams was a hospital architect and after Holden worked for him from 1899 to 1907, they became partners. The firm was known for its mannerist revival style until 1914, but in the 1930s Holden became famous for his build-ings for London Transport, including several underground railway stations.

131:1 HOLFORD, WILLIAM GRAHAM (1906-75)

Born in South Africa and articled to an accountant there. He then studied architecture at the University of Liverpool. His major achieve-ments are listed in AJ 125 (17 January 1957): 81. Publications: with Gabriel White (A 59), ARCHITECTURE TODAY, 1961, numerous publications on planning. Obituaries: AJ 162 (29 October 1975): 888; AR 159 (April 1976): 223; ARCHITECT AND BUILDER (South Africa) 25 (November 1975): 30; B 229 (24 October 1975): 53; HOUSING REVIEW 24 (November-December 1975): 141-42 by Rich-ard Edmonds; PLANNER 61 (December 1975): 386-87; RIBAJ 83 (January 1976): 37; TPR 47 (January 1976): 1-4 by Myles Wright.

131:2 Colley, H.V. "Construction of New London Bridge." CONCRETE 5 (April 1971): 123-24.

Holford was consultant architect for the new London Bridge, completed in 1972.

131:3 Petrie, Waldo. "Hay's Antics." AJ 154 (3 November 1971): 962-63.

Holford and Associates has evolved a strategy plan for Hay's Wharf, adjacent to London Bridge.

131:4 Shennan, Alfred E. "The Architects and Their Post-War Work in Liverpool." AJ 116 (25 December 1952): 768-77.

> Holford proposed a medical teaching center for Liverpool.

131:5 Wilson, L. Hugh. "The Precincts of St. Paul's." TPIJ 43 (December 1956): 10-13.

> There have been numerous designs for buildings in the area of St. Paul's. After the bombing during the Second World War, Holford wanted to encourage well-designed twentieth-century buildings. His proposals were approved in principle by the City of London Corporation.

132:1 HOPPER, THOMAS (1776-1856)

> Trained under his father, a Rochester surveyor, but otherwise self-taught. The RIBA has drawings. Obituary: B 14 (1856): 481. F.L. Dowsland wrote an undergraduate thesis at the University of Newcastle, 1962, titled "Thomas Hopper, 1776-1856, Architect."

132:2 Fedden, Robin. "Neo Norman." AR 116 (December 1954): 380-85.

> The life and work of Hopper complements his dictum that "it is an architect's business to understand all styles, and to be prejudiced in favour of none. He alone seems to have appreciated the wide possibilities of a Norman Revival." His style is generally discussed and Penrhyn Castle, Anglesey, Caernarvon, ca. 1827-47, is well illustrated.

132:3 Hague, Douglas B., and Hussey, Christopher. "Penrhyn Castle, Caernarvon." CL 118 (14, 21, 28 July 1955): 80-83 (Hague), 140-43, 192-95 (Hussey).

> This medieval castle on the Isle of Anglesey, Caernarvonshire, was extended by Samuel Wyatt in 1782 and enlarged by Hopper beginning in 1827. The third part of this article describes and provides extensive photographic coverage of the neo-Norman style.

132:4 Hussey, Christopher. "Purley Halls, Berkshire." CL 147 (5, 12 February 1970): 310-13, 366-69.

> This Jacobean manor of 1609 was altered and landscaped at the beginning of the eighteenth and nineteenth centuries, in the latter period by Hopper, who reroofed the building and modified its interior spaces.

132:5 O'Neill, Terence. "Neo-Norman Castles: Letter to the Editor."

CL 118 (18 August 1955): 344.

Further information on Shane and Gosford castles, County Antrim, elaborating upon Christopher Hussey's article "Penrhyn Castle, Caernarvon" CL 118 (21 July 1955): 140–43 (see 132:3).

132:6 Oswald, Arthur. "Arthur's: The End of a Famous London Club." CL 87 (1 June 1940): 546–50.

Hopper designed Arthur's, a clubhouse in London, 1826–27, in the Italian Renaissance style. Some of Hopper's other works are also mentioned.

132:7 Parks, G.H. "Stoneleigh Abbey." BIRMINGHAM ARCHAEOLOGICAL SOCIETY: TRANSACTIONS AND PROCEEDINGS 79 (1960–61): 76–84.

In this article, which actually appeared in 1964, we are told that Hopper made three suggestions for the alteration of this nine hundred-year-old structure in Warwickshire. He wanted a classical north entrance, additional accommodations in the south wing, and the changing of the chapel into a dining room or library.

133:1 HOWELL, KILLICK AND PARTRIDGE [and later Amis] (Partnership 1959-)

William Gough Howell (1922–74), John Alexander Wentzel Killick (–1971), John Albert Partridge (1924–   ), and Stanley Frederick Amis (1924–   ). Partridge trained at the Regent Street Polytechnic, London, the other three trained at the AAL, and all worked in the housing division of the LCC.

133:2 Chisholm, Judith. "People v. Architects." A 2 (January 1972): 44–45.

"People can exist without architecture but architects cannot exist without people." Seventy-two staff and thirteen hundred students use Acland Burghley School, London, an "architecturally, highly successful" school, where criticism seemed to condemn what was provided and lament what was not.

133:3 Cullen, Gordon. "Anti-Prairie Planning." AR 120 (July 1956): 52–54.

This hypothetical development incorporating a whole range of different residential accommodations is based upon the formality of London streets and squares.

133:4 Howell, W.G. "Architects' Approach to Architecture." RIBAJ 77
(March 1970): 100-108.

One of Howell's basic approaches is that of "vertibrate
buildings: the architecture of structured space . . . architecture in which the interior volume is defined and articlated
by actual, visible structure."

133:5 Howell, Killick, Partridge and Amis. "Attitudes to Architecture."
ARENA 82 (November 1966): 95-119.

Each of the four partners was asked "to perform, and then
to lead a discussion" about the historical qualities that he
admired and that led to his own work.

133:6 MacLeod, Robert. "A New Gothic Revival." ARENA 82 (November
1966): 120-21.

Functionalism has passed out of architecture and the work
of the firm "is illustrative of the point" that architecture
"must perforce be whimsical, arbitrary, and let in the rain
in all the wrong places."

133:7 Segal, Walter. "Cambridge Manners." AJ 150 (December 1969):
1516-18.

Downing College, Cambridge, provided the architects with
"an opportunity for their design virtuosity, and the tempta-
tion to reinterpret some of the canons of the classical past
was too strong to be ignored." The roof of the combination room mimics the classical portico of the adjoining facade. The discussion questions the validity of this approach
to design, citing other examples.

134:1 JACKSON, THOMAS GRAHAM (1835-1924)

Articled to George Gilbert Scott, 1858, and began practice in 1862.
RIBA gold medalist, 1910. Publications: ARCHITECTURE, 1925; AR-
CHITECTURE IN FRANCE AND ITALY, 1915; BYZANTINE AND RO-
MANESQUE ARCHITECTURE, 1913; THE CHURCH OF ST. MARY THE
VIRGIN, OXFORD, 1897; DALMATIA, THE QUARNERO AND ISTRIA,
1887; GOTHIC ARCHITECTURE IN FRANCE, ENGLAND AND ITALY,
1915; MODERN GOTHIC ARCHITECTURE, 1873; REASONS IN AR-
CHITECTURE, 1906; RECOLLECTIONS, 1950; THE RENAISSANCE OF
ROMAN ARCHITECTURE, 1921-22; WADHAM COLLEGE, OXFORD,
1893; WINCHESTER CATHEDRAL, 1910; and with R.N. Shaw, ARCHI-
TECTURE: A PROFESSION OR AN ART, 1892. The RIBA has draw-
ings. Obituaries: RIBAJ 32 (1924-25): 49; NIY (1924): 512.
C.R. Warren is researching Jackson.

134:2 George, Ernest. "The Royal Gold Medal, 1910: Presentation to Mr. Thomas Graham Jackson." RIBAJ 17 (1909-10): 621-29.

This article lists and illustrates the works of this eclectic designer.

134:3 Jackson, Basil H., ed. RECOLLECTIONS. London and New York: Oxford University Press, 1950. 283 p.

"These recollections were begun by my father in 1904. . . . They are intended for the eyes only of my own family [but] much of these recollections would be of general interest, and possibly . . . 'adventitious value.'" Jackson's life, training, and works.

134:4 Mallows, C.E. "The Complete Work of T.G. Jackson." AR 1 (1897): 136-60.

Jackson's educational, religious, and residential works are illustrated mainly by drawings and sketches by Jackson and others.

134:5 Warren, Edward. "An Appreciation." AR 56 (December 1924): 245.

Jackson was a restorationist, who added to several public schools and colleges.

134:6 Wight, P.B. "Jackson's 'Gothic Architecture.'" AREC 40 (1916): 282-84.

In praise of Jackson's important GOTHIC ARCHITECTURE IN FRANCE, ENGLAND AND ITALY, 1915, a work that investigates the origin and philosophy of the Gothic. The book's contents are described.

135:1 JACOBSEN, ARNE (1902-71)

Danish architect who designed St. Catherine's College, Oxford. Obituaries: AF 134 (May 1971): 64; AR 151 (July 1971): 63-64; A rec 149 (June 1971): 35; B 220 (2 April 1971): 54; RIBAJ 78 (May 1971): 183 by Ove Arup.

135:2 Faber, Tobias. ARNE JACOBSEN. New York: Praeger, 1964. 175 p.

Introductory essay plus annotated section of illustrations arranged according to building type. St. Catherine's College, Oxford, pp. 76-77; furnishings, p. 165.

135:3   Scott, N. Keith. "Appraisal of St. Catherine's." A&BN 226 (14 October 1964): 721-36.

> "A long, low grey and white antiseptic structure of great clarity and ordered precision stretched into a seeming infinity. . . . In years to come, this group of buildings, I think, will only improve for the landscape will mature."

135:4   Shriver, Paul Erik. "Jacobsen." AR 125 (February 1959): 140-42.

> A review of an exhibition held at the RIBA. Jacobsen's educational background is described and some of his architectural contributions in Denmark are illustrated.

135:5   Webb, Michael. "A Jewel among the Dreaming Spires: St. Catherine's College, Oxford." CL 139 (17 February 1966): 348-50.

> In 1966 Oxford did not have many significant new buildings, except St. Catherine's College, 1959. It houses 250 students.

136:1 JAMES, CHARLES HOLLOWAY (1893-1953)

Articled to W.B. Wood of Gloucester and assisted Edwin Lutyens, Raymond Unwin, and Barry Parker. Partnered with S. Rowland Pierce and James Bywaters. Publications: THE MODERN SMALL ENGLISH HOUSE, 1924; SMALL HOUSES FOR THE COMMUNITY, 1928; ROYAL LEAMINGTON SPA, 1947; with S. Rowland Pierce, A PLAN FOR NORWICH, 1945. Obituaries: AAJ 68 (April 1953): 175-76; AJ 117 (12, 19 February 1953): 214, 235; B 184 (13 February 1953): 264; RIBAJ 60 (March 1953): 206; T&CP 21 (April 1953): 182.

136:2   Phillips, Randal. "An Architect's Own House: Hornbeams, Hampstead." CL 86 (5 August 1939): 124-25.

> "It is sober without being dull, modern without being freakish, and is planned to suit present day needs."

137:1 JOHANSEN, JOHN MacLANE (1916-)

American architect who designed the American Embassy, Dublin. See Wodehouse, Lawrence. AMERICAN ARCHITECTS FROM THE FIRST WORLD WAR TO THE PRESENT, Detroit: Gale Research Co., 1977.

137:2   Donat, John. "U.S. Embassy, Dublin." In WORLD ARCHITECTURE vol. 2, pp. 82-87. New York: Viking Press, A Studio Book, 1965.

An enumeration of his early life, education, and travel prior to a discussion of his proposed restoration of Glasgow Cathedral and the design for the Scott Monument. He died on the foggy evening of 6 March 1844, when he "fell into the Canal, and in this melancholy way met his death, unseen by any human eye." An appendix, titled "Hints Regarding The National Monument," is included.

142:3 Gray, W. Forbes. "The Scott Monument and Its Architect." AR 96 (July 1944): 26-27.

John Ruskin dismissed the monument as a "small, vulgar, Gothic steeple. Ruskin wanted a natural site, rugged and craggy with figures." The competition and the winning project are described.

142:4 Wrinch, Ann Martha. "George Kemp and the Scott Monument." CL 150 (5 August 1971): 322-23.

This article repeats, in condensed form, much of the material by Bonnar (see 142:2). The competition for the commission to design the monument and its siting, design, style, and cost are discussed. In 1842 calotype of Kemp is illustrated.

143:1 KERR, ROBERT (1823-1904)

Publications: THE CONSULTING ARCHITECT, 1886; THE ENGLISH GENTLEMAN'S COUNTRY HOUSE, 1864; THE GENTLEMAN'S HOUSE, 1871; A HISTORY OF ARCHITECTURE IN ALL COUNTRIES, 1891-99; NEWLEAFE DISCOURSES ON FINE ART ARCHITECTURE, 1846. Obituaries: AA&BN 86 (1904): 50; AAN 19 (November 1904): 213; RIBAJ 12 (12 November 1904): 14-15.

143:2 Girouard, Mark. "Bear Wood, Berkshire." CL 144 (17, 24 October 1968): 964-67, 1060-63.

Kerr "was the author of a standard book on Victorian country house planning, and Bear Wood is his most important building and a fascinating example of the complex accommodation thought necessary for a rich Victorian family." The exterior has a bold fervor, and the interior, richly carved and paneled woodwork.

144:1 KNIGHTLEY, THOMAS EDWARD (1823-1905)

Articled to John Wallen, practiced from about 1853 on, and partnered with Thomas Batterbury beginning in 1901. Obituaries: AA&BN 88 (1905): 106; RIBAJ 12 (1904–5): 636.

144:2 Taylor, Nicholas. "Ceramic Extravagance." AR 138 (November 1965): 338–41.

Birkbeck Bank, London, built 1851 (bankrupt 1911 when the premises were taken over by Westminster Bank), was demolished in 1965. Its elaborateness is well illustrated.

145:1 KNOTT, RALPH (1878-1929)

Articled to Wood and Aislie and worked for Aston Webb. Partnered with E.S. Collins in London, 1921. Obituaries: AR 65 (March 1929): 159; B 136 (1929): 237, 255. RIBAJ 36 (1928-29): 296. Architect of County Hall, London, for the LCC. See ARCHITECT AND CONTRACT REPORTER 79 (1908): 102-6; AR 23 (March 1908): 156-60; 52 (September 1922): 59-73. The RIBA has one perspective drawing.

146:1 KNOWLES, JAMES THOMAS (1831-1908)

Trained in the office of his father, James Knowles. Obituary: RIBAJ 15 (1907-8): 276. The RIBA has drawings. P. Metcalf wrote a doctoral dissertation at the Courtauld Institute, London, 1971, titled "The Rise of James Thomas Knowles: Victorian Architect and Editor."

146:2 Hussey, Christopher. "15, Kensington Palace Gardens: Its Redecoration." CL 85 (25 February 1939): 198-202.

Designed in the Italianate style during the 1850s by Knowles and his father, the house was refurbished in 1938.

147:1 LAING, DAVID (1774-1856)

Articled to John Soane. Publications: HINTS FOR DWELLINGS: CONSISTING OF ORIGINAL DESIGNS FOR COTTAGES, FARM HOUSES, VILLAS, ETC., 1800; PLANS ETC. OF BUILDINGS, PUBLIC AND PRIVATE, EXECUTED IN VARIOUS PARTS OF ENGLAND INCLUDING THE CUSTOM HOUSE, LONDON, 1818. Obituary: B 14 (5 April 1856): 189.

147:2 Stratton, Arthur. "The Custom-House, London." AR 42 (July 1917): 1-4.

house, especially its interiors, is well illustrated; a plan
designating the additions is reproduced.

151:4 _____. "Killyleagh Castle, Co. Down." CL 147 (19, 26 March--
9 April 1970): 690-93, 774-77.

This seventeenth-century mansion was tripled in size by
Lanyon in an Elizabethan revival style. Rowan also sees
Lynn's hand in much of the work.

152:1 LASDUN, DENYS LOUIS (1914-)

Trained at the AAL; worked for Wells Coates; was a member of Tecton
(see 159:1); practiced with Linsey Drake, ca. 1945-51, and as Fry,
Drew, Drake and Lasdun, 1951-58; thereafter practiced alone.
Knighted, 1976. Publication: UNIVERSITY OF EAST ANGLIA PLAN,
1969.

152:2 AR. "Denys Lasdun: The Evolution of a Style." Vol. 145 (May
1969): 345-58.

Lasdun's architecture caters "to what lies deep in our nature (a sense of belonging, a desire for sensual exploration)." His work, 1951-69, is surveyed.

152:3 Baird, George. "Paradox in Regent's Park: A Question of Interpre-
tation." ARENA 81 (April 1966): 272-76.

The Royal College of Physicians, London, is one of two
buildings that Baird uses to discuss the question of "meaning" in architecture.

152:4 Boyarsky, Alvin. "The Architecture of Etcetera." AD 35 (June
1965): 268-70.

"Refreshingly enough, three of Britain's leading architects
[the firms of the Smithsons, Stirling and Gowan, and Denys
Lasdun] working from separate points of departure, different
yet principled, have recently shown that society's needs are
still capable of fertilizing their imagination." This article
is followed by Lasdun's account of his approach to architecture as presented at the RIBA, 9 February 1965 (see 152:6).

152:5 Curtis, William. A LANGUAGE AND A THEME: THE ARCHITEC-
TURE OF DENYS LASDUN AND PARTNERS. London: RIBA Publications, 1976. 119 p.

A dozen buildings and projects are discussed and thoroughly
illustrated.

152:6   Lasdun, Denys Louis. "An Architect's Approach to Architecture." RIBAJ 72 (April 1965): 184-95; AD 35 (June 1965): 271-91 (see 152:4).

> This is the first in a continuing series of articles in which architects are invited to discuss their approach to design. Lasdun surveys the past hundred years and the architects and buildings during that period that have inspired him before explaining his own work.

152:7   Miller, Russell. "Denys Lasdun--Architect." ARCHITECT AND BUILDER (South Africa) 21 (March 1971): 8-10.

> "He has given--and is still giving--the British capitol buildings of outstanding distinction and quality." His work throughout Britain is surveyed.

152:8   Webb, Michael. "A Palatial College for Physicians." CL 137 (29 April 1965): 998-1001.

> In praise of the Royal College of Physicians in a period when "modern architecture in Britain is castigated on many grounds. . . . The architect has given his client not merely what he demanded in the brief, but what he never dreamed of asking for."

153:1   LEIPER, WILLIAM (1839-1916)

A pupil of Boucher and Cousland, Leiper worked for Campbell Douglas, William White, and J.L. Pearson. Began practice in Glasgow ca. 1865. Obituary: RIBAJ 23 (1915-16): 302.

153:2   McNab, William Hunter. "William Leiper, R.S.A., J.P." RIBAJ 23 (26 August 1916): 302-4.

> An appreciation with a lengthy list of works.

153:3   Worsdall, Francis. "A Victorian Architect: William Leiper, RSA., 1839-1916." SCOTTISH FIELD 113 (June 1966): 30-31.

> A detailed study with biographical material and mention of numerous structures.

154:1   LESCAZE, WILLIAM EDMOND (1896-1969)

Swiss-born American architect. The RIBA has drawings of the CBS headquarters, Los Angeles. See Wodehouse, Lawrence. AMERICAN ARCHITECTS FROM THE FIRST WORLD WAR TO THE PRESENT, De-

Basil Ward, "The Whole Man"; D. Talbot Rice, "Scholarship and Writings"; and A.R.N. Roberts, "Teacher and Friend."

155:10 Roberts, A.R.N. "Life and Work of W.R. Lethaby: A Centenary Lecture." B 192 (18 January 1957): 145-46.

Report on a lecture on Lethaby's life, work, and achievements mentioned in 155:9.

155:11 Rubens, Godfrey. "William Lethaby's Buildings." In EDWARDIAN ARCHITECTURE AND ITS ORIGINS, edited by Alastair Service, pp. 130-41. London: Architectural Press, 1975.

Lethaby and his buildings are not exactly well known since a considerable portion of his time was devoted to writing and teaching rather than to designing.

155:12 Weir, Robert W.S. "William Richard Lethaby." AAJ 75 (June 1957): 6-14.

An obituary relating Lethaby to the foundation of the Art Worker's Guild. His works and opinions are listed at length.

156:1 LINDSAY, IAN GORDON (1906-66)

Publications: GEORGIAN EDINBURGH, 1948; with R.G. Cant, OLD STIRLING, 1948. Obituaries: AR 141 (January 1967): 5-6; B 211 (2 September 1966): 102; EAAY 11 (1967): 130-32; RIBAJ 74 (April 1967): 168.

156:2 Anson, Peter F. "Saint Ninian's Tynet, Banffshire: The Oldest Post-Reformation Catholic Church in Scotland." LITURGICAL ARTS 20 (February 1952): 45-46.

Lindsay restored this church.

156:3 McWilliam, Colin. "Ian Lindsay." EAAY 11 (1967): 130-32.

An investigator and restorer of historic Scottish architecture, Lindsay studied at Cambridge and was apprenticed to Reginald Fairlie.

LLEWELYN—DAVIES, RICHARD.
See DAVIES, RICHARD LLEWELYN

157:1 LORIMER, ROBERT (1864-1929)

Articled to Robert Rowand Anderson and worked for G.F. Bodley in

London prior to setting up practice in Edinburgh, 1892. Obituaries: AJ 70 (18 September 1929): 417; AR 66 (October 1929): 206-7; B 137 (20 September 1929): 478; CL 66 (21 September 1929): 398-400; NIY (1929): 579; RIBAJ 36 (1928-29): 771, 792. Publication: with Sir Robert Rowand Anderson, EXAMPLES OF SCOTTISH ARCHITECTURE FROM THE 12TH TO THE 17TH CENTURY, 1921-33. Peter D. Savage wrote a doctoral dissertation "The Work of Robert Lorimer" at the University of Edinburgh, 1976.

157:2   Begg, John.   "The Late Sir Robert Lorimer."   B 137 (20 September 1929): 478.

> "Lorimer's services to architecture in Scotland, at any rate, can hardly be overstated. He went far to wipe out the stain of much of the egregious 'Scottish Baronial.'"

157:3   Deas, F.W.   THE SCOTTISH NATIONAL WAR MEMORIAL.   Edinburgh: Committee of the Scottish National War Memorial, 1928. 36 p.

> The "official guide," with descriptions but no illustrations.

157:4   _____.   "The Work of Sir Robert Lorimer."   EAAY 10 (1933): 113-26.

> His domestic architecture followed R.N. Shaw's but had a distinctly Scottish flavor. Deas classifies Lorimer's work by building type.

157:5   E., J.M.   "The Late Sir Robert Lorimer: An Appreciation."   AJ 70 (18 September 1929): 417.

> "With the death of Sir Robert Lorimer an era of Scottish architecture comes to an end." The era had begun with Robert Rowand Anderson, who had promoted an interest in native tradition.

157:6   Hussey, Christopher.   THE WORK OF SIR ROBERT LORIMER.   London: Country Life, 1931. 111 p.

> "Sir Robert Lorimer combined in his buildings the spirit of old romantic things . . . with the originality and common-sense of today." His most important undertakings are discussed by building type under chronological headings. A list of works begins 1891.

157:7   H[ussey], C[hristopher].   "The Work of the Late Sir Robert Lorimer." CL 66 (21 September 1929): 398-400.

The last of a series of articles, this one is devoted to Whipsnade Zoo, Regent's Park Zoo, and Highgate Flats, London.

160:1 **LUGAR, ROBERT (ca. 1773-1855)**

Practiced in London. Publications: ARCHITECTURAL SKETCHES FOR COTTAGES, RURAL DWELLINGS AND VILLAS, 1805; THE COUNTRY GENTLEMAN'S ARCHITECT: DESIGNS FOR FARM HOUSES AND YARDS, 1807; PLANS AND VIEWS OF BUILDINGS EXECUTED IN ENGLAND AND SCOTLAND IN THE CASTELLATED AND OTHER STYLES, 1823; PLANS AND VIEWS OF ORNAMENTAL DOMESTIC BUILDINGS, EXECUTED IN CASTELLATED AND OTHER STYLES, 1836; VILLA ARCHITECTURE: A COLLECTION OF VIEWS, WITH PLANS OF BUILDINGS EXECUTED IN ENGLAND, SCOTLAND, ETC., 1828.

160:2 Cornforth, John. "Swinton, Yorkshire." CL 139 (7, 14, 21 April 1966): 788-92, 872-75, 944-48.

Building operations continued at Swinton from its beginnings in 1695. Lugar added the west tower, its dominant feature.

161:1 **LUTYENS, EDWIN LANDSEER (1869-1944)**

A pupil of Ernest George, Lutyens began practice in 1889. RIBA gold medalist, 1921. AIA gold medalist, 1924. Publications: with Patrick Abercrombie, A PLAN FOR THE CITY AND COUNTY OF KINGSTON UPON HULL, 1945; with Charles Bressey, HIGHWAY DEVELOPMENT SURVEY, 1938. A.C. Benson and Lawrence Weaver edited THE BOOK OF THE QUEEN'S DOLL'S HOUSE. London: Methuen, 1934, 92 pls., 24 in color (limited edition: 1500 copies). Avery Architectural Library, Columbia University, has seven sheets of miscellaneous drawings. The RIBA has drawings (see 161:45). Obituaries: AAJ 59 (January 1944): 47-48; A&BN 177 (7 January 1944): 3; AJ 99 (6, 10 February 1944): 2-3, 116; AR 95 (February 1944): xlv; JSAH 3 (October 1943): 15. Y.J. Czeiler wrote an undergraduate architectural thesis, "Lutyens In Northumberland," at the University of Newcastle, 1955; P. Robillard wrote an undergraduate architectural thesis, "The Early Life and Work of Sir Edwin Lutyens," at the University of Newcastle, 1962. D.A. Baker is researching the work of Lutyens at Lindisfarne Castle, N. Sidor is researching his early country houses, J.A. Sparks is researching his early work and N. Taylor is researching Lutyens's work generally. R. Gradidge wrote the chapter "Lutyens and Neo-Georgian Architecture" for SEVEN VICTORIAN ARCHITECTS (see A37).

161:2   Betjeman, John. "Memorial to a Great Architect." CL 109 (2 February 1951): 324-25.

> In reviewing the memorial volumes on Lutyens (see 161:4), Betjeman begins: "Lutyens added distinction to whatever he did. He is one of the few architects whose work is instantly recognizable."

161:3   Binney, Marcus. "An Architecture of Law and Order: The Lutyens Centenary Exhibition at the RIBA." CL 145 (10 April 1969): 876-77.

> Drawings by Lutyens and photographs of his work were exhibited at the RIBA. But Lutyens was unpopular in 1969 because of "his lack of social consciousness, . . . his tenacious attachment to classical forms. . . . A decade or two must elapse before he can satisfactorily be the subject of a large retrospective exhibition."

161:4   Butler, A.S.G. THE ARCHITECTURE OF SIR EDWIN LUTYENS. 3 vols. London: Country Life, 1950. Vol. 1; COUNTRY HOUSES. 61 p., 110 pls. Vol. 2; GARDENS, LAYOUTS AND TOWN PLANNING, BRIDGES, IMPERIAL DELHI, JOHANNESBURG ART GALLERY, THE WASHINGTON EMBASSY, UNIVERSITY BUILDINGS." 52 p., 121 pls., 277 figs. Vol. 3, TOWN AND PUBLIC BUILDINGS; MEMORIALS; THE METROPOLITAN CATHEDRAL, LIVERPOOL. 59 p., 107 pls., 173 figs.

> These memorial volumes thoroughly illustrate and describe all of Lutyens's major commissions.

161:5   Byron, Robert. "New Delhi." AR 69 (January 1931): 1-30.

> The whole January 1931 issue is devoted to a detailed coverage of the government buildings at New Delhi, with impressions, history, significance of the city, and plans and photographs of individual buildings.

161:6   Chipkin, C.M. "New Delhi." SOUTH AFRICAN ARCHITECTURAL RECORD 43 (November 1958): 21-28.

> See 16:5.

161:7   Dougill, Wesley. "Liverpool's Two Cathedrals." B 154 (14 January 1938): 54-58.

> Begun in 1933, the Metropolitan Cathedral, Liverpool, by Lutyens covers a nine-acre site, and consists only of a crypt up to ground level. This article offers interesting photographs of the crypt, where the "brickwork is generally of

Mells Park burned in 1917 and in 1924 Lutyens rebuilt it.
This article is illustrated by plans and photographs of the
interior and exterior.

161:22 Howling, G.T. "Liverpool Metropolitan Cathedral: A Comparison of
the Scott and Lutyens Designs." B 188 (4 March 1955): 366–68.

Adrian Gilbert Scott reworked Lutyens's design to make it
smaller because of rising costs. The Scott scheme was estimated to cost four million pounds compared to the estimate
for the continuation of the original design at twenty-seven
million pounds and to require a building time of sixty years.

161:23 _____. "Lutyens: Some Reflections." B 196 (13 February 1959):
313.

A report of a meeting at the AAL in appreciation of Lutyens's
charm, personality, and creative ability. Basil Spence pre-
dicted that Lutyens would come back into favor again.

161:24 Hussey, Christopher. "Ashby St. Ledgers, Northamptonshire." CL
110 (27 July; 3, 10, 17 August 1951): 274–77, 348–51, 420–23,
496–99.

This fifteenth-century manor house, much altered in the
seventeenth century, was greatly extended by Lutyens,
1904–25. Connecting ranges and interiors were mainly
affected (see plans on pp. 351 and 423 of this article for
comparative analysis), as were garden layouts and some
thatched village houses.

161:25 _____. "Blagdon, Northumberland." CL 112 (18, 25 July 1952):
188–91, 260–63.

Built and added to in the eighteenth century, this work's
garden layout was devised by Lutyens.

161:26 _____. "The British Embassy, Washington." CL 85 (14, 21 January 1939): 38–42, 64–68.

Georgian colonial in style, these extensive buildings, 1927–
30, are on a tight site, a fact which was considered in
their design. "The solution arrived at is indeed brilliant."

161:27 _____. "Crooksbury, Surrey." CL 96 (6, 13 October 1944):
596–99, 640–43.

Lutyens's first country house, built in 1890, enlarged in
1898, and rebuilt in 1914. Plans illustrate phases of its
enlargement.

161:28 _____. "An Early Lutyens Castle in the Air." CL 125 (22 January 1959): 148-49.

Reference is made to Emily Lutyens's book CANDLES IN THE SUN, in which she described the "sweetness" of Lutyens's architecture. Sketchbooks by Lutyens, 1893-96, illustrating, among other projects, a "dream-palace of fantastic splendour" had recently come to light.

161:29 _____. THE LIFE OF SIR EDWIN LUTYENS. 1950. Reprint. London: Country Life, 1953. 602 p.

A thorough, well illustrated biography to complement Butler's memorial volumes (see 161:4).

161:30 _____. "Middleton Park, Oxfordshire." CL 100 (4, 12 July 1946): 28-31, 74-77.

Building this structure during 1934-38, on the site of an eighteenth-century house, Lutyens used the orders, evolved at Delhi, on its south-front entrance.

161:31 _____. "The Salutation, Sandwich, Kent." CL 132 (13, 20 September 1962): 564-67, 650-54.

This Georgian revival of 1911, including the gardens by Gertrude Jekyll, is thoroughly described inside and out.

161:32 _____. "Sir Edwin Lutyens." CL 95 (14 January 1944): 68-71.

"Incontestably Lutyens was the greatest architect of our time." His career is surveyed.

161:33 _____. "A Vision of the New London." CL 92 (9 October 1942): 692-96.

Plans for the St. Paul's Cathedral precinct were exhibited at the Royal Academy. The area around the cathedral was opened up with an axis along Ludgate Hill as Christopher Wren intended but never realized, and with a southern access to the river Thames. Other major thoroughfares of London were also considered and illustrated.

161:34 Kinney, L.W. "Lutyens's First Public Work." CL 141 (23 March 1967): 662.

This letter by Kinney states that: "Your London Offices [COUNTRY LIFE] in Tavistock Street were not Sir Edwin Lutyens's first public work, as in 1895 he designed the Liberal Club in South Street," Farnham, Hampshire.

161:47 Smithson, Peter. "The Viceroy's House in Imperial Delhi." RIBAJ 76 (April 1969): 152-54.

> "The puzzle of Lutyens's design is the inexplicable leap from the ordinary sort of banal mixture of styles and poorish English Palladian planning to the very Roman thing that actually got built."

161:48 Summerson, John. "The Lutyens Memorial Volumes." RIBAJ 58 (August 1951): 390-91.

> See 161:4. A fitting tribute at the death of the architect and the end of the era to which he belonged.

161:49 Venturi, Robert, and Brown, Denise Scott. "Learning from Lutyens." RIBAJ 76 (August 1969): 353-54.

> Le Corbusier considered New Delhi, the capital, to be an accomplishment earning respect for Lutyens, an architect who was equally admired by Frank Lloyd Wright. In comparison, Alison and Peter Smithson's articles (see 161:46-47) "are condescending and irrelevant." Peter Smithson's article--entitled "The Viceroy's House in Imperial Delhi,"-- "is similarly based on its irrelevant polemicism, an unnecessary condescension."

161:50 Weaver, Lawrence. HOUSES AND GARDENS BY E.L. LUTYENS. London: Country Life, 1913. 344 p.

> "The year 1913 sees him in some sort at a parting of the ways. . . . This is a convenient time, therefore, to attempt a survey of his past achievement in domestic architecture."

161:51 _____. LUTYENS' HOUSES AND GARDENS. London: Country Life, 1921. 203 p.

> Examples of residential architecture, 1890-1912, that successfully relate to the landscape are presented. "They reveal the marriage of fine design with a just sense of materials."

162:1 LYNN, WILLIAM HENRY (1829-1915)

An assistant and later a partner of Charles Lanyon (see 151:1), 1854-89. The RIBA has drawings (see 162:5). Obituaries: B 109 (1915): 206, 219--a brief announcement but with an extensive listing of works; RIBAJ 22 (25 September 1915): 506.

162:2 B. "The Queen's University, Belfast." Vol. 99 (22 October 1910): 460–63.

>An announcement of the results of the competition for extensions to Charles Lanyon's Tudor-styled university buildings of 1849. Lynn submitted the most "masterly" designs. Other submissions are illustrated and described.

162:3 Bence-Jones, Mark. "The Building Dreams of a Viceroy." CL 148 (1, 8 October 1970): 816–19, 900–904.

>Lynn was chosen to gothicize Clandeboye, County Down, an eighteenth-century pile owned by Lord Dufferin. Dufferin was viceroy to Canada, where he wanted to have a gate designed (sketch illustrated). He also wanted Lynn to design an embassy for Constantinople.

162:4 Dixon, Hugh. "William Henry Lynn." QUARTERLY BULLETIN OF THE IRISH GEORGIAN SOCIETY 17 (January–June 1974): 25–30.

>Biographical notes and a list of fifty-six works.

162:5 Webb, Aston. "Leaves from the Life of W.H. Lynn." RIBAJ 24 (January 1917): 91–92.

>An announcement that Lynn's scrapbook of newspaper clippings, photographs of buildings, and sketches had been presented to the RIBA. "He was the greatest Irish architect of this century."

163:1 **LYONS, ERIC (1912–)**

>Trained at the Regent Street Polytechnic, London. Partnered with Geoffrey P. Townsend in 1938–39 and 1945–54. Thereafter the partnership was known as Lyons, Israeli and Ellis.

163:2 Allen, N.P. "Housing Schemes for the Professional Classes." TPR 29 (January 1959): 227–40.

>Parkleys, Ham Common, London, 1952, is described and illustrated as a comprehensive project on a modest economic scale of 182 residences.

163:3 Jordan, Robert Furneaux. "SPAN, the Spec Builder as Patron of Modern Architecture." AR 125 (February 1959): 109–20.

>Lyons is willing to interest himself "seriously in developer's problems rather than ignore the low standard of speculative builder's designs." Four of his projects are considered in

165:8 _____ . CHARLES RENNIE MACKINTOSH: IRONWORK AND ME-
TALWORK AT GLASGOW SCHOOL OF ART. Glasgow: Glasgow
School of Art, 1969. Unpaged.

> Thirty-two examples of architectural ironwork at the Glas-
> gow School of Art are illustrated, dimensioned, and photo-
> graphed.

165:9 BD. "Chairmannerisms." 15 March 1974, p. 31.

> Various famous chair designs, including those by Mackin-
> tosh (which are now respected enough to be made as repro-
> ductions), are listed. Quotations are taken from Felippo
> Alison (165:3).

165:10 Betjeman, John. "1830–1930--Still Going Strong: A Guide to the
Recent History of Interior Decoration." AR 67 (May 1930): 231-
72.

> Interiors by Mackintosh are illustrated (pp. 236-37, 242),
> and one is captioned "Prelude to Le Corbusier: A Bedroom
> by C.R. Mackintosh."

165:11 Billcliffe, Roger. ARCHITECTURAL SKETCHES AND FLOWER DRAW-
INGS BY CHARLES RENNIE MACKINTOSH. London: Academy Editions, 1977. 96 p., incl. 102 black and white and 21 color illus.

> A brief introduction relates the drawings of Mackintosh's
> early career to his architecture; his later drawings were
> independent of his architectural thought process.

165:12 _____ . FLOWER DRAWINGS BY CHARLES RENNIE MACKINTOSH.
Glasgow: Hunterian Museum, University of Glasgow, 1977. 18 p.

> A catalog of forty-two drawings and paintings with a brief
> introduction.

165:13 Binney, Marcus. "An Architect of Unfulfilled Promise." CL 144
(7 November 1968): 1182-83.

> A whole generation of outstanding architects, born in the
> 1860s, "achieved an international reputation by the turn of
> the century . . . [but] failed to fulfill the promise they
> had shown in the 1890's. Mackintosh was one of many; he
> resigned his Glasgow partnership in 1913, never to receive
> another major commission." His work and influence are
> assessed.

165:14 Blackie, Walter W. "Memories of Charles Rennie Mackintosh."
SCOTTISH ART REVIEW 11 (1968): 6-11.

Personal recollections by the client of Hillhouse in Helensburgh with regard to the building materials used there and his associations with the architect.

165:15 Bliss, Douglas Percy. CHARLES RENNIE MACKINTOSH AND THE GLASGOW SCHOOL OF ART. Glasgow: Glasgow School of Art, 1961. 24 p.

A well-illustrated booklet on the Glasgow School of Art, supplemented by two brief essays, "His Life and Work" and "An Estimate of His Achievement."

165:16 BRITISH ARCHITECT. "Liverpool Cathedral Project Drawings." Vol. 59 (13 March 1903): two plates by Honeyman, Keppie and Mackintosh.

165:17 BUILDER'S JOURNAL AND ARCHITECTURAL ENGINEER. "Scotland Street School." Vol. 24 (28 November 1906): 267-69.

Accommodations, costs, and principal contractors for this Glasgow school are listed. Photographs and plans.

165:18 Davidson, Hamish R. "Memories of Charles Rennie Mackintosh." SCOTTISH ART REVIEW 11 (1968): 2-5, 29.

Hamish R. Davidson was the grandson of one of Mackintosh's clients, William Davidson, for whom Windyhill in Kilmacolm, was built. William Davidson also purchased Mackintosh's own house at 78 Ann Street (now 78 Southpark Avenue), Glasgow, when it was sold in 1919 after Mackintosh had moved to England. Davidson also organized the Mackintosh Memorial Exhibition in 1933.

165:19 Finch, Paul. "Planners Vote to Demolish Mackintosh School Building." BD, 22 February 1974, p. 11.

It would be costly to move the Martyr's School, Glasgow, or to realign the proposed interchange that passes through the site, so the planning committee voted ten to four to demolish the school.

165:20 Glasgow Corporation, Education Department. CHARLES RENNIE MACKINTOSH. Glasgow: 1969. 8 p.

This was a centennial pamphlet, which reproduced two articles by Louise Annand on Mackintosh--one a reprint of 165:4, the other, "Charles Rennie Mackintosh," SCOTTISH EDUCATIONAL JOURNAL 51 (9 February 1968): 145.

Mackintosh "sought his inspiration . . . in the traditional architecture of his country and in the ever-varying glyptic forms of nature." Howarth believes that Queen's Cross Church ranks with the Glasgow School of Art "as one of his major works" though he states toward the end of his article that it "is not one of Mackintosh's best buildings." The church is described with plan, photographs, and a drawing.

165:33 _____. "Some Mackintosh Furniture Preserved." AR 100 (August 1946): 33-34.

Furniture from 78 Southpark Avenue, Glasgow, where Mackintosh and his wife had lived, was purchased by the University of Glasgow, 15 November 1945.

165:34 Huston, Desmond Chapman. "Charles Rennie Mackintosh: His Life and Work." ARTWORK 4 (Spring 1930): 20-31.

"The first attempt at a biographical appreciation, and the source used by most subsequent writers--but contains factual errors," is the way Howarth refers to this article in his biography (see 165:27, p. 310).

165:35 _____. "Decay." In A CREEL OF PEAT-STRAY PAPERS, pp. 159-67. London: Adelphi Press, 1910.

A brief essay dedicated to Margaret Macdonald Mackintosh and Charles Rennie Mackintosh.

165:36 _____. THE LAMP OF MEMORY: AUTOBIOGRAPHICAL DIGRESSIONS. London: Skeffington, 1950.

Huston was a good friend of Mackintosh and his wife and makes numerous mentions of the former throughout his book.

165:37 Huxtablė, Ada Louise. "Mackintosh: Revolution as the Scent of Heliotrope." NEW YORK TIMES 17 November 1968, sect. 2, p. 27.

At the Edinburgh Festival in 1968, a centenary exhibition of the works of Mackintosh was staged. "This exhibition," recreating his interiors of 1900-1917, "was indeed a revelation." The show was later taken to the V&A. "Mackintosh was involved in a reformation that was also a gentle exploration of beauty and a probing analysis of architectonic surfaces and spaces."

165:38 IDEAL HOME. "Now and Then: A Transformation." Vol. 2 (August, September 1920): 53-55, 92-95.

"An article describing how an old-fashioned and unsightly house was brought right up-to-date" for W.J. Bassett-Lowke at 78 Derngate, Northampton. The conversion of the whole house necessitated partition and staircase changes. "Before" and "after" photographs complement a text describing the color scheme, materials, furniture, and lightfittings. The first part of the article concentrates on the living areas and the second on the bedrooms and kitchen facilities.

165:39 Kossatz, Horst-Herbert. "The Vienna Secession and Its Early Relations with Great Britain." STUDIO INTERNATIONAL 181 (January 1971): 9-20.

A very general article on nineteenth-century cultural relationships between Austria and Great Britain. Mackintosh is viewed as one tradition within the arts-and-crafts movement and, although his and his Glasgow contemporaries, work was viewed as weird and caused indignation, it appealed to Viennese taste.

165:40 McGrath, Raymond. TWENTIETH CENTURY HOUSES. London: Faber and Faber, 1934. 232 p.

In chapter 5, entitled "Examples," Windyhill, Kilmacolm is considered in detail and background to the life and work of Mackintosh is also provided: "His houses go back three hundred years for their simple Scottish qualities . . . for the great qualities of the old Scottish farmhouses."

165:41 Mackie, Campbell. "Charles Rennie Mackintosh." B 145 (7 July 1933): 8.

Report on the Mackintosh Memorial Exhibition held in Glasgow. Mackintosh anticipated the 'Machine Age', which is giving us new materials and new ways of using long-known materials--metals, glass and the like."

165:42 Mackintosh, Charles Rennie. "Cabbages in an Orchard." SCOTTISH ART REVIEW 11 (1968): 1.

An explanation by Mackintosh of one of his paintings. "Anything in the sketch you cannot call a tree or a cabbage--call a gooseberry bush."

165:43 Macleod, Robert. CHARLES RENNIE MACKINTOSH. Feltham, Mdx.: Country Life, 1968. 159 p.

Although his works are discussed there, the emphasis in chapter 1, "Background," is on tracing some of the sources of Mackintosh's design criteria to the work of his contemporaries and of earlier generations of architects.

165:44 Mainds, Allan D. "Charles Rennie Mackintosh." LISTENER 10 (1933): 98–100.

The young Scottish school of design, based in Glasgow and led by Mackintosh, manifested itself in Europe as the successor to the arts-and-crafts movement. A general assessment.

165:45 Moffat, W. Muirhead. "Scottish Collectors: Mr. Smith and Mackintosh." SCOTTISH ART REVIEW 14 (1973): 1–5.

George Smith, a Glaswegian collector, began acquiring Mackintosh furniture after the publication of Howarth's biography (165:27). Eight photographs of Smith's collection.

165:46 O'Neill, Eithne. "Hermann Muthesius on Mackintosh." SCOTTISH ART REVIEW 11 (1968): 12–17, 30.

Muthesius praised Mackintosh in 1902 when he discussed the differences between Scottish and English architecture, and between Edinburgh and Glasgow, in his three-volumed book DAS ENGLISCHE HAUS, Berlin: Wasmuth, 1904–5. Mackintosh was having an impact in Vienna, whereas the English were rejecting continental ideas.

165:47 Paterson, John L. "Charles Rennie Mackintosh." EAAY 12 (1968): 111–16.

A centennial appreciation of Mackintosh's work that also mentions the work of his European contemporaries.

165:48 Pevsner, Nikolaus. CHARLES R. MACKINTOSH. Milan: Il Balcone, 1950. 152 p. Reprinted and translated in STUDIES IN ART, ARCHITECTURE AND DESIGN. London: Thames and Hudson, 1968. Vol. 2, VICTORIAN AND AFTER, pp. 152–75.

This first biography of Mackintosh is well illustrated. It is a general survey of all aspects of his life and work.

165:49 _____. "Charles Rennie Mackintosh (1867–1933)." CL 85 (15 April 1939): 402–3.

Too little is known of the Glasgow School and of Mackintosh. His background and attitudes and the art nouveau qualities and spatial considerations of his work are emphasized. Space is "the most essentially architectural value of Mackintosh's work."

165:50 _____. "No Grace for Mackintosh." AR 118 (August 1955): 117–18.

The Glasgow Corporation purchased the Cranston Tea Rooms, Ingram Street, in 1951 for twenty-one thousand pounds but has been unable to find a suitable occupant to pay a reasonable rent. Pevsner praises the National Gallery, Glasgow, and its expensive collection and suggests that Mackintosh's architecture is a work of art and should be considered as a national treasure.

165:51 Rykwert, Joseph. "Charles Rennie Mackintosh, 1868-1928." DOMUS no. 462 (March 1968): 32.

A very brief note in English, with a portrait of Mackintosh and one example of his stained glass designs.

165:52 Sekler, Eduard. "Mackintosh and Vienna." AR 145 (December 1968): 455-56. Reprinted in THE ANTI-RATIONALISTS, edited by Nikolaus Pevsner and J.M. Richards, pp. 136-51. London: Architectural Press, 1973.

Mackintosh was invited to exhibit at the Secession, Vienna, in 1900 by an enthusiastic crowd of admirers. The correspondence with the Secessionists and the exhibits are mentioned.

165:53 Shand, Philip Morton. "C.R. Mackintosh." AAJ 75 (January 1959): 163-67.

An assessment of Mackintosh, relating him to aspects of art nouveau and to the modern movement.

165:54 _____. "Mackintosh, Charles Rennie." DICTIONARY OF NATIONAL BIOGRAPHY, 1922-30, edited by J.R.H. Weaver, pp. 546-47. London: Oxford University Press, 1937.

"Sensitive individuality made him difficult for anyone to deal with who did not understand his temperament." Shand was a friend of the Mackintoshes.

165:55 _____. "Scenario for a Human Drama: Glasgow Interlude." AR 77 (January 1935): 23-26.

This is the fifth article in a series whose "purpose [is] . . . to bridge the gap that lies between the eighteenth century English house and the modern house." "Towards the end of the last century building technique and design were hopelessly out of date." Mackintosh's significance for the modern house is discussed.

165:56 Smith, William James. "An Architectural Anthology: Glasgow--'Greek' Thomson, Burnet and Mackintosh." QRIAS 85 (1951): 11-13, 56-60.

"Mackintosh only defended the past so far as it was living and likely to live."

165:57 _____. "Architecture, Glasgow and Mackintosh." PROCEEDINGS OF THE ROYAL PHILOSOPHICAL SOCIETY OF GLASGOW 75 (1951): 55-67.

In praise of distinguished Glaswegians; of Glasgow's institutions, learned societies, and growth; and of the Glasgow architects--from eighteenth century practitioners through Mackintosh and his contemporaries--who made the growth possible. "Mackintosh's individual greatness lay in his originality as a perpetual fount of ideas and in his artistic skill in carrying them out."

165:58 STUDIO. "The Glasgow School of Art." Vol. 19 (1900): 48.

Four interiors.

165:59 _____. "The International Exhibition of Modern Decorative Art at Turin--The Scottish Section." Vol. 26 (1902): 91-104.

A well-illustrated article on the Scottish contribution to the exhibition--furniture, interiors, and illustrations by Margaret M. and Charles Rennie Mackintosh, Frances and J. Herbert McNair, and E.A. Taylor.

165:60 STUDIO YEAR BOOK OF DECORATIVE ART. 1917. Pp. 122-23.

Two block prints by Mackintosh are illustrated.

165:61 _____. "The Hill House." 1907. Pp. 32-33.

Three illustrations: two woodcuts and a photograph. Brief mention of Hill House and the "elaborately mannered drawings" of it.

165:62 Taylor, E.A. "A Neglected Genius: Charles Rennie Mackintosh." STUDIO 105 (June 1933): 344-52.

Some lesser-known watercolors by Mackintosh are illustrated, one in color. He was inspired by natural beauty--"I have known him to enthuse over a maize cob and the intricate pattern the grains made."

165:63 Taylor, J. "Modern Decorative Art In Glasgow." STUDIO 39 (1906): 31-36.

Miss Cranston's Tea Rooms (or Houses as they are referred to in this article) were not literally for tea drinking but were social gathering places, where one could eat, play billiards, or simply smoke. "Each area of these rooms and many of the fittings were designed by Mackintosh."

165:64 Thomson, Alexander. "More Threats to Mackintosh in Blighted City." AJ 161 (19 February 1975): 389.

Queen's Cross Church, one of the few grade A historic listed buildings, and Ruchill Parish Church Hall are in danger, threatened by redevelopment policies of the city of Glasgow. The hall could be used after repairs, but the church has lost its congregation and thus, even if saved, would have to be converted to secular use.

165:65 TIMES. "Obituary: Mr. C.R. Mackintosh: Pioneer of Modernist Architecture." 14 December 1928, p. 16.

The TIMES states wrongly that Mackintosh died in Spain in this account of his life, education, prizes, and works. His influence in Europe is also commented upon: "In Holland in particular his work is held in high esteem." Howarth's biography (165:27) states "obituary notices appeared in the TIMES and in the Scottish press." However, no obituary appears to have been published in the SCOTSMAN.

165:66 Tonge, John. "Charles Rennie Mackintosh: Celtic Innovator." SCOTTISH ART REVIEW 3 (1950): 13-17.

A brief essay on the life and work of Mackintosh, lamenting that his work and significance have been overlooked: "When he died late in the Winter of 1928, only the GLASGOW EVENING NEWS in Scotland paid tribute to the first Scottish architect since [Robert] Adam and Charles Cameron to win fame abroad."

165:67 Tulloch, John. "Preservationists Rally to Aid of Threatened School." BD 21 September 1973, p. 5.

The Glasgow Engineers Department want to build an interchange on the site of the Martyr's School, necessitating the school's demolition. The school, designed 1895, was "the first opportunity that Mackintosh had to design something for himself."

165:68 Walker, David [M.] "Charles Rennie Mackintosh." AR 144 (December 1968): 355-63. Reprinted in EDWARDIAN ARCHITECTURE AND ITS ORIGINS, edited by Alastair Service, pp. 216-35. London: Architectural Press, 1975.

The arts-and-crafts movement, art nouveau, a variety of British vernacularisms, and the impact of his contemporaries were all ingredients of Mackintosh's personal idiom.

165:69 _____. "The Early Work of Charles Rennie Mackintosh." In THE ANTI-RATIONALISTS, edited by Nikolaus Pevsner and J.M. Richards, pp. 116-35. London: Architectural Press, 1973.

> The impact of contemporary architects and of the partners in the firm with which Mackintosh was associated is analyzed with relation to the development of his style. Vernacularisms and the vernacular revival played an important part in Mackintosh's development.

165:70 White, Gleeson. "Some Glasgow Designers and Their Work." STUDIO 11 (1897): 86-100, 226-36.

> These two lengthy, well-illustrated essays describe the metal and wood work and mural and book illustrations of Margaret Macdonald Mackintosh and Frances Macdonald, Mackintosh, J. Herbert McNair, and Talwin Morris. "The STUDIO was the first art magazine to appreciate his genius which will be recognizable to anyone turning to the pages of its July issue in 1897" (quote from E.A. Taylor, see 165:62).

165:71 Young, Andrew McLaren. ARCHITECTURAL JOTTINGS BY CHARLES RENNIE MACKINTOSH. Glasgow: Glasgow Institute of Architects, n.d. 32 p. Reprinted from the GLASGOW INSTITUTE OF ARCHITECTS YEARBOOK, 1968.

> Twenty-nine pages of sketches of old buildings by Mackintosh from the collections of James Meldrum, the Glasgow School of Art, and the University of Strathclyde School of Architecture (Glasgow) and from the University of Glasgow Mackintosh Collection. "They have been chosen for themselves rather than to demonstrate any argument about the lessons their author learned while he was making them."

165:72 _____. CHARLES RENNIE MACKINTOSH (1868-1928). Edinburgh: An Exhibition sponsored by the Edinburgh Festival Society and arranged by the Scottish Arts Council, 1968. 71 p., 32 pls.

> An introduction by Young and "Bibliographical Notes" are followed by a list of 350 items in this exhibition catalog.

166:1 MACLAREN, JAMES MARJORIBANKS (1843-90)

> Collaborated with William Dunn and A.D. Stewart on "A Tower for London." (J.M. Richards. AR 88 [November 1940]: 141-44.) Dunn later worked with Robert Watson, Maclaren's draftsman.

166:2 BRITISH ARCHITECT. "The Late Mr. J.M. Maclaren." Vol. 34 (7 November 1890): 340-41.

Worked for Campbell Douglas and Sellars, where the Queen
Anne style was in vogue and also for William Young.
Maclaren's other associations are also listed.

166:3   Goodhart-Rendel, H.S. "Rogue Architects of the Victorian Era."
A&BN 195 (22, 29 April 1949): 359-62, 381-84.

"Rogue architects" like "rogue elephants" are those who
have "worked apart from the herd." Maclaren was "an
architect for connoisseurs," building for Donald Currie at
Fortingal, Perthshire.

166:4   McAra, Duncan. "James Maclaren (1843-90): An Architect for
Connoisseurs." SCOTTISH ART REVIEW 12 (1970): 28-30.

Extolls Maclaren as a major Victorian architect and presents
some of his contributions, notably those in the vernacular
traditions.

166:5   Service, Alastair. "James Maclaren and the Godwin Legacy." AR
154 (August 1973): 111-18. Reprinted in EDWARDIAN ARCHITEC-
TURE AND ITS ORIGINS, edited by Alastair Service, pp. 100-118.
London: Architectural Press, 1975.

When Maclaren left Scotland for London about 1877, he
had in his pocket an introduction to a leading individualist
architect, Edward Godwin. Godwin's philosophy of design,
the American tradition of Henry Hobson Richardson, and the
vernacular revival all are reflected in Maclaren's work.

167:1   MACKMURDO, ARTHUR HEYGATE (1851-1942)

Studied under T. Chatfield Clarke, traveled to Italy with John Ruskin
in 1874, and set up practice the following year. See Sirr's correspondence at the RIBA. W.M.P. Haslam wrote an M.A. thesis at the
Courtauld Institute, London, 1968, entitled "A.H. Mackmurdo's Artistic Theory."

167:2   Pevsner, Nikolaus. "Mackmurdianum." AR 132 (July 1962): 59-
60.

Here Pevsner publishes a letter sent to him by Mackmurdo
in 1941. In it Mackmurdo reminisces about R.N. Shaw,
whose style had evolved from Gothic to Queen Anne.
Mackmurdo, however, has greater admiration for Philip
Webb.

167:3   _____. "A Pioneer Designer: Arthur H. Mackmurdo." AR 83

(March 1938): 141-43. Reprinted in STUDIES IN ART: ARCHITEC-
TURE AND DESIGN. London: Thames and Hudson, 1968. Vol. 2,
VICTORIAN AND AFTER, pp. 132-39.

William Morris generally influenced Mackmurdo's design
ability, which paralleled the "rapid development of his architectural style."

167:4 Pond, Edward. "Mackmurdo Gleanings." AR 128 (December 1960):
429-31. Reprinted in THE ANTI-RATIONALISTS, edited by Nikolaus
Pevsner and J.M. Richards, pp. 111-15. London: Architectural
Press, 1973.

Excepting an occasional exhibition, most of Mackmurdo's
work was residential. Illustrated.

167:5 Vallance, Aymer. "Mr. Arthur H. Mackmurdo and the Century
Guild." STUDIO 16 (1899): 183-92.

Mackmurdo having freed himself from "the toils of prim
Neo-Gothic artificiality . . . recognized proportion to be
the fundamental element of beauty." His education, travel,
associations, establishment of the Century Guild, and edi-
torship of the HOBBY HORSE for seven years are discussed,
and his designs are considered and illustrated.

168:1 MacNEILL, JOHN B. (ca. 1793-1880)

Worked in England for Thomas Telford from about 1824 until Telford's
death in 1834. Thereafter, MacNeill set up a practice in Glasgow
and London before returning to Ireland in 1836 to become consulting
engineer to the Irish Railway Commission. Obituary: B 38 (13
March 1880): 328.

168:2 Sheehy, Jeanne. "John B. MacNeill." QUARTERLY BULLETIN OF
THE IRISH GEORGIAN SOCIETY 17 (January-June 1974): 22-24.

Biographical material and list of major works.

169:1 MARTIN, JOHN LESLIE (1908-)

Trained at Manchester University; headed the Hull School of Architecture, 1934-39; deputy architect of the London, Midland and Scottish
Railway, 1939-48; deputy architect of the London County Council,
1948-55; thereafter professor of architecture at Cambridge University
and associate in practice with Colin St. John Wilson (see 273:1).
Publications: ARCHITECTURAL GRAPHICS, 1957; DESIGN GRAPHICS,
1962; with Sadie Speight, THE FLAT BOOK, 1937.

169:2 Lasdun, Denys. "Picton Street, Camberwell." AAJ 72 (June 1956): 22-24.

Lasdun emphasizes the high standard of quality achieved by Martin and other London County Council architects from 1946 to 1956, notably at Picton Street.

169:3 Martin, Leslie. "Architects' Approach to Architecture." RIBAJ 74 (May 1967): 191-200.

His faith is in the 1920s and '30s when a "systematic re-examination of human needs, . . . form of building, or environment [was] constantly re-assessed and thought out afresh." He describes his work.

169:4 Silver, Nathan. "Translating the Root Form for Today's Campus." PA 47 (April 1966): 156-67.

Harvey Court at Gonville and Caius College and Peterhouse College, Cambridge, follow a traditional pattern and achieve simplicity in their use of brick and other basic materials.

169:5 Robson, Geoffrey. "Law Library Building, Oxford." RIBAJ 73 (November 1966): 505-10.

"This is one of the few buildings in England since the war which I should like to have planned." Robson feels that a concern for needed expansion was not catered to in this building, designed by Martin and Wilson. He also considers it to be romantic and functional but to fail due to the inconsistency of its materials.

169:6 Stevens, Thomas. "The Work of Sir Leslie Martin." AD 35 (September 1965): 429-48.

Selected works, 1935-65, are briefly surveyed, but post-1959 building types, notably university buildings, such as the group of library buildings at Oxford, are emphasized.

170:1 MATTHEW, ROBERT HOGG (1906-75)

Graduated in Edinburgh, 1931, and began to work for the Department of Health of Scotland in 1936, becoming chief architect of that department in 1945 and then architect to the LCC, 1946-52. Professor of architecture at Edinburgh University. From 1952 on, he practiced in Edinburgh with Stirrat Johnson-Marshall. RIBA gold medalist, 1968. Publications: BELFAST REGIONAL SURVEY PLAN, 1964; THE CLYDE VALLEY REGIONAL PLAN, 1946. Obituaries: AD 45

(September 1975): 576; AIAJ 64 (August 1975): 66; AJ 162 (2 July 1975): 13; AR 158 (July 1975): 54 by Guy Oddie; A Rec 158 (September 1975): 33, 37; B 228 (27 July 1975): 39; DESIGN 324 (December 1975): 66; INDIAN INSTITUTE OF ARCHITECTS JOURNAL 41 (October/December 1975): 27; RIBAJ 82 (July–August 1975): 5, by Leslie Martin; T&CP 43 (September 1975): 385.

170:2 AJ. "Men of the Year." Vol. 129 (15 January 1959): 78–91.

Matthew's background, education, partnership, major projects, and a statement by him on the lack of directed research in schools of architecture. As head of the Edinburgh University School of Architecture, he intended, in 1959, to create a post-graduate research department.

170:3 Browne, Michael. "University of York: First and Second Phases." AR 138 (December 1965): 408-20.

The University of York is innovative in that it set out to solve "the intellectual problems of university planning" and is thus "a possible prototype of an approach to university design in general." System building for each type of structure was based upon those devised by CLASP (Consortium of Local Authorities Special Programmes). The system was modified for climatic and fireproofing reasons. The buildings rely upon the landscape for their effect and it is questioned "whether these particular buildings would create a satisfactory environment without such elements."

170:4 Ellis, Clough Williams. ROYAL FESTIVAL HALL. London: Max Parrish, 1951. 128 p.

Robert Matthew, architect to the LCC and Leslie Martin, its deputy architect, were responsible for all aspects of the design of Royal Festival Hall. This book is a detailed record of all aspects of the servicing of this complex structure.

170:5 Haddock, Mary. "Architects and Their Offices." B 213 (15 September 1967): 132-34.

Stirrat Johnson-Marshall was chief architect to the Ministry of Education prior to practicing with Matthew in Edinburgh. Architects employed by this practice work in teams of fifteen to forty-five. Further detailed information on the workings of the office is provided.

170:6 Laird, Michael. "Turnhouse: Edinburgh Airport Terminal." PROSPECT 2 (Summer 1956): 12-17.

Description, appreciation, criticism, plans, and photographs.

170:7 McKean, John Maule. "RMJM at Stirling." AR 153 (June 1973): 348-66.

> RMJM is the Robert Matthew/Johnson-Marshall partnership. The article provides criticism, detailed photographic analysis, and phasic plans of selected buildings. It is the new trend in university design, de-emphasizing the social engineering of students and providing instead a low-profile architectural expression.

170:8 Rock, Tim. "George Square: Town versus Gown in Edinburgh." AR 143 (June 1968): 433-44.

> Hume Tower for the Faculty of Arts and Social Sciences at Edinburgh University is assessed with respect to the historic eighteenth-century square on which it stands.

170:9 Sharp, Dennis. "The Architecture of Robert Matthew." CL 147 (25 June 1970): 1242-44.

> Biographical information and a survey of his work in public and private practice.

170:10 Steele, Alex. "Developing Commonwealth Games Facilities in Scotland." EAAY 14 (1970): 90-96.

> Steele was coordinator and adviser for the erection and planning of numerous sports facilities. The swimming pool was a commission of Robert Matthew/Johnson-Marshall. Photographs and description.

170:11 Wharton, Kate. "Talking to Sir Robert Matthew." A&BN 5 (5 February 1970): 34-35.

> Matthew talks about his homes and their environments and the housing of others. Various other building types are also discussed. Two of his sketches are illustrated.

171:1 MAUFE, EDWARD (1883-1974)

Articled to W.A. Pite. Won the competition for Guilford Cathedral in 1936. Knighted, 1954. RIBA gold medalist, 1944. The RIBA has drawings. Publication: MODERN CHURCH ARCHITECTURE, 1946. Obituaries: AJ 161 (8 January 1975): 67-68; B 227 (20, 27 December 1974): 27.

171:2 Broadbent, F.G. "Sir Edward Maufe." PAX: THE REVIEW OF THE BENE-
DICTINES OF PRINKNASH, GLOS. 65 (Spring/Summer 1975): 9-12.

>An appreciation of Maufe by Broadbent, architect at Prink-
nash Abbey, which Maufe admired.

171:3 Fry, E. Maxwell. "Mr. Ambrose Heal's House, Bayline, Beaconsfield." AJ 67 (27 June 1928): 909-12.

>This "charming" brick addition is described and illustrated.

171:4 Guilford House Gallery. THE WORK OF SIR EDWARD MAUFE, RA.
Guilford: 1973. Unpaged twelve-sided catalog and cover.

>An exhibition catalog of fifteen items, including portraits
and awards, but in the main, photographs of Maufe's work.

171:5 Hall, H. Austen. "Shepherd's Hill, Buxted, Sussex: The House of
Mr. Edward Maufe." AJ 71 (8 January 1930): 81-88.

>Maufe took a nondescript farm building and made it into
a home for himself. Plans and numerous photographs of its
interior and exterior.

172:1 MENDELSOHN, ERIC[H] (1887-1953)

Named Erich at birth but dropped the h when he became a British citizen
in 1938. Practiced in Britain, 1933-38, and partnered with Serge Cher-
mayeff (see 54:1), 1933-36. Designed thirteen buildings in Britain. See
AF 86 (May 1947): 73-77; A Rec 114 (November 1953): 10-11. The
RIBA has drawings. For his work in America, 1941-53, see Wodehouse,
Lawrence. AMERICAN ARCHITECTS FROM THE FIRST WORLD WAR TO
THE PRESENT, Detroit: Gale Research Co., 1977, wherein are noted
two biographies--by Wolf von Eckardt and Arnold Whittick. Publications:
MENDELSOHN: STRUCTURES AND SKETCHES, translated from the Ger-
man, London: 1924; THREE LECTURES ON ARCHITECTURE, 1944. Obit-
uaries: ARCHITECT AND ENGINEER 195 (October 1953): 26-27; AF
99 (September 1953): 45; A Rec 114 (November 1953): 10-11; B 185
(September 1953): 473; RIBAJ 60 (October 1953): 508.

172:2 Lea, F.M. QUALITATIVE STUDIES OF BUILDINGS: THE DE LA
WARR PAVILION, BEXHILL ON SEA AND THE GILBEY BUILDING,
OVAL ROAD, LONDON, N.W.1. London: Her Majesty's Station-
ery Office, 1966. 59 p.

>This is a technical, qualitative study of the "long-term
durability and functional performance" of two buildings
"discussed in relation to their owners' and designers' original intentions." History, description, construction, materials, finishes, and performance assessments are considered for each building.

172:3　Pevsner, Nikolaus.　"Mendelsohn by Himself."　AR　131 (March 1962): 161-63.

>An evaluation based upon correspondence and an exhibition held at the RIBA, 1962.

173:1　MICKLETHWAITE, JOHN THOMAS (1843-1906)

Pupil of George Gilbert Scott, 1862; practiced alone beginning in 1869 and with Somers Clarke, 1876-92.　Publications: MODERN PARISH CHURCHES, 1874; contributed to H.J. Feasey's WESTMINSTER ABBEY HISTORICALLY DESCRIBED, 1899.

173:2　Niven, W.　"J.T. Micklethwaite, F.S.A., Architect."　AR　20 (December 1906): 317.

>An appreciation of Micklethwaite, surveyor to Westminster Abbey, London, and St. George's Chapel, Windsor.

174:1　MILLS, EDWARD DAVID (1915-　)

Studied at the Regent Street Polytechnic, London.　Practiced since 1937.　Publications: ARCHITECTURE, 1945; ARCHITECTURE DETAIL SHEETS, 1955; FACTORY BUILDING, 1967; THE MODERN CHURCH, 1956 (see E 49); THE MODERN FACTORY, 1951; THE NEW ARCHITECTURE IN GREAT BRITAIN, 1946-1953, 1953 (see A 77).

175:1　MOORE, TEMPLE LUSHINGTON (1856-1920)

Articled to George Gilbert Scott, Jr. 1875.　The RIBA has drawings. Obituary: RIBAJ　27 (1919-20): 429.　S. Parkinson is preparing a biography.

175:2　Goodhart-Rendel, H.S.　"The Churches of Temple Moore: With a Note on the Use of the Styles."　AR　59 (January and February 1926): 12-17, 56-63.

>"Even in this un-Gothic age--all Gothic things were possible" as a series of churches and their fittings show.　"A List of the Ecclesiastical Works of Temple Moore" appears on pp. 61 and 63, and includes new buildings, restorations, additions, furniture, and fittings.

175:3　_____.　"The Work of Temple Moore."　RIBAJ　35 (1927-29): 471-87.

Most of Moore's work was Gothic revival and Goodhart-Rendel attempts to judge it objectively. "In the prosaic world of today," the latter laments, "the loss of the romantic world of yesterday that has left to us the treasures that are the works of Temple Moore."

175:4 Long, E.T. "Churches of a Victorian Squire." CL 144 (26 September 1968): 770-72.

Between 1856 and 1910, Sir Tatton [Sykes] rebuilt or founded seventeen churches." Moore was one of the four major architects he employed.

175:5 Wright, Canon W. "Nairobi Cathedral: An Extension." B 177 (28 October 1949): 540.

Moore's design was altered and its construction begun after his death.

176:1 MORO, PETER (1911-)

Worked for Tecton (see 159:1), 1936-38; partnered with R.L. Davies (see 73:1), 1938-40; worked for the LCC on the Royal Festival Hall, 1948-51; and practiced privately thereafter.

176:2 Webb, Michael. "Monuments to a Theatrical Revival." CL 138 (2 September 1965): 563-65.

Considerations of the Nottingham Playhouse and the Arnaud Theatre, Guilford.

177:1 MORRIS, HUGH (1913-)

177:2 Morris, Hugh. "Architects' Approach to Architecture." RIBAJ 73 (April 1966): 155-63.

Morris bares his soul, enters the confessional, states his architectural preferences, and discusses the Hook New Town project.

178:1 MORRIS AND STEEDMAN (Partnership 1957-)

James S. Morris (1931-) and R. Steedman (1929-). Both trained at the Universities of Edinburgh and Pennsylvania and both worked in the United States and in Switzerland prior to setting up practice in Edinburgh.

178:2 Girouard, Mark. "House That Juts over a Valley." CL 127 (11 February 1960): 284-86.

> The Wilson house at Lasswade, near Edinburgh, at the top of a precipitous slope overlooking an eighteenth-century landscape, is long and narrow because of site conditions. The elevation facing the road is blank, but on the other side, glass predominates.

178:3 _____. "Modernity beside a Scottish Loch." CL 130 (7 December 1961): 1401-3.

> The Winkler house at Taychreggan, Argyllshire, is situated on the edge of Loch Awe, set in magnificent scenery.

179:1 MORRISON, RICHARD (1767?-1849)

> First vice-president of the IAI, 1839-44, at a time when its president was not an architect. The Bank of Ireland, Dublin, has Morrison's drawings, including one of the conversion of Parliament House to a bank. The National Library, Dublin, has a drawing of St. George's Church, Dublin, 1793. Obituary: B 7 (24 November 1849): 557, which states that Morrison was the son of John Morrison, an architect of Cork. Richard trained in Dublin under James Gandon (1742-1823).

180:1 NESFIELD, WILLIAM EDEN (1835-88)

> A pupil of William Burn in London, 1851-53, and of his [Nesfield] uncle, Anthony Salvin. RIBA gold medalist, 1918. The V&A and RIBA have drawings of several designs. Nesfield was joint editor with his son of the AR. Publication: SPECIMENS OF MEDIAEVAL AR- CHITECTURE, CHIEFLY SELECTED FROM EXAMPLES OF THE 12TH AND 13TH CENTURIES IN FRANCE AND ITALY, 1862. Obituaries: AA&BN 23 (1888): 206; B 44 (1888): 225, 268.

180:2 Brydon, John McKean. "Plas Dinam, Llandinam: By W. Eden Nes- field." AR 4 (June-November 1898): 62-65.

> Plans, photographs, and elevations of this house built in 1872.

180:3 _____. "William Eden Nesfield." AR 1 (1897): 235-47; 2 (1898): 25-32, 283-95. Reprinted in EDWARDIAN ARCHITECTURE AND ITS ORIGINS, edited by Alastair Service, pp. 26-38. London: Archi- tectural Press, 1975.

> Brydon lists and comments upon Nesfield's background, ed- ucation, training, and major works.

180:4   Girouard, Mark. "Kinmel, Denbighshire." CL 146 (4, 11 September 1969): 542-45, 614-17.

"The house was transformed into a mixture of a Wren palace and a French chateau by W.E. Nesfield in 1870-74." He began with Home Farm and proceeded with alterations to the main house. Sketches, photographs, and description.

180:5   Hebb, John. "William Eden Nesfield." RIBAJ 10 (23 May 1903): 396-400.

Background, early years, and publications by and about Nesfield precede a listing of his works, 1860-81.

181:1 NEWTON, ERNEST (1856-1922)

Articled to Richard Norman Shaw, 1873, began practice in 1879. RIBA gold medalist, 1918. Publications: A BOOK OF COUNTRY HOUSES, 1903; SKETCHES FOR COUNTRY RESIDENCES DESIGNED TO BE CONSTRUCTED IN THE PATENT CEMENT SLAB SYSTEM OF W.H. LASCELLES, 1883; edited ENGLISH DOMESTIC ARCHITECTURE, 1923 (E 51). The RIBA has drawings. Obituaries: B 122 (1922): 180-81; RIBAJ 29 (1921-22): 191, 212.

181:2   Collingwood, Frances. "Ernest Newton (1856-1922): A Great Domestic Architect of His Day." B 191 (7 September 1956): 400.

From 1879 to 1889 he designed small suburban houses and "managed to demonstrate how an effect of spaciousness may be obtained by means of detailed planning and the unity of materials." Collingwood also comments upon his mature years and his publications.

181:3   K[een], A[rthur]. "An Exhibition of Some Works of the Late Ernest Newton." AR 53 (June 1923): 218.

Extolls the work of Newton, emphasizing his logical planning.

181:4   Keen, Arthur. "Ernest Newton--An Appreciation: His Skill as a Planner." AJ 55 (1922): 229-31.

"The great houses that he produced from about 1910 onwards are probably the best and most characteristically English houses of this generation."

181:5   Lethaby, W[illiam] R[ichard]. "The Late Ernest Newton, R.A." AR 51 (March 1922): 79.

Life, education, training, and professional commitment.

181:6 Newton, William Godfrey. THE WORK OF ERNEST NEWTON, RA. London: Architectural Press, 1925. 212 p.

A brief appreciation followed by photographs, drawings, plans, and details from a wide and varied practice.

181:7 Worthington, Hubert. "Uppingham: The Work of Ernest Newton, RA., and Sons." AR 56 (July 1924): 32-36.

Newton, an old Uppinghamian, designed classrooms and hall in the style of the Early English Renaissance as memorial additions to his old school.

182:1 NICHOLSON, PETER (1765-1844)

A journeyman-cabinetmaker who published dictionaries and numerous books on carpentry, construction, perspective, and the orders of architecture.

182:2 Nares, Gordon. "Corby Castle, Cumberland." CL 115 (7, 14 January 1954): 32-35, 92-95.

Medieval and seventeenth century in origin, Corby Castle, notably in its elevations and entrance hall, was enlarged by Nicholson in 1812-17, in the Greek revival style.

183:1 NICHOLSON, WILLIAM ADAMS (1803-53)

Articled to J.B. Papworth, 1821-24, and began practice in Lincoln, 1828. Obituary: B 11 (23 April 1953): 262.

183:2 Girouard, Mark. "Picturesque Gothic in Decay." CL 127 (3 March 1960): 430-33.

Bayons Manor, Lincolnshire, was designed by its owner with the help of Nicholson "whose other known work is rather dull." Nicholson was a Lincoln architect with an antiquarian interest.

184:1 OLIVER, THOMAS (1791-1857)

Practiced in Newcastle upon Tyne beginning in 1821. Publications:

THE TOPOGRAPHICAL CONDUCTOR, OR DESCRIPTIVE GUIDE TO NEWCASTLE AND GATESHEAD, 1851; A TOPOGRAPHICAL VIEW OF GREAT BRITAIN AND IRELAND, 1831.

184:2 Jones, Margaret E. "Thomas Oliver and His Plans for Central Newcastle." ARCHAEOLOGIA AELIANA 29 (1951): 239-52.

As an assistant of John Dobson, Oliver continued the facades of many streets and squares designed and begun by his master. Details and plans of Oliver's work are provided.

185:1 PAIN BROTHERS

James Pain (ca. 1779-1877), George Richard Pain (ca. 1793-1838), and Henry Pain. As menioned in 185:5, Henry worked in Limerick with James and George. All were grandsons of William Pain. James and George trained under John Nash and assisted him in Ireland, where they settled in Cork; James later moved to Limerick. Lord Inchiquin has an album of drawings of Dromoland. Obituary of James: B 35 (29 December 1877): 1303-4.

185:2 Bence-Jones, Mark. "Two Pairs of Architect Brothers." CL 142 (10 August 1967): 306-9.

This is the second article by the author on the architects of Cork. The first: CL 142 (3 August 1967): 250-53, briefly mentions G.R. Pain's work at Christ Church. The father of the Pain brothers was a London builder, and their grandfather, a writer on architecture, who published THE BRITISH PALLADIO. "According to some sources, the Courthouse, though built by the Pains was actually designed by Kearns Deane. It is also listed as one of Sir Thomas Deane's buildings in his obituaries."

185:3 _____. "A Vanished Gothic Castle in Ireland." CL 133 (18 April 1963): 840-41.

Michelstown Castle, County Cork, was built in a Tudor revival style during 1823-25 at a cost of one hundred thousand pounds. It burned down in 1922.

185:4 Hill, Henry H. "Some Forgotten Books and a Family of Architects." B 100 (23 June 1911): 769-73.

This well-illustrated article considers the "slenderness and elegance" of the Gothic designs by James and George as well as the writings of their grandfather William Pain (1730?-1790?).

185:5 Wicks, James. "James Pain and George Richard Pain." BLACK-
MANSBURY 9 (June and August 1972): 79-80.

> Brief biographies with notes, references, mention of some
> works, and a "Narrative Pedigree of the Pain Family, Ar-
> chitects."

186:1 PAPWORTH, GEORGE (ca. 1781-1855)

Obituary: B 13 (31 March 1855): 150-51 states that George was a
pupil of his elder brother John Buonarotti Papworth (see 187:1) of
London. George worked in Northampton and later in Dublin and
throughout Ireland. His commissions and clients are listed.

187:1 PAPWORTH, JOHN BUONAROTTI (1775-1847)

Son of John Papworth (1750-99), a stuccoist for William Chambers.
The younger Papworth was advised to become an architect because of
his drawing ability. Became student at RAL in 1798. The RIBA has
a portfolio of his drawings, which will be published as a separate
catalog. Publications: ESSAY ON THE PRINCIPLES OF DESIGN IN
ARCHITECTURE, 1826; HINTS ON ORNAMENTAL GARDENING,
1823; RURAL RESIDENCES, 1818. Obituary: B 5 (26 June 1847):
300.

187:2 Crook, J. Mordaunt. "Broomhall, Fife." CL 147 (29 January 1970):
242-46.

> Papworth was one of eighteen architects who submitted de-
> signs for Broomhall between 1766 and 1841. A design of
> 1823 is illustrated.

187:3 Joy, Edward T. "A Versatile Victorian Designer: J.B. Papworth."
CL 147 (15 January 1970): 130-31.

> A general appreciation.

187:4 Papworth, Wyatt. JOHN B. PAPWORTH, ARCHITECT TO THE KING
OF WURTEMBURG: A BRIEF RECORD OF HIS LIFE AND WORKS.
London: privately printed, 1879. 140 p.

> Wyatt Papworth was John B. Papworth's second son. This
> biography of his father's life and times includes a twenty-
> four-page autobiographical sketch "recording events in a
> part of his life of which we could have no knowledge."

187:5 Verey, David. "Cheltenham." A&BN 193 (12 March 1948): 240-53.

The development of Cheltenham during the early part of the nineteenth century, including Papworth's contribution, is surveyed.

187:6 Williamson, R.P. Ross. "Minor Masters of the XIXth Century: John Buonarotti Papworth, Architect to the King of Wurtemburg." AR 79 (June 1936): 279-81; 80 (August 1936): 93.

After Williamson cites Papworth's achievements and innovations, he discusses his works mainly in London.

188:1 PARKINSON, JOSEPH (1783-1855)

188:2 Hussey, Christopher. "Rotherfield Park, Hertfordshire." CL 103 (23, 30 April, 7 May 1948): 826-29, 878-81, 926-29.

Parkinson designed house, landscape, and village in a Tudorish style, 1815-21. It is a fine example of the sort of picturesque group recommended by Uvedale Price.

189:1 PATERSON, ROBERT (1825-89)

Articled to George Beattie.

189:2 McWilliam, Colin. "The Cafe Royal, Edinburgh." THE SCOTTISH GEORGIAN SOCIETY BULLETIN 3 (1974-75): 15-19.

"The Cafe Royal has few rivals for the title of finest Victorian restaurant in Britain." Its interiors and its owners are described in detail.

189:3 Rowan, Alistair. "Saving the Cafe Royal, Edinburgh." CL 146 (27 November 1969): 1381.

The French-styled building containing this excellent Edinburgh restaurant was threatened with demolition in 1969. Built in 1863, it still has many of its original interiors. Three weeks later Rowan presented further information on, and photographs of, his subject on the correspondence page, under "A Historic Interior." CL 146 (18 December 1969): 1651.

190:1 PAXTON, JOSEPH (1801-65)

Famous as a landscape gardener and the designer of the competition-winning Crystal Palace, London, 1851. Associated with his nephew George Henry Stokes (1827/8-74). Publication: PAXTON'S MAGAZINE OF BOTONY AND REGISTER OF FLOWERING PLANTS, 1834-49.

Obituaries: B 23 (17, 24 June 1865): 421, 423, 442-44; RIBAJ
(1865-66): 28. George F. Chadwick wrote a doctoral dissertation,
"Sir Joseph Paxton," in 1959 at the University of Manchester.

190:2 Anthony, John. JOSEPH PAXTON. Aylesbury, Bucks.: Shire Publications, 1973. 48 p.

> A brief but reasonably well-illustrated booklet covering
> Paxton's early as well as later and better-known works.

190:3 AR. "Another Side to Paxton." Vol. 110 (October 1951): 262-63.

> Five buildings by Paxton are illustrated and briefly de-
> scribed. They are typical of designs of the period and not
> as innovative as the Crystal Palace.

190:4 Banham, Reyner. "The Environmentalist." PROGRAM (Spring 1962):
57-64.

> Paxton comes of age as an environmentalist!

190:5 Beaver, Patrick. THE CRYSTAL PALACE. London: Hugh Evelyn,
1970. 151 p.

> "The Crystal Palace was a microcosm of Victorian life, in-
> dustry and leisure, reflecting every aspect of its age."
> This is a well-illustrated social survey in addition to being
> a study of the building.

190:6 Bird, Anthony. PAXTON'S PALACE. London: Cassell, 1976. 189 p.

> The latest book about the building.

190:7 Chadwick, George F. "The Glass Buildings of Sir Joseph Paxton."
RIBAJ 73 (February 1966): 59-60.

> A brief report of a lecture given at the RIBA on the cen-
> tenary of Paxton's death. Ten qualities of the Crystal Pal-
> ace are listed.

190:8 _____. "Paxton and Sydenham Park." AR 129 (February 1961):
122-27.

> Typically Victorian and conventional, Paxton's gardens at
> Sydenham, where the Crystal Palace was reerected after
> the 1851 Exposition, are presented and evaluated.

190:9 _____. "Paxton and The Great Stove." AH 4 (1961): 77-92.

> "The recent discovery of account books for the period of

Sir Joseph Paxton's association with Chatsworth has thrown further light on several important aspects of his work there."

190:10 _____. SIR JOSEPH PAXTON, 1803–1865. London: Arts Council in association with Victorian Society, 1965. 24 p.

One hundred and fifty-five drawings, photographs, and Paxtoniana are presented in this catalog, which contains detailed biographical information, year by year.

190:11 _____. THE WORKS OF SIR JOSEPH PAXTON. London: Architectural Press, 1961. 275 p.

In no way attempting to duplicate the material of Violet Markham's PAXTON AND THE BACHELOR DUKE (190:19), Chadwick explains in his introduction that he is concerned with "garden, building, and landscape, and Paxton's influence upon the mid-nineteenth century scene."

190:12 Fitch, James Marston. "The Palace, the Bridge and the Tower." AF 87 (October 1947): 88–95.

This is a chapter from Fitch's book AMERICAN BUILDING, glorifying structural aspects of nineteenth-century design, including that of the Crystal Palace.

190:13 Girouard, Mark. "Genius of Joseph Paxton." CL 138 (9 December 1965): 1606–8.

A review of Paxton's achievements with relation to the exhibition of which 190:10 is the catalog.

190:14 _____. "Lismore Castle, Co. Waterford." CL 136 (13 August 1964): 389–93.

Paxton started life as a gardener at Lismore to the sixth duke of Devonshire. He became the duke's "intimate friend and advisor, and manager of his affairs." Together they created Lismore as it is today. A.W.N. Pugin was one of its decorators and some of his designs "for carpets and ceiling decoration are now in the Print Room of the Victoria and Albert Museum."

190:15 Hitchcock, Henry-Russell. THE CRYSTAL PALACE: THE STRUCTURE, ITS ANTECEDENTS AND ITS IMMEDIATE PROTOGENY. Northampton, Mass.: Smith College, 1951. 39 p.

This catalog states that "it is generally recognized—perhaps somewhat exaggeratedly—as the greatest single architectural achievement of the Victorian Age in Britain." It burned

down in 1936, but from the late nineteenth century to that
date, little interest had been taken in it.

190:16 Hobhouse, Christopher. 1851 AND THE CRYSTAL PALACE. Rev.
ed. London: J. Murray, 1950. 181 p.

In this book's preface, Osbert Lancaster traces twentieth-
century attitudes toward the Victorian era and the beginnings of its acceptance in the 1930s. When the fate of
Crystal Palace was being questioned, Edwin Lutyens stated
that "it should be kept under glass." "Fortunately Hobhouse was only spasmodically up to date. . . . Certain
aspects of the Victorian era struck him as supremely funny"
says Lancaster, but he was also intelligent in assessing the
exhibition building and its contents.

190:17 Kamm, Josephine. JOSEPH PAXTON AND THE CRYSTAL PALACE.
London: Methuen, 1967. 168 p.

Paxton is presented against the background of his times,
not only as the designer of the Crystal Palace, but as a
gardener's boy who introduced rare plants into Britain.

190:18 King, Richard Louis. "Joseph Paxton and the Crystal Palace." IN-
DUSTRIAL ARCHAEOLOGY 6 (1969): 124-31.

"Virtue of honest toil" led to the 1851 exhibition, a "fu-
sion of aesthetic and industrial technology." The events
leading up to 1851 are again recounted.

190:19 Markham, Violet R. PAXTON AND THE BACHELOR DUKE. London:
Hodder and Stoughton, 1935. 350 p.

Granddaughter of Paxton, Violet Markham owned the correspondence and papers of this landscape architect and his
most important client, the duke of Devonshire. Markham
emphasizes Paxton's personal life, fame, and fortune: "For
as I see it," writes Markham, "Joseph and Sarah Paxton as
human beings are of interest no less great than the story of
Crystal Palace."

190:20 Oswald, Arthur. "Tatton Park, Cheshire: A Property of the National
Trust." CL 136 (30 July 1964): 292-96.

This is the final segment of an article on the landscape tradition and Paxton's contribution. See 285:3 for a reference
to the complete article.

190:21 Seddon, Richard. "The 'Paxton' Pavilion at Sheffield." AR 129
(February 1961): 137-38.

Paxton's pavilion was transferred to the Sheffield Corporation in 1957 and restored in 1961. Its origin, differences
from other Paxton structures, and construction are explained.

191:1 PEARSON, JOHN LOUGHBROUGH (1817-98)

Worked for I. Bonomi, Anthony Salvin, and Philip Hardwick. In
1843 began independent practice. Obituary: AA&BN 58 (1897):
94; RIBAJ 5 (1898): 113, 121. D.W. Lloyd wrote a chapter on
Pearson in Nikolaus Pevsner's SEVEN VICTORIAN ARCHITECTS
(see A37).

191:2 Long, E.T. "Churches of a Victorian Squire." CL 144 (26 September 1968): 770-72.

Pearson completed two restorations at Bishop Wilton and
Kirkburn, Yorkshire, in 1859 and 1856 respectively for
Tatton Sykes.

191:3 Newberry, John E. "The Work of John L. Pearson, RA." AR 1
(1897): 69-82.

Examples of his work are provided to give "some idea of
the nature and extent of Mr. Pearson's large practice." A
listing of his works by county is appended.

192:1 PENNETHORNE, JAMES (1801-71)

Trained under John Nash and A.C. Pugin. RIBA gold medalist, 1865.
Knighted, 1870. Publication: ELEMENTS AND MATHEMATICAL
PRINCIPLES OF GREEK ARCHITECTS AND ARTISTS, 1844. Obitu-
aries: B 29 (16 September 1871): 717-18; RIBAJ (1871-72): 5.

192:2 Chancellor, E. Beresford. "A Neglected Town-Planner." B 148 (7
June 1935): 1055.

Pennethorne continued in the Nash tradition by adding
streets and parks to London.

192:3 Hughes, Pennethorne. "The Last State Architect." CL 111 (22
February 1952): 500-501.

James Pennethorne was the son of John Nash's wife and
was sired by the Prince Regent, a client of Nash! Nash
was impotent. He employed his wife's illegitimate son,
who eventually became the surveyor of crown properties;
Pennethorne's work in this position is discussed.

192:4 Hussey, Christopher. "Highcliffe Castle, Hants." CL 91 (24 April, 1, 8 May 1942): 806-9, 854-57, 902-5.

> Robert Adam built the first Highcliffe, Hampshire, in 1773. It was razed in 1794 and rebuilt during 1807-35 in the French Flamboyant Gothic style. "At some stage . . . [A.W.N.] Pugin was actually summoned to advise on Highcliffe. . . . An uncertain tradition associates James Pennethorne, Nash's assistant, with the building."

193:1 PHIPPS, CHARLES JOHN (1835-97)

> Started practice in 1857. Obituaries: B 72 (1897): 488; RIBAJ 4 (1897): 380.

193:2 Spain, Geoffrey, and Dromgoole, Nicholas. "Theatre Architects of the British Isles." AH 13 (1970): 77-89.

> Fifty-five theaters by Phipps, constructed from 1863 to 1897 are listed.

194:1 PILKINGTON, FREDERICK THOMAS (1832-99)

> Son of Thomas Pilkington. Articled in London, educated at the University of Edinburgh, and practiced in Edinburgh with J. Murray Bell (1839-77), before transferring to London in 1860. D. Ross is researching his work.

194:2 Goodhart-Rendell, H.S. "Rogue Architects of the Victorian Era." A&BN 195 (29 April 1949): 382-83.

> "He was a real rogue; nobody can mistake his work, and no other architect would wish, if he could help it." He had a "strong liking for the ugly."

195:1 PILKINGTON, WILLIAM (1758-1848)

> Pupil of and in 1782, successor to Robert Taylor (1714-88) as surveyor to the Board of Customs.

195:2 Lees-Milne, James. "Otterden Place, Kent." CL 148 (27 August 1970): 510-14.

> Pilkington almost completely rebuilt this Tudor mansion at the beginning of the nineteenth century. One of his drawings, dated 1802, is illustrated.

196:1 PITE, ARTHUR BERESFORD (1861-1934)

Son of the architect Alfred Robert Pite (1832-1911) and articled to
W.G. Habershon, with whom he later partnered, 1860-78. He also
worked for Philip Hardwick. The RIBA has drawings. See also E 57.
Obituaries: A&BN 140 (30 November 1934): 260; RIBAJ 42 (8
December 1934): 213.

196:2 Fyfe, Theodore. "The Late Professor Beresford Pite." B 147 (7 December 1934): 969.

"It will probably be as a designer in brickwork that Pite
will ultimately secure his place among English architects."
His work and career are presented.

196:3 Goodhart-Rendel, Harry Stuart. "Ricardo and Pite: Extracts from a
Paper . . . Read before the RIBA." A&BN 144 (6 December 1935):
283-87; RIBAJ 43 (7 December 1935): 117-31.

See 209:2.

196:4 Service, Alastair. "Arthur Beresford Pite." In EDWARDIAN ARCHI-
TECTURE AND ITS ORIGINS, edited by Alastair Service, pp. 394-
404. London: Architectural Press, 1975.

Although, his work was inspired by the arts-and-crafts movement, and the mannerist, baroque, and Byzantine revivals,
these influences were treated in a personalized manner.

197:1 PLAYFAIR, WILLIAM HENRY (1789-1857)

Trained under William Stark (-1813). The University of Edinburgh
owns some drawings. Obituary: B 15 (11 April 1857): 208. M.D.
Langdon is writing an M.S. thesis at the University of Edinburgh, on
Playfair. D. Russell wrote an undergraduate architectural thesis,
"William Henry Playfair," at the University of Newcastle in 1958.

197:2 Gordon, Esme. THE ROYAL SCOTTISH ACADEMY OF PAINTING,
SCULPTURE, AND ARCHITECTURE, 1862-1876. Edinburgh: Charles
Skilton, 1976. 272 p.

A history of the Scottish Academy and its members, many
of whom were architects. Playfair was architect of the
academy's building, which is discussed thoroughly.

197:3 Lines, R. Charles. "Floors Castle, Kelso: Scottish Borders Home of
the Duke and Duchess of Roxburghe." CONNOISSEUR 145 (March
1960): 70-75.

Playfair added to this eighteenth-century castle a large ballroom, which has since been altered. Essentially this article is concerned with furnishings and decoration.

198:1 POCOCK, WILLIAM FULLER (1779-1849)

Studied under Charles Beazley and at the RAL. Publications: ARCHITECTURAL DESIGNS FOR RUSTIC COTTAGES, RURAL DWELLINGS, AND VILLAS, WITH APPROPRIATE SCENERY, 1807; DESIGNS FOR CHURCHES AND CHAPELS, 1819; MODERN FURNISHINGS FOR ROOMS, 1811; OBSERVATIONS ON BOND OF BRICKWORK, 1839. The RIBA has drawings.

198:2 Pocock, William Wilmer. "William Fuller Pocock." BLACKMANS-BURY 9 (February and April 1972): 1-20; (June and August): 21-78; (October and December): 45-67, 107-8.

> This reprint of a privately circulated pedigree dated 1883 was written by Pocock's son, who is mentioned in the reminiscences. Numerous letters are quoted.

199:1 POWELL AND MOYA (Partnership 1946)

Philip Powell (1921-   ) and John Hidalgo Moya (1920-   ). Both studied at the AAL and worked for Frederick Gibberd. Moya was born in Los Gatos, California. During 1946-50 the partnership included Powell's brother Michael Powell (-1971). The RIBA has drawings.

199:2 Clifford, H. Dalton. "A House That Surveys the Weald." CL 124 (7 August 1958): 286-87.

> Toys Hill, Kent, is a weekend house, stretching along the contours of the landscape in a linear manner, providing magnificent views.

199:3 Haddock, Mary. "Architects and Their Offices." B 212 (14 April 1967): 96-98.

> "With interest intensified in the kind of work an office like this turns out," all aspects of its work is considered.

199:4 Hitchcock, Henry-Russell. "Pimlico." AR 113 (September 1953): 176-84.

> Housing at Churchill Gardens, Pimlico, London, is favorably assessed with relation to the modern movement as a whole.

Powell and Moya are described as "mature architects with their own quiet personal command of design."

199:5 Levey, Michael. "3 New Art Galleries." AD 38 (October 1968): 483-89.

A critique of a new art gallery for Christ Church College, Oxford, which is one of the three galleries discussed.

199:6 Powell, Philip. "Architects' Approach to Architecture." RIBAJ 73 (March 1966): 116-27.

Powell elaborates to a large extent upon Churchill Gardens, Pimlico, won in competition, and its precedents.

200:1 PRICHARD, JOHN (1818-86)

Pupil of A.W.N. Pugin; practiced in Llandaff. Partnered at times with J.P. Seddon (229:1), 1852-62. Assisted and succeeded William Burges (42:1). D.R. Buttress wrote an M.A. thesis, "An Architectural History of Llandaff Cathedral," at the University of Manchester, 1964. J. Lawson is researching Prichard.

200:2 James, John H. A HISTORY AND SURVEY OF THE CATHEDRAL CHURCH OF LLANDAFF. 2d ed. Cardiff: Western Mail, 1929. 47 p.

A history with plans and numerous measured drawings. Prichard restored this old cathedral.

201:1 PRIOR, EDWARD SCHROEDER (1852-1932)

Articled to Richard Norman Shaw. Publications: THE CATHEDRAL BUILDERS OF ENGLAND, 1905; EIGHT CHAPTERS ON ENGLISH MEDIAEVAL ART, 1922; A HISTORY OF GOTHIC ART IN ENGLAND, 1912; with Arthur Gardner, AN ACCOUNT OF MEDIAEVAL FIGURE SCULPTURE IN ENGLAND, 1912. Obituaries: AF 57 (October 1932): 18; B 143 (1932): 328; RIBAJ 39 (1931-32): 858-89. The RIBA has drawings. Christopher N. Grillet wrote an undergraduate architectural thesis, "The Architecture of Professor Edward Schroeder Prior," at the University of Cambridge in 1952; N. Smith wrote an undergraduate architectural thesis, "The Work of Edward Schroeder Prior," at the University of Newcastle in 1958. L. Walker is researching Prior.

201:2 Goodhart-Rendel, H.S. "Rogue Architects of the Victorian Era." A&BN 195 (22, 29 April 1949): 359-62, 381-84; RIBAJ 56 (April 1949): 251-59.

Prior's buildings had strong plans and unconventional elevations.

201:3　Grillet, Christopher [N.]　"Edward Prior." AR 112 (November 1952):
302-8. Reprinted in EDWARDIAN ARCHITECTURE AND ITS ORIGINS,
edited by Alastair Service, pp. 142-51. London: Architectural Press,
1975.

Eight of Prior's buildings, designed 1885-1907, are presented, one in detail.

202:1　PUGIN, AUGUSTUS WELBY NORTHMORE (1812-52)

Son of Augustus Charles Pugin (1762-1832), under whom he studied.
Began the practice of architecture soon after 1833. Met James Gil-
lespie (-Graham)--see 110:1--as early as 1929 and was employed by
him when Pugin was shipwrecked off Leith, Scotland. Publications:
AN APOLOGY FOR THE REVIVAL OF CHRISTIAN ARCHITECTURE
IN ENGLAND, 1843; CONTRASTS . . ., 1836; DESIGNS FOR
GOLD AND SILVER SMITHS, 1836; DESIGNS FOR IRON AND BRASS
WORK IN THE STYLE OF THE XV AND XVI CENTURIES, 1836; DE-
TAILS OF ANCIENT TIMBER HOUSES OF THE 15TH AND 16TH CEN-
TURIES, 1836; EXAMPLES OF GOTHIC ARCHITECTURE, 3 vols.,
1831-38; FLORIATED ORNAMENT, 1849; GLOSSARY OF ECCLESI-
ASTICAL ORNAMENT AND COSTUME, 1844; GOTHIC FURNITURE
IN THE STYLE OF THE 15TH CENTURY, 1835; A LETTER TO A.W.
HAKEWELL, ARCHITECT: IN ANSWER TO HIS REFLECTIONS ON
THE STYLE OF THE REBUILDING OF THE HOUSES OF PARLIAMENT,
1835; THE PRESENT STATE OF ECCLESIASTICAL ARCHITECTURE IN
ENGLAND, 1843; A TREATISE ON CHANCEL SCREENS AND ROOD
LOFTS, 1851; THE TRUE PRINCIPLES OF POINTED OR CHRISTIAN
ARCHITECTURE, 1841. For other minor publications, refer to Phoebe
[A.] Stanton, PUGIN, pp. 210-11. London: Thames and Hudson,
1971 (see 202:21). The V&A has sketch books and drawings and the
RIBA has drawings and correspondence (see 202:13). The drawings
will be published in a separate volume of the catalog. Obituary: B
10 (25 September 1852): 605-7. D. Simpson wrote an M.A. thesis,
"Pugin and the Medieval Revival," at Keele University in 1974;
Phoebe A. Stanton wrote a doctoral dissertation, "Welby Pugin and
the Gothic Revival," at the Courtauld Institute, University of London
in 1950; and S.O. Wilson wrote an undergraduate architectural thesis
"The Life and Work of A.W.N. Pugin, 1812-52," at the University
of Newcastle in 1961. A. Wedgwood is preparing catalogs of Pugin
drawings at the V&A and RIBA.

202:2　Bryson, John.　"The Balliol That Might Have Been:　Pugin's Rejected
Designs."　CL 133 (27 June 1963): 1558-61.

College archives and unpublished letters form the basis of this article. George Basevi's plans were rejected partially because of Pugin's criticism of them, but although it was agreed that Pugin could redesign the scheme, it was stipulated that he could not be employed in the execution of the work because he was a Catholic. "When the designs reached Balliol, civil war broke out between Master and Fellows." The master rejected the designs, but the college wanted to keep them without paying for them. They were ultimately loaned to Alfred Waterhouse for his extensions to this Oxford college.

202:3 Cornforth, John. "Adare Manor, Co. Limerick." CL 145 (22 May 1969): 1302-6.

The manor was rebuilt during 1836-50. "Pugin made the designs for the staircase with its stone ballustrade for the first flight and a wooden one from the first landing to the first floor." This is the second of three articles by the author on the manor; the third (CL 145 [29 May 1969]: 1366-69), on Philip Harwick's contribution, states: "The 3rd Earl would have probably made an ideal patron for Pugin, but . . . Pugin was a sick man and it was out of the question to ask him to complete the house."

202:4 De Ballaigue, Geoffrey, and Kirkham, Pat. "George IV and the Furnishing of Windsor Castle." FURNITURE HISTORY 8 (1972): 1-34.

"Pugin's contribution was not limited to reproducing designs of existing pieces" even though he was employed in 1827 to do precisely that.

202:5 Ferrey, Benjamin. RECOLLECTIONS OF A.N. WELBY PUGIN AND HIS FATHER AUGUSTUS PUGIN WITH NOTICES OF THEIR WORKS. London: Edward Stanford, 1861. 473 p.

In writing this book for the generation that knew Pugin or of him, Ferrey accepted the fact that other monographs would ultimately be written by those who could view Pugin in his historical context. "More importance is attached to the early period in which Pugin's talents were distinguished. . . . Contains a good deal of information badly arranged." (Kenneth Clark. In THE GOTHIC REVIVAL, p. 122. London: Constable, 1928.)

202:6 Girouard, Mark. "Alton Castle and Hospital, Staffordshire." CL 128 (24 November 1960): 1226-29.

This craggy castle, set high above a river valley, has an almshouse, chapel, and school.

202:7 _____ . "Three Centuries of Commerce: City of Waterford, Ireland."
CL 140 (22 December 1966): 1695-98.

> Thomas Wyse, a fighter for Catholic emancipation, "had
> been one of the commissioners for the rebuilding of the
> Houses of Parliament [London]. In this connection he must
> have met Augustus Welby Pugin, whom he employed to de-
> sign an unassuming Gothic front for his house on the edge
> of Waterford, the Manor of St. John. One suspects that
> he also had something to do with the choice of Pugin as
> architect for the Presentation Convent (Fig. 6) which ad-
> joins the manor" of 1842.

202:8 Harries, John Glen. PUGIN. Aylesbury, Bucks.: Shire Publications,
1973. 48 p.

> A brief but thorough monograph covering Pugin's life, works,
> philosophy, and influence.

202:9 Hussey, Christopher. "Alton Towers, Staffordshire." CL 127 (2, 9
June 1960): 1246-49, 1304-7.

> The first part of this article is concerned with the valley
> garden and its buildings, constructed in 1814-27. Pugin
> added to a ruinous fantasy of 1830-40 between 1840 and
> 1852. Several Pugin features are mentioned and illustrated.

202:10 _____ . "Chirk Castle, Denbighshire." CL 110 (21, 28 September;
5, 12 October 1951): 896-99, 980-83, 1064-67, 1148-51.

> Continuously inhabited since about 1300, and added to at
> various times. The family rooms were "again altered c.
> 1835-37 under Pugin." Very little mention, however, is
> made of Pugin's contribution.

202:11 Jelley, F.R. "Six of the Best: A.N.W. Pugin, 'Man of Amazing
Intellect.'" B 210 (17 June 1966): 100.

> Jelley had just discovered Pugin's CONTRASTS . . ., pub-
> lished in 1836, and wanted everyone to know about its
> "robust literary pugilism at its best."

202:12 Mostyn, Elfrida. "Abney Hall, Cheshire." CL 133 (19, 25 April
1963): 846-49, 910-13.

> Pugin was the inspiration of the furniture and decorations
> at Abney, but the work was executed by John Gregory
> Crace in 1852-57, as illustrated in the second half of this
> article.

202:13 NRA. A.W.N. PUGIN CORRES. London: HMC, 1969. 29 p.

> Lists the RIBA collection of 350 letters from Pugin and members of his family.

202:14 Oswald, Arthur. "Albury Park, Surrey." CL 108 (25 August, 1 September 1950): 598-602, 674-78.

> This seventeenth-century mansion was remodeled in the Tudor manorial style by Pugin for Henry Drummond, who acquired the estate in 1819. Pugin's work is illustrated, but this article is more concerned with the original work, and particularly with its interiors.

202:15 Piper, John. "The First Home of A.W.N. Pugin." AR 98 (October 1945): 90-93.

> The "more remarkable than beautiful" St. Marie's Grange, Salisbury, 1835.

202:16 Port, M.H., ed. THE HOUSES OF PARLIAMENT. New Haven and London: Yale University Press, 1976. 352 p., 212 illus., 11 pls.

> See 18:12.

202:17 Pugin, Edward Welby, ed. PHOTOGRAPHS FROM SKETCHES BY AUGUSTUS WELBY N. PUGIN. 2 vols. London: S. Ayling, 1865.

> Five hundred photographs, mounted two per sheet.

202:18 Rope, H.E.G. PUGIN. Hassocks, Sussex: Pepler and Sewell, 1935. 42 p.

> "A consideration of Pugin and Catholic apologist and writer . . . a master of English prose." Three hundred copies of this publication were printed.

202:19 Schwartz, Rudolph. A PUGIN BIBLIOGRAPHY: AUGUSTUS WELBY NORTHMORE PUGIN, 1812-1852. Charlottesville, Va.: American Association of Architectural Bibliographers, 1963. 12 p.

> A listing of all publications by and on Pugin, including articles on related aspects of the nineteenth century.

202:20 Sirr, Harry. "Augustus Welby Pugin: A Sketch." RIBAJ 25 (1917-18): 213-26.

> This is more than a sketch; rather, it is a detailed study of Pugin's life, publications, attitudes, influence, and works.

202:21 Stanton, Phoebe [A]. PUGIN. London: Thames and Hudson, 1971.
216 p.

> Phoebe Stanton had been researching Pugin for more than
> twenty years when she published this biography. One there-
> fore expected a more in-depth study of this most important
> nineteenth-century architect, but this is apparently still to
> come from her! The book has an extensive catalogue raisonne
> and is interesting in that engravings of vernacular architec-
> ture are examined as design sources.

202:22 _____. "Pugin: Principles of Design versus Revivalism." JSAH 13
(October 1954): 20-25.

> Stanton found upon investigation that Pugin's "architecture
> and work in the arts of decoration were singularly free from
> archaeological pretentions and . . . of direct borrowing
> from the Gothic" even though one's first impressions might
> suggest otherwise.

202:23 _____. "Some Comments on the Life and Work of Augustus Welby
Northmore Pugin." RIBAJ 60 (December 1952): 47-54.

> Pugin's religion, individualism, personality, illness due to
> overwork, and four career phases are analyzed.

202:24 Summerson, John. "Pugin and Butterfield." AR 152 (August 1972):
97-99.

> A review of Stanton's PUGIN (202:21). "It gives us plenty
> to think about until we can welcome the arrival of Dr.
> Stanton's definitive work."

202:25 _____. "Pugin at Ramsgate." AR 103 (April 1948): 163-66.

> Pugin's house the Grange, Ramsgate, and its adjoining
> Church of St. Augustine are illustrated and described.

202:26 _____. "Pugin Effigy: A Christmas Reminiscence." A&BN 164
(27 December 1940): 181-82.

> The effigy was of Pugin's son Cuthbert, a discovery by
> Summerson as he investigated St. Augustine's, Ramsgate.

202:27 Symondson, Anthony. "Medieval Taste in Victorian Churches." CL
141 (1 June 1967): 1400-1403.

> "Butterfield did for the Church of England what Pugin had
> done for the Church of Rome." Ecclesiastical metalwork
> and embroidery are illustrated.

202:28 Trappes-Lomax, Michael. "Architect and Something More." LITUR-
GICAL ARTS 2 (Third Quarter 1933): 100-104.

>"The trouble was that Pugin made two fundamental mistakes.
>The first was in failing to see that art and religion were
>totally different things; the second, in believing that only
>one form of art--the Gothic--was suitable for Christians."

202:29 _____. PUGIN: A MEDIAEVAL VICTORIAN. London: Sheed and
Ward, 1932. 358 p.

>All aspects of the life, times, writings, clients, and works
>of Pugin are considered.

202:30 Waterhouse, Paul. "The Houses of Parliament." AR 6 (June-December 1899): 234-39; 7 (January-June 1900): 98-109.

>A general essay on the building and its designers, which
>also contains illustrations by Patten Wilson of designs for
>wood carving by Pugin.

202:31 _____. "The Life and Work of Welby Pugin." AR 3 (December
1897-May 98): 167-75, 211-21, 264-73; 4 (June-November 1898):
23-27, 67-73, 115-18, 159-65.

>The contents of this quotation "We are by this time suffi-
>ciently removed from the Gothic revival to be able to look
>back upon it with dispassion of temperate criticism" is the
>subject of this article. Numerous drawings, not by Pugin,
>plus plans and photographs.

202:32 Watkin, D.J., ed. SALE CATALOGUES OF LIBRARIES OF EMINENT
PERSONS. VOLUME 4; ARCHITECTS, pp. 239-83. London: Mansell
Information/Publishing, 1972.

>The sales of Pugin's possessions took place on 27-29 Janu-
>ary and 8 June 1853 and "remind us that he was half
>French." Another sale in February disposed of carvings he
>had collected and one in April, of paintings, drawings,
>and engravings.

203:1 PUGIN, EDWARD WELBY (1834-75)

Son of A.W.N. Pugin, under whom he studied, continuing his father's
practice after 1852. The RIBA has drawings to be published in a separate volume of the catalog and the V&A has notebooks, ca. 1865.
Obituaries: A 13 (12 June 1875): 350; ART JOURNAL 37 (1875):
279; B 33 (12, 19, 26 June 1875): 522-23, 559, 586, provides an
extensive listing of his works.

203:2 Girouard, Mark. "Carlton Towers, Yorkshire." CL 141 (26 January; 2, 9 February 1967): 176-80, 230-33, 280-83.

> This mansion of the seventeenth and eighteenth century was transformed by Pugin, 1873-75, even though only a fraction of his proposals materialized.

204:1 REIACH, ALAN (1910-)

> Trained at the Edinburgh College of Art during 1928-35, articled to Robert Lorimer in 1935, and began practice in 1949. Publication: with Robert Hurd, BUILDING SCOTLAND: A CAUTIONARY GUIDE, 1941.

204:2 Laird, Michael. "Enterprising Speculation." PROSPECT 1 (Spring 1956): 31-34.

> A speculative housing scheme at Joppa, Edinburgh.

204:3 _____. "Two Scottish Churches." AJ 128 (18 September 1958): 408-10.

> A description of Easterhouse Church, Glasgow, giving its plan and photographs of its interior and exterior.

204:4 Macnab, George A. "Heriot-Watt University at Riccarton." EAAY 16 (1972): 78-83.

> The commission for a college to accommodate three thousand students on 242 acres was given in 1967. Aims of the plan and the "systematic, modular basis" of the buildings are described.

204:5 Rock, Tim. "George Square: Town versus Gown in Edinburgh." AR 143 (June 1968): 433-44.

> The relation of Appleton Tower for the Faculty of Arts and Social Sciences at Edinburgh University to the historic eighteenth-century square on which it stands is assessed.

205:1 REID, ROBERT (1776-1856)

> Partnered with Robert Sibbald in Edinburgh. Was the last holder of the office of master of the king's works for Scotland until 1840.

205:2 Cantacuzino, Sherban. "New Uses for Old Buildings." AR 151 (May 1972): 281-82.

St. George's Church, Edinburgh, 1814, was converted into
the Public Records Office.

205:3 Rowan, Alistair. "Paxton House, Berwickshire." CL 142 (17, 24,
31 August 1967): 364-67, 422-25, 470-73.

Built in the late 1730s, and altered at various times, the
east wing was added by Reid in 1811-14. The final portion
of this article covers this aspect of the building's history.

206:1 REILLY, CHARLES HERBERT (1874-1948)

A pupil of his father, Charles Thomas Reilly, he worked for John
Belcher and partnered with Stanley Peach. RIBA gold medalist, 1943.
Knighted, 1944. Publications: ARCHITECTURE AS A COMMUNAL
ART, 1944; MCKIM, MEAD AND WHITE, 1924; REPRESENTATIVE
BRITISH ARCHITECTS OF THE PRESENT DAY, 1931; SCAFFOLDING
IN THE SKY, 1938 (see 206:5); SOME ARCHITECTURAL PROBLEMS
OF TODAY, 1924; SOME MANCHESTER STREETS AND THEIR BUILD-
INGS, 1924; THE THEORY AND PRACTICE OF ARCHITECTURE, 1932;
and wrote the introduction to Lawrence Wolfe's THE REILLY PLAN: A
NEW WAY OF LIFE, 1945. The RIBA has one drawing of the com-
petition for the Cathedral Church of Christ, Liverpool. Obituaries:
AAJ 63 (February 1948): 175; A&BN 193 (6 February 1948): 111;
AR 103 (April 1948): 180-83; B 174 (6 February 1948): 161; RIBAJ
55 (February 1948): 212-13; TPIJ 34 (March-April 1948): 103.

206:2 Budden, L[ionel] B[ailey]. "Charles Reilly." RIBAJ 55 (March
1948): 212-13.

Under Reilly's chairmanship the Liverpool University School
of Architecture changed from its pursuit of various stylistic
trends to a commitment to modernism.

206:3 _____ , ed. THE BOOK OF THE LIVERPOOL SCHOOL OF ARCHI-
TECTURE. Liverpool: University Press, 1932. 68 p.

One thousand copies were printed to commemorate Reilly's
chairmanship of the School of Architecture, 1904-29. The
first four parts of the book cover Reilly's life and career,
from 1874 to 1932.

206:4 Holford, William. "Sir Charles Reilly." AR 103 (April 1948):
180-83.

"It may be too early to assess the value of his contribution
to education. . . . Charles Reilly had a special quality
as a teacher which is difficult to describe in words."

206:5 Reilly, Charles Herbert. SCAFFOLDING IN THE SKY: A SEMI-
ARCHITECTURAL AUTOBIOGRAPHY. London: Routledge and Sons,
1938. 352 p.

> Autobiographical comments and description of professional
> commitment.

207:1 RENNIE, JOHN (1794-1874)

> Obituary: B 32 (12 September 1874): 773. C.T.G. Boucher wrote
> a doctoral dissertation, "John Rennie," at the University of Manchester,
> 1955.

207:2 A. "Sir John Rennie." Vol. 14 (1875): 224-25, 237.

> Background, education, travel, and works.

207:3 ARCHITECTS' AND BUILDERS' JOURNAL. "John Rennie's Bridges."
Vol. 38 (1913): 155-57.

> Several bridges are mentioned but the article is essentially
> about Waterloo Bridge, London, which Rennie designed
> although its attribution had been given to others.

207:4 Betjeman, John. "The Truth about Waterloo Bridge." AR 71 (April
1932): 125-27.

> Betjeman questions the demolition of a bridge where archi-
> tecture and engineering are one. He examines the reasons
> for condemning the old bridge and concludes that a wider
> bridge was not needed.

207:5 Russell, John. "An Byronic Engineer." AR 94 (November 1943):
119-20.

> Rennie continued his more famed father's business as an
> engineer with his brother George. A large portion of the
> article is devoted to Rennie's extensive travels.

208:1 RHIND, DAVID (1808-83)

> A pupil of A.W.N. Pugin and a fellow student of Charles Barry.
> Obituary: B 43 (12 May 1883): 635, which lists some of Rhind's
> major works in Edinburgh. The RIBA has one drawing.

209:1 RICARDO, HALSEY RALPH (1854-1928)

> Began practice in 1878. The RIBA has drawings. Obituaries: B 134

(1928): 326; RIBAJ 35 (1928): 312.

209:2 Goodhart-Rendel, Harry Stuart. "Ricardo and Pite." A&BN 144
(6 December 1935): 283-87; RIBAJ 43 (7 December 1935): 117-31.

> "A general sketch of the work of two remarkable men whose
> more worthy commemoration remains to be made. Biograph-
> ical facts have been excluded from it, and only those per-
> sonal traits remarked that throw light on peculiarities in
> the work itself." Twenty-two thumbnail illustrations ac-
> company the article.

210:1 RICHARDSON, ALBERT EDWARD (1880-1964)

Articled to Thomas Page, 1895; assisted E. Hellicar, Leonard Stokes,
and F.T. Verity; partnered with C. Lovett Gill in 1908 and later
with E.A.S. Houfe. RIBA gold medalist, 1947. Knighted, 1956.
The RIBA has correspondence of 1925, 1938, and 1942-43, and three
drawings, and the V&A has drawings of two projects. Publications:
GEORGIAN ENGLAND, 1931; AN INTRODUCTION TO GEORGIAN
ARCHITECTURE, 1949; MONUMENTAL CLASSICAL ARCHITECTURE
IN GREAT BRITAIN AND IRELAND DURING THE EIGHTEENTH AND
NINETEENTH CENTURIES, 1914 (see A 97); ROBERT MYLNE, 1955;
THE SIGNIFICANCE OF THE FINE ARTS, 1955; THE SMALLER EN-
GLISH HOUSE OF THE LATE RENAISSANCE, 1660-1830, 1925; with
H.O. Corfiato, THE ART OF ARCHITECTURE, 1938, and DESIGN
IN CIVIL ARCHITECTURE, 1956; with H.D. Eberlein, THE ENGLISH
INN, 1925; with C. Lovett Gill, LONDON HOUSES, 1660-1830,
1911, and REGIONAL ARCHITECTURE OF THE WEST OF ENGLAND,
1924. Obituary: A&BN 225 (12 February 1964): 255-56 (see
210:3); B 106 (1964): 273-74.

210:2 Fulford, Roger. "The Sedbergh School Library." CL 124 (10 July
1958): 80-81.

> The interior of this early eighteenth-century Yorkshire li-
> brary was remodeled by Richardson.

210:3 Goulden, Contran. "Sir Albert Richardson." A&BN 225 (12 February 1964): 255-56.

> An obituary notice, with anecdotes and good background
> coverage, of "a staunch opponent of modern art and archi-
> tecture in all their forms."

210:4 Howling, G.T. "Restoration of St. Alfege's, Greenwich." B 182
(14 March 1952): 401-5.

Bombed and burned on 19 March 1941, this early seventeenth-century church was rebuilt by Richardson.

210:5 Hussey, Christopher. "Woburn Abbey, Bedfordshire." CL 118 (1, 8
September 1955): 434-37, 489-91.

Neglect and dry rot necessitated demolitions at the abbey
and Richardson was commissioned to design a new court
and to restore the truncated ends of demolished elements.

210:6 Taylor, Nicholas. "Sir Albert Richardson: A Classic Case of Edward-
ianism." AR 140 (September 1966): 199-206. Reprinted in EDWARD-
IAN ARCHITECTURE AND ITS ORIGINS, edited by Alastair Service,
pp. 444-59. London: Architectural Press, 1975.

Richardson's buildings, including even his later commissions,
which he termed "stripped classical," always had a classical
flavor.

211:1 RICKARDS, EDWIN ALFRED (1872-1920)

Obituary: AR 48 (October 1920): 100-101; B 119 (1920): 247,
251, 333; RIBAJ 27 (1920): 470-73. The RIBA has drawings. In
1956 John Warren wrote an undergraduate architectural thesis at the
University of Newcastle entitled "Edwin Alfred Rickards: A Spumanti
Spirit of Edwardian Baroque."

211:2 Warren, John. "Edwin Alfred Rickards." In EDWARDIAN ARCHI-
TECTURE AND ITS ORIGINS, edited by Alastair Service, pp. 338-50.
London: Architectural Press, 1975.

Rickards studied at the RAL and worked for a considerable
number of architectural firms. He eventually partnered with
Henry Vaughan Lanchester (150:1) and James A. Stewart,
with the aim of entering twelve competitions; in fact, they
entered more than twenty. Their designs were in a wide
variety of baroque revival styles of the seventeenth century
adapted from different geographic areas.

212:1 RICKMAN, THOMAS (1776-1841)

Practiced as a doctor, 1801-3, and in various other occupations.
Publications: AN ATTEMPT TO DISCRIMINATE THE STYLES OF
ENGLISH ARCHITECTURE FROM THE CONQUEST TO THE REFORMA-
TION, 1817; with Dawson Turner, SPECIMENS OF ARCHITECTURAL
REMAINS IN VARIOUS COUNTIES IN ENGLAND, 1938. The RIBA
has drawings and fifty-seven volumes of diaries. The Ashmolean

Museum, Oxford, has more than two thousand sketches of Gothic buildings. In 1962 E.D. Colley wrote an M.A. thesis "The Life and Works of Thomas Rickman, FSA., Architect," at the University of Manchester; B.A. James wrote an RIBA diploma thesis, "The Architectural Work of Thomas Rickman," and J. Bailey is writing a Ph.M. thesis at the University of Leeds on Rickman.

212:2 Hadfield, Miles. "In the Gothic Taste." CL 119 (21 June 1956): 1373.

St. George's, Birmingham, 1820–23, "is famous for the iron shafts carrying Gothic arches of cast open tracery which support the gallery at the west end.

212:3 _____. "Rickman Churches in Birmingham." CL 124 (7 August 1958): 284. Reply by George E. Powell, CL 124 (11 September 1958): 600–603. Reply by Hadfield, CL 124 (13 November 1958): 1127.

Hadfield's first letter concerns the church of St. George Birmingham, famed for its cast iron. The church was to be demolished because of the depopulation of the area. Powell replied that the area was not being depopulated but that a combination of factors, including porous sandstone and dry rot, had left the church in such a poor state that its demolition was inevitable. Powell also stated that the building of the church for 1,100 pounds less than its 14,000-pound estimate was equally part of the problem and quotes a source of 1822 to back up his argument.

212:4 James, Ann. "Rickman and the Fitzwilliam Competition." AR 121 (April 1957): 270–71.

"Rickman was one of four architects to submit three designs each" for this Cambridge museum competition (one architect submitted four designs). Of Rickman's three designs, one was Gothic and two were classical. His architectural output prior to 1820 had been classical, as seen in his design of a sweetshop for his sister based upon the Choragic Monument of Thrasyllus, Athens.

212:5 Jelley, F.R. "Six of the Best: Thomas Rickman." B 211 (7 October 1966): 102.

An evaluation of Rickman's AN ATTEMPT TO DISCRIMINATE THE STYLES OF ENGLISH ARCHITECTURE . . .

212:6 Rickman, Thomas Miller. THOMAS RICKMAN: LIFE AND WORK. London: George J.W. Pitman, 1901. 89 p.

Most of the material for this biography was extracted from
Rickman's diaries. The seven editions of AN ATTEMPT TO
DISCRIMINATE THE STYLES OF ENGLISH ARCHITECTURE
. . ., 1817–81, are discussed.

212:7   Whiffen, Marcus. "The Architectural Review, Gothic Number: Act
2: Romantic Gothic; Scene 2: Rickman and Cambridge." AR 98
(December 1945): 160–65.

Landscape and the early Gothic revival complemented each
other in Rickman's St. John's College, Cambridge, 1825–31.
However, this early building does not have the flimsiness
associated with the late eighteenth century and is well constructed, its overrun in cost partially due to its need for
expensive foundations on its riverside site.

213:1 RISS, EGON (-1964)

Studied in Vienna and came to Britain in 1938. Was division architect to the Scottish Coal Board. Well known for his design of Rothes
Colliery, Thornton, Fife, 1956.

214:1 ROBERTS, HENRY (1802/3-76)

Entered the RAL, 1825, worked for Robert Smirke, and began practice
in London in 1844. Publications: THE DWELLINGS OF THE LABOUR-
ING CLASSES, 1850; THE MODEL HOUSE FOR FAMILIES, 1851.
The RIBA has drawings. Obituary: RIBAJ 1875–76, p. 39 (announcement only).

214:2   Foyle, Arthur M. "Henry Roberts, 1802–1876." B 184 (2 January
1953): 5–8.

His life, work, and major projects are discussed, and a few
of the last are illustrated. He designed model houses for
Streatham Street, London, 1849, and designs for four-family
units, 1851.

214:3   Oswald, Arthur. "Restoring Halls of the City Companies: Some Recent Work at Fishmongers' Hall and Leathersellers' Hall." CL 112
(14 November 1952): 1564–67.

Fishmongers' Hall, 1834, was badly damaged during the Second World War. It "is now generally recognized to be not
only the masterpiece of a little known architect but one of
the finest works of the Greek revival.

215:1 **ROBERTSON, HOWARD MORLEY (1888-1963)**

Born in the United States and trained at the AAL and Ecole des Beaux-Arts, Paris. Practiced with Edwin Stanley Hall and, starting in 1919, with John Murray Easton as Easton and Robertson (see 87:1). RIBA gold medalist, 1949. Knighted, 1954. Publications: ARCHITECTURE ARISING, 1944; ARCHITECTURE EXPLAINED, 1926; DOMESTIC ARCHITECTURE AND THE SECOND GREAT WAR, 1940; THE FOUR INNS OF COURT, 1930; MODERN ARCHITECTURAL DESIGN, 1932; THE PRINCIPLES OF ARCHITECTURAL COMPOSITION, 1924; with F.R. Yerbury, EXAMPLES OF MODERN FRENCH ARCHITECTURE, 1928. The RIBA has drawings. Obituaries: AAJ 79 (July-August 1963): 38-39; AF 118 (June 1963): 13; B 204 (10 May 1963): 915; RIBAJ 80 (1963): 247-48; TIMES 6 May 1963.

215:2 Banham, Reyner. "Howard Robertson." AR 114 (September 1953): 160-68.

"The article examines the career of Howard Robertson in relation to the growth of [the modern] movement, and attempts to evaluate the special, and characteristic, contribution which he has made to the rise of a new architecture in England," wrote the editors of AR. This is a lengthy article with numerous, if small, illustrations of the works of an architect whose "work has significance for students of architecture."

215:3 Myerscough-Walker, Herbert Raymond. "Building: Its Planned Development." B 159 (8 November 1940): 426-28.

Robertson, as president of the RIBA, and George Hicks, a member of Parliament, answer a series of questions on the building industry.

215:4 Payne, Harold. "The Layman at Bay." AR 65 (May 1929): 217-18.

A lecture was held at the AAL in praise of the beauty of the past and present in architecture. Payne objected that modern architecture seems devoid of the need of an architect. Robertson replied, explaining the purpose of an architect in the design of modern buildings.

216:1 **ROBSON, EDWARD ROBERT (1835/6-1917)**

A partner of John James Stevenson (245:1). Publication: SCHOOL ARCHITECTURE, 1874 (see E 61). Obituary: RIBAJ 24 (1916-17): 92-96, 104, 129. N. Jackson is researching Robson.

216:2 Gregory-Jones, David. "The London Board Schools." AR 123 (1958): 393-98. Reprinted in EDWARDIAN ARCHITECTURE AND ITS ORIGINS, edited by Alastair Service, pp. 88-97. London: Architectural Press, 1975.

> Robson was the first London School Board architect from 1870, when the boom in building schools began. His style was Queen Anne and his buildings were tall for urban sites.

217:1 ## ROCHEAD, JOHN THOMAS (1814-78)

> A pupil of David Bryce and, starting in 1837, of Hurst and Moffatt of Doncaster. He returned to Edinburgh to work for David J. Hamilton before practicing independently, 1841-70.

217:2 Worsdall, Francis. "John Thomas Rochead, 1814-1878." SCOTTISH FIELD 111 (September 1964): 37-39.

> A detailed, well-illustrated study mentioning numerous works by Rochead.

218:1 ## RUNTZ, ERNEST AUGUSTUS (ca. 1859-1913)

> Practiced as Runtz and Ford beginning in 1898. Obituaries: B 105 (1913): 437; RIBAJ 21 (1913-14): 29.

218:2 Street, Arthur Edmund. "By Way of Comparison." AR 15 (March 1904): 89-93.

> Two theaters in London, the Gaiety and the Palace, are compared.

219:1 ## SAARINEN, EERO (1910-61)

> Finnish-born, American architect. See also Wodehouse, Lawrence. AMERICAN ARCHITECTS FROM THE FIRST WORLD WAR TO THE PRESENT. Detroit: Gale Research Company, 1977.

219:2 Atkinson, Fello. "U.S. Embassy Building, Grosvenor Square, London." AR 129 (April 1961): 252-58.

> A well-illustrated article concerning the American Embassy in London, which relates the building to its geographic position as well as to its chronological position in American architecture.

219:3 Dorfles, Gillo. "Eero Saarinen: The TWA Terminal and the American Embassy, London." ZODIAC 8 (1961): 84-89.

Is the embassy glamorous, pompous, and undemocratic?

220:1 SALMON, JAMES, JR. (ca. 1874-1924)

Son of William Forest Salmon (1843-1911) and grandson of James Salmon, Sr. (1805-88). James, Jr. was apprenticed to William Leiper but joined his father ca. 1890 and the two partnered with John Gaff Gillespie (-1926) as Salmon, Son and Gillespie until 1913. Obituary: RIBAJ 31 (1923-24): 513. Including material from Glasgow newspapers of the period, P.A. Galashan wrote an undergraduate architectural thesis, "James Salmon: Art Nouveau Architect," at Robert Gordon's Institute of Technology, Aberdeen, in 1975.

220:2 Worsdall, Francis. "Plans That Went Awry." SCOTTISH FIELD 112 (March 1965): 26-28.

Dennistoun, Glasgow, was planned by Salmon but the plans were completely modified during construction.

220:3 Walker, David [M]. "Salmon, Son, Grandson, and Gillespie." SCOTTISH ART REVIEW 10 (no. 3, 1966): 17-21, 28-29.

The architects, their works, and those who influenced them are discussed. A list of works is supplied at the end of the article.

220:4   . "The Partnership of James Salmon and John Gaff Gillespie." EDWARDIAN ARCHITECTURE AND ITS ORIGINS, edited by Alastair Service, pp. 236-49. London: Architectural Press, 1975.

Most of their designs were competition projects in Glasgow, where they had a practice of some note although it operated in the shadows of Burnet and Mackintosh.

221:1 SALVIN, ANTHONY (1799-1881)

Worked for John Nash prior to beginning practice in 1828. The HMC has proposals for Inverary Castle in its Argyll Collection and correspondence in various other collections. The RIBA has drawings. J. Allibone is working on a Ph.M. thesis on Salvin at the University of London. Obituaries: B 41 (31 December 1881): 809-10; BN 41 (1881): 818; RIBAJ 1881-82, p. 59.

221:2 Cornforth, John. "Hutton-in-the-Forest, Cumberland." CL 137 (4, 11, 18 February 1965): 232-35, 286-89, 352-56.

Six major building periods over a five hundred-year period ended with Salvin's contribution. The work's south facade and towers date from 1826 and thus are an early commission, which Salvin modified in 1867. Other nineteenth-century architects also contributed to the fabric.

221:3 Girouard, Mark. "Peckfordton Castle, Cheshire." CL 138 (29 July, 5 August 1965): 284-87, 336-39.

Built 1844-50 in the style of a twelfth-century medieval castle, Peckfordton is quite well composed as can be seen from Salvin's drawings and a watercolor, which are illustrated. Interiors are bold and impressive.

221:4 Hussey, Christopher. "Harlaxton Manor, Lincolnshire." CL 121 (11, 18 April 1957): 704-7, 764-67.

Although Salvin designed Harlaxton in 1831 (see 221:8, which states 1830-37) in a Tudor-manor revival style, "it is now established that it was completed and enlarged c. 1838-55 partially by William Burn."

221:5 _____. "Mamhead, Devon." CL 117 (26 May, 2 June 1955): 1366-69, 1428-31.

R.W. Newman purchased Mamhead in 1822, demolished the existing house, and commissioned Salvin to design a Tudor-style mansion, 1828-33. Good illustrations of its interior and exterior.

221:6 _____. "Muncaster Castle, Cumberland." CL 87 (8, 15 June 1940): 570-74, 592-95.

The present castle was reconstructed in 1860. Its historic and artistic treasures are mentioned in the second part of the article.

221:7 _____. "Scotney Castle, Kent." CL 120 (6, 13 September 1956): 470-73, 526-29.

"An unaltered example of William IV Tudor," designed by Salvin in 1835 and built during 1837-44. The new house is within view of the old castle, which became a romantic ruin.

221:8 Oswald, Arthur. "Country Homes, Gardens, Old and New: Harlaxton Hall, Lincolnshire." CL 82 (9 December 1937): 374-79.

Built on the site of a sixteenth-century house, Harlaxton Hall was designed in 1830-37 by Salvin, who incorporated features of "Manorial Gothic" in its design. The building

was for sale in 1937 and its future depended upon finding
a buyer with a viable use for it.

221:9 _____. "Encombe, Dorset." CL 133 (24 January 1963): 164–68,
214–17.

Salvin altered this Georgian house of 1734 in the 1870s.

221:10 Piper, John. "Decrepit Glory: A Tour of Hafod." AR 87 (June
1940): 207–10.

In 1853 Salvin added an Italianate wing to Hafod, a Moghul revival building of the late eighteenth century by John
Nash and others.

222:1 SCHULTZ, ROBERT WEIR (1861-1951)

A Scot by birth, who changed his name in 1914 to Robert Schultz
Weir. He trained under Robert Rowand Anderson in Edinburgh and
worked for R.N. Shaw and for Ernest George and Peto in London.
Publications: THE MONASTERY OF SAINT LUKE OF STIRIS . . .,
1901; edited THE CHURCH OF THE NATIVITY AT BETHLEHEM, 1910.
Obituary (his surname here is Weir): B 180 (11 May 1951): 663.
The Warburg Institute of the University of London has the collection
of the Byzantine Research and Publications Fund, which contains drawings by Schultz, ca. 1890–1918. The NMRS has drawings of Sanquhar
Castle, Dumfriesshire, 1895. Buteshire National Historical Society,
Rothesay, also has his drawings. Dorothy D. Bosomworth Reynolds is
working on a Ph.M. thesis at the University of London on Byzantine
influences on British architecture and design, 1840–1914, and is including the work of Schultz.

222:2 Crook, J. Mordaunt. "Patron Extraordinary: John 3d Marquess of
Bute." In VICTORIAN SOUTH WALES ARCHITECTURE, INDUSTRY
AND SOCIETY, pp. 3–22. Victorian Society Conference Report no.
7. London: 1969.

Tucked into this article on South Wales is a detailed mention of Weir's work for Bute in Scotland, notably at Falk-
land Palace.

222:3 Green, W. Curtis. "Recent Decoration at the Roman Catholic Cathedral, Westminster." AR 40 (July 1916): 7–12.

"An acknowledged authority of Byzantine art," Weir designed the Chapel of St. Andrew, which is described and
illustrated.

223:1 SCOTT, GEORGE GILBERT (1811-78)

Articled in 1827 to a London architect, James Edmeston, and worked for Peto and Grissel, builders, and for Henry Roberts before assisting Sampson Kempthorne. Scott practiced with William Bonython Moffatt (1812-87) and with John Oldrid Scott (1841-1913). George Scott had more than 975 commissions (see 223:13). For Scott's work at the University of Glasgow, see John Duncan Mackie, THE UNIVERSITY OF GLASGOW, 1954. Knighted, 1872. The HMC has correspondence in various collections. The V&A has some designs. See the Cockerell Collection at the RIBA (and 223:16). The RIBA has Moffatt's drawings and is preparing a catalog. Publications: ADDITIONAL CATHEDRALS, 1854; DESIGN FOR THE NEW LAW COURTS, 186?; GLEANINGS FROM WESTMINSTER ABBEY, 1861; LECTURES DELIVERED AT THE ROYAL ACADEMY, 1866?; LECTURES ON THE RISE AND DEVELOPMENT OF MEDIAEVAL ARCHITECTURE, 1879; ON THE CONSERVATION OF ANCIENT ARCHITECTURAL MONUMENTS AND REMAINS, 1864; PERSONAL AND PROFESSIONAL RECOLLECTIONS, 1879 (see 223:15, 16); A PLEA FOR THE FAITHFUL RESTORATION OF OUR ANCIENT CHURCHES, 1850; REMARKS ON SECULAR DOMESTIC ARCHITECTURE, 1857; THOUGHTS AND SUGGESTIONS ON THE ARTISTIC EDUCATION OF ARCHITECTS, 1864; A NATIONAL MEMORIAL TO HIS ROYAL HIGHNESS THE PRINCE CONSORT, 1873; and numerous articles on conservation and restoration. Obituaries: A 19 (1878): 193, 201-2, 209-11, 213; AA&BN 3 (1979): 117, 150-51; RIBAJ 1878-79, pp. 3, 193-208. David Cole is preparing a catalog of Scott's works. M.G. Broderick is working on a doctorial dissertation at Columbia University on Scott's ecclesiastical architecture; W.J. Hennessey is working on a doctoral dissertation at Columbia University on Scott's Albert Memorial, London; and P.C. Jamieson wrote an M.A. thesis in 1964 at the University of London entitled "St. Pancras Station: A Case History."

223:2 Addleshaw, G.W.O. "Architects, Sculptors, Designers and Craftsmen, 1770-1970, Whose Work Is to Be Seen in Chester Cathedral." AH 14 (1971): 74-112.

Detailed information on Scott's major contribution.

223:3 Begley, W.W. "Sir Gilbert Scott and the Nikolai Kirche of Hamburg." B 132 (17 July 1927): 964-65.

Begley gauges the importance of Scott's major commissions during the three phases of the Gothic revival. Scott won the competition for the Hamburg church in 1845.

223:4 Berbiers, John L. "The Planned Villages of Halifax." B 211 (15 July 1966): 79-80.

Akroyden and its 350 dwellings were planned by Scott and his pupil W.H. Crossland. The plan was amended and illustrated in James Hole's THE HOUSES OF THE WORKING CLASSES, 1866.

223:5 Briggs, Martin Shaw. "Sir Gilbert Scott, RA." AR 24 (August, September, October, December 1908): 92-100, 147-52, 180-85, 290-95.

The four installments of this article are subtitled "Early Days," "The Cathedral Builder: The Flowing Tide, 1846-1856," "The Great Competitions," and "The Last Decade."

223:6 Burden, Alfred W.N. "Sir George Gilbert Scott." AAN 17 (February 1902): 17-19.

Scott's background, choice of architectural style, travel, and major works are assessed by his one-time pupil and assistant.

223:7 Cole, David. "Some Early Works of George Gilbert Scott." AAJ 66 (December 1950): 98-108.

Most of these works are in the south of England.

223:8 Ferriday, Peter. "The Grandest Folly of Them All: The Architecture of St. Pancras Station and Hotel." CL 138 (18 November 1965): 1314-17.

Scott won the limited competition (of eleven architects) in 1865 and provided a larger, taller, more expensive hotel than was anticipated. It was opened in 1873 and closed in the 1930s.

223:9 Girouard, Mark. "Kelham Hall, Nottinghamshire." CL 141 (18, 25 May 1967): 1230-33, 1302-5.

Kelham Hall burned in 1857 and Scott used the commission to rebuild as an "opportunity to design his most important country house, and erect a prototype for the St. Pancras Hotel." The plan illustrated on p. 1232 is based upon one drawn by Scott. The second half of the article illustrates some of the fine interiors.

223:10 Handley-Read, Charles. "The Albert Memorial Re-Assessed." CL 130 (14 December 1961): 1514-16.

Prince Albert died one hundred years to the day previous to this issue of CL. After his death "began a decade of intense effort to honour the Prince" in a memorial.

Handley-Read quotes from the range of opinions provoked
by the memorial over the years, from those who thought it
"the finest monumental structure in Europe," to others who
considered that this "confection of gingerbread . . . aught
to be under a glass shade on a giant's mantelpiece."

223:11 Handley-Read, Lavinia. "Legacy of a Vanished Empire: The Design
of the India Office." CL 148 (9 July 1970): 110-12.

Scott situated the India Office in the southwestern corner
of his design for the Foreign Office, Whitehall, but Matthew
Digby Wyatt was responsible for the initial concept, the
interiors, and a courtyard. The building relies for inspiration on Early Renaissance Italy and is adorned with sculp-
tured reliefs.

223:12 Hearn, M.F. "On the Original Nave of Ripon Cathedral." BRITISH
ARCHAEOLOGICAL ASSOCIATION JOURNAL 35 (1972): 39-45.

Scott published an article, "Ripon Minster," in ARCHAE-
OLOGICAL JOURNAL 31 (1874): 310-18, in which he
illustrated in three drawings his reconstruction of the twelfth-
century nave and elevations. "His paper was composed primarily to describe and justify the restoration he had just
completed."

223:13 Roberts, H.V. Molesworth. "Sir George Gilbert Scott." RIBAJ 65
(April 1958): 207.

A statistical analysis of Scott's career. "The total number
of his architectural 'jobs' (new buildings, alterations and
restorations), by himself alone or in association with his
sons or others, appears to be 903; those by his early partnership Scott and Moffatt, number 72--total, 975! This
number includes unidentifiable places but excludes 21 that
may have been mere consultations." His practice, ca.
1834-78, lasted forty-four years, which means that his firm
prepared a design every two weeks, on average.

223:14 Rowan, Alistair. "Eastnor Castle, Herefordshire." CL 143 (7, 14,
21 March 1968): 524-27, 606-9, 668-71.

Smirke was the architect of the castle as described and illustrated in the first two installments of this article. Scott
designed most of the castle's Victorian interiors while others
were designed by A.W.N. Pugin, and ca. 1866 George E.
Fox added a Renaissance revival library. Scott's sketch of
the central hall is illustrated.

223:15 Scott, G[eorge] Gilbert [, Jr.], ed. PERSONAL AND PROFESSIONAL
RECOLLECTIONS BY THE LATE SIR GEORGE GILBERT SCOTT, RA.
London: Sampson Low, Marston, Searle and Rivington, 1879. 436 p.

> "Designed originally for the information of his family,"
> these recollections are placed "before the public fairly and
> honourably." All aspects of Scott's life and work are cov-
> ered. See also 224:1-3.

223:16 Stamp, Gavin. "Sir Gilbert Scott's Recollections." AH 19 (1976):
54-73.

> The five-volume manuscript of Scott's RECOLLECTIONS
> (223:15) was given to the RIBA in 1974. Begun in 1864,
> it was the first autobiography of a British architect. This
> article provides commentary and explanations.

224:1 SCOTT, GEORGE GILBERT, JR. (1837-97)

Eldest son of George Gilbert Scott. Publications: HISTORY OF
ENGLISH CHURCH ARCHITECTURE, 1881; edited: PERSONAL AND
PROFESSIONAL RECOLLECTIONS, 1879 (see 223:15). E.T. Long is
researching his work. For the RIBA's collection of Scott's papers, see
224:3; the RIBA is preparing a catalog.

224:2 Millard, Walter. Notes on Some Works of the Late Geo. Gilbert
Scott . . . The Younger." AR 5 (December 1898-May 1899): 58-
66, 124-32.

> Scott's ecclesiastical architecture is illustrated and discussed.
> "In any work of art it is the actual human interest that
> really touches us, apart from all consideration as to what
> so called style or period the thing may be said to be de-
> signed in."

224:3 NRA. DESCRIPTION OF THE PAPERS OF GEORGE GILBERT SCOTT,
JUNIOR, DEPOSITED AT THE ROYAL INSTITUTE OF BRITISH ARCHI-
TECTS. London: HMC, 1973. 16 p.

> A listing of Scott's office papers. The RIBA also owns a
> number of drawings.

225:1 SCOTT, GILES GILBERT (1880-1960)

Second son of George Gilbert Scott, Jr. Articled to Temple Lushington Moore and began practice in 1903. Obituaries: AAJ 75 (May
1960): 230-31; AR 127 (April 1960): 227, 424-26; B 198 (19

February 1960): 345-46, 360; RIBAJ 67 (March 1960): 149, (April 1960): 221-22. For his restoration work at the Houses of Parliament, see Maurice Hastings, PARLIAMENT HOUSE: THE CHAMBER OF THE HOUSE OF COMMONS, 1950. The RIBA is preparing a·catalog of the Scott family including Giles Gilbert Scott.

225:2 Cambridge University Library. CAMBRIDGE UNIVERSITY LIBRARY, 1400-1934. Cambridge: 1934. 15 p.

Issued upon the opening of the new building by George V, 22 October 1934; the building was erected with the help of the Rockefeller Foundation.

225:3 Bagenal, Hope. "The Cathedral Church of Christ Liverpool." AR 50 (26 July 1921): 13-26.

The article is illustrated by numerous drawings and complementary photographs of the construction in progress, including views of the external surfaces of the vaulting, rarely seen when a structure is completed.

225:4 Birnstingl, H.G. "The Liverpool Cathedral." AF 44 (May 1926): 281-88.

A history and costing of Liverpool Cathedral. "A visible testimony of the fundamental nobility of mankind; an expression, as magnificent as any that he has ever erected, to his faith."

225:5 Budden, Lionel B[ailey]. "Liverpool Cathedral." AJ 60 (10 September 1924): 371-91.

"It may be advisable once again briefly to indicate its situation and the disposition of its main elements."

225:6 Burdett, Osbert. "Our Greatest Memorial Building." AJ 65 (22 June 1927): 897-904.

The new Charterhouse Chapel, Godalming, Surrey, was consecrated 18 June 1927. Its style is Gothic.

225:7 Clist, Hubert. "Some Notes on the Charterhouse Memorial Chapel." A&BN 116 (23 July 1926): 101.

"What a pity it is that Sir Giles Scott did not design all the school buildings at Charterhouse."

225:8 Cotton, Vere E. LIVERPOOL CATHEDRAL: THE OFFICIAL HANDBOOK OF THE CATHEDRAL COMMITTEE. Liverpool: Littlebury Bros., 1924. 150 p.

A history and detailed description of all aspects of the cathedral, including its furnishings and decoration, both interior and exterior. This publication is very similar to another work by Cotton, THE BOOK OF LIVERPOOL CATHEDRAL, Liverpool: University Press, 1964. 221 p. In the latter, Cotton differentiates between the cathedral as designed and won in competition by Scott and its continuously changing structure, which has been built over a sixty-year period.

225:9 _____. "Liverpool Cathedral: The Progress of the Building." CL 84 (13 August 1938): 156-59.

In 1938 the tower and central crossing were approaching completion.

225:10 Dorsfield, Wilberforce. "The Cathedral Church of Liverpool." AREC 31 (January 1912): 27-43.

Description, with interesting photographs of work in progress, drawings, and plan.

225:11 Dougill, Wesley. "Liverpool's Two Cathedrals." B 154 (14 January 1938): 54-58.

Begun in 1904, the Anglican cathedral had, by 1925, another section near completion. The building's progress and labor force are mentioned.

225:12 Goodhart-Rendel, H.S. "The New Chamber." A&BN 181 (12 January 1945): 19-21.

The old decoration of the demolished House of Commons was "lifeless and uninteresting." Scott proposed to change all that and, additionally, to introduce air conditioning.

225:13 Green, Arthur. "The Erection of the Liverpool Cathedral." ARCHITECTS' AND BUILDERS' JOURNAL 35 (7, 21 February 1912): 143-46, 194-98.

"A practical account of the erection of Liverpool Cathedral, describing in detail exactly those items in which the architect and the builder are most interested."

225:14 Hastings, J.M. "The Traditional Seating in the House of Commons." AR 97 (February 1945): 34-38.

After the destruction of the House of Commons in a bombing raid, it was decided that the traditional seating had been of sufficient symbolic importance to be identically replaced.

225:15 Hastings, Maurice. "The House of Commons." AR 108 (September 1950): 161-81.

The precedents for the internal arrangement of the House of Commons are both traditional and historical, as well as the basis of the British type of democracy. Why change it?

225:16 Little, Bryan. "Sir Giles Gilbert Scott." A&BN 217 (20 April 1960): 511-16.

"An appreciation of this well known architect illustrated with a cross section of his work."

225:17 Marriott, Basil. "Coronation Decorations: Sir Giles Scott's Designs for the City." B 184 (9 January 1953): 89.

These decorations consisted of suspended and attached forms.

225:18 Oswald, Arthur. "The Guildhall Restored." CL 116 (23 December 1954): 2246-48.

The third roof of the fifteenth-century Guildhall, London, was designed by Horace Jones, the city architect, in 1865. After this roof was destroyed in 1940, a fourth roof was added by Scott in the 1950s.

225:19 Reilly, C[harles] H[erbert]. "Liverpool Cathedral: The Second Section." AJ 71 (26 February 1930): 352-54.

Building progress was faster than expected. The south porch is described as useless.

225:20 _____. "The Work of Sir Giles Gilbert Scott, RA." AJ 61 (7 January 1925): 13-35.

"Giles Gilbert Scott with the Liverpool Cathedral competition became at once one of the most important and certainly the most interesting figure in English architecture." His work is surveyed and illustrated.

225:21 Worthington, Hubert. "Sir Giles Gilbert Scott: An Appreciation." RIBAJ 67 (April 1960): 193-94.

Brief outline of his life with an emphasis on Liverpool Cathedral.

226:1 SCOTT, MACKAY HUGH BAILLIE (1865-1945)

Practice began in 1889. Publications: HOUSES AND GARDENS,

1906 (see 226:5); with Raymond Unwin contributed to TOWN PLAN-
NING AND MODERN ARCHITECTURE AT THE HAMPSTEAD GARDEN
SUBURB, 1909. The RIBA has drawings. Obituary: RIBAJ 52
(March 1945): 143.

226:2 Betjeman, John. "Baillie Scott and the 'Architecture of Escape.'"
LONDON STUDIO 116 (October 1938): 177-80.

Betjeman states: "How proud is the possessor of early numbers of the STUDIO. . . . Baillie Scott has continued on
in the old early STUDIO tradition." Betjeman explains and
illustrates his viewpoint.

226:3 _____. "M.H. Baillie Scott, FRIBA." STUDIO 130 (July 1945):
17.

His "designs were like himself, modest and countrified."
An appreciation of his work.

226:4 Kornwolf, James D. M.H. BAILLIE SCOTT AND THE ARTS AND
CRAFTS MOVEMENT. Baltimore and London: Johns Hopkins Press,
1972. 588 p.

Although relying on British gothicists and proponents of the
arts-and-crafts tradition, Scott's planning and internal space-
relationships are more akin to late nineteenth-century American architecture. An extensive listing of over three hundred of his designs.

226:5 Scott, Mackay Hugh Baillie. HOUSES AND GARDENS. London:
George Newnes, 1906. 417 p.

Each chapter considers another of the various interior and
exterior elements of the house. All illustrations are of
Scott's own work; some reproductions are of watercolors.

226:6 Taylor, Nicholas. "Baillie Scott's Waldbuhl." AR 138 (December
1965): 456-58.

Waldbuhl, Uzwil, Switzerland, was designed from 1909 to
1911. The interiors of this timber structure illustrate "Scott's
distinctive genius."

227:1 SCOTT, MICHAEL (1905-)

Worked for Jones and Kelly, 1923-27, and has practiced since 1929.
RIBA gold medalist, 1974.

227:2 Atkinson, Fello. "Miesian in Eire: Tobacco Factory and Offices, Dundalk, Co. Louth, Ireland." AR 149 (January 1971): 45-54.

> The factory owner-clients were sympathetic with Mies van der Rohe's aesthetics after their round-the-world trip, including a one-night stopover in Chicago, visiting factory buildings. In Scott's design the administrative area has been integrated into the production floor. Scott and Partners did not use services consultants "but employed their own engineering staff. The neatness achieved is of course an important part of what one must call the Miesian idiom."

227:3 Gibney, Arthur. "No Rat-Race in Dublin." RIBAJ 73 (September 1966): 409-16.

> Ireland was late in accepting the modern movement but "anyone, certainly any stranger in Ireland, confronted by, say, Scott and Partners' church at Knockanure, or by the television studios at Donnybrook, would be pardoned for wondering if he was in Ireland at all."

227:4 Irish Times. In WHO'S WHO, WHAT'S WHAT, AND WHERE IN IRE-LAND, p. 321. London and Dublin: Geoffrey Chapman, 1973.

> Scott and his partners seem to be the only contemporary architects listed in this reference work. Their buildings and backgrounds are listed.

227:5 Jordan, R. Furneaux. "Television Centre, Dublin." AR 133 (February 1963): 102-7.

> A foursquare building, two stories high, surrounding a core of studio space. The ground floor includes loading and workshop areas and the upper floor accommodates offices. It is Miesian in spirit.

227:6 Tallon, Ronald. "Knockanure Church." In WORLD ARCHITECTURE II, edited by John Donat, pp. 74-81. New York: Viking Press, 1965.

> The people of the parish had to give approval for this church, which is described and illustrated.

227:7 Wharton, Kate. "Talking to Michael Scott." A 1 (February 1971): 33.

> Scott feels that "buildings all over the world are bad," not only in Ireland.

228:1 SEDDING, JOHN DANDO (1838-91)

Articled to G.E. Street, 1858-65; practiced with his brother Edmund

Sedding (1836-1868) and in London, beginning in 1875. Publications: GARDEN CRAFT: OLD AND NEW, 1891; ART AND HANDICRAFT, 1893. The RIBA has sketchbooks and drawings. Obituary: RIBAJ 1891-92, pp. 109-10.

228:2 Cooper, J. Paul, and Wilson, Henry. "The Work of John D. Sedding." AR 3 (1897-98): 35-41, 69-77, 125-33, 188-94, 235-42, 197-98; 4 (1898): 33-36. Reprinted in EDWARDIAN ARCHITECTURE AND ITS ORIGINS, edited by Alastair Service, pp. 258-79. London: Architectural Press, 1975.

Cooper was a pupil of Sedding, and Wilson was Sedding's partner. They wrote this article six years after Sedding's death, illustrating the type of Gothic structure with its arts-and-crafts flavoring, that was built in the 1880s.

228:3 Cram, Ralph Adams. "John D. Sedding: Some Considerations of His Life and Genius." ARCHITECTURAL REVIEW (Boston) 1 (1891): 9-11.

Sedding is placed on the Gothic-revival podium with Pugin and Street. He linked the Gothic spirit with Christian civilization.

228:4 Morris, James A. "Attainable Ideals." AR 6 (June-December 1899): 98-105, 146-53.

Working drawings of church fitments and some of Sedding's pen and ink drawings are used by Morris to lecture young architects "on the spirit and pursuit of our art."

228:5 Pite, [Arthur] Beresford. "A Review of the Tendencies of the Modern School of Architecture: The Influence of J.D. Sedding." RIBAJ 8 (1900-1901): 85-87.

"He had literary and poetic instinct as well as training and experience in the best Gothic of the late Revival period coupled with marked originality and freshness of design."

228:6 Roberts, H.V. Molesworth. "John Dando Sedding (1838-91)." B 184 (9 January 1953): 87-88.

Reference is made to three objects designed by Sedding and displayed in an exhibition of Victorian and Edwardian decorative arts at the V&A.

228:7 _____. "Notes on Some English Architects." BLACKMANSBURY 7

(February and April 1970): 9-25.

"Even where the Gothic precedent was more or less followed, a new vision of its possibilities seems to have been
caught--see J.D. Sedding's St. Peter's, Ealing, [London]."

229:1 SEDDON, JOHN POLLARD (1827-1906)

Articled in 1847 to Thomas Leverton Donaldson and practiced during
1852-62 with John Prichard. The V&A has furniture designs. Publi-
cations: ANCIENT EXAMPLES OF DOMESTIC ARCHITECTURE IN THE
ISLE OF THANET, 1872; KING RENE'S HONEYMOON CABINET,
1896; MEMOIRS AND LETTERS OF THE LATE THOMAS SEDDON, AR-
TIST, 1858; PROGRESS IN ART AND ARCHITECTURE, 1852; RAMBLES
IN THE RHINE PROVINCES, 1868. Obituaries: B 90 (1906): 150;
BN 90 (1906): 203; RIBAJ 13 (1905-6): 194, 221. The RIBA has
drawings. J. Symonds is writing a Ph.M. thesis at the University of
London on Seddon.

229:2 Pevsner, Nikolaus. "A Byzantine in Herefordshire." CL 142 (21
September 1967): 672.

Structural defects, damp, and decay are playing havoc with
this Byzantine-inspired church at Hoarwithy, Herefordshire.

230:1 SEIFERT, RICHARD (1911-)

Educated at the University of London, began practice in 1934, and
continued practice after the war.

230:2 Haddock, Mary. "Architects and Their Offices." B 212 (10 February 1967): 94-96.

The office has an informal air with none of the high-powered
organization associated with such a large concern.

230:3 Huxtable, Ada Louise. "London's New Buildings Are Closer to Miami."
NEW YORK TIMES, 12 June 1971, pp. 31, 58.

The firm Richard Seifert and Partners is building many of
the new London skyscrapers in a pop-art style and, in so
doing, are making London look more like the worst of the
United States.

231:1 SELLARS, JAMES (1843-88)

Apprenticed to Hugh Barclay, 1857-64, and to James Hamilton, 1864-

67; in 1870 joined Campbell Douglas, who made him a partner the following year.

231:2　Keppie, John. "The Late James Sellars, Architect, Glasgow." SCOTTISH ART REVIEW 1 (1888): 191-93.

"Throughout Scotland a widespread feeling of regret. There is no architect north of the Tweed whose work is better known or more appreciated." His major projects are illustrated and described.

231:3　Walker, David M. "James Sellars, Architect, Glasgow." SCOTTISH ART REVIEW 11, no. 1 (1967): 16-19.

Sellars continued in the earlier classical tradition of Alexander Thomson. His background, early career, and major works are discussed.

232:1　SHARPE, EDMUND (1809-77)

Articled to Thomas Rickman, 1836, and partnered with Edwin Graham Paley (1823-95), 1841-51. RIBA gold medalist, 1875. Publications: AN ACCOUNT OF THE CHURCHES VISITED DURING THE LINCOLN EXCURSION OF THE ARCHITECTURAL ASSOCIATION, 1871; THE ARCHITECTURAL HISTORY OF ST. MARY'S CHURCH, NEW SHORE-HAM, 1861; ARCHITECTURAL PARALLELS, 1848; THE CHURCHES OF THE NENE VALLEY, NORTHAMPTONSHIRE, 1880; DECORATED WINDOWS, 1849; THE MOULDINGS OF THE SIX PERIODS OF BRITISH ARCHITECTURE, 1871; THE ORNAMENTATION OF THE TRANSITIONAL PERIOD OF BRITISH ARCHITECTURE, 1877; THE SEVEN PERIODS OF ENGLISH ARCHITECTURE, 1851; SUPPLEMENTAL SKETCHES OF THE COLLECTIVE ARCHITECTURAL HISTORY OF CHICHESTER CATHEDRAL, 1861; A TREATISE ON THE RISE AND PROGRESS OF DECORATED WINDOW TRACERY IN ENGLAND, 1849; A VISIT TO THE DOMED CHURCHES OF CHARENTE, FRANCE, 188?. The RIBA has drawings. Obituaries: AA&BN 2 (9 June 1877): 177-78; B 35 (19 May 1877): 491-93; (26 May): 521; (2 June 1877): 550, 562; BN 22 (1877): 484; RIBAJ 1877-78, pp. 8-9. Robert Jolley wrote an M. Arch. thesis, "The Work of Edmund Sharpe, (1809-77)" at the University of Liverpool, 1966 (see 232:3). D. McLaughlin is researching the work of Paley, Sharpe and Hubert James Austin.

232:2　Jolley, Robert. "Edmund Sharpe and the 'Pot' Churches." AR 146 (December 1969): 426-31.

Sharpe utilized terra-cotta for the decoration of his churches because of its durability--it has a tradition going back thousands of years. However, he learned the characteristics of the material by trial and error. He countered arguments concerning mechanical repetition by stating that all his details were well thought-out.

232:3 _____. "Edmund Sharpe (1809-77): A Study of a Victorian Architect." M. Arch. thesis, University of Liverpool, 1966, copy in the RIBA Library. 300 p.

The life and career of a thorough-going gothicist.

233:1 SHAW, JOHN (1803-70)

A pupil of his father, John Shaw (1776-1832). Publication: A LETTER ON ECCLESIASTICAL ARCHITECTURE: AS APPLICABLE TO MODERN CHURCHES, 1839. The RIBA has a drawing of Eton College, Windsor, 1844. Obituary: B 28 (6 August 1870): 630.

233:2 Goodhart-Rendel, H.S. "Rogue Architects of the Victorian Era." A&BN 195 (22, 29 April 1949): 359-62, 381-84; RIBAJ 56 (April 1949): 251-59.

John, not [Richard] Norman Shaw is credited with the Queen Anne revival, which took place in the 1840s, not in the 1870s; however, the term "Queen Anne" must be taken in its broadest, nonderivative sense.

234:1 SHAW, RICHARD NORMAN (1831-1912)

Articled to William Burn starting ca. 1846, prior to study at the RAL. He assisted Salvin and Street and partnered with W.E. Nesfield (see 180:1), 1862-68. The V&A has drawings of Old Swan House, 48 Cadogan Square, London, and Bedford Park Estate, London. For the RIBA holdings, see 234:13-14; the RIBA drawings are extensive. Publications: ARCHITECTURAL SKETCHES FROM THE CONTINENT, 1858; ARCHITECTURE: A PROFESSION OR AN ART, 1892; SKETCHES FOR COTTAGES AND OTHER BUILDINGS, 1878. Obituaries: AIAJ 1 (1913): 137; AR (December 1912): 300-308, (234:12); RIBAJ 20 (1912-13): 55, 88. In 1966 D.J. Curry wrote an undergraduate architectural thesis, "Richard Norman Shaw In Northumberland," at the University of Newcastle; Andrew Saint is researching Shaw (see 234: 19).

234:2 Austin, Phyllis. "The Enchanted Circle." AR 133 (March 1963): 205-7.

Shaw designed numerous buildings in Britain's first planned garden suburb, Bedford Park, London, at the Turnham Green

Underground Station. Phyllis Austin, the daughter of a journalist, was born at Bedford Park.

234:3 Beattie, Susan. "New Scotland Yard." AH 15 (1972): 68-81.

Shaw's aim was "to erect an architectural monument for the police worthy of its purpose," to be designed "in the round, free from the facade emphasis that characterized much public building." This article is based upon Home Office papers in the Public Record Office, London.

234:4 Blomfield, Reginald Theodore. RICHARD NORMAN SHAW, RA., ARCHITECT, 1831-1912. London: B.T. Batsford, 1940. 115 p.

"To Shaw more than anyone is due the recovery of architecture from the dull conventions of the Victorian era . . . and advance[ment] the best . . . of the 18th century." A "List of Buildings Designed by . . .," 1866-1907, is on pp. 106-8.

234:5 Brandon-Jones, John. "The Work of Philip Webb and Norman Shaw." AAJ 71 (July-August 1955): 40-47, cover.

Brandon-Jones's interest in the origins of work by Lutyens led him to enquire into the work of Webb and Shaw. Their work is discussed and several plans and elevations of their buildings are reproduced. See also 268:5.

234:6 Falkner, Harold. "The Creator of 'Modern Queen Anne,' The Architecture of Norman Shaw." CL 89 (15 March 1941): 232-35.

An appreciation of Shaw's value as an architect-originator after 1872 echoing Blomfield's opinion in his biography of Shaw (234:4).

234:7 Girouard, Mark. "Adcote, Shropshire." CL 148 (22 October 1970): 1056-59.

"Adcote is the most controlled, coherent, and masterly of the big country houses designed by Norman Shaw." Its interiors, exteriors, and plan are illustrated.

234:8 _____. "Craigside, Northumberland." CL 146 (18, 25 December 1969): 1640-43, 1694-97.

This huge, sprawling, rambling house, built in 1870-83, "expresses the quintessence of late Victorian romanticism" and "nicely demonstrates the development of [Shaw's] style as he became the favoured architect of the Victorian industrialist at home." The house was built piecemeal on an awkward site. Exteriors are illustrated in the first segment of the article and interiors in the second.

234:9 _____. "The Victorian Artist at Home." CL 152 (16 November 1972): 1278-81.

Shaw designed houses for several artists--Luke Fildes and Marcus Stone (on Melbury Road, London, 1875) and George Houghton (Campden Hill, London, 1877).

234:10 Greeves, T. Affleck. "London's First Garden Suburb: Bedford Park, Chiswick." CL 142 (7, 14 December 1967): 1524-29, 1600-1602.

Shaw designed numerous buildings--houses, church, and inn (illustrated here in drawings and photographs)--for this speculative garden suburb.

234:11 Hussey, Christopher. "180, Queen's Gate, London." CL 120 (30 August 1956): 424-27.

The interior decoration and furniture of this residence of 1883 by Shaw are by William Morris and J.E. Millais.

234:12 Keen, Arthur. "Some Personal Reminiscences of Norman Shaw." AR 32 (December 1912): 300-308.

Keen worked for Shaw and recounts Shaw's approach to design and methods of working. Several buildings are illustrated and discussed.

234:13 NRA. KEEN/SHAW CORRESPONDENCE. London: HMC, 1970. 3 p.

Arthur Keen presented this correspondence of 1878-96 to the RIBA.

234:14 _____. R. NORMAN SHAW MSS. London: HMC, n.d. 6 p.

Lists papers owned by the RIBA.

234:15 Newton, William G. "Sir Reginald Blomfield's Life of Norman Shaw: A Review." RIBAJ 48 (February 1941): 61-62.

"Sir Reginald's reading of Shaw's development is that all his life he was working his way to the 'monumental classic, the goal of his ambition, which he never quite reached.'"

234:16 Pevsner, Nikolaus. "Richard Norman Shaw." AR 99 (March 1941): 41-46. Reprinted in EDWARDIAN ARCHITECTURE AND IT ORIGINS, edited by Alastair Service, pp. 40-54. London: Architectural Press, 1975.

> Shaw's variety of styles produced a wide range of individual and pioneering buildings. His career is outlined and his developments, with relation to his major contemporaries, are discussed.

234:17 Pite, [Arthur] Beresford. "A Review of the Tendencies of the Modern School of Architecture: The School of Mr. Norman Shaw and of Mr. Bodley." RIBAJ 8 (1900-1901): 90-91.

> Shaw's later phase of the Gothic revival evolved into the modern school of Mr. Bodley.

234:18 Ricardo, Halsey. "Parr's Bank, Liverpool." AR 10 (September 1901): 146-55.

> An appreciation and description, with plans, sections, elevations, and photographs of inside and out.

234:19 Saint, Andrew. RICHARD NORMAN SHAW. New Haven and London: Yale University Press, 1976. 291 p.

> The publisher's announcement states: "In this fully documented and illustrated biography of Shaw, Andrew Saint captures the charm and individuality of Shaw's personality, vividly narrated his long and varied career, and set it into the fast changing architectural context of the time."

234:20 Sturges, W. Knight. "The Long Shadow of Norman Shaw." JSAH 9 (December 1950): 15-20.

> "This article investigates the remarkable confluence of the ideas of Norman Shaw with reviving colonialism in this country [United States] during the 1870's and '80's."

234:21 Williams, John H.H. "Revelations in Vintage Concrete." CONCRETE 6 (November 1972): 30-34.

> Shaw used concrete in several projects, including his design for No. 8 Lloyds Avenue, London, 1908, where he employed the Kahn System introduced from the United States.

234:22 Wight, M. "A Vanished House By Norman Shaw." CL 146 (13 November 1969): 1249.

> Illustrating Preen Manor, Shropshire, this article notes that this and many other Shaw buildings were demolished after the First World War.

235:1 SHEPPARD, RICHARD HERBERT (1911-)

Trained at the AAL and began practice in 1938, later practicing with
Geoffrey Robson (1918-   ). Publications: BUILDING FOR DAY-
LIGHT, 1948; BUILDING FOR PEOPLE, 1948; CAST IRON IN BUILD-
ING, 1945; PREFABRICATION IN BUILDING, 1946.

235:2 Banham, Reyner. "Criticism." AR 136 (September 1964): 174-79.

An analysis comparing Arne Jacobsen's St. Catherine's College, Oxford, "built almost exactly [as] his original architectural vision" intended, to Churchill College, Cambridge.
"Churchill admits very little to the first sweep of the eye,
and demands intensive exploration before planning methods
or architectural intentions become as clear." The dining
hall of the latter is too heroic, the entrance too impressive,
and the whole "informal but grand."

235:3 Jordan, Robert Furneaux. "Churchill Memorial College." A&BN
216 (12, 19 August 1959): 2-4, 52-58.

Discussion of what a college should be is followed by a
brief statement about the Sheppard scheme (not illustrated),
including its costs. The second part of the article illustrates other noteworthy entries in the competition. See
also E13.

235:4 Webb, Michael. "Massive Simplicity beside the Cam." CL 138
(25 November 1965): 1394-97.

"The architecture well reflects the mood of the 1960's and
must command respect for the soundness of its [Churchill
College] planning and construction."

236:1 SIMPSON, ARCHIBALD (1790-1847)

Obituary: B 5 (8 May 1847): 217. R.S. Smith is researching
Simpson's work in Aberdeen.

236:2 RIAS. THE ARCHIBALD SIMPSON CENTENARY CELEBRATIONS, 9TH
MAY 1947. Edinburgh: 1947. 21 p.

With a list of his works on pp. 17-18, this exhibition catalog spans the years 1811-46.

237:1 SKIDMORE, OWINGS AND MERRILL (Partnership 1939-)

See Wodehouse, Lawrence. AMERICAN ARCHITECTS FROM THE FIRST

WORLD WAR TO THE PRESENT. Detroit: Gale Research Co., 1977.

237:2 Richards, J.M. "Administration and Research Building, Hayes Park, Middlesex." AR 138 (August 1965): 109-16.

>The Heinz Company has a clean-cut building in England for which Richards has high praise although he questions its function and aesthetics.

238:1 SMIRKE, ROBERT (1781-1867)

>A pupil for a short period of 1796 (the same year in which he entered the RAL) of John Soane. Began practice in 1806. RIBA gold medalist, 1853. The RIBA has letters in the Smirke and Cockerell Collections, 1801-3, and twenty-three drawings and sketch books. See also 238:9. The BM has correspondence. The V&A has drawings of the General Post Office, St. Martin le Grand, London. Smirke illustrated several books. Publications: REMAINS OF TWO TEMPLES AND OTHER ROMAN ANTIQUITIES DISCOVERED AT BATH, 1802; SPECIMENS OF CONTINENTAL ARCHITECTURE, 1806. Obituaries: B 25 (1867): 287, 335, 604-6; RIBAJ 1866-67, pp. 197-207. J. Mordaunt Crook wrote a doctoral dissertation, "The Career of Sir Robert Smirke, RA," at Oxford University, in 1958 according to A46, 1961 according to A91.

238:2 Chancellor, E[dwin] Beresford. "Sir Robert Smirke." AJ 54 (21 September 1921): 337-41.

>Concerns his major buildings in London.

238:3 Collingwood, Frances. "Robert Smirke (1781-1867)." B 212 (14 April 1967): 92.

>At the centennial of Smirke's death, Collingwood reassesses him as the leading architect of his age. He was a logical choice for major buildings because of his technical know-how, caution, and conventionality.

238:4 Colvin, Howard. "The Architect of Stafford House." AH 1 (1958): 17-30.

>Three architects--Smirke, Benjamin Wyatt, and Barry--worked on Stafford House, London, but who did what? The discovery of a book of some of the correspondence has solved this problem. Smirke was the first employed and the building was begun according to his plan. When the duke of York's family objected to the design, Wyatt was brought in,

whereupon Smirke ordered the building-work stopped. Wyatt
was then accused of infringing the rules of the Architects'
Club. Barry succeeded Wyatt and altered a roof lantern,
but it is not possible to estimate his other involvement.

238:5 Cornforth, John. "Bowood, Wiltshire, Revisited." CL 151 (8, 15,
22 June 1972): 1448-51, 1546-50, 1610-13.

In the third installment of this article, a drawing dated
1823 illustrates Smirke's work at Bowood, 1817-18.

238:6 _____. "Normanby Park, Lincolnshire." CL 130 (17 August 1961):
346-49.

The house of 1825-30 was designed for the same family that
has inhabited Normanby since 1590. Some interiors were
altered in 1905-7.

238:7 _____. "Stafford House Revisited." CL 144 (7, 14 November
1968): 1188-91, 1257-61.

Smirke was executant architect at Stafford (now Lancaster)
House of the work designed 1827-38, by Benjamin Dean
Wyatt.

238:8 Crook, J. Mordaunt. "Architect of the Rectangular: A Reassessment
of Sir Robert Smirke." CL 141 (13 April 1967): 846-48.

An assessment at the centennial of Smirke's death: "the
quality of his work suffered from over-production."

238:9 _____. "Sir Robert Smirke: A Centenary Florilegium." AR 142
(September 1967): 208-10.

The RIBA owns Smirke's manuscripts, including a treatise on
architectural elements, style, and personalities.

238:10 _____. "Sir Robert Smirke: A Pioneer of Concrete Construction."
NEWCOMEN SOCIETY TRANSACTIONS 38 (1965-66): 5-22, pls.
5-9.

A consideration of attitudes toward the use of concrete construction and its use by Smirke in piles, foundations, and
the like.

238:11 Hussey, Christopher. "Burton Park, Sussex." CL 80 (11 July 1936):
38-43.

Built in 1828, Burton Park is the third house on this particular site.

238:12 Kendrick, Thomas. "The British Museum, 1753–1953." CL 113 (11 June 1953): 1876–78.

> Primarily a survey of the workings of the museum, with only a brief note on Smirke's work, 1823–52.

238:13 Liscombe, Rhodri. "Economy, Character and Durability: Specimen Designs for the Church Commissioners." AH 13 (1970): 43–57.

> Smirke submitted six church designs, which have recently come to light, to the Office of Works. The source of his inspiration and his attitude toward the design of economical religious buildings are discussed.

238:14 Nares, Gordon. "The Royal College of Physicians." CL 113 (27 March 1953): 906–9.

> A background history of this famed institution. Its library and portraits in its fourth home, designed by Smirke in 1828, are presented.

238:15 Pevsner, Nikolaus. "British Museum: Some Unsolved Problems of Its Architectural History." AR 113 (March 1953): 179–82.

> Pevsner considers the sources of Smirke's inspiration and compares the museum to similar structures in Britain and elsewhere.

238:16 Ramsey, Stanley C. "London Clubs." AR 35 (May 1914): 115–18.

> Ninth in a series of articles on London's clubs, this article discusses Smirke's Union Club, 1822.

238:17 Rowan, Alistair. "Eastnor Castle, Herefordshire." CL 143 (7, 14, 21 March 1968): 524–27, 606–9, 668–71.

> An earlier house was demolished and Smirke built the present Eastnor, 1811–20, in a castellated style. One of the drawings of the building, preserved at Eastnor, is illustrated in the second part of this article, which also includes interiors and a plan.

238:18 Smirke, Edward. "Memoir of the Late Sir Robert Smirke." RIBAJ 1866–67, pp. 197–207.

> Edward Smirke was Robert's brother and read this paper before the RIBA. It details his brother's travels, research, and professional life.

238:19 Stillman, Damie. "The Gallery for Lansdowne House: International

Neoclassical Architecture and Decoration in Microcosm." ART BUL-
LETIN 52 (March 1970): 75-80.

> Lansdowne House was designed by Robert Adam in the 1760s.
> Seven proposals for a gallery were submitted between 1760
> and 1819; Smirke's was built.

238:20 Stratton, Arthur. "Covent Garden." AR 41 (April and May 1917):
67-72, 99-104.

> Covent Garden's eighteenth-century theater burned down in
> 1808. Smirke's new building was opened the following
> year.

238:21 _____. "The Custom House, London." AR 42 (July 1917): 1-4.

> Smirke not only saved David Laing's Custom House, 1812,
> from sinking into the ground but ca. 1825 also remodeled
> the facades.

238:22 Watkin, D.J., ed. SALE CATALOGUES OF LIBRARIES OF EMINENT
PERSONS. London: Mansell Information/Publishing, 1972. In vol.
4, ARCHITECTS, pp. 223-38.

> "The original size of the collection remains a matter for
> speculation but what survived in 1868 suffices to indicate
> his sense of belonging to the French rather than the English
> classical tradition." Sale of 28 May 1868.

239:1 SMIRKE, SYDNEY (1798-1877)

Younger brother of Robert Smirke, in whose office he trained. RIBA
gold medalist, 1860. The RIBA has correspondence of 1824-26, in
the Robert Smirke and C.R. Cockerell collections and drawings. The
HMC has letters in various collections. Publications: A MODE OF
ASSISTING THE EYE IN THE RIGHT PERCEPTION OF COLOUR IN
PICTURES, 1856; SUGGESTIONS FOR THE ARCHITECTURAL IMPROVE-
MENT OF THE WEST PART OF LONDON, 1834. See Richard Hamilton Essex, ILLUSTRATIONS OF THE ARCHITECTURAL ORNAMENT
AND EMBELLISHMENTS AND PAINTED GLASS OF THE TEMPLE
CHURCH, LONDON: WITH AN ACCOUNT OF THE RECENT RES-
TORATION OF THE CHURCH BY SYDNEY SMIRKE, 1845. Obitu-
aries: AA&BN 2 (15 December 1877): 404; B 35 (15 December
1877): 1256; RIBAJ 1878-79, pp. 5-6. J. Mordaunt Crook has prepared an essay on Smirke for SEVEN VICTORIAN ARCHITECTS, edited
by Nikolaus Pevsner (see A37).

239:2 Collard, A.O. "The Late Sydney Smirke." 19 (1911-12): 609-11.

This account of the main events of his life reproduces the list of events in Smirke's career, 1855-87, that he had submitted in his application for the fellowship of the RIBA.

239:3 Hussey, Christopher. "Lambton Castle, Durham." CL 139 (24, 31 March 1966): 664-67, 726-29.

Lambton Castle was formerly known as Harraton Hall, which was rebuilt in the nineteenth century by Smirke according to plans prepared by John Dobson, 1862-65, and demolished in the 1930s.

239:4 Ramsey, Stanley C. "London Clubs." AR 35 (March 1914): 56-59.

Eighth in a series of articles on London clubs, this article discusses Smirke's collaboration with Basevi on the Conservative Club.

240:1 SMITH, GEORGE (1783-1869)

Entered the RAL, 1801, and worked for various architects before opening practice, ca. 1810. COLLECTION OF DESIGNS FOR HOUSEHOLD FURNITURE, 1808, was the first publication on neoclassical furniture and the break from the styles of Robert Adam.

240:2 Stratton, Arthur. "The Royal Exchange, London." AR 42 (August and September 1917): 26-29, 45-50.

Starting in 1816, Smith made alterations to this seventeenth-century building. It burned down in 1838.

241:1 SMITH, JAMES (1808-63)

Had an architect-builder's practice with his father, a builder, in Glasgow. Married David Hamilton's daughter and partnered with Hamilton's son James, 1843-44. Smith then partnered with John Baird (1816-93)--not, however, the John Baird of entry 14:1.

241:2 Worsdall, Francis. "Poor Mr. Smith." SCOTTISH FIELD 110 (December 1963): 50-51.

"It is the fate of some men to be remembered only as the father of their children. James Smith is one of these." Some of his works are listed.

242:1 SMITH, WILLIAM (fl. ca. 1850-1890)

Son of John Smith (1781-1852) of Aberdeen. One time city architect of Aberdeen. The HMC's Haddo House Collection has plans and elevations of Balmoral Castle, Aberdeenshire, of which he was architect after the death of his father.

242:2 Carter, Charles. "Balmoral through Artist's Eyes." CL 128 (25 August 1960): 366-68.

The article illustrates and explains why "Balmoral Castle has been a favourite subject with painters only during the last century."

242:3 Duff, David. VICTORIA IN THE HIGHLANDS: THE PERSONAL JOURNAL OF HER MAJESTY QUEEN VICTORIA. London: Frederick Muller, 1968. 398 p.

A complete account of the building of Balmoral; pp. 137-45 are particularly relevant.

242:4 Werner Company of Chicago. BEAUTIFUL BRITAIN: THE SCENERY AND THE SPLENDOURS OF THE UNITED KINGDOM. London: 1894. 192 p.

The foundation stone of Balmoral was laid in 1855, after the purchase of the property by the prince consort.

243:1 SMITHSON, PETER AND ALISON (Partnership ca. 1950)

Peter Denham Smithson (1923-   ) and his wife Alison Margaret Gill Smithson (1928-   ), both of whom studied at the University of Durham. Publications: ORDINARINESS AND LIGHT, 1970; TEAM 10 PRIMER, 1968; URBAN STRUCTURING, 1960; WITHOUT RHETORIC--AN ARCHITECTURAL AESTHETIC, 1955-1972, 1973, an explanation of the theories upon which their work is based. The RIBA has a large collection of their drawings.

243:2 Baker, Jeremy. "A Smithson File." ARENA 81 (February 1966): whole issue.

"Intended to be a definitive description of the Smithsons' work in their first forty years . . . all their published essays, competition entries and completed building designs . . . arranged in chronological order. All their unpublished works have been noted."

243:3 Banham, Reyner. "The New Brutalism." AR 118 (December 1955): 354-61.

"One cannot begin to study the New Brutalism without realizing how deeply the New Art-History has bitten into progressive English architectural thought." The Smithsons' school at Hunstanton, Norfolk, is mentioned in this broadly scoped article.

243:4 Eisenman, Peter. "Robin Hood Gardens, London E14." AD 42 (September 1972): 557-73, 588-92.

"The Smithsons' buildings are consigned forthwith to the mainstream of the modern movement; they are analysed as works of art in the heroic tradition." Special emphasis is given to Robin Hood Gardens.

244:1 SPENCE, BASIL URWIN (1907-76)

A pupil of Edwin Lutyens, Spence won the competition for Coventry Cathedral in 1951. Practiced as a member of Spence, Bonnington and Collins and of Spence, Glover and Ferguson. Publications: PHOENIX AT COVENTRY, 1962 (see 244:17); with Henk Snook, OUT OF THE ASHES: A PROGRESS THROUGH COVENTRY CATHEDRAL, 1963 (see 244:18). The RIBA has drawings of Coventry Cathedral. Obituaries include: BD 26 November 1976, p. 8; RIBAJ 84 (January 1977): 40-41.

244:2 Banham, Reyner. "Coventry Cathedral--Strictly 'Trad, Dad.'" AF 117 (August 1962): 118-19.

"There can be little doubt that Coventry Cathedral is the worst setback to English church architecture for a very long time." It is as traditional and establishment-ridden as the architectural jury that awarded it first premium.

244:3 Beaumont, J. Duncan, and Woods, Ian R.J. "Duncanrig, Secondary School at East Kilbride." PROSPECT 3 (Autumn 1956): 8.

Plans, photographs, and description.

244:4 Burford, James. "St. Michael's, Coventry: The Evolution of the New Cathedral Church." B 192 (11 January 1957): 56-57, 83.

It is traditional in that meaning has been given to the work through "human impact which gives life to dead forms [and] . . . empowers them . . . to accumulate and to pass on and re-create the emotion which went to their disposition and array." Changes in the design as it evolved are listed.

244:5 Collins, Peter. "The Lessons of Coventry Cathedral." RAICJ 39 (September 1962): 61-68.

Collins considers the controversy surrounding the building
with a note that at "the wish of Sir Basil Spence, the July
RIBAJ announced, it had been decided that Coventry Cathedral will not after all be the subject of an appraisal,"
in its own pages, Collins criticizes the cathedral point by
point.

244:6   Fifloot, E.R.S.   "Edinburgh University Library: The Consumer's View."
        EAAY   13 (1969):   112-13.

A library is compared to a department store and the differences are shown.

244:7   Girouard, Mark.   "Success and Failure at Coventry."   CL   131 (31
        May 1962):   1292-93.

Coventry Cathedral should be judged on how far it will, in
Spence's words, "turn a casual visitor into a worshipper."
The cathedral interior's failure to direct the visitor toward
its east end is "the most damaging criticism that can be
levelled against the building."   This argument is spelled
out in detail.

244:8   Glover, J. Hardie.   "Edinburgh University Library."   EAAY   13
        (1969):   103-11.

Arrangement, plan, structure, internal environment, furniture, and finishes are described and plans, photographs,
and a section are provided.

244:9   Hussey, Christopher.   "The Problem of Coventry Cathedral."   CL   110
        (14 September 1951):   810-11.

Is there a lack of "close-knit integrity between the ruins
and Spence's new design?   His aesthetic is to stress the
visual and commemorative significance of the bombed cathedral."   Sectional and detailed drawings and a perspective
view are illustrated.

244:10 Jordan, Robert Furneaux.   "Cathedral Church of St. Michael, Coven-
        try."   AR   132 (July 1962):   24-42.

Built during an awkward period in the history of architecture, Coventry Cathedral is neither modern nor, like Chartres,
splendorous.   It must therefore be judged in the context of
its period and in the spirit of the courageous intentions of
its designer.

244:11 _____.   "Coventry Cathedral."   STUDIO   164 (August 1962):   54-57.

"One can only feel astonishment when the big things are so right, that the blunders should be so childish and, one would think, foreseeable." Although its clear, etched-glass, west window allows one's eye to wander to distractions, its other aspects are praised.

244:12 Laird, Michael. "Two Scottish Churches." AJ 128 (18 September 1958): 408-10.

Clermiston Church, Edinburgh, by Spence is described and photographs of its interior and exterior are reproduced.

244:13 Morris, A.E.T. "Trawsfyndd Power Station." OA&P 32 (May 1969): 542-48.

"This appraisal is only briefly concerned with the rights and wrongs of locating such a massive group of buildings in outstandingly beautiful, relatively wild countryside." The program and siting of this successful building are described.

244:14 Richards, J.M. "Coventry." AR 111 (January 1952): 3-7.

The competition for a new cathedral at Coventry originally stipulated that the building had to be designed in the English Gothic style. This requirement was changed and Spence produced a contemporary design, but is it a good one?

244:15 Rock, Tim. "George Square: Town versus Gown in Edinburgh." AR 143 (June 1968): 433-44.

Spence produced his master plan for George Square (designed by James Brown in 1766) in 1954, and from the latter year until 1960, Edinburgh University, as landlord and developer, fought the Scottish National Trust for the right to demolish and rebuild. The fight created better architecture than might otherwise have been produced. The square, but not the scale of the original eighteenth-century buildings, has been preserved and the new scale has impinged upon the Edinburgh skyline from several vantage points. Spence's university library is critically analyzed and plans, sections, and photographs are provided.

244:16 Scott, Keith. "Coventry Cathedral Appraised." A&BN 221 (23 May 1962): 738-39, 749-58.

"Thank God that Basil Spence was moved to compete for had he not, one shudders to think of the building which might now confront us." A descriptive article sympathetic to the architect's sincerity and integrity.

244:17 Spence, Basil. PHOENIX AT COVENTRY: THE BUILDING OF A CATHEDRAL. London: Geoffrey Bles, 1962. 141 p.

Scene one begins on the beaches of Normandy, 1944, where, before going to sleep, Spence admitted to a mate that his ambition was "to build a cathedral." Scene two takes place in a dentist's chair six years later, when Spence passed out after being administered a local anesthetic. "My dream was wonderful . . . but I could not see the windows until I went right in and turned half back--the walls were zig-zagged!"

244:18 Spence, Basil, and Snook, Henk. OUT OF THE ASHES: A PROGRESS THROUGH COVENTRY CATHEDRAL. London: Geoffrey Bles, 1962. 141 p.

Spence "builds on the past, learns from the past, seeks to mould the past into a creative and courageous present." The cathedral is explained from its conception to completion.

244:19 Williams, H.C.N. COVENTRY CATHEDRAL. London: Hodder and Stoughton, 1966. 68 p.

Concerning the city, its ministry, and its new cathedral with its numerous significant works.

244:20 Wright, Lance. "Coventry Cathedral Six Years Later: An Analysis That Concludes with Success." AIAJ 50 (August 1968): 50-55.

Describing Coventry Cathedral as "an uplifting place to take a girl friend on a wet Sunday afternoon," Wright points out that tourists flock there in large numbers on sunny days too. "Coventry Cathedral is a building which stands firmly outside the evolutionary development of architecture."

244:21 Wright, Michael. "RIBA Architecture Awards 1968." RIBAJ 75 (September 1968): 407-13.

The 1968 award in Scotland was recommended for Spence's University of Edinburgh Library.

245:1 STEVENSON, JOHN JAMES (1831-1908)

A pupil of David Bryce, 1856-58 and of George Gilbert Scott, 1858-60, Stevenson worked for Campbell Douglas, 1860-69, and thereafter partnered with E.R. Robson (see 216-1). Publication: ARCHITECTURAL RESTORATION: ITS PRINCIPLES AND PRACTICE, 1877. The V&A has drawings of the Red House, Bayswater Hill, London. Obituary: RIBAJ 15 (1907-8): 455, 482.

245:2 Girouard, Mark. "Ken Hill, Norfolk." CL 142 (12, 26 December 1967): 1654-58, 1704-7.

Ken Hill and other designs by Stevenson in the style of the Queen Anne revival are described and illustrated; the origins of the style are also covered.

245:3 Macleod, Robert. In CHARLES RENNIE MACKINTOSH, pp. 15-16. London: Country Life, 1968.

"Stevenson recommended for Scotland the adoption of the Scottish Baronial style," as a vernacular expression linked to a regional area.

246:1 STILLMAN AND EASTWICK-FIELD (Partnership 1949-   )

John Cecil Stillman (1920-   ), John Charles Eastwick-Field (1919-   ), and Elizabeth Eastwick-Field (1919-   ). All trained at the University of London. J.C. Stillman and J.C. Eastwick-Field jointly authored THE DESIGN AND PRACTICE OF JOINERY, 1961.

246:2 Haddock, Mary. "Architects and Their Offices." B 212 (13 January 1967): 67-69.

Their offices and attitudes toward design, management, and facilities are described.

247:1 STIRLING, JAMES (1926-   )

Educated at the University of Liverpool, Stirling worked for Lyons, Israeli and Ellis prior to his partnership (1956-63) with James Gowan (1923-   ); Gowan trained at the AAL. See also A50. Stirling practiced independently from 1963 to 1967 and with Michael Wilford starting in 1971. The RIBA has drawings (see 247:3).

247:2 Banham, Reyner. "History Faculty, Cambridge." AR 144 (December 1968): 328-41.

Standardized details and industrialized components of the Engineering Building, University of Leicester, appear again at Cambridge. Banham defends the building against all criticism: if it was too hot in the building, it was because the heat was at full blast to dry the building out immediately after its completion. "There are bound to be complaints about lighting because it is a fashionable thing to complain about." The supporters of the building "were not in the market for either pseudo-jewel-casket like the Beinecke Library at Yale, nor a joke fortification like the new library at Trinity College, Dublin. . . . The History Faculty just has a lot of undergraduates and a lot of current literature."

247:3 _____. JAMES STIRLING. London: RIBA Publications, 1974. 96 p.

An exhibition catalog of material from the RIBA's drawing collection. Illustrated with numerous sketches, drawings, and photographs, the catalog also contains a lecture, an article, comments, and a list of projects, all by Stirling, articles by and about him, biographical information, and a list of his lecture visits.

247:4 Boyarsky, Alvin. "Stirling 'Dimostrationi.'" AD 38 (October 1968): 454-78.

"It has fallen to James Stirling to express the revolutionary intentions of a new generation in the medium of hard building." Nikolaus Pevsner terms Stirling's architecture "violent self-expression" and thereby rejects it in preference for the simplicity of past nonexpression. The History Faculty Building, Cambridge University, and the Florey Building, Queen's College, Oxford University, are well illustrated and thoroughly analyzed.

247:5 Frampton, Kenneth. "Information Bank." AF 129 (November 1968): 36-47.

Mainly a visual presentation of the History Faculty Building, Cambridge, plus a general appraisal of Stirling's work.

247:6 Futagawa, Y. LEICESTER ENGINEERING DEPARTMENT, CAMBRIDGE HISTORY FACULTY. Tokyo: Global Architecture, 1971. 48 p.

Japanese text but superb color photography, not only in this volume, but in all volumes in the series illustrating modern buildings.

247:7 Jacobus, John. "Engineering Building, Leicester University." AR 135 (April 1964): 252-60.

Its leftover site and the need for north light having dictated its form, this building incorporates a hundred-foot-high water tower into its top. Materials (red brick, tile, glass, and aluminum) were chosen for climatic conditions. Architects and engineering consultants were on the same wavelength.

247:8 _____. JAMES STIRLING BUILDINGS AND PROJECTS, 1950-1974. London and New York: Oxford University Press, 1975. 184 p.

Photographs and drawings of all of Stirling's projects, with limited annotative information. His lectures, articles, and statements are listed.

247:9 Korn, Arthur. "The Work of James Stirling and James Gowan." A&BN 215 (7 January 1959): 8-23.

Classified as leaders of a new generation of architects, their work, mainly residential, is illustrated. Included in the illustrations are preliminary studies in the design process.

247:10 Richards, J.M. "Criticism: House near Cowes, Isle of Wight." AJ 128 (24 July 1958): 119-22.

Modular planning principles in the design of a small house on an open site are questioned in this detailed criticism.

247:11 Stamp, Gavin. "Gleaming, Elegant and Gay But . . ." BD, 19 March 1976, pp. 14-15, 17. Reprint of "Stirling's Worth: The History Faculty Building." THE CAMBRIDGE REVIEW, 30 January 1976.

Stirling's History Faculty Building at Cambridge, won in competition in 1963, was rotated ninety degrees due to problems of land ownership and built without change of design in 1968. Its glass roof leaks and it is cold in winter and warm in summer. Three cooling fans situated in the roof were so noisy and vibrated so much that Stirling removed the fuses when a television team on location found that the noise and vibrations upset the cameras. The high water table keeps the basement damp, and water penetrates the ventilation system. Heating costs are high. Technology has been used to solve problems created by the building, but a more traditional library design would not have needed sophisticated technology.

247:12 Stirling, James. "An Architect's Approach to Architecture." RIBAJ 72 (May 1965): 231-40.

Stirling tells us who inspired him, what competitions he entered, and how his appraoch evolved.

248:1 STOKES, LEONARD ALOYSIUS (1858-1925)

Articled to S.J. Nicholl, 1871-74. Worked for T.E. Collcutt, G.E. Street, and G.F. Bodley, prior to setting up practice in 1883. RIBA gold medalist, 1919. Worked for G.E. Street on the restoration of Christ Church, Dublin. The RIBA has drawings. Obituaries: A 115 (1926): 30-34; AR 59 (February 1926): 1; B 130 (1926): 7; RIBAJ

133 (1926): 148-49. T.R. Spence is researching Stokes.

248:2 Roberts, H.V. Molesworth. "Leonard Aloysius Stokes." AR 100 (December 1946): 173-77. Reprinted in EDWARDIAN ARCHITECTURE AND ITS ORIGINS, edited by Alastair Service, pp. 362-71. London: Architectural Press, 1975.

> Stokes was "successful in middle and later life, [but] faded into obscurity shortly after." He designed in the Gothic style but evolved into a more functional phase especially in a series of telephone exchanges, one in Aberdeen.

249:1 STREET, GEORGE EDMUND (1824-81)

Articled to Owen Carter, worked for Scott and Moffatt, 1844, and began his own practice in Wantage in 1848, in Oxford ca. 1851, and in London in 1855. RIBA gold medalist, 1874. Professor at the RAL. The V&A has drawings of St. Mary's Church, Holmbury, Surrey, and of Bristol Cathedral. The RIBA has sketches, drawings, and other original materials in the Wyatt and the Papworth correspondence collections. Publications: BRICK AND MARBLE ARCHITECTURE IN ITALY, 1855; THE CATHEDRAL OF THE HOLY TRINITY, COMMONLY CALLED CHRIST CHURCH CATHEDRAL, DUBLIN: AN ACCOUNT OF THE RESTORATION OF THE FABRIC, 1882; NEW LAW COURTS, 1869; SOME ACCOUNTS OF GOTHIC ARCHITECTURE IN SPAIN, 1865; with an introductory essay by Georgiana Goddard King, UN- PUBLISHED NOTES AND REPRINTED PAPERS, 1916. Stephen Thompson wrote SEPULCHRAL MONUMENTS OF ITALY: MEDIAEVAL AND RENAISSANCE, 1883, containing full extracts from Street's manuscript notes. David Cole is preparing a catalog of Street's works. Obituaries: A&BN 11 (1882): 13-14; B 41 (24, 31 December 1881): 777-79, 784-85; B 42 (7 January 1882): 26; (4 February): 54-55, 147; (11 February): 414.

249:2 Goodhart-Rendel, H.S. "George Edmund Street." B 184 (3 April 1933): 519-20.

> Discusses the work of Street's early years and the major competitions for which he submitted projects. His pupils and last years are mentioned.

249:3 Hitchcock, Henry-Russell. "G.E. Street in the 1850's." JSAH 19 (December 1960): 145-71.

> Hitchcock attempts to rectify the fact that Street's "work has not received in the present century as much attention as that of Butterfield and his name is certainly not as well known as Scott's." The article covers the wide span of Street's career and is illustrated, sometimes in color.

249:4 Hussey, Christopher. "Haddo House, Aberdeenshire." CL 140 (18, 25 August 1966): 378-81, 448-52.

To Haddo House, built by William Adam, 1731-34, Street added a chapel in the early English Gothic style, 1876-81. The staircase leading to the chapel has Scottish painted decorations.

249:5 Long, E.T. "Churches of a Victorian Squire." CL 144 (26 September 1968): 770-72.

Street was responsible for the restoration of a large number of churches for Tatton Sykes. They are listed with their dates.

249:6 Millard, Walter. "George Edmund Street's Sketches at Home and Abroad." RIBAJ 25 (1917-18): 97-103.

Street's sketchbooks were presented to the RIBA by his son. Two sketches are reproduced.

249:7 _____. "Some Records of the Work of George Edmund Street." RIBAJ 24 (1916-17): 17-24.

Many of the drawings by Street, owned by the RIBA, were exhibited. They are discussed and five are reproduced.

249:8 Port, M.H. "The New Law Courts Competition, 1866-67." AH 11 (1968): 75-93, pls. 17-24.

At the centenary of the competition, the Law Courts are reexamined. The cramped quarters of the old courts, the lobbying for a new building, and the choice of site preceded the selection of architects for the limited competition, which resulted in eleven Gothic designs; each scheme is assessed. Edward Barry's plan was preferred, but Street's elevation was more acceptable, so, Barry having been awarded the design of the National [Portrait] Gallery's new accommodation, Street was given the more prestigious Law Courts.

249:9 Street, Arthur Edmund. MEMOIR OF GEORGE EDMUND STREET, RA., 1824-1881. London: John Murray, 1888. 441 p.

"Originally intended to be no more than a private record of some of my father's opinions and a few of his more important works, it suffers, I am aware, from a want of continuity and cohesion natural to such beginnings and to an inexperienced writer."

249:10 Summerson, John. "The Law Courts Competition of 1866-67." RIBAJ 77 (January 1970): 11-18.

The competition stipulated that "designs would be judged
wholly on questions of convenience and efficiency and
without respect to style or artistic intention." The article
illustrates and comments upon each entry.

250:1 TATHAM, CHARLES HEATHCOTE (1772-1842)

Was a clerk to S.P. Cockerell, 1788, and studied in Italy under
Henry Holland's patronage, 1791-94. Tatham's writings on archaeo-
logical and historical subjects include: ETCHINGS: REPRESENTING
THE BEST EXAMPLES OF ANCIENT ORNAMENTAL ARCHITECTURE,
3d ed., 1796; REPRESENTATION OF A GREEK VASE IN THE POS-
SESSION OF C.H. TATHAM, 1811.

250:2 Udy, David. "The Neo-Classicism of Charles Heathcote Tatham."
CONNOISSEUR 177 (August 1971): 269-76.

George Smith's COLLECTION OF DESIGNS FOR HOUSE-
HOLD FURNITURE, 1808, was the first publication on neoclassical furniture and the break from the styles of Robert
Adam. Tatham forwarded the precedent set by Smith by
stressing the need to use antique models in furniture design.

250:3 Proudfoot, Christopher, and Watkin, David. "A Pioneer of English
Neo-Classicism: C.H. Tatham." CL 151 (13, 20 April; 8 June
1972): 918-21, 1481-86.

Tatham also designed in the Gothic such works as Ochter-
tyre Mausoleum, Perthshire, 1809. The second part of this
article is concerned with Tatham's furniture designs.

251:1 TAYLER AND GREEN (Partnership 1939-72)

Herbert Tayler (1912-   ), born in Java, and David John Green
(1912-   ). Both studied at the AAL, 1929-34. The Suffolk County
Record Office, Ipswich, has all of the Tayler and Green office drawings, documents, and accounts, 1939-73, and some of their AAL student drawings.

251:2 Girouard, Mark. "Designed for Expansion." CL 125 (5 March
1959): 454-55.

Robin Hill, Surrey, built in 1946 and extended in 1952,
"is not only a house full of novel and stimulating ideas
but . . . it sits in a position as beautifully and naturally
as though it had been built for years."

252:1 **TAYLOR, GEORGE LEADWELL (1780-1873)**

Publications: THE ARCHITECTURAL ANTIQUITIES OF ROME MEAS-URED AND DELINEATED BY G.L. TAYLOR AND E. CRESY, 1821-22; THE ARCHITECTURE OF THE MIDDLE AGES IN ITALY, 1829; THE AUTO-BIOGRAPHY OF AN OCTOGENARIAN ARCHITECT, 1870-72, "being a record of his studies at home and abroad, during 65 years"; STONES OF ETRURIA AND MARBLES OF ANCIENT ROME, 1859.

252:2 Dalleywater, Roger J. "A Kentish Fonthill." CL 140 (29 December 1966): 1748.

Hadlow Castle, Kent, 1838-40, "was a deliberate attempt to outshine Fonthill," Wiltshire, by James Wyatt.

TECTON. See LUBETKIN, BERTHOLD

253:1 **TEULON, SAMUEL SANDERS (1812-73)**

Began practice about 1840. Obituary: RIBAJ 1872-73, p. 39.

253:2 Girouard, Mark. "Acrobatic Gothic." CL 148 (31 December

Elvetham Hall, Hampshire, and Bestwood Lodge, Notting-hamshire, both built in the 1860s, exhibit Teulon's Gothic gymnastics. Numerous illustrations provide an insight into his masterly, strange features.

253:3 _____. "Shadwell Park, Norfolk." CL 136 (2, 9 July 1964): 18-21, 98-102.

This small eighteenth-century house was enlarged twice in the nineteenth century, in 1840-43 by Edward Blore, and in 1856-60 by Teulon. Its nineteenth-century growth was considerable, as the later plan clearly illustrates. Blore's additions were Tudor, Teulon's were "original and provoca-tive . . . prickly, rocky, dramatic, assertive; they bristle with individuality."

254:1 **THOMAS, ALFRED BRUNWELL (1865/8-1948)**

Received his architectural training at the Westminster Art School. Obituaries: B 174 (30 January 1948): 134; RIBAJ 55 (April 1948): 271.

254:2 Thomas, Alfred Brunwell. "The Belfast City Hall." AR 20 (October 1906): 187-208.

> Described as "Classic Renaissance, carrying on the traditional architecture of the seventeenth and eighteenth centuries," it is a large and rich building.

255:1 THOMAS, PERCY E. (1883-1969)

Publication: PUPIL TO PRESIDENT, 1963 (see 255:2). RIBA gold medalist, 1939. Obituaries: B 217 (22 August 1969): 57; RIBAJ 76 (1969): 408.

255:2 Thomas, Percy E. PUPIL TO PRESIDENT (MEMOIRS OF AN ARCHITECT). Leigh-on-Sea, Essex: F. Lewis, 1963. 65 p.

> Thomas discusses his early years, career, and work from the early 1920s on and provides a list of his competition successes and major jobs as a consultant.

255:3 Weeks, Ronald. "The Design and Building of Clifton Cathedral." PAX: THE REVIEW OF THE BENEDICTINES OF PRINKNASH 63 (Autumn/Winter 1973): 60-69.

> Weeks, the job architect of St. Peter and St. Paul Roman Catholic Cathedral, discusses the client-architect relationship and the resultant design.

255:4 Wharton, Kate. "Genius of a Cathedral." A&BN 2 (1 January 1969): 22-29.

> Wharton considers the relationship of design to liturgy, as well as the various shapes possible, in the planning of a cathedral. At the time of this article, the cathedral was due for completion in 1971.

255:5 _____. "A Sequence of Space." A 1 (April 1971): 48-51.

> The Great Hall at the University College of Wales, Aberystwyth, proves that "a multi-purpose hall is a difficult architectural problem" to which there can be a satisfactory solution.

256:1 THOMPSON, FRANCIS (fl. early to mid-nineteenth century)

O.F. Carter wrote an RIBA diploma thesis, "Francis Thompson," in 1956.

256:2 Carter, O.F. "Railway Thompson." AR 143 (April 1968): 314–15.

> Thompson worked for railway companies, 1835–46, designing
> at least twenty-six stations and other buildings in a variety
> of styles. He was responsible for the masonry work of
> Robert Stephenson's Britannia tubular bridge.

257:1 THOMSON, ALEXANDER (1817–75)

Apprenticed to Robert Foote until 1832 and then to John Baird (1798–
1859). Partnered with John Baird (1816–93), 1849–57, with George
Thomson 1857–71, and with Robert Turnbull, 1871–75. The V&A has
material on Thomson in the Mitchell Johnson and Co. Collection, and
the Mitchell Library, Glasgow, has the manuscript of Thomas Gildard's
memoir of Thomson. Obituary: B 33 (10 April, 18 September 1875):
318–19, 840. T. Spence is writing an M. Arch. thesis at the University of Liverpool, on Thomson; Graham C. Law wrote an undergraduate architectural thesis entitled "Greek Thomson" at the University
of Cambridge in 1950; and J.M. McKean wrote an M.A. thesis "Alexander Thomson," at the University of Essex in 1971.

257:2 Addison, Joseph. "Some Aspects of Greek Architecture." RIBAJ 39
(9 January 1932): 165–80.

> This study of the neo-Greek style in Europe refers to some
> of Thomson's works.

257:3 Barclay, David. "'Greek' Thomson: His Life and Opinions." AR
15 (May 1904): 182–94.

> Discusses Thomson's life and works and includes elaborate,
> measured drawings of plans, sections, and elevations of his
> most impressive projects.

257:4 Blomfield, Reginald. "'Greek' Thomson: A Critical Note." AR 15
(May 1904): 194–95.

> "Thomson of Glasgow was possibly the most original thinker
> in architecture of the nineteenth century . . . but drew
> his inspiration mainly from books and drawings. . . . His
> taste in ornament seems to have been bad." His "barba-
> risms" ran riot in Glasgow warehouses, but his revival of
> the Greek style had life, compared to the work of earlier
> more archaeologically inspired architects.

257:5 Budden, Lionel B. "The Work of Alexander Thomson." B 99 (3 December 1910): 815–19.

> Thomson was a classicist but not in the Palladian sense.

"For several years he stumbled about in a state of mental chaos, designing pseudo-Gothic cottages. . . . but emerged from Victorian mediocrity in a single gigantic stride."

257:6 Edwards, A.T. "Modern Architects: Alexander ('Greek') Thomson." ARCHITECTS' AND BUILDER'S JOURNAL 39 (1914): 334-36.

In praise of Thomson's work, notably his St. Vincent Street Church, Glasgow.

257:7 Gomme, Andor, and Walker, David M. "The Individual Contribution of Alexander Thomson." In ARCHITECTURE OF GLASGOW, pp. 123-52. London: Lund Humphries, 1968.

Chapter 6 of this book discusses Thomson's work, claiming that it is less Greek than we expect: some of it is Egyptian and his domestic work is almost nonstylistic.

257:8 Goodhart-Rendel, H.S. "Rogue Architects of the Victorian Era." A&BN 195 (22 April 1949): 359-62; RIBAJ 56 (April 1949): 251-59.

The Greek revival was a past style at the time that Thomson was using it. He was thus a rogue elephant "working apart from the herd" and not a pioneer with followers. He had "great originality of outlook . . . and with a little more attention to propriety, he might have proved no rogue but a leader."

257:9 Law, Graham [C.]. "Greek Thomson." AR 115 (May 1954): 307-16.

Law carefully documents Thomson's background and early beginnings before discussing his major works in detail. The extent of his practice and some minor commissions are also mentioned. "The Greek revival in England seems to have had practically no influence on Thomson. . . . Thomson's work was practically unknown in England . . . he had few imitators even in Glasgow."

257:10 Macaulay, James. "Greek Thomson in Danger." AR 136 (August 1964): 145-46.

Thomson built three famous Glasgow churches. The Germans destroyed one, and the other two, in poor repair, are owned by the Glasgow Corporation. "The convenor of the city's planning committee has said that Glasgow may only be able to retain one."

257:11 McNeill, Peter, and Walker, David M. "A Note on Greek Thomson." GLASGOW REVIEW 2 (Summer 1965): 44-48.

A description of his life, antecedents, influence, works, and style precedes "List of Works," 1849-77, under building-type headings.

257:12 Smith, William James. "An Architectural Anthology: Glasgow-- 'Greek' Thomson, Burnet and Mackintosh." QRIAS 85 (1951): 56-60, 11-13.

"Thomson was perhaps the first nineteenth century architect to repudiate the archaeological facade."

257:13 Worsdall, Francis. "'Greek' Thomson." SCOTTISH FIELD 109 (February 1962): 46-49.

"The pre-eminent architect of Victorian Glasgow, the finest Victorian city in Britain, to quote John Betjeman."

258:1 TINSLEY, WILLIAM (1804-85)

Born at Clonmel, Ireland, where he and his brother were the third generation of a firm of builders. Influenced by James Pain, whom he succeeded as architect to the Board of Ecclesiastical Commissioners. Immigrated to the United States in 1851.

258:2 Bence-Jones, Mark. "William Tinsley: Victorian or Georgian." QUARTERLY BULLETIN OF THE IRISH GEORGIAN SOCIETY 3 (April-June 1960): 13-20.

Biographical information and list of works in Ireland.

258:3 Forbes, John D. VICTORIAN ARCHITECT: THE LIFE AND WORK OF WILLIAM TINSLEY. Bloomington, Ind.: University Press, 1953. 153 p.

His works on both sides of the Atlantic are illustrated and discussed.

259:1 TITE, WILLIAM (1798-1873)

Articled to David Laing in London, 1812. RIBA gold medalist, 1856. President of the RIBA on two occasions. The RIBA has material in the Cockerell Collection. Published widely in professional journals and wrote: DESCRIPTIVE CATALOGUE OF ANTIQUITIES FOUND IN THE EXCAVATIONS OF THE ROYAL EXCHANGE, 1848. Obituary: RIBAJ, 1873-74, pp. 209-12.

259:2 A. "Sir William Tite." Vol. 9 (1873): 215-16, 225; vol. 10 (1874): 283, 296, 305, 323.

> A leader in the profession of "policy and discussion." His important commissions are listed. The sale of his library consisted of 3,526 lots, two hundred autograph letters, and 200 lots of drawings. Some other details of the sale are also given.

259:3 Briggs, Martin S. "Sir William Tite, MP.: His Life and Work." B 178 (13, 20 January 1950): 39-42, 95-98.

> "Early Competition Designs," "Work at the Mill Hill School [London]," "Election as Fellow of the Royal Society," and the "Royal Exchange Building" are the major topics covered.

259:4 Stratton, Arthur. "The Royal Exchange, London." AR 42 (September 1917): 45-50.

> Tite won the second limited (limited to five architects) competition for the rebuilding of the Royal Exchange after it burned down in 1838. Work began in 1841; the building still stands. Cockerell's design is also illustrated.

260:1 TOWNSEND, CHARLES HARRISON (1850-1928)

> Obituary: RIBAJ 36 (1928-29): 211. A. Luty and M. O'Connor are independently researching Townsend.

260:2 Malton, John. "Art Nouveau in Essex." In THE ANTI-RATION-IONALISTS, edited by Nikolaus Pevsner and J.M. Richards, pp. 159-69. London: Architectural Press, 1973.

> Townsend and William Reynolds-Stephens were commissioned to design a church at Great Warley, Essex. All of the church's details are art nouveau.

260:3 Musgrave, Noel. "Survival of the Richest: The Whitechapel Art Gallery." RIBAJ 73 (July 1966): 315.

> Intended "to be a place where slum-dwellers could meet on equal terms, well-off and cultivated people," the White-chapel (in 1966) was running at a loss and it was feared that it would be forced to close. (This fear did not come to pass.)

260:4 Service, Alastair. "Charles Harrison Townsend." In EDWARDIAN ARCHITECTURE AND ITS ORIGINS, edited by Alastair Service, pp. 162-82. London: Architectural Press, 1975.

Townsend's vertical compositions were free from historic styles and in many respects were inspired by American precedents, particularly those established by Henry Hobson Richardson.

261:1 **TURNER, RICHARD (fl. mid-nineteenth century)**

261:2 Hix, John. "Richard Turner: Glass Master." AR 152 (November 1972): 268–93. See also John Hix in THE GLASS HOUSE, pp. 117–21, figs. 179–84. London: Phaidon, 1974.

Turner built the Palm House, Belfast, 1839, by Charles Lanyon, from his [Turner] Dublin works and then the Palm House at Glasnavin, Dublin, in 1843; the latter was enlarged in 1869.

261:3 Ferriday, Peter. "Palm House at Kew." AR 121 (February 1957): 127–28.

See 45:3.

261:4 McCracken, Eileen. THE PALM HOUSE AND BOTANIC GARDEN, BELFAST. Belfast: Ulster Architectural Heritage Society, 1971. 66 p.

"This monograph on the Belfast Botanic Garden has been written primarily to draw attention to the need for the repair and preservation of the Palm House which is in danger of demolition." It is a thorough monograph and provides an in-depth bibliography of printed and manuscript sources.

262:1 **VOYSEY, CHARLES FRANCIS ANNESLEY (1857-1941)**

Articled to J.P. Seddon, for whom he worked. He also assisted George Devey and practiced independently beginning in 1881. The V&A has design drawings for furniture and wallpaper. RIBA gold medalist, 1940. the RIBA has correspondence in the Sirr Collection and drawings (see 262:17). Publications: INDIVIDUALITY, 1915; REASON AS THE BASIS OF ART, 1906. Obituaries: A&BN 165 (21 February 1941): 129–30; AJ 93 (20 February 1941): 124, 126; AR 89 (May, 1941): 112–13; B 160 (21 February 1941): 197; RIBAJ 48 (March 1941): 88. D.T.I.G. Davies wrote a 1958 RIBA diploma thesis, "C.F.A. Voysey, Architect and Designer"; A.W. Guthrie wrote an undergraduate architectural thesis, "C.F.A. Voysey, 1857-1941," at the University of Newcastle, 1963; and John Brandon-Jones is researching Voysey.

262:2 Adams, Thomas. "The True Meaning of Town Planning: A Reply to

Mr. C.F.A. Voysey." AR 46 (September 1919): 75-77. In reply to Voysey's "On Town Planning." AR 46 (July 1919): 25-26.

Voysey claimed that "town planning is the outcome of a belief in a fundamental principle which is false. The principle is collectivism. The drilling and controlling of the multitude--the formalism of Prussian militarism." Adams replies that Voysey "does not discuss town planning at all . . . I do not agree with Mr. Voysey in his acceptance of individualism as a creed in a civic state . . . Mr. Voysey is really one of the best friends of town planning" in that his houses present an approach to all aspects of architecture.

262:3 B., M. "Some Recent Work of C.F.A. Voysey, An English Architect." HOUSE AND GARDEN 3 (1903): 254-60.

At the time of this article, Voysey's architecture, roughly cast and painted green was being accepted in England. Several examples are cited.

262:4 Betjeman, John. "C.F.A. Voysey." AJ 91 (29 February 1940): 234-35; AF 72 (May 1940): 348-49.

Voysey at eighty-three was awarded the RIBA gold medal. An appreciation of his attitudes, influence, and importance.

262:5 _____. "Charles Annesley Voysey." In EDWARDIAN ARCHITECTURE AND ITS ORIGINS, edited by Alastair Service, pp. 152-56. London: Architectural Press, 1975.

Possibly the most famous of the arts-and-crafts architects, Voysey forwarded simplicity in design and was ahead of his time.

262:6 Brandon-Jones, John. "C.F.A. Voysey, 1857-1941." AAJ 72 (May 1957): 239-62.

Voysey's background, training, practice, architectural development, attitudes, buildings, and designs are discussed and a detailed list of his designs and projects is presented.

262:7 Briggs, Martin S. "Voysey and Blomfield: A Study in Contrast." B 176 (14 January 1949): 39-42.

See 32:3.

262:8 Donat, Robert. "Uncle Charles." AJ 93 (20 March 1941): 193-94.

Film actor Robert Donat married Voysey's niece and recounts

personal reminiscences. Voysey designed his own clothes--
jackets without lapels and trousers without cuffs because
both harbor dirt and dust.

262:9 Gebhard, David. "C.F.A. Voysey--to and from America." JSAH
29 (October 1970): 272-73; 30 (December 1971): 304-12.

The December 1971 article is the developed version of a
paper reported in the October 1970 reference. Gebhard
questions the impact of Voysey on the United States and
the impact of American architecture upon London practitioners through publications, lectures, and exhibitions. The
American Shingle Style influenced Voysey.

262:10 _____. CHARLES F.A. VOYSEY. Santa Barbara: University of
California Art Gallery, 1970. 75 p.

Gebhard's twenty-five page introduction to this exhibition
catalog precedes a list of writings by Voysey, 1893-1936;
of writings about him, 1893-1968; and forty-one pages of
drawings (many of the drawings were loaned by the RIBA),
watercolors (reproduced in color), and photographs.

262:11 _____. CHARLES F.A. VOYSEY, ARCHITECT. Los Angeles: Hennessey and Ingalls, 1975. 184 p.

"Voysey evolved a highly individual style, rooted in vernacular Gothic of English cottage architecture . . . yet
heralded the twentieth century." He was interested in
"fitness" of structure, environment, and materials. Essentially an expansion of 262:10.

262:12 _____. "The Vernacular Transformed." RIBAJ 78 (March 1971):
97-102.

"Voysey's most direct connection with the twentieth century
does not basically lie with the modern movement, but with
the imagery and ideas."

262:13 Pevsner, Nikolaus. "C.F.A. Voysey." In STUDIES IN ART, ARCHI-
TECTURE AND DESIGN, vol. 2, pp. 140-51. London: Thames and
Hudson, 1968.

Translated from the Dutch periodical ELSEVIERS MAAND-
SCHIFT of May 1940 (no pagination provided), this article
places Voysey in the context of the period of design in
which he practiced, discussing his successes, design ability,
and mature architecture.

262:14 Richardson, Margaret. "Wallpapers by C.F.A. Voysey." RIBAJ 72 (August 1965): 399–403.

>Five examples of Voysey's wallpaper designs are illustrated in color. He used natural objects "juxtaposed and simplified into flat shapes, to form strongly repeated patterns."

262:15 Scott, M.H. Baillie. "On the Characteristics of Mr. C.F.A. Voysey's Architecture." INTERNATIONAL STUDIO 33 (1907-8): 19–24.

>Voysey's work "consists mainly in the application of serenely sane, practical and rational ideas to home making." Garden Corner, Chelsea, London, is illustrated to forward this viewpoint.

262:16 STUDIO. "An Interview with Mr. C.F.A. Voysey." Vol. 1 (1893): 231–37.

>Chosen for the interview because his designs were better known than their author, Voysey establishes limitations for the design of such materials and wallpaper patterns, which he says should be large and bold; scale is modified through color. Animal decoration should be symbolic. "To go to Nature is, of course, to approach the fountain-head, but a literal transcript will not result in good ornament." The danger is in overornamentation, but one must not be hidebound by tradition.

262:17 Symonds, Joanna. CATALOGUE OF THE DRAWINGS COLLECTION OF THE ROYAL INSTITUTE OF BRITISH ARCHITECTS: C.F.A. VOYSEY. Farnborough, Hants.: Gregg International Publishers, 1976. 95 p., 120 figs.

>Includes a detailed description and listing of 931 items, a chronological list of designs for buildings, and a subject index.

262:18 Townsend, Horace. "Notes on Country and Suburban Houses." STUDIO 16 (1899): 157–64.

>After a general statement in praise of Voysey's simplicity of design, selected examples of his residences are described and illustrated.

263:1 VULLIAMY, LEWIS (1791-1871)

Articled to Robert Smirke; entered the RAL in 1809. Publications: THE BRIDGE OF STA. TRINITA AT FLORENCE, 1822; EXAMPLES OF ORNAMENTAL SCULPTURE IN ARCHITECTURE FROM GREECE, ASIA

MINOR AND ITALY, 1823. The V&A has drawings of St. James, Clapham, London; and Christ Church, Woburn Square, London.

263:2 Hussey, Christopher. "Tregothnan, Cornwall." CL 119 (17, 24 May 1956): 1051-54, 1112-15.

> Built ca. 1650 and tudorized, 1816-18, Tregothnan was enlarged by Vulliamy, 1845-48.

264:1 **WALLIS, THOMAS (1873-1953)**

Worked for Sydney R.J. Smith and began partnership with J.A. Bowden in 1908. Later Wallis partnered with an American architect as Wallis, Gilbert and Partners although the American never came to Britain; together they used the Kahncrete Concrete System. Obituary: RIBAJ 60 (September 1953): 465.

264:2 Aptaker, Neil. "Hoover Limited." PERSPECTA 13/14 (1971): 190-93.

> Hoover factory, London, 1932, was, according to Gilbert "free from tradition . . . the pioneer of reinforced concrete." It had a flexible plan.

264:3 Snowdon, J.J., and Platts, R.W. "Great West Road Style: The Work of Wallis, Gilbert and Partners." AR 156 (July 1974): 21-27.

> Kahncrete was used in a series of industrial structures along the Great Western Road, London, and elsewhere.

265:1 **WATERHOUSE, ALFRED (1830-1905)**

Articled to Richard Lane of Manchester, where he also practiced before moving to London. RIBA gold medalist, 1878. President, RIBA, 1888-91. Obituaries: AA&BN 88 (1905): 65, 126-27; BRICK-BUILDER 14 (September 1905): 189; BRITISH ARCHITECT 64 (25 May 1905): 8; CONSTRUCTION NEWS 20 (28 October 1905): 1; RIBAJ 12 (30 September 1905): 605, 609-18; RIBAJ 13 (11 November 1905): 11-12; WESTERN ARCHITECT 4 (September 1905): 1. D. Adams wrote a Cambridge University B.A. thesis, "The Architecture of Alfred Waterhouse in Cambridge," in 1962; P. Roantree is researching Waterhouse; Stuart A. Smith wrote a doctoral dissertation, "Alfred Waterhouse: The Great Years, 1860-1875," at the University of London in 1970 and has produced a chapter on Waterhouse for SEVEN VICTORIAN ARCHITECTS (A37); and P.G. Velluet is writing an undergraduate architectural thesis at the University of Newcastle on Waterhouse.

265:2 AA&BN. "Alfred Waterhouse." Vol. 88 (1905): 65, 126-27.

"Alfred Waterhouse . . . more than any of his contemporaries succeeded in making 'Victorian Gothic' something more
and better than a mere bald, lifeless and ill-understood application of Gothic forms." His life, works, and style are
presented.

265:3 Axon, William E.A. AN ARCHITECTURAL AND GENERAL DESCRIP-
TION OF THE TOWN HALL, MANCHESTER. Manchester and London:
Abel Heywood and Son, 1878. 97 p., 17 unnumbered pls.

An "accurate account of a building probably unmatched for
size, completeness, and adaptability to its purpose" and a
record of the dedicatory proceedings.

265:4 Cooper, Thomas. "Alfred Waterhouse, RA, LLD." RIBAJ 12 (30
September 1905): 609-18.

Waterhouse practiced in Manchester, where he won the
competition for the Assise Courts, 1859. He moved to
London in 1865. Some of his major works are discussed,
but many more are listed.

265:5 Jenkins, Frank. "The Making of a Municipal Palace: Manchester
Town Hall." CL 141 (16 February 1967): 336-39.

First- and second-stage competition drawings and carefully
selected photographs of the hall's interior complement this
article.

266:1 WATERHOUSE, PAUL (1861-1924)

Son of Alfred Waterhouse (265:1), under whom Paul trained and with
whom he partnered, 1891-1901, after which he practiced alone. Publications: A COLLECTION OF CERTAIN OF HIS PAPERS AND AD-
DRESSES, 1930; OLD TOWNS AND NEW NEEDS, 1912; SIR CHRIS-
TOPHER WREN, 1632-1723, 1934. Obituaries: AIAJ 13 (1925):
77; ANNUAL REGISTER, part 2 (1924): 150; AR 57 (January 1925):
45; NIY, 1924, p. 517; RIBAJ 32 (1924-25): 141-42, 192, 202,
321.

266:2 Collingwood, Frances. "Paul Waterhouse, 1861-1924." B 201 (27
October 1961): 774.

The centenary of the birth of Paul Waterhouse, the second
of four generations of architects. The works of both Alfred
and Paul Waterhouse are listed.

267:1 **WEBB, ASTON (1849-1930)**

Articled to Banks and Barry and began practice, 1873. Collaborated with E. Ingress Bell (1837-1914). President, RIBA, 1902-4. Knighted, 1904. RIBA gold medalist, 1905. Edited: LONDON OF THE FUTURE, 1921. The RIBA has material in the Sirr Collection. Obituaries: AF 53 (September 1930): 37; RIBAJ 37 (1929-30): 710, 744.

267:2 Creswell, H. B[ulkeley]. "A Backward View." A&BN 208 (11 August 1955): 172-73.

Creswell worked for Webb at the time of the design of the Royal Naval College at Dartmouth. It is "modern" in that it belongs to all time.

267:3 _____. "Seventy Years Back." AR 124 (December 1958): 403-5. Reprinted as "Aston Webb and His Office," in EDWARDIAN ARCHITECTURE AND ITS ORIGINS, edited by Alastair Service, pp. 328-38. London: Architectural Press, 1975.

A description of a successful Edwardian practice, led by an architect whose facility for large-scale planning complemented his grandiose architecture.

268:1 **WEBB, PHILIP SPEAKMAN (1831-1915)**

Articled to John Billing of Reading and worked for G.E. Street prior to opening practice in London in 1856. Webb joined the firm of Morris, Marshall, Faulkner and Co. at its founding in 1861. The V&A has some correspondence, 1884-1915. J. Brandon-Jones is researching Webb. Obituaries: AR 37 (June 1915): 122; RIBAJ 22 (1914-15): 312, 339-41, 344, 369, 395.

268:2 Barman, Christian. "Philip Webb." RIBAJ 42 (25 May 1935): 832-33.

A review of Lethaby's PHILIP WEBB AND HIS WORK (see 268:11). Webb does not appear in the DICTIONARY OF NATIONAL BIOGRAPHY, but George Gilbert Scott does, so the article tends to be in praise of Webb and a subjective diatribe against Scott.

268:3 Brandon-Jones, John. "Letters of Philip Webb and His Contemporaries." AH 8 (1965): 52-72.

On his retirement from practice in 1901, Webb intended to destroy all his drawings and correspondence. George Jack and Charles Winmill persuaded him to do otherwise, selected drawings and sketches from his practice, which were eventually given to the RIBA. Emery Walker preserved his letters and loaned them to W.R. Lethaby, who published them in the B between 9 January and 4 December 1925; they were later incorporated into Lethaby's biography of Webb (see 268:11). Brandon-Jones now owns the letters concerning the years 1874-83. Two dozen letters are quoted from and some are illustrated in facsimile.

268:4 _____. "Notes on the Building of Smeaton Manor." AH 1 (1958): 31-32.

Smeaton Manor, Yorkshire, 1877, is symmetrical, which is unusual for a design by Webb. Approximately three dozen letters (and drawings) from Webb to his client Major Godman are quoted verbatim in this first volume of a magazine devoted to presenting original research material.

268:5 _____. "The Work of Philip Webb and Norman Shaw." AAJ 71 (June 1955): 9-21; (July-August 1955): 40-47.

Numerous buildings are illustrated with plans, photographs, and measured drawings. See also 234:5.

268:6 Briggs, Martin S. "Lethaby, Webb and Morris: Exhibition of Their Work at the RIBA." B 178 (24 February 1950): 254-55.

Drawings for this exhibition of like-minded designers are owned by the RIBA, but photographs and other exhibited items came from other sources. The influence and work of these three designers are assessed.

268:7 Girouard, Mark. "Standen, Sussex." CL 147 (26 February, 5 March 1970): 494-97, 554-57.

This is a significant work by Webb, not only because it is a major example of the domestic architectural revival of the 1890s, but because it survives unaltered; it dates from 1891-94.

268:8 _____. "The Victorian Artist At Home." CL 152 (16 November 1972): 1278-81.

The G.B. Boyce House, Glebe Place, Chelsea, London, 1868, and an earlier house, for Val Princep (an early example of a home built specifically for an artist, 1865), are described.

268:9 Handley-Read, Charles. "Jubilee Pyramid." AR 137 (March 1965): 234-36.

> "The Pyramid to fill the whole [of Trafalgar] Square. To receive all the statues now in London and many more. Queen Victoria was to sit on an elephant at the apex of the pyramid. The design was made in horrified anticipation of the crop of buildings and monuments that would rise to honour the Queen in 1887, the year of her first Jubilee."

268:10 Jack, George. "An Appreciation of Philip Webb." AR 38 (July 1915): 1-6, pls. 1-5. Reprinted in EDWARDIAN ARCHITECTURE AND ITS ORIGINS, edited by Alastair Service, pp. 16-25. London: Architectural Press, 1975.

> Webb was the architect of country houses rather than of public buildings proving that "country gentlemen were much more intelligent than the general public." Drawings for tapestries, as well as architecture, are illustrated. Jack worked for Webb and on p. 6 gives a chronological list of Webb's major commissions, 1860-1905.

268:11 Lethaby, William Richard. PHILIP WEBB AND HIS WORK. London: Oxford University Press, 1935. 234 p.

> Webb's life at Oxford, where he was born, his association with William Morris, and his architectural practice, 1859-1900, are all covered.

268:12 Macleod, Robert. "The Art of Moral Building: Some Late Victorian and Edwardian Architectural Ideas." B 211 (23 December 1966): 31-34.

> The thought process "which, led by William Morris and Philip Webb, found a new way of looking at building in relation to society."

268:13 Morris, G. "On Mr. Philip Webb's Town Work." AR 2 (1897): 199-208.

> Pencil sketches by E.A. Rickards of interior details are used to illustrate "refinement of details by Webb, their imaginative and elusive qualities."

268:14 Rooke, Noel. "The Work of Lethaby, Webb and Morris." RIBAJ 57 (March 1950): 167-75.

> Rooke studied under Lethaby. Although Webb and Morris were considerably older than Lethaby by twenty-six and twenty-three years respectively, they were influenced by and collaborated with him.

WEIR, ROBERT SCHULTZ. See SCHULTZ, ROBERT WEIR

269:1 **WHITE, WILLIAM (1825-1900)**

Worked for George Gilbert Scott and began practice about 1847. Obituary: RIBAJ 7 (1899-1900): 118, 145-46, 148; lists an extensive number of works in England.

269:2 Girouard, Mark. "Humewood Castle, Co. Wicklow." CL 143 (9 May 1968): 1212-15.

White "had a facility for dashing out bold compositions on the basis of convenient and ingenious plans." White estimated that Humewood would cost fifteen thousand pounds, but it ultimately cost twenty-five thousand, leading to an unpleasant court proceeding. The castle is slightly Scottish baronial.

269:3 Thompson, Paul. "The Writings of William White." In CONCERNING ARCHITECTURE: ESSAYS PRESENTED TO NIKOLAUS PEVSNER, edited by John Summerson, pp. 226-37. London: Allen Lane, 1968.

"Of all the leading architects of the mid-Victorian Gothic school, William White came nearest ot complete oblivion." His buildings, writings, and opinions are assessed, with good footnote coverage of source material.

270:1 **WILD, JAMES (1814-92)**

Articled to George Basevi starting in 1840. Obituary: RIBAJ 9 (1892-93): 275-76.

270:2 Goodhart-Rendel, H.S. "Rogue Architects of the Victorian Era." A&BN 195 (22, 29 April 1949): 359-62; RIBAJ 56 (April 1949): 251-59.

Wild's style in some works was vaguely Byzantine.

271:1 **WILLIAMS, EVAN OWEN (1890-1968)**

Trained as an engineer. Knighted for his contribution to the Palace of Industry, Wembley Exhibition, 1923. Obituary: B 216 (30 May 1969): 61.

271:2 Gold, Michael. "Sir Owen Williams, KBE." ZODIAC 18 (1968): 11-30.

A photographic and descriptive essay on his major projects.

271:3 Perlmutter, Roy. "Engineer's Aesthetic vs Architecture: The Design and Performance of the Empire Pool, Wembley." JSAH 31 (March 1972): 56-60.

The building is described and its structure is analyzed in detail.

271:4 Ritchie, Thomas. "A New Restaurant at Wembley Stadium." A&BN 153 (25 February 1938): 249-51.

A new restaurant designed within a rigid, existing structural system. The problem is stated and the solution explained.

272:1 WILSON, CHARLES (1810-63)

Apprenticed to D. and J. Hamilton, 1827, and worked for them until 1837 when he began practice with his brother as J. and C. Wilson, until 1839. He then practiced independently until late in life when he partnered with Charles Heath Wilson, not a relative. The NMRS has drawings. John Hepburn is researching Wilson. Obituary: B 21 (7 March 1863): 173.

272:2 Thomson, D. "The Works of the Late Charles Wilson, Esq." GLASGOW PHILOSOPHICAL SOCIETY 13 (13 March 1882): 552-69.

His various commissions are described chronologically and stylistically.

273:1 WILSON, COLIN ST. JOHN (1922-)

Trained at Cambridge University and partnered at one time with Leslie Martin (see 169:1).

273:2 Webb, Michael. "A Painter's House near Cambridge." CL 142 (2 November 1967): 1110-11.

Christopher Cornford's house has achieved "a marvellous economy of means . . . by a masterly control of mass, space, texture and light."

274:1 WILSON, HENRY (1863-1934)

274:2 Taylor, Nicholas. "Byzantium in Brighton." AR 139 (April 1966):

274-77. Reprinted in EDWARDIAN ARCHITECTURE AND ITS ORI-GINS, edited by Alastair Service, pp. 280-88. London: Architectural Press, 1975.

> Trained under John Oldrid Scott and later John Belcher; assisted Arthur Beresford Pite and J.D. Sedding, continuing the latter's practice after Sedding's death in 1891. He was sufficiently interested in the Byzantine revival to design a free version of the Byzantine style at St. Bartholomew's, Brighton, 1897-1908.

275:1 WILSON, LESLIE HUGH (1913-)

Architect of Canterbury, 1945-56, and of Cumbernauld, 1956-62; practices with J.L. Womersley (see 278:1).

275:2 AJ. "Men of the Year." Vol. 125 (17 January 1957): 80-92; vol. 143 (19 January 1966): 157.

> Wilson explains his approach to design at Cumbernauld.

275:2 Nuttgens, Patrick. "Cumbernauld New Town Centre." AR 142 (December 1967): 440-51.

> One-fifth of the total area of the town center had been completed by 1967 when this article was published. The center's function, structure, and circulation are described.

275:3 Whittick, Arnold. "The Plan for Irvine." T&CP 35 (October 1967): 449-56.

> Irvine, Ayrshire, southwest of Glasgow, was designated a new town in 1966. The reason for creating the town in this area are appraised; so, too, are Wilson's concepts, details, and open space.

276:1 WINMILL, CHARLES CANNING (1865-1945)

276:2 Winmill, Joyce M. CHARLES CANNING WINMILL, AN ARCHITECT'S LIFE: BY HIS DAUGHTER. London: J.M. Dent and Sons, 1946. 148 p.

> An ardent preservationist, Winmill was reared in the arts-and-crafts tradition. He worked for John T. Newman, attended the AAL, and in 1888 became an assistant of Leonard Stokes. From 1892 to 1923, Winmill worked for the LCC. He then worked independently.

277:1 **WOMERSLEY, CHARLES PETER (1924-)**

Trained at the AAL.

277:2 Womersley, Charles Peter. "Architects' Approach to Architecture."
RIBAJ 76 (May 1969): 189-96.

> "After five years learning sociology at the AA, I left to
> get some practical training." Womersley works and prac-
> tices in Edinburgh.

278:1 **WOMERSLEY, J. LEWIS (1910-)**

Practiced in London, 1933-38 and was architect of Northampton,
1946-53, and of Sheffield, 1953-64. Practices with Leslie Hugh Wilson (see 275:1).

278:2 Darke, Roy. "Urban Evaluations: Sheffield Revisited." BUILT EN-
VIRONMENT 1 (November 1972): 557-61.

> The conclusion is that the Park Hill and Hyde Park housing
> developments are successful and that complaints by tenants
> tend to be concerned with the faults of high-density living
> accommodations rather than with criticism of this particular
> scheme.

279:1 **WOOD, EDGAR (1860-1935)**

Articled to James Muratroyd of Manchester and began practice in
1885. Practiced with James Henry Sellers (1861-1954), from 1900 to
1922; Sellers practiced independently thereafter. Wood's obituaries:
A&BN 144 (25 October 1935): 87; B 149 (25 October 1935): 740;
RIBAJ 43 (21 December 1935): 212. John H.G. Archer wrote a
RIBA diploma thesis, "The Life and Work of Edgar Wood and J.H.
Sellers" in 1955 and also an M.A. thesis "Edgar Wood and the Architecture of the Arts and Crafts and Art Nouveau Movements in Britain,"
at the University of Manchester in 1968.

279:2 Archer, John H.G. "An Introduction to Two Manchester Architects:
Edgar Wood and John Henry Sellers." RIBAJ 62 (December 1954):
50-53.

> Background to the careers of both architects is provided.
> Wood sought out Sellers after seeing one of his buildings
> and thereafter they partnered together. They built several
> schools, but after 1922 Sellers practiced in the Neo-Georgian
> style. They seem to have done their best work when their
> respective talents were combined.

279:3   _____ . "Edgar Wood: A Noteable Manchester Architect." LAN-CASHIRE AND CHESHIRE ANTIQUARIAN SOCIETY TRANSACTIONS 73-74 (1963-64): 153-87. Reprinted as EDGAR WOOD (1860-1935) A MANCHESTER 'ART NOUVEAU' ARCHITECT. Manchester: Lancashire and Cheshire Antiquarian Society, 1966. 34 p.

> "Edgar Wood enjoyed a national and international reputation in his lifetime but has since been neglected, partly because he has no major buildings in any prominent place in Manchester or elsewhere." After a brief essay, twenty-two pages are devoted to a "Chronological Account of Wood's Life Combined With A Catalogue Raisonne of His Work." His work was mainly residential.

279:4   _____ . "Edgar Wood and J. Henry Sellers: A Decade of Partnership and Experiment." In EDWARDIAN ARCHITECTURE AND ITS ORIGINS, edited by Alastair Service, pp. 372-84. London: Architectural Press, 1975.

> Wood made the transition from the arts-and-crafts ideals to the steel-framed and concrete structures of the twentieth century because of his partnership with Sellers. Sellers practiced in several different areas of northern England prior to the partnership; details are provided.

279:5   _____ . PARTNERSHIP IN STYLE. Manchester: Manchester City Art Gallery, 1975. 96 p.

> An exhibition catalog containing a brief essay on each of the two architects--Wood and Sellers.

280:1 WOOD, SANCTION (1814-86)

Trained under Robert Smirke and Sydney Smirke. Built numerous railway stations in England. Obituary: RIBAJ 3 (1886-87): 20.

280:2 Sheehy, Jeanne. KINGSBRIDGE STATION. Ballycotton, County Cork: Gifford and Craven, 1973. 10 p.

> The engineer for the Great Southern and Western Company (of Ireland), John Macneill selected designs of "great merit" and of "merit" from the twenty submitted for this station. They were then forwarded to London where Wood's design was chosen. Good footnoting of source material.

281:1 WOODWARD, BENJAMIN (1815-61)

Practiced with Thomas Deane, 1846-61 (77:1). Obituary: RIBAJ 1861-62, p. 12.

281:2 Curran, Constantine. "Benjamin Woodward, Ruskin and the O'Sheas."
STUDIES: AN IRISH QUARTERLY REVIEW OF LETTERS, PHILOSOPHY
AND SCIENCE 29 (June 1940): 255-68.

Of Woodward, Curran states: "Born apparently in 1815, we
know nothing of his parentage nor of his education." Prior
to his joining Deane, Sir Thomas was a classicist, and after
Woodward's death, Deane's medieval revivals were less dis-
tinct. The work of the O'Shea brothers, sculptors, is also
discussed, and quotations of criticism from IRISH BUILDER,
15 May 1866, are related. The account of the meeting of
Woodward and Ruskin is taken from Edward Tyas Cook's THE
LIFE OF JOHN RUSKIN, vol. 1, p. 455. London: G. Allen
and Company, 1911.

282:1 WORNUM, GEORGE GREY (1888-1957)

Educated at the AAL and articled to his uncle R.S. Wornum. He
also worked for Simpson and Ayrton and began practice in 1910. Associated with P.D. Hepworth in 1919, with Louis de Soissons (see
78:1) and with Edward Playne in 1950. RIBA gold medalist, 1950.
Publication: with John Gloag, HOUSE OUT OF FACTORY, 1946.
Obituaries: A&BN 211 (20 June 1957): 800; AJ 125 (20 June
1957): 910; B 192 (21 June 1957): 1115; RIBAJ 64 (August 1957):
439.

282:2 MacEwan, Malcolm. "RIBA Working Groups." RIBAJ 78 (March
1971): 119-20.

The subcommittee of the RIBA responsible for its headquarters
building is still apologizing for the aesthetics, but no longer
for the planning, of Wornum's design of 1932. The eco-
nomics of the 1971 situation are explained.

282:3 Turner, Philip J. "The Library of the Royal Institute of British Architects." JRAIC 13 (September 1936): 172-75.

The library is described and illustrated.

283:1 WORTHINGTON, THOMAS (1826-1909)

Obituary: RIBAJ 17 (1909-10): 91, 223-24.

283:2 Ogden, Paul. "Thomas Worthington." RIBAJ 17 (1909-10): 223-
24.

Background and major works are listed. "He was probably the first to design a hospital in England on the pavilion principle" and had accepted advice on the planning of the hospital from Florence Nightingale.

284:1 WYATT, BENJAMIN DEAN (1775-ca. 1850)

Eldest son of the architect James Wyatt (1746-1813), with whom he studied beginning in 1819. The RIBA has limited correspondence in its collection of the Wyatt family's papers. Publications: OBSERVATIONS ON THE PRINCIPLES OF THE DESIGN FOR THE THEATRE NOW BUILDING IN DRURY LANE, 1811; and a similar book OBSERVATIONS ON THE PRINCIPLES OF THE DESIGN FOR THE THEATRE IN DRURY LANE, AS ERECTED IN 1812, 1813.

284:2 Binney, Marcus. "The Theatre Royal, Drury Lane." CL 148 (10 December 1970): 1116-19.

Wyatt wrote in OBSERVATIONS . . ., 1811, that "I have compleated a design which I believe to be free from every serious objection." He also brought the audience nearer to the stage.

284:3 Colvin, Howard. "The Architects of Stafford House." AH 1 (1958): 17-30.

See 238:4.

284:4 Cornforth, John. "Stafford House Revisited." CL 144 (7, 14 November 1968): 1188-91, 1257-61.

Now known as Lancaster House, London, the building was completed by Wyatt, 1827-38. The second part of the article is devoted to the gold-leaf ornamentation of the Louis XIV or "flamboyant style" interiors (some illustrated in color), which Wyatt claimed to have introduced into nineteenth-century British architecture.

284:5 Dale, Anthony. "James Wyatt and His Sons." A&BN 193 (26 March 1948): 294-96.

A commentary on the Wyatts, including Benjamin, from a series of letters owned by descendants. "The letters shed no light on architectural accomplishments."

284:6 Hussey, Christopher. "Restoration of Lancaster House." CL 114

(12 November 1953): 1572-73.

Wyatt began the building in 1825. It was completed and enlarged by Robert Smirke and Charles Barry in 1842. Opulent interiors.

284:7 Oswald, Arthur. "Great London Mansions: Londonderry House, Park Lane." CL 82 (10 July 1937): 38-44.

Built as Holdernesse House, ca. 1760-65, the house was remodeled by Benjamin and Philip Wyatt, 1825-28.

284:8 Stanley-Morgan, R. "Benjamin Wyatt and His Noble Clients." AR 145 (February 1969): 101-5.

Wyatt made proposals for a Waterloo Palace to glorify the duke of Wellington. Instead he made additions and alterations to Apsley House, London. This article is based upon sixty letters to and from Wyatt.

285:1 WYATT, LEWIS WILLIAM (ca. 1778-1853)

Pupil at the RAL until 1802, when he set up practice. Publication: PROSPECTUS OF A DESIGN FOR VARIOUS IMPROVEMENTS IN THE METROPOLIS, 1816. Obituary: GENTLEMAN'S MAGAZINE, 1853, p. 670.

285:2 Goodison, Nicholas, and Hardy, John. "Gillows at Tatton Park." FURNITURE HISTORY 6 (1970): 1-39.

The design of the library at Tatton Park is attributed to Wyatt. Drawings survive.

285:3 Oswald, Arthur. "Tatton Park, Cheshire: A Property of the National Trust." CL 136 (16, 23, 30 July 1964): 162-65, 232-36, 292-96.

Samuel Wyatt designed the house in the 1780s and his nephew Lewis added neoclassical elements to it in 1807. The second part of the article covers the interiors, and the third, the landscaping, including that by Paxton.

286:1 WYATT, MATTHEW DIGBY (1820-77)

Publications: AN ARCHITECT'S NOTE-BOOK IN SPAIN, 1872; THE ART OF ILLUMINATING AS PRACTICED IN EUROPE FROM EARLIEST TIMES, 18??; FINE ART, 1870; THE INDUSTRIAL ARTS OF THE NINETEENTH CENTURY, 1851; NOTICES OF SCULPTURE IN IVORY,

1855; ON THE ARCHITECTURAL CAREER OF THE LATE SIR CHARLES BARRY, 1860 (see 18:16); SPECIMENS OF ORNAMENTAL ART, 1852; SPECIMENS OF THE GEOMETRICAL MOSAIC OF THE MIDDLE AGES, 1848; VIEWS OF CRYSTAL PALACE AND PARK, 1854. Obituaries: AA&BN 2 (2 June 1877): 169-70; RIBAJ, 1877-78, pp. 7-8.

286:2 Pevsner, Nikolaus. "Matthew Digby Wyatt." In STUDIES IN ART, ARCHITECTURE AND DESIGN, vol. 2, pp. 96-107. London: Thames and Hudson, 1968.

> "As for his buildings only a few can be looked at, just enough I hope, to come to a judgement on his gifts as an architect." Additionally, Pevsner considers those theorists who influenced Wyatt.

286:3 _____. MATTHEW DIGBY WYATT: THE FIRST CAMBRIDGE SLADE PROFESSOR OF FINE ART. Cambridge: University Press, 1950. 44 p., 6 pls.

> At the end of this transcript of his lecture, Pevsner lists Wyatt's writings, architecture, and other works.

287:1 YORKE, ROSENBERG AND MARDALL (Partnership 1946-)

> Francis Reginald Stevens Yorke (1906–62) studied at the University of Birmingham and collaborated with Marcel Breuer (see Wodehouse, Lawrence. AMERICAN ARCHITECTS FROM THE FIRST WORLD WAR TO THE PRESENT, Detroit: Gale Research Co., 1977) during the 1930s; Eugene Rosenberg (1907-   ) was born and studied in Prague; and Cyril Leonard Sjostrom Mardall (1909-   ) studied at the Northern Polytechnic, London, and at the AAL. Yorke's publications: THE MODERN HOUSE, 1934; THE MODERN HOUSE IN ENGLAND, 1937 (see E80); with Frederick Gibberd, MASTERWORKS OF INTERNATIONAL APARTMENT BUILDING DESIGN, 1959, and THE MODERN FLAT, 1937 (see E81); with Colin Penn, A KEY TO MODERN ARCHITECTURE, 1939 (see A114); with Penelope Whiting, THE NEW SMALL HOUSE, 1953 (see E82; see also E79). Obituaries of Yorke: AF 117 (August 1962): 13; AR 132 (October 1962): 279-80, by E. Maxwell Fry; B 202 (8 June 1962): 1223; RIBAJ 69 (August 1962): 303.

287:2 Atkinson, Fello. "U.S. Embassy Building, Grosvenor Square, London." AR 129 (April 1961): 252-58.

> The firm (Yorke, Rosenberg and Mardall) site-supervised this Eero Saarinen building.

287:3 Banham, Reyner. THE ARCHITECTURE OF YORKE, ROSENBERG, MARDALL, 1944-72. London: Lund Humphries, 1972. 128 p.

Banham assesses, analyzes, and appraises the wide range
and variety of building types designed by the firm. Good
visual coverage.

287:4 Chalk, Warren. "Slightly below the Knee: Thoughts on Architecture
and YRM." AD 36 (June 1966): 274-93.

A chronological list of works, 1947-64, are listed and illustrated. Gatwick Airport and other building types are
analyzed. Chalk praises the businesslike way in which this
teaching office is run as a team.

288:1 YOUNG, WILLIAM (1843-1900)

Worked for various Scottish architects but practiced in London. Pub-
lications: MUNICIPAL BUILDINGS OF GLASGOW, 1890; PICTUR-
ESQUE ARCHITECTURAL STUDIES AND PRACTICAL DESIGNS FOR
GATE LODGES, COTTAGE HOSPITALS, VILLAS, ETC., 1872;
SPON'S ARCHITECTS' AND BUILDERS' POCKET BOOK, 1st-14th
eds., 1873-87; SPON'S ARCHITECTS' AND BUILDERS' PRICE BOOK,
15th-25th eds., 1888-98. TOWN AND COUNTRY MANSIONS AND
SUBURBAN HOUSES: WITH NOTES ON THE SANITARY AND AR-
TISTIC CONSTRUCTION OF HOUSES, 1879. Obituaries: AR 8
(July-December 1900): 234-35; RIBAJ 8 (1900-1901): 21, 44-47.

288:2 Hunt, John. "Gosford, East Lothian." CL 150 (21 October, 4
November 1971): 1048-50, 1200-1202.

Gosford was begun in 1790 according to designs by Robert
Adam but was altered in 1800 after his death. "It was
the victim of changing whims all through the 19th century
and did not assume its final proportions until 1891 by Young.
It achieves a degree of overall harmony which is both wel-
come and surprising considering the very fussy detail of
Young's exterior work." Its extremely rich interiors are
described and illustrated.

288:3 Young, Clyde. "The New War Office." AR 20 (November 1906):
301-16.

Description with good visual coverage.

INDEXES

GENERAL INDEX

This index is alphabetized letter by letter and numbers refer to entry numbers unless preceded by a "p." (to indicate that it refers to a page number). In the case of individual architects, underlined numbers refer to main entries. Indexed are names and partnerships of major American architects, authors, and titles of books, dissertations, and theses. Subject areas of particular interest and importance to the study of architecture are also indexed. Titles of works written by individual architects are listed under their main heading within the text and in some cases are shortened. Names of firms are not inverted but are indexed as they appear in the annotations. Buildings discussed within the text are separately indexed under the Building Location Index.

General Index

Adam, William 110:5; 249:4
Adams, D. 265:1
Adams, Harry Percy 130:1, 3
Adams, Holden and Pearson 130:1
Adams, S.S. 58:1
Adams, Thomas 262:2
Adams and Thompson 103:1
Adaptability 265:3
Addison, Joseph 257:2
Additions A78; 38:3,4
Addleshaw, G.W.O. A1; 223:2
Adkins, J. Standen 37:2; 55:2
Admiralty 119:1
Adshead, Stanley Davenport 2:1, 2
A. E. COGSWELL, ARCHITECT WITHIN
    A VICTORIAN CITY 60:2
AESTHETIC MOVEMENT A2
Aesthetics A61, 114; B92; 29:12;
    105:5; 112:2, 8; 190:18;
    227:2; 237:2; 244:9; 282:2
"A. H. Mackmurdo's Artistic Theory"
    167:1
Ahrends, Burton and Koralek 3:1-10
Ahrends, Peter 3:1
Air conditioning 225:12
Aitchison, George, The Younger
    4:1-3
Aitken, George Shaw D1; 5:1, 2
Albert, Prince Consort 101:2; 223:10;
    242:3
Aldous, Tony 115:2
Alexander, C. 54:1
"Alexander Thomson" 257:1
"Alfred Waterhouse: The Great Years,
    1860-1875" 265:1
Alison, Felippo 165:3, 9
Allen, Gordon E2
Allen, N.P. 163:2
Allen, Phyllis E50
Alley, P.B. 72:1
Allibone, J. 221:1
Allison, J.T. 103:1
Allsopp, Bruce B2, 3
Alterations. See Restorations
Aluminium 247:7
AMERICAN ARCHITECT & BUILDING
    NEWS 15:2; 265:2
AMERICAN ARCHITECTS FROM THE
    CIVIL WAR TO THE FIRST
    WORLD WAR 47:1

AMERICAN ARCHITECTS FROM THE
    FIRST WORLD WAR TO THE
    PRESENT 54:1; 120:1;
    137:1; 154:1; 172:1; 219:1;
    237:1; 287:1
AMERICAN ARCHITECTURE COMES
    OF AGE A35
American architecture, theory, influ-
    ences and tradition A35,
    102; E11, 47, 61, 63; 14:2;
    44:10; 95:3; 102:2; 166:5;
    219:2; 226:4; 230:3; 260:4;
    262:9; 264:1
AMERICAN BUILDING 190:12
Amis, Stanley Frederick 133:1
AMPHION, OR THE NINETEENTH
    CENTURY A53
Anderson, Adam 6:1, 2
Anderson, Robert Rowand p. xvii;
    7:1, 2; 157:1, 5; 221:1
Andrews, Malcolm 92:2
Angus (Scotland) architecture D4
Annand, Louise 165:4, 20
ANNUAL REVIEW OF PERIODICAL
    ARTICLES A90
ANOTHER BLOW FOR LIFE 113:4
Anson, Peter F. 63:2; 156:2
ANTHOLOGY OF HOUSES, AN E56
Anthony, John 190:2
Antiquarians 33:1; 84:3; 112:9; 183:2
Antiquities C8
ANTI-RATIONALISTS, THE 56:2;
    165:52, 69; 167:4; 260:2
Antrim (Ireland) architecture C5, 14
Applied arts A80
Aptaker, Neil 264:1
ARCHAEOLOGICAL JOURNAL 223:12
Archaeological research and sites 59:1,
    3; 105:2; 202:22; 250:1; 257:4,
    12
ARCHAEOLOGICAL SURVEY OF
    COUNTY DOWN, AN C20
Archaeological surveys p. xviii
Archer, John H.G. 279:1-5
ARCHIBALD SIMPSON CENTENARY
    CELEBRATIONS, 9TH MAY
    1947 236:2
Archigram 8:1-12
ARCHIGRAM 8:1, 10, 11
ARCHITECT 138:2; 259:2

302

General Index

General Index

General Index

General Index

General Index

Memorials, monuments and mausolea
32:4; 33:6; 105:2; 142:1-4;
157:3, 8, 10; 161:2, 4;
181:7; 202:26; 212:4; 223:1,
10; 225:6, 7; 250:3; 268:9
Mendelsohn, Eric p. xxi; 54:1; 172:1-
3
Metalwork D3; 42:13; 111:3; 165:41,
70
ecclesiastical 202:27
Metcalf, Priscilla B41; 146:1
Mewes, Charles 74:1, 4
Mewes and Davis 74:4
M.H. BAILLIE SCOTT AND THE ARTS
AND CRAFTS MOVEMENT
226:4
Micklethwaite, John Thomas 173:1
Middle class A11
MIDDLESEX B73
Middleton and Bailey 18:1
Mies van der Rohe 137:2; 227:2, 5
Millais, J.E. 234:11
Millard, Walter 224:2; 249:6, 7
Miller, Russell 152:7
Millikin, Sandra A9
Mills, Edward David A77; E49;
174:1
Mills, John Fitsmaurice 108:1
Ministry of Education, Johnson-Marshall
at 170:5
Ministry of Public Buildings and Works
109:1
Ministry of Works p. xvii
Mitchell, Peter Chalmers 159:1
Mitchell Library, Glasgow, Thomson
material 257:1
MODERN ARCHITECTURE A102
MODERN ARCHITECTURE IN BRITAIN
A32
MODERN ARCHITECTURE IN EN-
GLAND A59
Modern Architecture Research Society
Group A75; 103:9
MODERN BRITISH DOMESTIC ARCHI-
TECTURE 165:26
MODERN BUILDINGS IN LONDON
B43
MODERN CHURCH, THE E49
MODERN ENGLISH ARCHITECTURE
A74

MODERN ENGLISH HOUSE, THE
E54
MODERN FLATS E81
MODERN HOME, THE E66
MODERN HOMES E24
MODERN HOUSE IN ENGLAND, THE
E80
MODERN HOUSES IN BRITAIN,
1919-39 p. xxi; E34
Modern movement (contemporary archi-
tecture and architects) A25,
32, 36, 43, 61, 64, 65, 68,
72, 75, 77, 89, 99, 102, 114;
B1, 12, 33, 35, 41; C1, 2,
22; D6; E1, 3, 34, 49, 51,
66, 73, 79; 3:2; 13:3; 44:2,
3; 46:5; 64:4; 87:2, 4; 88:2,
5; 91:2; 112:8; 116:3; 117:2;
136:2; 141:2; 163:3; 165:31,
53, 55, 59, 65, 69; 178:3;
199:4; 206:2; 210:3; 215:2,
4; 228:5; 234:17; 243:4, 14;
247:6; 262:12; 267:2
MODERN MOVEMENTS IN ARCHI-
TECTURE A63
MODERN SCHOOL BUILDINGS E20
MODERN SMALL COUNTRY HOUSES
E64
Modifications. See Restorations
Modular planning 10:4; 204:4; 247:10
Moffat, Milne and Paterson 118:3
Moffat, W. Muirhead 165:45
Moffatt, William Bonython 223:1
Moghul revival 221:10
MOIRA RURAL DISTRICT COUNCIL
p. xix
Molesworth, Robert H. 155:6
Monks Hall Museum 103:10
MONUMENTAL CLASSIC ARCHITEC-
TURE IN GREAT BRITAIN
A97
MONUMENTAL FOLLIES E6
Moon, R.C. 108:3
Moore, Temple Lushington 175:1-5;
225:1
Moorish revival style 33:3
Moro, Peter 28:11; 176:1, 2
Morris, A.E.T. 244:13
Morris, Francis O. A78
Morris, G. 161:40; 268:13

General Index

General Index

General Index

General Index

BUILDING LOCATION INDEX

All buildings within town boundaries are listed under the name of the town. Since British counties are not divided into townships, as in the United States, buildings not located in towns (such as castles, manor houses, and abbeys, some of which were in existence prior to the setting up of county boundaries) are listed independently.

AUSTRALIA

Adelaide, cathedrals at 46:15
Melbourne, Cathedral 46:6, 15

FRANCE

Chartres, Cathedral 244:10
Lille, Cathedral 42:1
Mayence, Cathedral 84:2
Ypres, Menin Gate 32:4

GERMANY

Hamburg, Nikolai Kirche 223:3

GREAT BRITAIN including Ireland (Eire)

Aberystwyth, University College, Hall 255:5
Abney Hall, Cheshire 202:12
Adare Manor, County Limerick 125:3; 202:3
Adcote, Shropshire 234:7
Albury Park, Surrey 202:14
Alloa, St. John's Church 7:1

Alton Castle (Towers) and Hospital, Staffordshire 202:6, 9
Ashby St. Ledgers, Northamptonshire 161:24
Aylesbury, Buckinghamshire 190:2
Ballywalter Park, County Down 151:3
Balmoral Castle, Aberdeenshire 242:1-4
Barham Court, Kent 161:16
Bath, Brydon's work at 39:3
Bayons Manor, Lincolnshire 183:2
Beaconsfield, Heal house, Bayline 171:3
Bear Wood, Berkshire 143:2
Belfast
    Botanical Garden 261:4
    City Hall 254:2
    Palm House 261:2
    Queen's University 162:2
Bestwood Lodge, Nottinghamshire 253:2
Bexhill on Sea, De La Warr Pavilion 172:2
Birmingham
    Edward VI School 53:1
    St. George's 212:2
    Teachers Training College 97:2
    University of, Mining and Metallurgy Building 10:4

Building Location Index

Building Location Index

Building Location Index

350

GREECE

INDIA

ITALY

KENYA

LIBYA

MONACO

NIGERIA

REPUBLIC OF SOUTH AFRICA

SWITZERLAND

TURKEY